ENVIRONMENT, SOCIETY, AND
THE COMPLEAT ANGLER

Cultural Inquiries in English Literature, 1400–1700

Rebecca Totaro, General Editor

ADVISORY BOARD

Joe Campana
Rice University

Hillary Ecklund
Loyola University, New Orleans

Katherine Eggert
University of Colorado, Boulder

Wendy Beth Hyman
Oberlin College & Conservatory

Julia Reinhardt Lupton
University of California, Irvine

Vin Nardizzi
The University of British Columbia

Gail Kern Paster
Folger Shakespeare Library

Garrett Sullivan
Penn State University

Tiffany Werth
University of California, Davis

Jessica Wolfe
University of North Carolina, Chapel Hill

Books in the Cultural Inquiries in English Literature, 1400–1700, series acknowledge the complex relationships that link disciplines in the pre-modern period and account for the lived experience represented in literary and cultural texts of the time. Scholars in this series reconnect fields often now considered distinct, including cuisine, ecology, cartography, the occult, meteorology, physiology, drama, popular print, and poetry.

OTHER BOOKS IN THE SERIES:

Emily Griffiths Jones, *Right Romance: Heroic Subjectivity and Elect Community in Seventeenth-Century England*

Nancy L. Simpson-Younger and Margaret Simon, eds., *Forming Sleep: Representing Consciousness in the English Renaissance*

Scott Oldenburg, *Labor, Household, Plague: A Weaver-Poet in Shakespeare's London*

Jennifer Linhart Wood, ed., *Dynamic Matter: Transforming Renaissance Objects*

ENVIRONMENT, SOCIETY, AND

THE COMPLEAT ANGLER

Marjorie Swann

THE PENNSYLVANIA STATE UNIVERSITY PRESS
UNIVERSITY PARK, PENNSYLVANIA

Library of Congress Cataloging-in-Publication Data

Names: Swann, Marjorie (Marjorie E.), author.
Title: Environment, society, and The compleat angler / Marjorie Swann.
Other titles: Cultural inquiries in English literature, 1400–1700.
Description: University Park, Pennsylvania : The Pennsylvania State University Press, [2023] | Series: Cultural inquiries in English literature, 1400–1700 | Includes bibliographical references and index.
Summary: "Analyzes the environmental and social complexities of Izaak Walton's famous fishing treatise The Compleat Angler. Examines the complex portrayal of the natural world through an ecocritical lens and explores other neglected aspects of Walton's writings, including his depictions of social hierarchy, gender, and sexuality"—Provided by publisher.
Identifiers: LCCN 2022061058 | ISBN 9780271095196 (hardback) | ISBN 9780271095202 (paper)
Subjects: LCSH: Walton, Izaak, 1593–1683. Compleat angler. | Fishing in literature. | Environmentalism in literature. | Human ecology in literature.
Classification: LCC SH433 .A1989 2023 | DDC 799.12—dc23/eng/20230215
LC record available at https://lccn.loc.gov/2022061058

Copyright © 2023 Marjorie Swann
All rights reserved
Printed in the United States of America
Published by The Pennsylvania State University Press,
University Park, PA 16802–1003

The Pennsylvania State University Press is a member of the Association of University Presses.

It is the policy of The Pennsylvania State University Press to use acid-free paper. Publications on uncoated stock satisfy the minimum requirements of American National Standard for Information Sciences—Permanence of Paper for Printed Library Material, ANSI Z39.48–1992.

CONTENTS

List of Illustrations | vi

Acknowledgments | vii

Note on the Text | viii

Introduction | 1

1 The Environmental Imagination of Izaak Walton | 11

2 Creating the Brotherhood of the Angle | 59

3 The Great Chain of Eating | 106

4 Charles Cotton and the Properties of Angling | 146

Epilogue: Haunted by Walton | 195

Notes | 205
Bibliography | 231
Index | 251

ILLUSTRATIONS

1. Cartoon, *Outdoor America* magazine, July 1926 | 4

2. Image of the eel from Izaak Walton, *The Compleat Angler*, 2nd ed. (1655) | 13

3. Image of the fisherman from the *Treatyse of Fysshynge wyth an Angle* in the *Boke of Saint Albans*, 2nd ed. (1496) | 62

4. Title page of Charles Cotton, *The Compleat Angler, Part II* (1676) | 175

ACKNOWLEDGMENTS

I have incurred many debts while writing this book. An Andrew W. Mellon Foundation Fellowship at the Huntington Library jump-started my research, and a sabbatical at Hendrix College allowed me to complete the manuscript. Vin Nardizzi has encouraged and supported my work ever since I presented my first conference paper about Walton, and all phases of this project have been improved by Todd Borlik's generous comments and suggestions. Throughout my time at Hendrix College, Provost Terri Bonebright helped me unstintingly, and John Shutt, the wizard of interlibrary loans, worked his magic tirelessly on my behalf.

At Penn State University Press, Rebecca Totaro, Kathryn Bourque Yahner, and Maddie Caso have assisted me greatly. The anonymous readers for the Press provided painstaking and constructive feedback at a time when they should been on vacation to recover from the stress and exhaustion of the COVID pandemic. Nicholas Taylor meticulously copyedited my manuscript. And I appreciate Scott Kovarovics and Mary Rubin at the Izaak Walton League of America for enabling me to use an illustration from the organization's archives.

I must express more personal and long-standing thanks as well. In Staffordshire, Tony Bridgett played Piscator to my Viator, acting as my guide to Izaak Walton's hometown of Stafford, the River Dove, and Charles Cotton's fishing temple in Beresford Dale. Robert Guiver shared with me his wealth of knowledge about Walton in the form of his own publications and allowed me to visit his wonderful collection of Waltoniana. Anthony Wilson's provocative and compelling essays in the newsletter of the Izaak Walton Cottage Chapter of the Izaak Walton League of America showed me the ongoing relevance of Walton's environmentalism, and Anthony continues to sustain my thinking via our email conversations. Finally, I am most grateful for the superhuman patience and good humor of my husband, William M. Tsutsui, who has for years now cheerfully endured being trapped in a ménage à trois with Izaak Walton.

NOTE ON THE TEXT

All quotations from the first (1653) and fifth (1676) editions of *The Compleat Angler* by Izaak Walton are from Jonquil Bevan's edition of Walton's book (Clarendon Press of Oxford University Press, 1983), references to which are included, in parentheses, in the body of the text. The capitalization and formatting from Bevan's volume have been retained in nearly all instances; when alterations have been made, they are noted in the text.

Unless otherwise noted, biblical quotations are from the King James translation.

When quoting directly from primary sources, I have modernized *i*, *j*, *ſ*, *þ*, *u*, *v*, and *vv* as necessary and have included letters omitted in elisions, but otherwise I have retained original spelling.

When I use non-inclusive language, it reflects the worldview or social dynamics portrayed in the text(s) under discussion.

The year is taken to begin on January 1.

Introduction

At high noon on a snowy, frigid Saturday in January 1922, fifty-four men gathered for lunch in the Venetian Gothic splendor of the Chicago Athletic Club. Professionally disparate (their ranks included salesmen, journalists, lawyers, a jeweler, a commercial artist, and a clergyman), in private life all members of the group "were first and foremost fly fishermen."[1] As they feasted on broiled Lake Superior whitefish in an oak-paneled dining room, the men swapped angling tips and fish stories. But then the tone of the meeting turned somber. One of the conveners of the lunch, publicist and advertising executive Will H. Dilg, began to address the group. Dilg "demanded of us an accounting," a participant later recalled. "He showed us denuded hills, once rich in forests; polluted cesspools that once were glorious rivers alive with fish; a mere trace of wildfowl that once had darkened the sky; and asked us pointedly if this were the sort of heritage we were proud to hand down to coming generations." Dilg refused to allow his dining companions to retreat into the comfort of their postprandial coffee and cigars. "WHAT SHALL WE DO TO SAVE OUR FISHING?" Dilg challenged his audience.[2] In response to Dilg's impassioned call to action, the group decided they must preserve the natural environment of the United

States by creating a national alliance of conservationist-sportsmen—and they proudly named their new fraternity of environmentalists after "the patron saint of anglers everywhere," Izaak Walton.³ The founders of the Izaak Walton League of America identified with their patronym, one chronicler explained, "not only because of [Walton's] love of angling, but also because of his deep appreciation of the outdoors, his true sportsmanship and advanced ideas on conservation."⁴

The Izaak Walton League immediately adopted a broad and aggressive purview, its leadership styling the fledgling organization as the "Defender of Woods, Waters and Wild Life."⁵ Its holistic perspective on conservation distinguished the League from other environmental groups active in the 1920s, which focused instead on isolated features of the American outdoors.⁶ And the League's structure—in which each member of the national organization also belonged to and socialized within a local chapter—further set the new group apart from its competitors. Like other fraternal service organizations that boomed during the 1920s, the Izaak Walton League deliberately constituted its membership as a band of brothers: historian Stephen Fox observes that "a typical chapter of the [L]eague resembled not one of the older conservation groups but rather a Rotary Club that liked to go fishing."⁷ The League's combination of conviviality and breadth of vision struck a chord, and within three years of its founding the organization had recruited upward of one hundred thousand members based in chapters across the United States at a time when the Sierra Club (founded in 1892) and the Audubon Association (founded in 1905) each had fewer than seven thousand members.⁸ The Izaak Walton League of America "was a phenomenon—the first conservation group with a mass membership," and the group quickly began to flex its political muscle.⁹ In 1923, the League thwarted attempts by business interests to build roads in the Superior National Forest in Minnesota.¹⁰ Simultaneously, upon learning that developers planned to drain the watershed of a three-hundred-mile-long stretch of the upper Mississippi the organization sprang into action, and by 1924 the Izaak Walton League had pressured the federal government to transform the endangered watershed into a wildlife preserve financed by a congressional appropriation. The largest previous sum earmarked for such a purpose had been $40,000; by contrast, the Izaak Walton League landed a whopping $1.5 million for its cause. The success of the "Ikes," as League members proudly dubbed themselves, was unprecedented, and at the League's third annual convention in 1925 Will Dilg (now the group's president) boasted that "in the world of conservation, our League stands forth like a towering mountain set in the center of a vast prairie."[11]

In 1926, an issue of the League's magazine featured a cartoon portraying the organization's militant members as chips off the formidable old block of their seventeenth-century namesake (see fig. 1). The image is dominated by a gigantic Izaak Walton who stands, bare-headed and barrel-chested, at the edge of a coniferous forest.[12] Walton carries in his left hand a huge war flag emblazoned with "Izaak Walton League," while his enormous right hand rests on the shoulder of Teddy Roosevelt, "the first conservationist in the White House," who's risen from the dead to help the Ikes defend a battlement with their clenched fists.[13] League policy objectives—"Unremitting Opposition to Illegal, Destructive, and Unfair Methods in Hunting and Fishing," "Outdoor Recreation for Youth," "Game Farms and Fish Hatcheries for Increased Propagation and Distribution of Fish and Game," "Opposition to Injurious Drainage," "Federal Control to Protect and Conserve Our Forests"—are inscribed on the rectangular stones that form the crenellated wall guarded by the pugilistic Ikes. In the foreground of the cartoon, a gang of environmental villains retreats after unsuccessfully trying to breach the conservationists' defenses, and we can read the damning ID labels ("Game Hog," "Water Polluter," "Forest Exploiter," "Poacher," "Bad Sportsmanship") on the hats of the vanquished miscreants. This cartoon, its caption proudly proclaims, documents "A Battle the Izaak Walton League Is Winning."

The League's depiction of its eponym as the John Brown of conservationists was rooted in a long tradition of popular enthusiasm for Walton's narrativized fishing manual *The Compleat Angler*. First published in 1653 as a cheap little octavo that a fisherman could carry in his pocket, Walton's *Angler* appeared in five editions during the author's lifetime.[14] Thanks to its sustained grassroots appeal, the book has been almost constantly in print since the first posthumous edition appeared in 1750 and remains "one of the most enduring literary classics in the English language."[15] The bare-bones plot of the treatise is simple: a small group of men goes on a springtime fishing trip in rural Hertfordshire. Led by Walton's alter ego, the experienced angler Piscator, the vacationing anglers talk about fish, land fish, and eat fish—taking care each evening to wash down their catch of the day with plenty of alcohol. As a convivial fraternity of recreational sportsmen motivated by their shared passion for the outdoors, the intertwined structure and ethos of the Izaak Walton League of America thus mirrored dynamics

FIGURE 1 | Cartoon by John T. McCutcheon, "A Battle the Izaak Walton League Is Winning," *Outdoor America* 4, no. 12 (July 1926): 4.

fundamental to the angling "brotherhood" that Walton had portrayed centuries earlier. And by proclaiming the author of *The Compleat Angler* as the new organization's tutelary genius, the upstart Izaak Walton League deftly capitalized on Walton's abiding popularity during its highly effective branding campaign in the 1920s. But we should not simply (dis)regard the League's self-serving appropriation of Walton and his angling treatise as a popular, early twentieth-century—and thus misguided and outmoded—example of "presentism."[16] For in their lived response to Walton's famous book, the founders of the Izaak Walton League of America gave material form to insights that have often been missing from scholarly assessments of *The Compleat Angler*.

Although his anglers' fish-centric discussions of the natural world make up the bulk of Walton's text, literary historians have paid surprisingly little attention to the environmental emphasis of *The Compleat Angler*. Fixated narrowly on oceans, scholars affiliated with the "blue cultural studies" have overlooked Walton's depiction of riparian ecosystems, while works of environmentally inflected literary history as a whole continue to uphold the canon—and the imperatives of academic job security and professional prestige—by teasing out ecological references in Shakespeare and Milton rather than examine a popular fishing treatise in which the natural world holds center stage.[17] Thus, most recent commentators continue to read *The Compleat Angler* through a New Historicist lens that focuses on Walton's veiled criticism of interregnum religion and politics. From this perspective, Walton's book primarily constitutes a conservative "polemic," and therefore the "naturalist materials" that predominate in *The Compleat Angler* should be interpreted (and then ignored) as "the occasion of the book rather than the center of its argument."[18] Walton had staunchly supported the beleaguered monarchy during the British Civil Wars, going so far as to risk imprisonment or execution by serving as a royalist agent after the Battle of Worcester in 1651, and he remained a Prayer Book loyalist throughout the 1650s.[19] Although these traditional allegiances certainly shape some aspects of *The Compleat Angler*, in other ways the experiences of Walton's anglers in the Hertfordshire countryside question both the moral fortitude of the English church and the ideological underpinnings of the abolished Stuart monarchy. And Walton's multifaceted portrayal of the natural environment never functions solely as the vehicle of religiopolitical commentary. Because "nature and culture are mutually constitutive," concepts of nature are necessarily "ideas of kinds of societies" and vice versa: thus, only by analyzing Walton's complex, interwoven depiction of both the biosphere and his fishermen's social world can we understand the rich and distinctive ecosocial vision presented in *The Compleat Angler*.[20]

Walton first published his angling treatise for a readership that inhabited "an early modern world of scarcity and uncertainty" wracked by environmental crises.[21] In the middle of the seventeenth century, "the earth experienced some of the coldest weather recorded in over a millennium" during an especially severe phase of the Little Ice Age, a period of unusually cold, wet, and unstable weather that caused crop failures, food shortages, and disease throughout the Northern Hemisphere.[22] These dire conditions gave English landowners added impetus to fulfill more intensively what they regarded as their God-given mandate to exert human dominion over the earth, and initiatives designed to increase agricultural productivity (and profits)—enclosure, drainage of wetlands, felling of trees, and cultivation of wastes—destroyed both rural ecosystems and human communities. The misery produced by the Little Ice Age exacerbated the religious and political unrest that would culminate in the civil wars, and militarized conflict further ravaged the natural environment.[23] Perpetually searching for new sources of revenue, King Charles I had opportunistically mismanaged forests and sold vast numbers of oak trees, and as combat raged during the 1640s deer parks were repeatedly invaded by both soldiers and discontented local residents, with thousands of deer slaughtered and trees felled.[24] When hostilities finally ceased in 1651, hedges and orchards had been cleared for miles beyond the defenses of fortified towns, warfare had destroyed crops and livestock, and forests, parks, and chases had been devastated. Yet this period of armed combat also inadvertently produced environmental benefits. Although wildlife decreased overall during the seventeenth century, so many men left Caernarvonshire to fight for the king "that the Justices of the Peace had to offer a 10-shilling bounty for killing foxes, hunting them having ceased due to the war."[25] And during the blockade of Newcastle in 1643–44, when Londoners could no longer obtain coal, the clouds of sulfurous smoke that normally choked the English capital were so reduced that chronically stunted and sickly plants "were observed to bear such plentiful and infinite quantities of Fruits, as they never produced the like either before or since."[26] Ironically, however, this wartime amelioration of London's air quality came at the cost of increased deforestation as impoverished and desperate residents of the city resorted to cutting down trees for fuel, with Parliament authorizing the "organized plunder" of royalist-owned woodlands located within sixty miles of London.[27]

The tumult of the civil wars also intensified emergent challenges to long-standing environmental worldviews. According to early modern English orthodoxy, whether acting as agricultural improvers, aristocratic hunters, or Baconian scientists, men who exploited the natural world were simply fulfilling their Christian duty to restore (patriarchal) human control over the postlapsarian earth. Yet this "breathtakingly anthropocentric" vision of the natural world as "redolent with human analogy and symbolic meanings" was increasingly undermined by new concepts of nature as "autonomous, only to be understood in non-human terms."[28] Keith Thomas argues that "the explicit acceptance of the view that the world does not exist for man alone can be fairly regarded as one of the great revolutions in modern Western thought," and during Walton's lifetime the stirrings of this paradigm shift catalyzed a deepening "crisis of distinctions" between the human and the nonhuman.[29] Some of Walton's contemporaries wistfully imagined how they might escape from the demands of normative heterosexuality and become more like plants, able to experience the asexual innocence of "vegetable love" and thus "procreate like trees, without conjunction."[30] Others argued that animals—even fish—possess reason and language, capacities long regarded as the defining characteristics of human superiority.[31]

Such challenges to man's status as the earthly apex of the Great Chain of Being became even more explicit and radical during the civil wars. In the mid-1640s, the vituperative Presbyterian clergyman Thomas Edwards included in his catalog of the "Errours of the Sectaries" the heretical statement that men should regard themselves as "no better then was meet, for God loves the creatures that creep upon the ground as well as the best Saints and there is no distance between the flesh of a Man, and the flesh of a Toad."[32] The Ranter Jacob Bauthumley published in 1650 what Edwards would have regarded as a sectarian nightmare, a tract in which Bauthumley declared that "God is in all Creatures, Man and Beast, Fish and Fowle, and every green thing, from the highest Cedar to the Ivey on the wall."[33] Bauthumley's attack on anthropocentrism threatened to eradicate traditional forms of religious authority, so all copies of his impious book were ordered to be incinerated, and Bauthumley himself was burned through the tongue with a hot iron as punishment for his blasphemy.[34] Although Izaak Walton's unorthodox ideas never attracted such violent opposition, his marginalization during the interregnum likewise enabled Walton to think innovatively about humankind's place in God's creation.[35] In the face of a polarized society devastated by warfare, climate change, ecological degradation, hunger, and disease, Walton used *The Compleat Angler* to develop an audacious model of a new kind of community in which men's love of the natural world—not fealty to the church, the state, or the family—becomes the foundation of both individual identity and social order. And in the process, Walton created one of the most innovative and influential environmental texts ever written.[36]

The chapters that follow analyze *The Compleat Angler* as a uniquely complex—and compelling—exploration of humankind's ecosocial existence. As chapter 1 details, Walton's fishing treatise presents a kaleidoscopic wealth of early modern perspectives on a wonderfully heterogeneous natural world. Walton was a staunch adherent of the prewar Church of England, and an Anglican-inflected Christian anthropocentrism thus pervades much of his book.[37] A devout mode of meditation underpins the joyful apprehension of numinosity that Walton's fishermen often experience in the English countryside, and many of the most famous passages in *The Compleat Angler* are imbued with what Todd Borlik helpfully terms "eco-spirituality."[38] The religiosity of Walton's text frequently modulates into versions of the pastoral mode; but as one would expect from a how-to manual, *The Compleat Angler* encompasses even more types of georgic, and Walton's anglers formulate nascent concepts of ecology, conservation, and sustainability as they seek to harvest fish within bountiful ecosystems subjected—like Izaak Walton himself—to the harsh weather that often battered seventeenth-century England during the Little Ice Age.

As Walton's doppelgänger-protagonist Piscator tries to catch fish, he revolutionizes English angling by transforming the sport into a sociable activity. Chapter 2 examines how Walton, rejecting the time-honored stereotype of the solitary fisherman, creates a convivial "brotherhood" of anglers both within and beyond his book. Just as the upheaval of civil war catalyzed new ways of thinking about humanity's relationship with the natural environment, so Walton, like many of his contemporaries during the interregnum, also imagined new kinds of social bonds. Drawing on familiar organizational models from both the religious and secular spheres, Piscator fosters in his community of anglers an unorthodox voluntary association rooted in its members' shared experiences of the outdoors. Piscator cannot, however, include elite men who dabble in Baconian science within the ranks of his angling fraternity. And like his biographies of notable Anglicans, Walton's fishing treatise is pervaded by unease about women, so the innovative model of ecosocial relationships developed in *The Compleat Angler* also remains staunchly female-free. Thus both Piscator and Walton are limited by early modern concepts of rank and gender when they seek converts to "turn Angler" and join their "brotherhood" of outdoorsmen.

Fishers of men must also be feeders of men in Walton's book, and chapter 3 analyzes the omnipresent fascination with food central to *The Compleat Angler*. Piscator flourishes as the paterfamilias of the Brotherhood of the Angle because he excels at providing irresistible meals to fish and fishermen alike. Both legitimizing and politicizing the piscivorous diet he advocates, Walton allies his protagonist's feats of fish cookery with those of Christ in the New Testament while also evoking the "fish days" proscribed during the interregnum. Yet fish was regarded as a dangerous foodstuff in the early modern period, and the recipes that Piscator provides—many of them also reflecting the continental cuisine associated with royalism—seek to minimize the adverse effects of fish consumption on human health. Since food preparation was stereotyped as demeaning women's work, however, Walton must simultaneously strive to portray Piscator's expertise in fish cookery as respectably masculine. Above all, Walton insists that his anglers inhabit a providentially bountiful natural world in which God miraculously feeds some creatures and generates others from the very food they eat—a protoecological dynamic paralleled in the genesis of the Brotherhood of the Angle itself.

The life of the Staffordshire gentleman Charles Cotton attests to the power of Izaak Walton's influence as an environmental thinker and writer during the early modern period. In the spring of 1676, as a personal favor to Walton, Cotton hastily wrote a treatise about fly-fishing. Included with the final edition of Walton's book as Part II of *The Compleat Angler*, Cotton's pioneering text—the first specialized fly-fishing manual ever published—remains a touchstone for modern fly fishermen. Perhaps because of its stylistic clarity and continued usefulness as a how-to book, Part II of *The Compleat Angler* has received little scholarly attention beyond narrowly focused histories of recreational fishing. Chapter 4 remedies this deficiency by analyzing Cotton's treatise as a work of imaginative literature that honors yet also conservatively revises the ecosocial dynamics of Izaak Walton's book. Whereas Walton's anglers deliberately bypass the Theobalds estate (and thus reject the aristocratic modes of environmental and social domination it represents) as they head into Hertfordshire, Cotton's fishermen visit his country house in Beresford Dale, an oasis of elite civilization on the banks of the River Dove located amid the rugged, intimidating terrain of the Peak District. Extending the membership dynamics of Walton's Brotherhood of the Angle, Cotton's protagonist Piscator Junior paradoxically invests the patrimonial resources of his estate so he may forge a nonlineal identity for himself as Izaak Walton's adopted son. Yet as Piscator Junior creates dozens of artificial flies from an amazing (and often exotic) array of furs, feathers, textiles, and precious metals, he channels the ethos of patrician environmental mastery emblematized by Theobalds into a new, explicitly genteel practice of fly-tying. Thus, rather than emulate his foster father Izaak Walton and forage for bait in a numinous English countryside teeming with invertebrates, Charles Cotton transforms the natural world into a globalized bazaar that caters to the rarefied tastes of a cosmopolitan landed elite—even in such an unlikely place as the Peak.

Cotton's depiction of fly-fishing as socially superior to bait-fishing finally renders his relationship with Izaak Walton equivocal, a dynamic that likewise shapes Norman Maclean's autobiographical novella *A River Runs Through It*. The epilogue of this study explores how Maclean uses *The Compleat Angler* to complicate what ecotheorist Joseph Meeker would term the "literary ecology" of Maclean's narrative. Depicting his brother Paul as a brilliant but troubled fly fisherman who lives by a destructive code of masculine self-sufficiency, Maclean portrays Walton's seventeenth-century angling treatise as the source text of a life-affirming worldview that could save his brother—but Paul seals his tragic fate by refusing to embrace the sustaining (and sustainable) mode of male identity modeled in *The Compleat Angler*. Maclean's celebrated story thus demonstrates the ongoing relevance and cultural vitality of Izaak Walton's vision of an environmentally rooted habitus that draws human beings into communion with both the natural world and one another.

CHAPTER 1

The Environmental Imagination of Izaak Walton

The Compleat Angler presents a rich and compelling vision of the ways in which humanity interacts with (and within) a complex natural world. Walton's very title alerts us to the diverse modes of environmental thought that shape his book. The adjective "compleat" both implies comprehensive plenitude and evokes the genre of the early modern English how-to manual; so in this context, the word "angler" characterizes the reader as a would-be self-improver who seeks to exploit aquatic ecosystems as effectively as possible.[1] Yet this suggestion of vast practical knowledge acquired for the sake of environmental mastery is immediately complicated by the book's subtitle: *or, The Contemplative Man's Recreation*. The adjective "contemplative" ascribes a spiritualized intellectualism to the angler's experience that might, at first glance, seem to conflict with the fisherman's practical goal of catching trout or salmon. Taken together, the title and subtitle thus stage a piscatory version of the traditional contest between the *vita activa* and the *vita contemplativa*. But the final word of Walton's subtitle further complicates interpretation. Etymologically, the word "recreation" suggests renewal, and for Walton's first readers "recreation" could simultaneously refer to a pleasurable pastime, to physical refreshment more generally, to a person or a specific place providing such refreshment, to mental or spiritual consolation, to a beneficial but enjoyable educational experience, and to a meal.[2] The title of Walton's book thus prepares us to encounter (and enjoy) disparate, even contradictory, representations of a "compleat" fisherman's relationship to a heterogeneous natural world.

Walton acknowledges that the complexity of his environmental vision shapes—and complicates—his use of literary modes.[3] In the prefatory epistle to the first edition of *The Compleat Angler* published in 1653, Walton advises his reader to expect a multimodal text. Channeling Horace, Walton suggests his treatise can provide readers with "*profit* or *pleasure*," and to ensure that his "discourse of *fish* and *fishing*" might not "read *dull*, and *tediously*," Walton reports he has "in severall places mixt some innocent Mirth" to leaven the instructional loaf—what Walton terms "the more usefull part"— of his book (59).[4] Yet the heterogeneity of *The Compleat Angler* exists not simply as a calculated source of audience appeal. Indeed, Walton continues, his how-to manual's "mixt" quality accurately represents the complexity of its author's own consciousness: "the whole discourse is a kind of picture of my owne disposition, at least of my disposition in such daies and times as I allow my self, when honest *Nat.* and *R.R.* and I go a fishing together" (59).

Still worried, however, that his reader might not welcome the interpretive demands of his multifarious text, Walton continues his sales pitch by noting yet another aspect of his book that he hopes will be a crowd-pleaser: "and let me adde this, that he that likes not the discourse, should like the pictures of the *Trout* and other fish, which I may commend, because they concern not my self" (59). Walton provides no images of the human characters in *The Compleat Angler*, but six engravings of different freshwater fish appear in the first edition of his book, each one entering the reader's field of vision at the very moment that Piscator names the species depicted, the illustrations' unorthodox and finickity placement on the printed page allowing them to function like hypertext.[5] Walton enhanced this feature of his book in the second edition of 1655 by adding four new images, including an eel (see fig. 2) that apparently smiles in anticipation of being stuffed and roasted according to the recipe that Walton provides immediately beneath its mug shot (319). Shifting worldviews, different modes of pleasurable self-renewal, the author's own protean sensibility fostered by shared experiences of angling, and animals that are both irreducibly Other and appropriated (often as entrées) by early modern culture: as we prepare to

FIGURE 2 | Image of the eel from Izaak Walton, *The Compleat Angler*, 2nd ed. (1655). RB 148257, detail, The Huntington Library, San Marino, California.

cross the threshold of his book, Walton introduces us to characteristics of his artistic vision that will become crucial to our understanding of *The Compleat Angler*.

Despite his unease about the demands he was placing on his reader, Walton greatly increased "the more usefull part" of his book in the four later editions that appeared during the author's lifetime. The second edition of *The Compleat Angler* was especially noteworthy in this regard as it added not only new pictures but also seven chapters to Walton's book, thus supersizing the 1653 text by nearly half its original length. Walton began the revision and expansion of his 1655 text with his dramatis personae: whereas the first edition opens with a dialogue between the master fisherman Piscator and the nonangler Viator ("Traveller"), in the second edition Walton changes Viator's name to "Venator" ("Hunter") and introduces a third interlocutor, Auceps ("Falconer"). At the same time, Walton devotes many more pages to descriptions of the appearance and behavior of nonhuman inhabitants of the planet.[6] By opening the 1655 narrative with a three-way bragging contest among Auceps, Venator, and Piscator, Walton immediately expands his scope of environmental consideration to include "the very birds of the air" and a vast array of creatures, ranging from ants to elephants, "which the earth breeds and nourisheth" (180, 184). Nonetheless, it is fish—their appearance, their food, their habitat, their behavior, how they can be caught, how their populations can be sustained in the wild, how they can be reared in ponds, and how they can be prepared for human consumption—that make up the main focus of Walton's voluminous additions.

For centuries, readers of *The Compleat Angler* have commented on the book's diverse mixture of literary materials and perspectives. In a commendatory poem added to the second edition of *The Compleat Angler* in 1655, John Floud compares Walton to Erasmus, who interspersed "some toys" in his "learned Colloquies" so as to "entice all Readers": "And such is this Discourse: there's none so low, / Or highly learn'd, to whom hence may not flow / Pleasure and information" (427). Given Floud's long-standing personal relationship with Walton—he was the brother of Walton's first wife, Rachel Floud, who had died in 1640 after nearly fourteen years of marriage—it is suggestive that his praise of the *Angler* revisits Walton's defensive prefatory comments about the work's "mixt" quality. Walton was always conscious that he was a tradesman who lacked a university education, and Floud preemptively counters any suggestion that the heterogeneity of Walton's book stems from ignorance or ineptitude by comparing it with the artistry of the legendary scholar Erasmus.[7] Floud's strategy of legitimizing Walton's complexity of form by tracing it to a forebear with sterling intellectual credentials has been more recently paralleled by modern scholars who argue we should regard *The Compleat Angler* as a Menippean satire that just happens to be full of fish.[8]

Some commentators have been less sanguine about the profusion of modes—and thus perspectives on the environment—in *The Compleat Angler*. Walton's first editor, Moses Browne, developed a system of redlining to protect eighteenth-century readers from the "more usefull" sections of Walton's text: in his preface to the 1759 edition of *The Compleat Angler*, Browne observes that "*the Parts which treat merely of* Directions for the Sport, [Browne has] *contrived so to distinguish and enclose with particular Marks . . . that they may be past over, and nothing but the entertaining Parts of the Book present themselves for those, to whom those other might appear dull and unpleasant.*"[9] Later critics have sometimes followed Moses Browne's example and encouraged readers to ignore significant portions of Walton's book. Charles Lamb assured Samuel Taylor Coleridge that "all the scientific part you may omit in reading," and more recently, literary historians quarrying the text for statements of conservative political ideology have likewise found that Walton's fish—and all the other creatures that swarm through his angling treatise—keep getting in the way of their interpretive agenda.[10] Walton's depiction of a fish-centric natural plenitude has thus led some readers to ignore vast expanses of his book. Walton, ever concerned to keep all members of his audience happy, would probably have approved of such narrowly selective reading strategies, but Walton's complexity of vision can be appreciated only if we try to assess his depiction of the natural world on its own terms: *compleatly*.

To understand Walton's book in all its fish-filled abundance, we must read *The Compleat Angler*, first and foremost, as an environmental text. Although he focuses on American literature of a later period, Lawrence Buell's ecocritical scholarship provides a salutary model of how we might approach Walton's angling manual. Nineteenth-century environmental writing, Buell observes, is often marked by "instability of form" because of authors' attempts to represent "an environmental plenum," and from this perspective, Buell argues, Henry David Thoreau's *Walden* "reflects Thoreau's commitment to not one but a cluster of distinct approaches to nature."[11] Rather than privileging one environmental mode over another as we try to make sense of *The Compleat Angler*, we should similarly strive to analyze Walton's book holistically as a sprawling, often bewildering profusion of perspectives on the natural world. Steeped in a culture that was intellectually inclined toward "accommodation rather than wholesale innovation," Walton was, like Thoreau two centuries later, "a negotiator among a menu of preexisting environmental discourses."[12] So the complexity of *The Compleat Angler* is, in part, rooted in the contradictions of early modern environmental thought that Walton had inherited. But in response to the conditions of crisis specific to mid-seventeenth-century England, Walton's love for the natural world also regularly leads him beyond the parameters of his society's time-honored "menu" of ideas. *The Compleat Angler* thus harnesses in productive tension a *copia* of dominant, residual, and emergent environmental worldviews: an explicitly Christian belief that nature embodies a divine order, multiform modes of pastoral and georgic, and pragmatic responses to the changing environmental conditions that shaped and challenged human life in seventeenth-century England.[13] Thanks to this polyphony, *The Compleat Angler* presents a richly complicated, sometimes paradoxical vision of the natural world.

GOD AND NATURE IN *THE COMPLEAT ANGLER*

Many facets of Walton's environmental imagination originate in his deeply felt embrace of traditional Christian interpretations of the Bible. Early in the post-1653 editions of *The Compleat Angler*, Walton's protagonist, the master fisherman Piscator, builds his argument for the supremacy of angling over hawking and hunting on the foundation of his reading of Genesis—"The *water* is the eldest daughter of the Creation, the Element upon which the Spirit of God did first move, the Element which God commanded to bring forth living creatures abundantly" (185)—and the book concludes with Piscator's new disciple testifying to his enhanced faith in "the goodness of the God of *Nature*" (371).[14] Walton's display of a panoply of environmental perspectives in *The Compleat Angler* is thus often framed by "the essentially optimistic idea that the order of nature on the earth was the result of the beneficent design of the Creator."[15]

But God sometimes stands in the wings of Walton's text while the earth's creatures function according to the principles established at the dawn of time by a (usually capitalized) personification called "Nature" who is both an artist and a life coach. At one point, for example, Piscator remarks of the bullhead that "Nature hath painted the Body of this Fish with *whitish, blackish, brownish* spots," and Walton's master angler elsewhere observes that the minnow cannot be "easily found and caught till *March*, or in *April*, for then he appears first in the River, Nature having taught him to shelter and hide himself in the Winter in ditches that be near to the River" (350, 246). Occasionally this personified Nature is explicitly gendered female, a version of the goddess Natura who had been imported from classical antiquity into Christian thought during the Middle Ages.[16] In this vein, Piscator quotes Sir Henry Wotton's versified celebration of springtime that begins "*This day dame Nature seem'd in love*," and as the anglers return to London at the end of the narrative, Piscator's disciple invites him to take a break so they can "rest [them] selves in this sweet shady Arbour, which nature her self has woven with her own fine fingers" (206, 366). Although such personifications represent nature "as a secondary creative force" that functions as "the 'vicar of God,'" the hint of autonomy lurking in these avatars becomes even more pronounced when Piscator implicitly speaks of "nature" as an inherent temperament, a usage that often appears in Walton's discussions of individual species of fish, such as the program note prefacing chapter 4:

"*Observations of the nature and breeding of the Trout; and how to fish for him*" (224).[17] So the very bedrock of many aspects of Walton's environmental vision—his devout, traditional belief that "nature" has been created and sustained by a beneficent deity—is in and of itself subtly multifaceted.

Early modern interpretations of Genesis were often unequivocally anthropocentric: God created human beings to "subdue" the earth and "have dominion" over all other life forms (Gen. 1:28). "Nothing we see, but means our good, / As our *delight*, or as our *treasure*," declared George Herbert. "The whole is, either our cupboard of *food*, / Or cabinet of *pleasure*."[18] This time-honored vision of nature existing solely for the benefit of human existence sometimes appears in explicit form in Walton's book: from the second edition of *The Compleat Angler* onward, for example, Venator enthuses, "How doth the earth bring forth *herbs, flowers* and *fruits*, both for *physick* [medicine] and the *pleasure* of mankind?" and in a dedicatory poem, the clergyman Thomas Weaver reminds Walton that fish "to your use / Owe their creation" (183, 429).[19] In other passages, Piscator praises bees for "how useful their honey and wax is both for meat and Medicines to mankind" and extols birds because they "both feed and refresh [man]; feed him with their choice bodies, and refresh him with their Heavenly voices" so that "his curious palate [is] pleased by day" and "their very excrements [feathers] afford him a soft lodging at night" (182, 180). The idea that the natural world exists primarily for the "use" of human beings similarly underwrites many of Walton's observations about fish: Piscator brags that angling is inherently superior to falconry or hunting because fish are "more advantagious to man; not only for the lengthning of his life, but for the preventing of sickness," especially praising the tench for being "very useful both dead and alive for the good of mankind," and in his final edition of 1676, Walton draws on Pliny to explain that fish can even have architectural value, as "the people of *Cadara* . . . make the Timber for their houses of those Fish-bones" of gargantuan sea fish and whales (186, 308, 195). The belief that God designed all creatures, great and small, to be exploited by humankind thus often gives a theological charge to Walton's depictions of human domination of the environment.

Piously freighted anthropocentrism likewise pervades the traditional concept of the Great Chain of Being that Walton frequently invokes. A metaphor of the ordered plenitude of God's creation, the Great Chain "stretched from the foot of God's throne to the meanest of inanimate objects," linking every particle of the creation in ordered, continuous succession from the deity downward through the heavenly host to humanity, ants, fungi, and stones.[20] While human beings clearly occupied a position below God and the angels in this cosmic hierarchy, they were also (in theory) decisively placed above all animals and other earthly entities. At the same time, however, analogies among the different levels of the Chain of Being also connected all the components of God's creation.[21] We find this vision of a web of correspondences amidst hierarchy in a passage from Du Bartas that Piscator quotes early in the tutorials he conducts for his angling disciple:

> *God quickned in the sea and in the rivers,*
> *So many Fishes of so many features,*
> *That in the waters we may see all creatures,*
> *Even all that on the earth are to be found,*
> *As if the world were in deep waters drown'd.*
> *For seas (as well as skies) have Sun, Moon, Stars;*
> *(As well as air) Swallows, Rooks, and Stares* [starlings];
> *(As well as earth) Vines, Roses, Nettles, Melons,*
> *Mushroms, Pinks, Gilliflowers, and many millions*
> *Of other plants, more rare, more strange than these,*
> *As very fishes living in the seas:*
> *As also Rams, Calves, Horses, Hares and Hogs,*
> *Wolves, Urchins* [hedgehogs], *Lions, Elephants and Dogs;*
> *Yea men and Maids, and which I most admire,*
> *The mitred Bishop, and the cowled Fryer.* (197)

Despite its Christianized anthropocentric foundations, this representation of the Great Chain of Being offers a model of the natural world that deemphasizes both God and humankind. The passage quoted by Piscator begins with God the Creator, but our attention is immediately captivated by the plethora of entities—celestial bodies, animals, birds, fish, and plants—that the poet describes as aquatic counterparts to the terrestrial creation: God disappears as the reader is overwhelmed by a flash mob of the denizens of the heavens, the earth, and the seas. Humanity is likewise sidelined since the poet does not describe nature's plenitude as existing to fulfill the needs of human beings, and the poet's insistence on analogy blurs the boundaries among the ostensibly hierarchical categories of the Great Chain of Being, a process that culminates in the hybrid fish-human identity of "*The mitred Bishop* [a fish that looks like a bishop], *and the cowled Fryer* [a fish that looks like a monk]."[22] Thus Walton's evocation of the Great Chain of Being in *The Compleat Angler* sometimes emphasizes the metaphor's inherent contradictions and decenters both God and humanity.

Other facets of Walton's depiction of a numinous natural world prove similarly complex. As the subtitle of *The Compleat Angler* indicates, Walton's depiction of the environment focuses centrally on the experience of contemplation. In recent years, scholars have often analyzed Walton's "contemplative" anglers as thinly disguised figures of political critique. At first glance, a passage that appears early in the 1653 edition seems to support such an interpretation. As Piscator tries to convince Viator that recreational fishing is "an Art, and an Art worth learning," Walton's master fisherman commends angling because in it, he claims, contemplation and action "meet together" (67, 69).[23] Piscator then develops this theme by focusing on the relationship that, he argues, has long existed between angling and contemplation:

> And first I shall tel you what some have observed, and I have found in my self, That the very sitting by the Rivers side, is not only the fittest place for, but will invite the Anglers to Contemplation: That it is the fittest place, seems to be witnessed by the children of *Israel*, who having banish'd all mirth and Musick from their pensive hearts, and having hung up their then mute Instruments upon the Willow trees, growing by the Rivers of *Babylon*, sate down upon those banks bemoaning the *ruines* of *Sion*, and contemplating their own sad condition. (70)

Piscator's evocation of Psalm 137—which Walton carefully glosses with a textual note to ensure that his reader recognizes the allusion—would have carried an implicit but powerful political message in 1653. As Kirsten Tranter argues, by introducing the exiled Children of Israel into Walton's book, Piscator mobilizes a "trope of Israel in captivity as England under Cromwell" that would have resonated strongly for interregnum readers who, like Walton, had supported the king and the established church during the civil wars.[24] Thus in this passage, Piscator presents riverside contemplation "as a political act of remembering in the context of exile."[25]

Yet Walton's contemplative fisherman functions as an allegorically closeted enemy of the Rump Parliament for just a moment. In the first words of the very next paragraph, Piscator pivots decisively away from the self-centered (and thus human-focused) lamentation of the Children of Israel in Psalm 137 to an environmental mode of contemplation in which the riparian natural world serves not only as the site but also as the object of contemplation: "And an ingenuous *Spaniard* sayes, *That both Rivers, and the inhabitants of the watery Element, were created for wise men to contemplate, and fools to pass by without consideration.* And though I am too wise to rank my self in the first number, yet give me leave to free my self from the last, by offering to thee a short contemplation, first of Rivers, and then of Fish: concerning which, I doubt not but to relate to you many things very considerable" (70). Beginning with the second edition of *The Compleat Angler*, published in 1655, Walton further emphasizes this shift in focus by adding Piscator's own testimony that he has "made many an hour pass away more pleasantly, as I have sate quietly on a flowry Bank by a calm River, and contemplated what I shall now relate to you" (194). In typically compendious fashion, Piscator subsequently provides a wide-ranging catalog of riparian "things very considerable": after describing extraordinary rivers throughout history and quoting from George Herbert, Piscator invokes the presentation of God's "manifold" creatures in Psalm 104—which Piscator commends for arousing "amazement" in "a contemplative Reader"—before enlisting Pliny and Du Bartas in quick succession as authorities on marvelous fish (71).[26] Piscator thus reframes contemplation as a mode of thought focused not on human society but on the natural world, and the lamenting Children of Israel are quickly swept away by a flood of aquatic wonders.

As Piscator leaves Psalm 137 behind, Walton abandons a narrowly political mode of thought and instead modulates into an environmentally focused form of meditation. This devotional response to nature relies implicitly on the concept that one can understand God not only by reading the Bible but also by studying nature, God's second "book" in which theological truths are revealed. We find this idea articulated explicitly by the Norwich physician Sir Thomas Browne: "Thus there are two bookes from whence I collect my Divinity; besides that written one of God, another of his servant Nature, that universall and publik Manuscript, that lies expans'd unto the eyes of all."[27] Developed in the early seventeenth century to counter the Roman Catholic tradition of Ignatian meditation, which entailed the contemplation of vividly imagined scenes from the life and Passion of Christ, Protestant meditation on the Book of Nature instead encouraged attentiveness to the ordinary sights and sounds of the natural world.[28] Practitioners of this mode of environmentally focused contemplation often cited scriptural precedent from the Old Testament to justify their methodology. The terms "meditate" and "meditation" appear frequently in early modern English translations of the Psalms: "I will meditate of the beautie of thy glorious majestie and thy wonderfull works," the Psalmist proclaims in the Geneva Bible's version of Psalm 145:5, affording an example of what Protestants categorized as "*Sudden, Occasional, or External Meditation*, [which] ariseth from such things as God by his providence offers to our eyes, ears and senses."[29] The writer of the Psalms, the biblical King David, thus became a model for Protestants seeking to know God by contemplating the natural world, and Walton overtly situates *The Compleat Angler* within this ancient meditative tradition. Fish are "fit for the contemplation of the most prudent and pious, and peaceable men," Piscator argues, as "testified by the practice of so many devout and contemplative men[,] as the Patriarchs or Prophets of old," and beginning with the third edition of 1661, Piscator concludes a catalog of astonishing aquatic creatures with a punch line from Psalm 107: "And doubtless this made the Prophet *David* say, *They that occupy themselves in deep waters see the wonderful works of God*" (74, 200).[30] Early modern English Protestants also found authority for a mode of contemplation *en plein air* in the King James translation of Genesis: "And Isaac went out to meditate in the field at the eventide" (24:63).[31] Although Walton does not refer to this passage in *The Compleat Angler*, the parallel between the meditative practices of the biblical patriarch and Piscator, the alter ego of another devout outdoorsman named "Izaak," would surely have been noticed by Walton's seventeenth-century readers.

The mode of environmental meditation that pervades *The Compleat Angler* aligns with the precepts and practice of Bishop Joseph Hall, one of the most important theorists and practitioners of meditation in the early modern period. Like Walton, Hall had been a friend of John Donne, and Hall's dazzling career—which began at Emmanuel College, Cambridge, and later included a stint as chaplain to Prince Henry—culminated with his becoming first the bishop of Exeter and then the bishop of Norwich. Hall's professional life concluded painfully during the civil wars, however: imprisoned by Parliament in 1642, Hall was subjected to draconian financial penalties after he was released from the Tower and was finally forced out of Norwich in 1647.[32] In addition to his treatise *The Arte of Divine Meditation* (1606), Hall wrote some very popular books of meditations that were subsequently reissued in his collected *Works*, as well as a stand-alone collection, *Occasional Meditations*, that was first published in 1630.[33] Hall's publications were a treasured part of Izaak Walton's personal library—he singled them out in his will when he bequeathed "Doctor Halls Works" to his daughter— and Hall's meditational theory and practice illuminate important aspects of Walton's depiction of the environment in *The Compleat Angler*.[34]

"Man is placed in this stage of the world to view the several natures and actions of the Creatures; to view them, not idly, without his use, as they do him," Hall insists.[35] "God made all these [creatures] for man and man for His own sake; both these purposes were lost if man should let the creatures pass carelessly by him, only seen not thought upon," Hall elaborates, explaining that "the creatures are half lost if we only employ them, not learn something from them. God is wronged if His creatures be unregarded; ourselves most of all if we read this great volume of the creatures and take out no lesson for our instruction" (74). Hall himself rarely pays attention to the entries about fish inscribed within the Book of Nature, but Piscator and his companions develop Hall's argument that "fishes" have been created by the deity "for the use and behoofe of man" as they contemplatively study the nonhuman inhabitants of their riverside surroundings.[36] Joseph Hall's seventeenth-century theory of meditation as embraced by Walton transposes early modern anthropocentrism into a new key: the natural world has been created by God for the sake of humanity, but now human superiority entails attentiveness to and reflection on the lower levels of the Great Chain of Being "as a supplementary source of revelation."[37] Hall's description of humanity's divinely ordained consumption of the environment—humankind's responsibility to "use" nature through meditation—thus complicates our understanding of Walton's discourse of use value in *The Compleat Angler*. For a contemplative man, Walton's designation of "the more usefull part" of his book—"the observations of the *nature* and *breeding*, and *seasons*, and *catching of fish*" (59)—refers not only to practical information intended to help the angler fill his creel but also to "examples" (74) that can be transformed into what Hall terms "extemporal" or "occasional" meditations (72, 123).[38]

Joseph Hall's own meditations on the Book of Nature are primarily emblematic in their interpretation of the nonhuman inhabitants of the earth.

In an evocative description of his approach to meditating on the natural world, Hall helps us to experience his devout mode of attention to detail in the midst of environmental plenitude:

> There is no creature of whom we may not learn something.... Who can be so stupid as not to take notice of the industry of the Bee, the providence of the Ant, the cunning of the Spider, the reviving of the Flye, the worms endeavour of revenge, the subtlily of the Foxe, the sagacity of the Hedge-hog, the innocence and profitablenesse of the Sheep, the laboriousnesse of the Oxe, the obsequiousness of the Dog, the timorous shifts of the Hare, the nimbleness of the Dear, the generosity of the Lion, the courage of the Horse, the fiercenesse of the Tiger, the chearful musick of Birds, the harmlessnesse of the Dove, the true love of the Turtle, the Cocks observation of time, the Swallows architecture, shortly, (for it were easie here to be endlesse) of the severall qualities, and dispositions of every of those our fellow-creatures, with whom we converse on the face of the earth; and who that takes notice of them, cannot fetch from every act, and motion of theirs, some monition of duty, and occasion of devout thoughts?[39]

Hall demonstrates here how one should evaluate the Book of the Creatures as a set of moral exempla. Following this method of environmental interpretation, when Hall hears birds "chirp and sing out of ... natural joy" early on a spring morning, he extrapolates that "no otherwise is the penitent and faithful soul affected to the true Sun of righteousness, the Father of lights," and when he contemplates a spider, Hall concludes, "What is this but an emblem of those spiritual free-booters that lie in wait for our souls? They are the spiders, we the flies. They have spread their nets of sin; if we be once caught, they bind us fast and hail us into hell" (142, 131).[40] Like the authors of medieval bestiaries or Aesop's *Fables*, Hall analyzes the behavior of birds and animals in search of the divinely authored moral doctrine that should guide a Christian's thought and behavior.

Piscator and his friends are avid readers, and as they share their favorite contemplative passages from works of prose and poetry *The Compleat Angler* becomes a multiauthor anthology of meditations on the Book of Nature. Some of the writers Walton showcases, working within the emblematic tradition favored by Hall, provide Piscator with botanical exempla in which we can "*see the proudest Oak / Most subject to the rending Thunder-stroke*" (162) and contemplate the transience of life:

> Sweet Rose, whose hew angry and brave
> Bids the rash gazer wipe his eye,
> Thy root is ever in its grave,
>   and thou must die.[41] (112)

Du Bartas—whose versified account of the Genesis creation story Piscator explicitly calls "a contemplation" (71)—frequently provides Walton's anglers with similarly moralized interpretations of aquatic creatures, such as Piscator's list of "lustful and chaste fishes" that ranges from the Don Juan of the oceans, "*The Adulterous* Sargus [sea bream]," to that scaly exemplar of "*chaste love*," the female mullet, which will, Piscator approvingly notes, choose to die ashore with her partner "*if the Fisher hath surprised her pheer* [mate]" (72–73). When Piscator sings "The Anglers Song" by William Basse, he provides a model of streamside contemplation through which we can draw life lessons from the behavior of trout:

> And when the timerous Trout I wait
> To take, and he devours my bait,
> How poor a thing sometimes I find
> Will captivate a greedy mind:
> And when none bite, I praise the wise,
> Whom vain alurements ne're surprise. (97)

In a passage that first appears in the 1661 edition, Walton depicts his own contribution to his book's digest of contemplative poetry as the product of extemporal meditation. Before reciting "The Anglers Wish," Piscator explains how he came to compose it: "I'le tell you Scholar, when I sate last on this *Primrose-bank*, and look'd down these Meadows; I thought of them as *Charles* the Emperour did of the City of *Florence*: *That they were too pleasant to be look'd on, but only on Holy-days*: as I then sate on this very grass, I turn'd my present thoughts into verse: 'Twas a wish which I'le repeat to you" (262). Piscator then presents an account of meditative fishing amid "*flowry Meads*" and "*Chrystal streams*" that combines emblematic interpretation of the Book of Nature—"*see the* Turtle-dove, / *Court his chast Mate to acts of love*"—with autobiography (including references to Walton's wife and a fishing spot near his hometown of Stafford) to heighten the poem's depiction of extemporal meditation as a lived experience (262).[42] Such angling-based contemplation, writes Walton, serves to "*raise my low pitch thoughts above / Earth, or what poor mortals love,*" and he looks forward to spending all his waking hours, from dawn to dark, beside the stream so he can "*There meditate my time away*"; Walton's poem then solemnly concludes with the speaker reporting that he prays "*to have / A quiet passage to a welcome grave*" (262). Taken as a whole, the conceptual structure of this poem—an opening observation of the natural world followed by analysis of its spiritual implications and a concluding prayer—typifies the structure of Joseph Hall's occasional meditations.[43] And as Piscator verbally recounts his contemplative experience for his angling pupil, he transforms his personal meditation into a kind of sermon, a productive blurring of genres likewise characteristic of Hall's contemplative works. "Protestant meditation," Frank Livingstone Huntley remarks, "is as public as it is private, intended not for the individual alone but for large numbers of people, congregations perhaps, of the devout."[44] Thus Piscator's recitation of "The Anglers Wish" firmly aligns Walton's poem—and the narrative in which it appears—with the style of meditation on the Book of Nature that Joseph Hall theorized and practiced.

Walton's anglers frequently interpret the natural world as spiritually didactic exempla. Exactly in line with Hall's meditational practice, Venator rhetorically asks "how doth the earth afford us a doctrinal example in the little *Pismire* [ant], who in the Summer provides and lays up her Winter provision, and teaches man to do the like?" (184); whereas Piscator, in a more apocalyptic mood, remarks of the typical behavior of perch that "if there be twenty or forty in a hole, they may be at one standing all catch'd one after another; they being . . . like the wicked of the world, not afraid though their fellows and companions perish in their sight" (311). Similar to the metaphor of the Great Chain of Being, however, this emblematic mode of meditation on the Book of the Creatures contains inherent contradictions that complicate an anthropocentric worldview. On the one hand, God has designed the world to serve as a moral primer for humanity; yet on the other hand, humans find themselves humbled by their similarities to fish and their inferiority to ants. In the very achievement of environmental mastery through meditation, Walton's anglers confront the precariousness of humanity's sense of superiority to the other creatures on the planet.

Walton's meditative response to the environment sometimes departs from this emblematic style of interpretation and displays instead an emergent mode of natural theology. Like the other explicitly Christian environmental concepts that shape *The Compleat Angler,* Walton's version of natural theology is rooted in the premise that because the world has been created by a benevolent deity, humans can perceive God's goodness in the details of His creation. Rather than reading the Book of the Creatures as a compendium of moral lessons written by God for the edification of humankind, however, the adherent of natural theology interprets nature as an intricate design that, in its all-encompassing scope and beauty, reveals God's providence and sagacity. Yet again, we find the lineaments of this mode of interpretation in Joseph Hall's meditational theory: "Every herb, flower, spire of grasse, every twig and leaf; every worm and fly; every scale and feather; every billow and meteor, speaks the power and wisdom of their infinite Creator."[45] Reaching its apogee in the works of John Ray, seventeenth-century natural theology celebrated "the admirable contrivance of natural things" that "could only have been produced by an infinitely wise and beneficent agent."[46] Thus, decades after Piscator first ventured into the Hertfordshire countryside, John Ray sought "*to Trace the Footsteps of* [God's] *Wisdom in the Composition, Order, Harmony, and Uses*" of the creation, and he argued that this activity "*serve*[s] *to Stir up and Increase in us the Affections and habits of Admiration, Humility and Gratitude.*"[47] As he finds proof of God's "*Infinite Power and Wisdom*" everywhere in nature, Ray stresses not only the plenitude of the environment but also God's "*admirable Contrivance of all and each*" of the creatures and "*the Provision that is made for their Sustenance.*"[48]

We find precursors to Ray's method of interpreting the natural world in several of the contemplative passages showcased in *The Compleat Angler.* Walton's master fisherman takes a spiritualized aesthetic pleasure in "those very many *flies, worms,* and little living creatures with which the Sun and Summer adorn and beautifie the river banks and meadows; both for the recreation and contemplation of the Angler" (104), and Piscator later reports that he can regard his catch of the day with similarly devotional connoisseurship: "I have caught many a *Trout* in a particular Meadow, that the very shape and inamelled colour of him, has joyed me to look upon him, and I have with *Solomon* concluded, *Every thing is beautifull in his season*"

(116).⁴⁹ In his evocative final speech added to the conclusion of *The Compleat Angler* in 1655, Piscator's angling disciple Venator combines an emblematic reading of the New Testament's carefree lilies of the field (cited as object lessons by Christ in Matthew 6:28 and Luke 12:27) with a vision of future extemporal meditation rooted in natural theology: "So when I would beget *content*, and increase confidence in the *Power*, and *Wisdom*, and *Providence* of Almighty God, I will walk the *Meadows* by some gliding stream, and there contemplate the *Lillies* that take no care, and those very many other various little living *creatures*, that are not only created but fed (man knows not how) by the goodness of the God of *Nature*, and therefore trust in him" (371). In these passages, we find evidence for Clarence Glacken's argument that natural theology generated important ecological concepts: "Once the focus is taken away from man, the emphasis is no longer on utility but on the wider interrelationships characteristic of all nature. . . . The wisdom of the Creator is self-evident, everything in the creation is interrelated, no living thing is useless, and all are related one to the other."⁵⁰ Walton's meditative use of natural theology, although rooted in Christian anthropocentrism, can thus decenter humanity and give rise instead to a nascent perception of ecology.

At many points in *The Compleat Angler*, Walton's combination of Protestant meditation and natural theology leads him into the peculiarly early modern territory of "wonder." Rooted in the premise that the deity's complex design of the natural world transcends human understanding, the category of the "wonderful" tacitly acknowledges that the omnipotent God of Nature can produce creatures and phenomena that defy the comprehension of mere mortals. The contemplative man who piously tries to read the Book of the Creatures may thus find himself reduced to open-mouthed astonishment at God's miraculous creativity, as Walton's fishermen frequently discover.⁵¹ Early in *The Compleat Angler*, as we have already seen, Piscator legitimizes his penchant for meditating on fishy wonders by citing as his model Psalm 104, "wherein for height of Poetry and Wonders, the Prophet *David* seems even to exceed himself; how doth he there express himselfe in choice Metaphors, even to the amazement of a contemplative Reader, concerning the Sea, the Rivers, and the Fish therein contained" (71). Following the Psalmist's example, Walton's master angler repeatedly encounters wonders both in and near the water. The design and construction skills of caddis fly larvae astonish Piscator: "the case or house in which this [caddisworm] dwells is made of small husks, and gravel, and slime, most curiously made of these, even so as to be wondred at, but not to be made by man no more than a *King-fishers* nest can, which is made of little Fishes bones, and have such a Geometrical inter-weaving and connexion, as the like is not to be done by the art of man" (346–47). Here, as in passages of emblematic meditation in *The Compleat Angler*, the interpretive lens of wonder-filled natural theology causes Piscator to elevate the skills and accomplishments of lower animals over those of human beings. When Piscator tutors Viator/Venator about using live flies as bait for trout, he likewise marvels at the incomprehensible diversity of insect life to be found in the English countryside: "You are to know, that there are as many sorts of Flies as there be of Fruits: I will name you but some of them: as the *dun flie*, the *stone flie*, the *red flie*, the *moor flie*, the *tawny flie*, the *shel flie*, the *cloudy* or blackish *flie*: there be of Flies, *Caterpillars*, and *Canker flies*, and *Bear flies*; and indeed, too many either for mee to name, or for you to remember: and their breeding is so various and wonderful, that I might easily amaze my self, and tire you in a relation of them" (103).[52] Once again, an emergent concept of ecology subtends Walton's meditative excursion into natural theology: such a bewildering—"wonderful"—plenitude of insects exists because the environment contains so many different host species of "Fruits," plants, and animals.

Some of the passages of prose and verse anthologized within *The Compleat Angler* likewise contribute to Walton's wonder-filled mode of natural theology. When Piscator considers the gymnastics of salmon as they swim upstream to spawn, he shares a compendium of mind-boggling environmental observations gleaned from other writers. In a passage added in 1655, Piscator begins by citing two of his favorite authors—first Gesner, then Camden—about the "wonder" of the salmon's prodigious leaps and then quotes a passage from Drayton's *Poly-Olbion* that describes the astonishing "*Summer-salt*" of this species of fish during the spawning season (275–76). Earlier in the narrative, Piscator lightly edits a poem by George Herbert to position it more firmly within a similar discourse of wonder. The verses he will present, Piscator says, constitute Herbert's "Divine Contemplation on Gods Providence," and we find a clear emphasis on natural theology in the first two stanzas that Piscator quotes:

> Lord, who hath praise enough, nay, who hath any?
> None can express thy works, but he that knows them;

And none can know thy works, they are so many,
And so compleat, but only he that ows [owns] *them.*

We all acknowledg both thy power and love
To be exact, transcendent and divine;
Who dost so strangely and so sweetly move,
Whilst all things have their end, yet none but thine. (196)

The initial stanza, like Piscator's lead-in, establishes the poem as a meditation on the wisdom, power, and beneficence of God as discerned in the plenitude of His creation: we are now firmly in the territory of natural theology, and by echoing the first word in the title of Walton's book itself, these lines encourage us to associate Walton's overall project with what Piscator presents here as Herbert's practice of devotional meditation. Yet the astonishing *copia* of God's handiwork, although perfect and "*compleat*" in the omniscient eyes of its Creator, cannot be comprehended by lesser beings like the poem's speaker: as so often happens in *The Compleat Angler*, we are able only to wonder at the complexity of the natural world, and Walton subtly revises Herbert's language to enhance this quality of astonishment. As originally printed in Herbert's poem "Providence," the seventh and eighth lines quoted by Piscator should read, "Who dost so *strongly* and so sweetly move, / While all things have their *will*, yet none but thine."[53] By substituting "*strangely*" for "*strongly*" and "*end*" for "*will*," Walton increases the power of God over a more wonder-filled creation than Herbert had originally depicted. Thus acting as a writer, anthologist, and editor of environmental texts, Walton creates in *The Compleat Angler* a bountiful literary ecosystem of meditations that both depict and embody the wonderful diversity of a numinous natural world.

But Walton's highly developed capacity for wonder can also result in startling incongruity. As Piscator lectures Viator/Venator about pike fishing, we discover how "the more usefull part" (59) of Walton's book can encompass both repulsive angling techniques and wonder-filled meditation at the same time. In the midst of a stomach-churning set of instructions about how to transform a live frog into pike bait, Piscator suddenly modulates into contemplation: "Put your hook into his [the frog's] mouth, which you may easily do from about the middle of *April* till *August*, and then the *Frogs* mouth grows up and he continues so for at least six months without eating, but is sustained, none, but he whose name is Wonderful, knows how" (126).

As we shall see, Walton was fascinated by accounts of miraculous eating and anorexia, and after mentioning the frog's mouth in his hook-baiting tutorial, Piscator cannot resist pursuing this favorite topic. Following his brief excursion into the natural theology of inappetence, however, Piscator matter-of-factly concludes his instructions for skewering a frog onto a fishing hook, advising the would-be pike angler to torture the unlucky amphibian "as though you loved him, that is, harme him as little as you may possibly, that he may live the longer" (126). Lord Byron alluded to this disturbing passage when he deemed Walton a "sentimental savage" and argued that "no angler can be a good man," but Walton himself saw no conflict between vivisecting a frog as bait and using it as a "wonderful" object of contemplation.[54]

Throughout *The Compleat Angler*, Walton praises the spiritual and psychological impact of meditating outdoors. As we have already seen, in his last speech in the book Venator describes streamside meditation as a guaranteed way to "beget *content*, and increase confidence in the *Power*, and *Wisdom*, and *Providence* of Almighty God" (371), and several of the poems that Walton anthologizes confirm this characterization. During the anglers' postprandial entertainment one evening, a fisherman named Coridon sings a song that opens with a panegyric to the mental-health benefits of meditation: "*Oh the sweet contentment / The country-man doth find! / . . . That quiet contemplation / Possesseth all my mind*" (239). Walton's own poem "The Anglers Wish" similarly begins by extolling the salutary psychological impact of emulating the biblical Isaac and meditating in the fields: "*I in these flowry Meads wou'd be: / These Chrystal streams should solace me; / To whose harmonious bubling noise, / I with my Angle wo'd rejoice*" (262). Several lines later, Piscator depicts how extemporal meditation on a natural object immediately heightens his sense of well-being, noting that he may "*feel the west wind / Breath health and plenty, please my mind / To see sweet dew-drops kiss these flowers, / And then, washt off by* April-*showers*" (262). Walton's wide-ranging exploration of *The Contemplative Man's Recreation* thus presents a Christianized, environmental affirmation of Aristotle's idea that in order to live happily, one must take time to meditate.[55]

VERSIONS OF PASTORAL

Walton's contemplative appreciation of the natural world in *The Compleat Angler* frequently draws on the pastoral mode. Rooted in the self-consciously stylized depictions of the lives of shepherds in the poetry of Theocritus and Virgil, pastoral provided sixteenth- and seventeenth-century English writers with a highly malleable repertoire of conventions through which they could simultaneously portray and interrogate the ecosocial aspects of human existence. The shepherds of early modern pastoral usually inhabit an Edenic world of perpetual springtime that allows them to lead simple, unhurried lives in harmony with nature. Their interpersonal relationships, unlike the weather, are often imperfect, but conflict among the shepherds is usually confined to the low-stakes arenas of amatory pursuits and impromptu singing competitions: in the pastoral mode, men do die from time to time and worms do eat them, but not for love or a second-place finish in *Arcadia's Got Talent*. Nonetheless, the qualities of idealism and simplicity intrinsic to pastoral are inevitably challenged by "the instabilities, tensions, and paradoxes embedded ... in the simultaneous realism and artifice" of this literary mode.[56] George Puttenham argued that "*pastorall Poesie*" is inherently double in nature, not created "of purpose to counterfait or represent the rusticall manner of loves and communication: but under the vaile of homely persons, and in rude speeches to insinuate and glaunce at greater matters, and such as perchance had not bene safe to have been disclosed in any other sort."[57] Early modern authors thus often used pastoral as a vehicle of political critique, and perhaps feeling that the "predatory art" of angling was more suitable for such calculated doublespeak, some English writers, influenced by the *Eclogae Piscatoriae* (*Piscatorial Eclogues*) of the Italian poet Jacopo Sannazaro, expanded the ecological and occupational dimensions of pastoral by populating its idyllic countryside with fishermen rather than shepherds.[58] In 1645, Izaak Walton combined both these sets of pastoral characters in his preface to Francis Quarles's *The Shepheards Oracles*: Walton depicts Quarles as an angler who, having gone trout fishing one May morning, overheard the "discourse" of a group of shepherds whose transcribed "Eglogues" now constitute Quarles's collection of poems.[59] So nearly a decade before he published his angling treatise, Walton was exploring the relationship between pastoral conventions and the realistic narrative of a springtime fishing trip, a juxtaposition that he revisits in different ways in *The Compleat Angler*.

Many commentators have regarded Walton's use of pastoral as crucial to an understanding of his fishing treatise. Because the pastoral mode can encompass multiple—often antithetical—perspectives, however, disparate definitions of pastoral underlie and finally fracture what may initially look like a critical consensus about the nature of Walton's artistic vision and achievement; moreover, taken on its own terms, each pastoral-centric reading of Walton's book proves problematic.[60] Walton's first editor, Moses Browne, wrote in his preface to the 1750 edition of *The Compleat Angler* that "*Mr. Walton was a Writer of the true pastoral Character*," and over the following centuries readers have frequently reiterated Browne's opinion, praising Walton's book as "a complete pastoral picture of angling as a way of life," "England's one perfect Pastoral," or, even more broadly, "the best pastoral in the language."[61] Such assessments usually focus on Walton's depiction of "fresh meads" that are "fairer than life itself": Walton's use of pastoral, from this vantage point, consists in the "detailed evocation of a charming countryside" that allows readers to imaginatively join Walton's fishermen as they leave the crowded squalor of the city and immerse themselves in a beautiful green world.[62] As we have seen, although Walton's meditative perspective on the environment leads him to consider everything from ants to kingfishers' nests with reverent attention, his anglers do indeed periodically gaze upon and give thanks for conventional scenes of rural beauty. In the most celebrated of these vignettes (which, as Jonquil Bevan has pointed out, echoes a passage from Sir Philip Sidney's *Arcadia*), Piscator recounts how, in his preceding fishing trip to Hertfordshire, he sat under a "broad *Beech tree* . . . near to the brow of that Primrose hil; there I sate viewing the Silver streams glide silently towards their center, the tempestuous Sea, yet sometimes opposed by rugged roots, and pibble stones, which broke their waves, and turned them into fome: and sometimes viewing the harmless Lambs, some leaping securely in the cool shade, whilst others sported themselvs in the cheerful Sun; and others were craving comfort from the swolne Udders of their bleating Dams" (88).[63] Walton's repeated evocation of "lovely flowers that adorn the verdant Meadows" (88) is an important component of his pastoral landscape description in *The Compleat Angler*, and we see in the passage quoted above Walton's habitual creation of compound terms that transform features of the landscape into floral displays: in addition to this "Primrose hil," the countryside adjacent to the River Lea features a "*Primrose-bank*" (262, added to the 1661 ed.), "*Cowslip-banks*" (261, added to the 1655 ed.), and multiple "honeysuckle-hedges" (231, 263, 362). Walton's floralization of rural topography departs strikingly from Sidney's description of "meadows enamelled with all sorts of eye-pleasing flowers," the artisanal diction of which "assimilat[es] . . . the natural to the human."[64] Taken by themselves, such moments of pastoral beauty might indeed cause a reader to regard *The Compleat Angler* as imbued with a "mellow vision of field and stream, of lambs frisking and children gathering lilies and cowslips."⁶⁵ And for Walton's first readers, inhabiting landscapes despoiled by years of civil war, such idyllic images of a verdant, flower-studded countryside surely would have elicited nostalgia for a green and pleasant land unscarred by warfare's environmental devastation, a connection emphasized in a poem that Viator/Venator recites near the very end of *The Compleat Angler*:

> *Here's no fantastick Mask nor Dance,*
> *But of our kids that frisk and prance;*
> *Nor wars are seen,*
> *Unless upon the green*
> *Two harmless Lambs are butting one the other,*
> *Which done, both bleating, run each to his mother:*
> *And wounds are never found,*
> *Save what the Plough-share gives the ground.* (160)

Other aspects of Walton's depiction of springtime in Hertfordshire are less easily analyzed as the soothing components of a "mellow" pastoralism, however. New Historicist scholars of *The Compleat Angler* argue that Walton, like other royalist writers during the civil wars and interregnum, adopted the pastoral mode as literary protective camouflage to express political dissent. From this perspective, to use Puttenham's terminology, Walton's pastoralism "glaunce[s] at greater matters" and his book is, above all, a work of royalist critique that describes a bucolic natural world solely to gesture to the political reality that it thus encodes. At times, Walton certainly uses pastoral as a self-consciously political discourse of royalist defiance—most importantly, I would argue, in the seasonal setting of Walton's narrative. Commentators have long noted that Walton goes to great lengths to make his story appear to unfold in real time. The first edition of *The Compleat Angler* was published early in May 1653, and Walton, seeking to create the illusion that his first readers were experiencing Piscator's journey as it occurred, carefully plotted the narrative so it unfolds during a span of several days at the beginning of that same month; later editors often highlighted this feature of Walton's text by dividing the book not into its original chapters but instead into the five days of the anglers' fishing expedition.⁶⁶ Walton thus tightly fastens his book's swirling mass of environmental perspectives, including his use of the pastoral mode, onto a realistically conceived framework of calendrical time. Walton establishes the time frame of his story in the very first sentence of the 1653 edition when Piscator greets Viator on "this fine pleasant fresh *May day* in the Morning" (63). And in case we missed this narrative timestamp, as the opening chapter concludes, Piscator reminds us again of the date when he praises some verses by John Dennys that he has just recited as "more pleasant and more sutable to *May Day*, then my harsh Discourse" (79).[67] Walton thus explicitly begins the narrative of *The Compleat Angler* on May 1—May Day—1653, and we should carefully consider the implications of this crucial detail.

The calendar of Walton's book makes perfect sense on a practical level. Walton's anglers regard trout as the ne plus ultra of fish—Piscator openly confesses that trout is the species "for which I love to angle above any fish"— and, as Walton's master angler goes on to observe, trout "usually . . . be in their perfection in the month of *May*" (98). May is also the best month to learn how to catch trout, for as Charles Cotton observes in his fly-fishing treatise, "almost any thing will take [catch] a Trout in *May*."[68] So trout-crazed anglers in early modern England would naturally have tried to emulate Piscator and go fishing during the month of May.

At the same time, however, astute readers of the first edition of *The Compleat Angler* would have recognized additional layers of meaning in the book's springtime setting. May Day was traditionally celebrated in early modern England as a holiday that immersed people in the natural world. The church had long tried to Christianize the first day of May by transforming it into the Feast of St. Philip and St. James the Less.[69] In *Scintillula Altaris*, Edward Sparke suggests that it is appropriate to celebrate St. Philip and St. James in the midst of the *"Glories* of the *Spring"* because *"These Too* cause *Spirituall Flourishing,* / Shew flowery Pastures, leade to Pleasant Brookes / In Sweet *Disclosures* of the *Sacred Books"*; but as the lameness of Sparke's rationale suggests, this cultural forced marriage never succeeded, and the traditional English observance of May Day remained firmly rooted in pre-Christian fertility festivals, "all veneration for the saints . . . submerged in a welter of secular and pagan activities" celebrating the springtime vitality of nature.[70] Writing in 1598, John Stow reported that Londoners "in the moneth of May, namely on May day in the morning, every man (except impediment) would walke into the sweet meadowes and greene woods, there to rejoyce their spirites with beuty and savour of sweete flowers, and with the noyce of birdes, praising God in their kinde," and Walton's urbanite anglers continue this tradition in 1653 by leaving London and heading into the countryside early on May Day.[71] As part of the time-honored "maying" customs practiced before the civil wars, the population of England would also create decorations from the flowers and fresh boughs they gathered in the fields and woods: this convention—although deeply transgressive in 1653—is likewise portrayed in *The Compleat Angler* when Walton's novice angler recalls how he sat beneath a waterside willow tree and "looking down the Meadows, could see here a Boy gathering *Lillies* and *Lady-smocks*, and there a Girle cropping *Culverkeys* and *Cowslips*, all to make Garlands sutable to this present Month of *May*" (150).[72] In these passages, Walton presents a purified version of May Day traditions, consonant with a "mellow" version of the pastoral mode. As contemplative anglers, Piscator and his friends do not put up a maypole, perform morris dances, or otherwise engage in the disorder and sexually charged "May-games" that had long outraged puritan critics like Philip Stubbes, who fulminated that on May Day, "of fortie, threescore, or a hundred maides going to the wood over night there have scarcely the third part of them returned home againe undefiled."[73] Stubbes wildly exaggerated the aphrodisiac effect of May Day—historians have discovered "that patterns of marital conception, let alone of bastard-bearing, have little relationship to seasonal revelry" in early modern England[74]—but nonetheless, his condemnation of May games during the 1580s was a harbinger of the widespread cultural conflict over traditional holiday celebrations that would only intensify during the first half of the seventeenth century.

As puritans continued to advocate the outlawing of games and festive pastimes on the sabbath and other dates of religious significance, the observance of holidays evolved into a deeply divisive cultural and political issue throughout England. Because celebrations involving maypoles were customarily held on Sundays, May Day became a particular focus for sabbatarian reformers and their adversaries during the Stuart period.[75] In 1617–18, King James I attempted to quell the sabbatarianism of radical Protestants by issuing his Book of Sports, a work that promoted the popular pursuit of traditional forms of "lawful recreation"—including May games—on Sundays and holidays, providing participation in such festivities did not lead to "impediment or neglect of divine service."[76] James's Book of Sports—often called the Book of Recreation by contemporaries—became increasingly controversial.[77] For King Charles I, puritan attacks on traditional festivities threatened the very identity of the English church, and in 1633 Charles reissued his father's anti-sabbatarian text and ordered that it be read from every pulpit. Like many of the policies conceived and implemented during the years of his personal rule, Charles I's advocacy of "recreation" only contributed to the demise of the monarchy, and on April 8, 1644, during the full-blown chaos of the civil wars, the festive celebration of May Day was banned by Parliament and the Book of Sports was ordered to "be called in, seized, suppressed, and publiquely burnt."[78] So when Izaak Walton published the first edition of *The Compleat Angler* in 1653, both May Day and the Stuart monarchs' Book of Recreation had been abolished for nearly a decade.

There is thus much more to the springtime setting of Walton's book than innocently "mellow" pastoral descriptions of flower-filled meadows: Walton clearly displays his royalist sympathies by opening the narrative of his *Contemplative Man's Recreation* on May 1, 1653.[79] As David Underdown observes, "Festive rituals were often symbolic expressions of opposition to government" in mid-seventeenth-century England, and between 1644 and the Restoration, May Day served as the occasion for repeated acts of transgression that unnerved both local and national officials.[80] The same year that Walton published the first edition of *The Compleat Angler*, May Day festivities in Wolverhampton resulted in the arrest of the participants: despite the revelers' claim that they were celebrating Cromwell's dismissal of the Rump Parliament rather than challenging ecclesiastical and political authorities, the Council of State "authorized the use of troops if necessary to restore order," and similarly prohibited, sometimes violent May Day festivities were common in many parts of the country throughout the 1650s.[81] Thus, when Walton first published *The Compleat Angler* in 1653, his evocation of maying traditions would have registered with an attentive reader as thinly veiled political defiance.

Our analysis of the springtime setting of *The Compleat Angler* becomes even more richly complicated when we note that May 1, 1653, fell on a Sunday.[82] As we have seen, the seventeenth-century controversy over May Day celebrations was just one symptom of a larger cultural dispute about how the people of England should respond to the Fourth Commandment: "Remember the sabbath day, to keep it holy. Six days shalt thou labour, and do all thy work: But the seventh day *is* the sabbath of the LORD thy God:

in it thou shalt not do any work, thou, nor thy son, nor thy daughter, thy manservant, nor thy maidservant, nor thy cattle, nor thy stranger that *is* within thy gates" (Exod. 20:8–10). Rather than viewing Sunday primarily as a day for leisure and recreation after attendance at church services, puritan sabbatarians argued that the entirety of Sunday should be dedicated "to an uninterrupted cycle of public and private devotional exercises and charitable works."[83] Sabbatarianism became the law of the land in England during the 1640s, and from 1644 through 1657 "increasingly rigorous legislation" sought to transform Sunday into a "whole-day Christian sabbath."[84] The ordinance prohibiting the traditional celebration of May Day began by insisting that the entire population "shall on every Lords-day, apply themselves to the sanctification of the same, by exercising themselves thereon, in the duties of Piety and true Religion, publickly and privately": any kind of work or commercial activity was forbidden on Sunday, as was travel "without reasonable cause," which would be fined.[85] Nine months later, the ordinance abolishing the Book of Common Prayer further specified that on Sundays there must be "an abstaining, not onely from all sports and pastimes, but also from all worldly words and thoughts," and any time not spent attending church must "be spent in Reading, Meditation, Repetition of Sermons" and similarly pious activities; another ordinance issued in October 1645 categorized as "scandalous persons" who should be denied communion those who "upon the Lords Day . . . use Hawking, Hunting, or Coursing, Fishing, or Fowling" as well as "any person that shall travel on the Lords Day without reasonable cause"; and an Act passed in 1650 forbade travelers from changing their lodgings on the sabbath and banned "drinking, or tipling" in public premises on Sundays.[86] Even the seemingly innocuous activity of walking in the fields on the sabbath was proscribed in London and other jurisdictions during the interregnum.[87] At the same time, however, the need for repeated proclamations urging the enforcement of existing sabbatarian laws suggests that many people did not readily embrace the strictures of a whole-day sabbath.[88]

So as they walk through the countryside on a May Day that is also the sabbath, Piscator and Viator not only perpetuate what were, in 1653, forbidden maying customs, but they also violate interregnum restrictions on Sunday activities. By traveling rather than attending church services on the sabbath and daring to have "a cup of Ale" and take up lodgings at an inn on a Sunday evening (79), Walton's anglers establish themselves as the kind of "scandalous persons" who should be denied communion and fined for their sins.[89] Walton thus uses the seasonal setting of *The Compleat Angler* to stage a defiant piece of political theater. And with hindsight, we realize that the subtitle of Walton's book, *The Contemplative Man's Recreation*, by echoing the popular name for the Stuart monarchs' Book of Sports, prepares us to understand Walton's fishing treatise as a work of politicized critique.

Yet, if the politics of *The Compleat Angler* thus complicate our analysis of Walton's use of the pastoral mode, Walton's "mellow" pastoralism in turn complicates our understanding of the book's politics. As we have already noted, Walton's G-rated May Day contains no phallic maypoles, unruly festivities, or erotically suggestive "green-gowns": even as Walton evokes the traditional holiday celebrations promoted by his dead king, his desexualized portrayal of pastoral components of maying customs (the enjoyment of the outdoors and the gathering of flowers) sanitizes Walton's depiction of May Day and places Piscator and his friends on a middle ground between defiant royalist promotion and puritan condemnation of the holiday.[90] Likewise, Walton's emphasis on a contemplative response to the natural world allows him to fill his anglers' May Day conversations with devout analyses of both God's creation and human exemplars of religious virtue: by spending their Sunday in meditation, Piscator and his disciple act in accordance with both the letter and the spirit of sabbatarian regulations even as their travel and consumption of alcohol defy the same strictures.

When Walton revised and expanded *The Compleat Angler* in later editions, he further countered a univocally political reading of the seasonality of his book. Beginning with the first edition published after the Restoration, Walton changed the opening line of his narrative so that it no longer specifies the first day of Piscator's fishing trip as May 1: Piscator instead hails Venator and Auceps on "this fine, fresh *May* morning" (173). The May setting of Walton's *Angler* was still politically resonant during the Restoration, for both houses of Parliament had voted to reestablish "the Government... by King, Lords, and Commons" on May 1, 1660, and Charles II arrived in London on May 29, 1660—his thirtieth birthday.[91] David Cressy notes that "Charles II was the May king, born in that month, and re-born to his kingdom, ever to be associated with maypoles and the revelling good fellowship of his father's and grandfather's Book of Sports."[92] Yet as Walton increased the amount of material devoted to descriptions of the natural world and its inhabitants in later editions of *The Compleat Angler*, the political charge of his book's May setting became overshadowed and subsumed into a less topical celebration of springtime.

The political stakes of the pastoral mode in *The Compleat Angler* are likewise complicated when Walton self-consciously evokes the poetry of Virgil. In his first *Eclogue*, Virgil presents a dialogue between two shepherds, Meliboeus and Tityrus, who converse beneath a large beech tree. Caught in the aftermath of civil war, the herdsman Meliboeus faces removal from his land, which will be given to a soldier from the victorious army; Tityrus, by contrast, has had his farm restored to him by a powerful benefactor.[93] This poem, with its depiction of an innocent man evicted from his rural property after warfare has devastated his fields, resonated powerfully in the 1650s with displaced royalist landowners who, because of self-exile or sequestration, found themselves compelled to abandon their estates.[94] As we have already remarked, in *The Compleat Angler*, the shade provided by a "broad *Beech tree*" (88)—a Hertfordshire scion of Virgil's tree—becomes a favorite site for Piscator's outdoor meditations, and from the second edition of 1655 onward, "*smooth-leav'd* beeches *in the field*" also give shelter to a humble but contented man in verses quoted by Venator (335).[95] But Walton explicitly invokes Virgil's first *Eclogue* when Piscator, concluding his mini-lecture to Viator about fly-fishing for trout, remarks that the two anglers have "sate as quietly and as free from cares under this *Sycamore*, as *Virgils Tityrus* and his *Meliboeus* did under their broad *Beech* tree: No life, my honest Scholar, no life so happy and so pleasant as the Anglers" (112). Three decades later, Walton's association with Virgil's politically charged text was celebrated by Thomas Flatman in his dedicatory verses for the edition of John Chalkhill's pastoral narrative poem *Thealma and Clearchus* that Walton published in 1683: Flatman addresses Walton as a "Happy Old Man, whose worth all mankind knows," echoing the reiterated vocative "Fortunate senex" with which Meliboeus addresses Tityrus in the first *Eclogue* and thus identifying Walton with Virgil himself.[96] Yet in *The Compleat Angler*, Walton's conflation of Meliboeus and Tityrus as "happy" rustics completely rewrites Virgil's narrative, calling into question the politics of his evocation of Virgil.[97] Walton's anglers, as we shall see in chapter 4, persistently challenge orthodox concepts of property, and by erasing the figure of the dispossessed landowner crucial to royalist appropriations of Virgil, Walton adds to his equivocal depiction of landownership. Moreover, by placing his anglers beneath a sycamore rather than a beech tree, Walton frames his rewriting of Virgil's first eclogue within a specifically Christian context: the sycamore was understood in the seventeenth century to be the same species of plant as the fig tree from the leaves of which the fallen Adam and Eve created the first clothes in human history.[98] Regarding the characters and setting of eclogue 1 from beneath "that Sycamore, / Whose leaves first sheltered man from drought and dew," Piscator disregards the basis of royalist polemic and instead aligns Virgilian pastoral with Walton's optimistic mode of Christian contemplation through which humankind can enhance its relationship with the Creator in a postlapsarian natural world.[99]

GEORGIC MODULATIONS

Such glimpses of Arcadia by no means dominate Walton's multifaceted depiction of the environment, however. Historically, pastoral "evolved from the practicalities" of its literary forebear, the georgic mode, and the repressed "practicalities" of georgic frequently return to qualify evocations of bucolic perfection in *The Compleat Angler*.[100] Named after Virgil's eponymous poems but originating even earlier in Hesiod's *Works and Days*, georgic both explains and celebrates the quotidian tasks of rural farmers. Pastoral and georgic thus exist not as diametrically opposed environmental templates but rather as "the ends of a spectrum of possibilities for writing about the countryside."[101] Like pastoral, georgic promotes the idea that human life can assume its most gratifying form in the country; but rather than a bucolic, premodern Club Med where the bounty of nature spontaneously fulfills shepherds' needs in a world of perpetual springtime, georgic presents a rural landscape of seasonal change where nature sustains human existence only through the difficult labor performed by skilled agricultural workers. During the seventeenth century, georgic and pastoral were often regarded as competing political codes: whereas the Stuart monarchs and their royalist supporters favored pastoral's depiction of "leisured, aristocratic *sprezzatura*" and implicit veneration of an idyllic status quo, georgic, by contrast, was associated with political and religious reform as well as scientific innovation.[102] In response to repeated crop failures and dearth, puritan promoters of agrarian improvement such as Ralph Austen, Walter Blith, and Samuel Hartlib sought to remedy the effects of the Fall on the natural world and reassert humanity's divinely ordained "dominion" over the earth in order to increase agricultural productivity.[103] Both pastoral and georgic were thus aligned with theologically and politically charged visions of Edenic perfection, and as early modern writers sought to define the optimal relationship between human beings and the natural world, English literature became marked by a shifting, dynamic imbrication of these two modes. Looking at the text's relative balance between georgic and pastoral elements, one might argue that *The Compleat Angler* demonstrates how this "'georgicization' of pastoral" created "a richly composite mode of rural panegyric" in seventeenth-century English literature and culture.[104] At the same time, however, in Walton's book, the georgic mode functions within a polyphony of environmental discourses and fruitfully maintains its distinctive identity even as it interacts with—and sometimes contradicts—other perspectives on the natural world, including Walton's versions of pastoral.

Although Walton was always strangely silent about his own successful career as a skilled craftsman, he unabashedly celebrates angling as "*an Art*" that must be developed through "*pleasant labour*" (57). Walton states in his preface to the reader that "no man is born an *Artist* nor an *Angler*," and Piscator later attests that one can become the latter only with "diligence, and observation, and practice, and an ambition to be the best in the Art" (60, 348). As an angling treatise, *The Compleat Angler* thus exemplifies the burgeoning genre of the seventeenth-century how-to manual. Inspired by the increasingly respectable georgic impulse to improve techniques of husbandry, Walton's contemporaries churned out instructional books on such topics as horse breeding, orcharding, farriery, farming, cattle breeding, gardening, and bee keeping, and Walton's project of teaching English anglers how to harvest freshwater fish more effectively springs from the same enthusiasm for agrarian improvement that led to the publication of handbooks about raising vegetables and cultivating silkworms.[105] *The Compleat Angler* overlaps with these how-to manuals most obviously in Piscator's instructions for creating fishponds, which Walton drew primarily from the English translation of a sixteenth-century French husbandry treatise.[106] But in addition to pond-reared carp and tench, Walton encourages his angler to raise many different, far less orthodox species of livestock. Walton primarily caught fish with live bait rather than fabricated lures or artificial flies, and his angling treatise provides instructions for the cultivation of multiple species of insects for use as fish bait. Piscator explains how to create a terrarium out of a "great earthen pot or barrel of three or four gallons" in which one can keep winged ants—regarded as a delicacy by multiple species of fish (152)—and he likewise reports that the larval form of the caddis fly, "kept three or four days in a woollen bag with sand at the bottom of it, and the bag wet once a day, will ... be a choice bait" for "any great fish" (156). One of the most revolting passages in *The Compleat Angler* contains Piscator's matter-of-fact account of different techniques for raising maggots during the winter: he recommends that one prepare as a growing medium either a rotting piece of "beasts liver"—suspended above a container of clay into which the maggots will fall as they mature—or the fly-blown carcass of either a cat or raptor, buried in a frost-free patch of moist earth, that can be dug up for just-in-time harvests of worms (153). In all such passages, the mucky-fingered georgic reality of bait husbandry obliterates any traces of decorous pastoralism from Walton's text.

Other descriptions of the procurement and use of bait species inflect the georgic mode in different ways. Because an angler needs special equipment to capture caddis fly larvae, Piscator explains how to fashion a caddisworm collecting stick; but when Piscator reports that he has been "much pleased to walk quietly by a Brook with a little stick in my hand, with which I might easily take these [caddis fly larvae], and consider the curiosity of their composure" (156–57), the georgic mode provides the angler not only with fish bait but also with a subject for contemplative wonder. Learning from the morally emblematic ant that farsightedly "lays up her Winter provision" (184), Walton's anglers also venture into georgic territory when they harvest bait they can use during the winter to catch roach, dace, and chub. At the beginning of November, Piscator counsels,

> (and so till Frost comes) when you see men ploughing up heath-ground, or sandy ground, or greenswards [grass-covered areas], then follow the plough, and you shall find a white worm, as big as two Magots, and it hath a red head (you may observe in what ground most are, for there the Crows will be very watchful, and follow the Plough very close); it is all soft, and full of whitish guts; a worm that is in *Norfolk*, and some other Countries called a *Grub*.... [G]ather a thousand or two of these, and put them with a peck or two of their own earth into some tub or firkin, and cover and keep them so warm, that the frost or cold air, or winds kill them not, and you may keep them all winter and kill fish with them at any time. (152–53)

The angler's activities of gathering and caring for grubs, like the autumnal "ploughing" that enables his gleaning of such fish bait, immerse him in the georgic mode. When Piscator advises that his foraging angler should emulate crows, however, a georgic task becomes indistinguishable from the opportunistic behavior of hungry animals, and the identities of the laboring fisherman and the "watchful" corvids become blurred. Bait-species georgic in *The Compleat Angler* can thus inspire meditation, root the angler in the unglamorous chores of husbandry, and associate him with creatures to which humans are supposedly superior.

Throughout his angling manual, Walton closely aligns his georgic vision with natural history. In his preface to the reader, as we have seen, Walton advises that "the more usefull part" of *The Compleat Angler* consists of "the observations of the *nature* and *breeding*, and *seasons*, and *catching of fish*" (59), and these categories of instruction regularly lead Piscator to provide firsthand descriptions of organisms—like caddisworms, grubs, and maggots—that do not normally inhabit the Golden Age countryside of the pastoral mode. In order to experience the great "pleasure" of catching a trout with "a naturall fly" (111), Piscator and his companions forage for insects likely to whet the appetites of hungry fish. So like field biologists, Walton's characters must identify and study not only fish but also a wide range of invertebrates, and Piscator helpfully provides detailed eyewitness accounts of the habitat and behavior of insects: the species of flies favored by trout, Piscator reports, "may be found thus, the *May-fly* usually in and about that month [May] neer to the River side, especially against [near the beginning of] rain; the *Oak-fly* on the Butt or body of an *Oak* or *Ash*, from the beginning of *May* to the end of *August*; it is a brownish fly, and easie to be so found, and stands usually with his head downward, that is to say, towards the root of the tree; the smal black fly, or *hawthorn* fly is to be had on any Hawthorn bush, after the leaves be come forth" (111). This same kind of sharp-eyed expertise in riparian entomology is likewise required of the fly fisherman, who must be able to adapt to local conditions as he fashions artificial flies in imitation of a trout's favorite *insecte du jour*:

> [A]n ingenuous Angler may walk by the River and mark what fly falls on the water that day, and catch one of them, if he see the *Trouts* leap at a fly of that kind, and having alwaies hooks ready hung with him, and having a bag also, always with him [filled with fly-tying

> materials].... [A]nd if he hit to make his *flie* right, and have the luck to hit also where there is store of *trouts*, and a right wind, he shall catch such store of them, as will encourage him to grow more and more in love with the Art of *fly-making*. (109)

In another passage, Piscator warns his disciple that to understand caddis-worms "and their several kinds, and to what flies every particular *Cadis* turns, and then how to use them first as they be *Cadis*, and after as they be *flies*, is an art, and an art that every one that professes to be an Angler has not leisure to search after, and if he had is not capable of learning" (347). To succeed in the "art" of angling, Walton's recreational fishermen must continually conduct research in natural history, and as a result, the georgic labor exerted by Walton's anglers is intellectual as well as physical.

As evidenced in the preceding passages, Piscator's angling tutorials are implicitly underwritten by the idea that to catch fish in a specific body of water, an angler must carefully study the surrounding ecosystem in all its complex particularity. Piscator's discussions of natural history thus often depict plants and animals living within interrelated networks: although the term *ecology* was not coined until the nineteenth century, Walton clearly understood the concept and encourages the seventeenth-century angler to do likewise. The environmental relationships encompassing a particular body of water (and thus the life of its fish) are definitively shaped by its surrounding vegetation, Piscator acknowledges: "Mulberries and those Black-berries, which grow upon Briers, be good baits for *Chubs* or *Carps*, with these many have been taken in Ponds, and in some Rivers where such Trees have grown near the water and the fruit customarily dropt into it" (346). When Piscator gazes at the countryside through the lens of natural history, trees lose their symbolic meanings and become instead noteworthy components of an ecological community: thus, rather than sheltering the lamenting Children of Israel, willows are significant because they provide effective erosion control around fishponds and serve as host plants for puss moth caterpillars (70, 357, 105).[107] As we have already noted, Walton's vision of a wonder-filled natural world often springs from his delighted astonishment at the abundance of invertebrates that inhabit the English countryside, and Piscator recognizes this plenitude of creatures exists only because of the corresponding diversity of habitat that supplies so many different sources of food and shelter. Piscator observes that "every plant has his particular flie or

Caterpillar, which it breeds and feeds" (249), and Walton's keen sense of the interrelatedness of flora and fauna leads him to coin the compound name "dock-worm" for a grub that uses plants of the genus *Rumex* as its host.[108] In this vein, Piscator remarks how worms "for colour and shape alter even as the ground out of which they are got: as the *marsh-worm*, the *tag-tail*, the *flag-worm*, the *dock-worm*, the *oak-worm*, the *gilt-tayle*, the *twachel* or *lob-worm* (which of all others is the most excellent bait for a *Salmon*) and too many to name, even as many sorts, as some think there be of several hearbs or shrubs, or of several kinds of birds in the air" (245). The breadth and intricacy of riparian ecology make the angler's study of natural history both demanding and richly rewarding.

Walton's vision of natural history is further complicated by his recognition that the English countryside is a socionatural environment long modified by the activities of human beings, and he thus often depicts the ecology of *The Compleat Angler* as fundamentally georgic. Husbandry sometimes infiltrates Piscator's descriptions of the behavior of fish and insects: an individual barbel "will root and dig in the sands with his nose like a hog," barbel en masse "flock together like sheep" (322), and a chub will bite at "the young *humble-bee* that breeds in long grasse, and is ordinarily found by the Mower of it" (222). Farm animals can enter Walton's narrative on the hoof: as we have seen, Piscator recounts viewing lambs and ewes from his vantage point beneath a "broad *Beech tree*" on a "Primrose hil" (88), and Walton's anglers drink "a draught of *Red-Cows milk*" provided by a milkwoman to whom Piscator and his disciple give some freshly caught fish (145). More often, however, we encounter domesticated livestock in the form of their dung, which insects transform into habitat. Indeed, Walton's connoisseurship of manure provides one of the most jarringly anti-pastoral features of *The Compleat Angler*. Piscator advises that the brandling—a species of worm irresistible to trout—"is usually found in an old dunghil, or some very rotten place near to it: but most usually in Cow-dung, or hogs-dung, rather than horse-dung, which is somewhat too hot and dry for that worm" (244), and he encourages us to hunt for "the *Dor* or *Beetle*, (which you may find under a Cow-tird) or a *Bob*, which you will find in the same place, and in time will be a Beetle; it is a short white worm" (221). Such passages force us to abandon the blissfully ignorant panoramic gaze of primrose-hill pastoral and confront instead the zoom-lens georgic reality of a pasture bestrewn with fecal matter: not the setting for Golden Age idealism, certainly, but a happy hunting ground for an avid angler in search of worms and grubs.[109] Elsewhere, the reeking farmyard manure pile again steams its way into the reader's consciousness as Piscator remarks that one can catch eels with lampreys, which "may in the hot months be found many of them in the River *Thames*, and in many mud-heaps in other Rivers, yea, almost as usually as one finds worms in a dunghill" (318). At such moments, the activity of harvesting fish bait from the feces of livestock transposes Walton's georgic mode into an unabashedly excremental key.

In other passages, human industry and architecture, rather than agriculture, create new types of zoological habitat. Just as worms and beetle larvae transform the dung of nonnative, domesticated animals into their homes and nurseries, both invertebrates and fish convert humanity's refuse and built environment into their own havens. Although brandlings, as we have seen, can thrive in piles of cow manure, Piscator reports that "the best of them are to be found in the bark of the Tanners which they cast up in heaps after they have used it about their leather" (244–45), and to please the palate of a chub, Piscator recommends that one should harvest as bait "the black *Bee* that breeds in clay [mortared] walls" (222).[110] Many of the aquatic ecosystems mentioned in Piscator's angling instructions are not pristine but altered by humans, yet they nonetheless support fish populations in unintended and surprising ways. While salmon have wondrously learned how to navigate rivers that have become human-engineered obstacle courses—"they will force themselves through *Flood-gates*, or over *Weires*, or *hedges*, or *stops* in the water, even to a height beyond common belief" (275)—other fish transform human structures into habitat: a barbel "sometimes . . . retires to deep and swift Bridges, or Flood-gates, or Weires, where he will nest himself amongst piles, or in hollow places, and take such hold of moss or weeds, that be the water never so swift, it is not able to force him from the place that he contends for" (322); similarly, eels "do not usually stir in the day time, for then they hide themselves under some covert, or under boards or planks about Flood-gates, or Weires, or Mills, or in holes in the River banks" (318); and in warm weather, roaches may be caught "near to the Piles or Posts of a Bridg, or near to any posts of a *Weire*" (341). As Piscator continues to discuss the behavior of roaches, the conceptual division between rural and urban environments as well as the distinction between the human-created and the natural erode, since the roach's preference for bridges as habitat means that "the largest and fattest" roaches in seventeenth-century England may be found "below *London-bridg*," with "great store of *Roach* taken" at Windsor and Henley-on-Thames as well (341). *The Compleat Angler* thus explores multiple modes of commensalism, a "process of cohabitation" through which animals adaptively inhabit and transform human-modified environments into "a resource base for their own ecology."[111] Walton's depictions of commensalism culminate in his portrayal of different subgroups of anglers developing in response to the distinctive qualities of England's varied aquatic ecosystems: "And lastly let me tell you, the *Roach* makes an Angler excellent sport, especially the great Roaches about *London*, where I think there be the best Roach-Anglers, and I think the best *Trout-Anglers* be in *Derby-shire*, for the waters there are clear to an extremity" (341). In the complex webs of life that Walton portrays in *The Compleat Angler*, not only do wild animals adapt to and exploit the by-products of human civilization, but humankind itself becomes differentially shaped by its interactions with the unique, highly localized "ethnozoological landscape[s]" of England's rivers.[112]

Walton's vision of the interdependency of humans and aquatic ecosystems likewise informs his repeated and vehement calls for conservation. Walton was by no means the first writer to fear the adverse impact of a "woefull want" of fish on the human population of early modern England. "Fishes decrease, and fishers multiply," Thomas Bastard had complained at the end of the sixteenth century, and Michael Drayton later questioned whether the nation's rivers would always be able to sate "mans gurmandize" with freshwater fish.[113] Walton goes beyond mere handwringing, however, and instead provides his readers with both a philosophy and practical models of conservation. As we have already seen, Walton's anthropocentrism is rooted in the traditional Christian belief that all entities of the natural world (including fish) were created by God for the benefit of humankind. This emphasis on the use value of the nonhuman components of the web of life, which readily provides a Christian rationale for the georgic mode, likewise often undergirds Walton's championing of practices and regulations that will preserve fish as a natural resource. Early in Walton's book, we learn that Piscator has embarked on his springtime journey into the Hertfordshire countryside as an agent of conservation. In the 1653 edition of *The Compleat Angler*, shortly after Piscator catches up with Viator on Tottenham Hill, he asks his new acquaintance why he is traveling. Viator replies that his purpose "is to bestow a day or two in hunting the *Otter*" with a friend at Amwell Hill (64), located about a mile and a half south of the city of Ware. Piscator immediately reveals that he, too, is traveling in order to hunt otters; but rather than seeking "pleasure" from the activity of hunting as Viator does, Piscator is motivated instead by his intense antipathy toward otters as a species: "my purpose is to bestow a day or two in helping to destroy some of those villanous vermin: for I hate them perfectly" (64). Piscator's desire to exterminate otters thus serves as the catalyst for the entire narrative of *The Compleat Angler*.

Ironically, the environmental consciousness that today strictly prohibits the hunting of otters in England has developed from the ethos of conservation that motivated Piscator in the seventeenth century to eradicate the same species.[114] "Fish totally dominate the diet" of English otters, and biologists conservatively estimate that an adult otter (which weighs on average between fifteen and twenty-two pounds) daily consumes 15 percent of its body weight in food, with a lactating female having been observed to eat 28 percent of her own weight in fish per day.[115] Piscator does not care to hunt foxes despite the fact that "they do as much mischief as the *Otters*" since foxes have no impact on fish. Piscator hates otters—and otters alone—"because they love fish so well, or rather, because they destroy so much": as an angler who strives above all to preserve the environmental conditions that enable his favorite recreation, Piscator necessarily becomes "an enemy to the *Otter*" (64). Piscator thus depicts his antipathy toward otters as an inevitable result of his love of angling: in order to preserve fish stocks, Piscator engages passionately in a seventeenth-century version of wildlife management.

Piscator's concern to preserve freshwater fisheries likewise shapes his attitude toward angling regulations—and the human miscreants who fail to obey them. Piscator laments that salmon fry "would about a certain time return back to the salt water, if they were not hindred by *weres* and *unlawful gins* [contrivances such as nets or traps], which the greedy Fisher-men set, and so destroy them by thousands," and he likewise forcefully denounces the "many Nets and Fish that are under the Statute size, sold daily amongst us" (213).[116] Piscator also vigorously advocates adherence to the legal statutes governing "fence-months," the breeding season during which fishing is prohibited.[117] When Piscator lectures about the importance of observing the fence months, however, he transforms conservation from an anthropocentric calculus into a religious obligation of environmental stewardship: "But above all, the taking [of] Fish in Spawning time, may be said to be against nature; it is like the taking the dam on the nest when she hatches her young: a sin so against nature, that Almighty God hath in the Levitical

Law made a Law against it" (213–14). Piscator may cross the line of legality by heading into the Hertfordshire countryside on a Sunday, but he is nonetheless strictly a law-and-order angler—who observes both secular statutes and divine edicts—when it comes to issues of conservation.

Moreover, Walton always wants the government, regardless of whether he agrees with its politics, to work aggressively to safeguard freshwater fish populations. In a passage that Walton added to his book in the second edition of 1655, Piscator argues that "the want of *Otter-killers*, and the not keeping the *Fence months* for the preservation of *fish*, will in time prove the destruction of all *Rivers*" (213), and Walton's alter ego makes specific suggestions as to how officials should take action on both these fronts. According to Piscator, the state should wield carrots and sticks alike to elicit environmentally responsible behavior from the human population of England. In the former category, Piscator suggests that the government should offer financial incentives to encourage the eradication of that archenemy of English fish, the otter: "in my judgment, all men that keep Otter dogs ought to have a Pension from the Commonwealth to incourage them to destroy the very breed of those base *Otters*, they do so much mischief" (64).[118] But Piscator also believes that the laws mandating close seasons, restrictions on fishing methods, and size limits must be strictly administered, so he vehemently censures government officials who do not fulfill their duty by enforcing these regulations. As he anatomizes the abuses of "the wise Statutes" designed to prevent "the destruction of Fish," Piscator declares that "the *conservators* of the waters should be ashamed" of their lax enforcement of the very laws they are charged to uphold in order to preserve England's freshwater fish populations (213).[119] In a passage that Walton added to *The Compleat Angler* in 1655, Piscator foresees that without sufficient conservation, citizens who want to eat fish "will be forced to eat flesh, or suffer more inconveniencies than are yet foreseen" (213).

By portraying freshwater fish as a resource that the government should preserve for the future welfare of the public as a whole, Walton expresses a nascent concept of sustainability, the idea that "a society must not undermine the ecological underpinnings on which it is dependent."[120] Although environmental historians argue that the concept of sustainability initially emerged in early modern debates about wood as a national asset that should be managed for the long-term benefit of society (as exemplified by John Evelyn's *Sylva*, first published in 1664), we find a much earlier discourse of sustainability in English fishing treatises.[121] Multiple angling writers before Walton raised conservation issues—the author of the late fifteenth-century *Treatyse of Fysshynge with an Angle* warns that a fisherman should not be "too ravenous" and deplete fish stocks, and in the Elizabethan *Arte of Angling*, we learn that William Samuel's master fisherman gives up his beloved sport during the spawning season—but Walton's complex views on conservation and sustainability align most closely with the ideas presented by Leonard Mascall in his late sixteenth-century *Booke of Fishing with Hooke and Line*.[122] As well as providing detailed instructions for eradicating a whole host of birds and animals that prey on fish, Mascall laments the widespread existence of both unsportsmanlike fishing methods and "water Bayles [bailiffs]" who "neglect their duties," and he wishes that "carefull men were put in office, and such as favours the common wealth."[123] In Mascall's demand for governmental enforcement of conservation measures combined with his reiterated concern "for the preserving of the common wealth," we find an emergent concept of sustainability that would later shape Walton's environmental vision—and the reception of *The Compleat Angler*.[124] Through his portrayal of Piscator, Walton created a vigorous, memorable new model of the angler-conservationist that would go on to inspire environmentally conscious sportsmen for centuries.

Implicit in the concept of "fence-months" that is so important to Walton's philosophy of conservation we find another feature of the georgic mode central to *The Compleat Angler*: seasonal change. Bucolic literature sometimes acknowledges the existence of nonidyllic weather and temperatures, but more usually in the pastoral mode "every season's like the month of May."[125] In georgic texts, by contrast, temperate springtime inevitably gives way to the searing heat of summer, followed by the cold and inclement weather of the autumn and winter. As we have already noted, the seasonal rhythms of agricultural husbandry shape the rural environment traversed by Piscator and his friends and thus structure the anglers' activities as well. Even more fundamentally, however, fish in *The Compleat Angler* are seasonally variable animals: they may sometimes be able to adapt to by-products of human life such as weirs and bridges, but finally fish can be understood (and caught) only if anglers recognize the profoundly formative influence that the changing seasons exert on the life cycles and behavior of these creatures. Fence months translate such seasonal knowledge into restrictions on human conduct: fish predictably breed at particular times of the year, so for the sake of sustainability (and, from Piscator's perspective, respect for God's providential Creation as well), anglers must refrain from catching fish during these periods. Moreover, by carefully charting the seasonal rhythms that shape the natural history of each species of fish, an angler will be able to accurately predict (and exploit) the annual cycles of piscine behavior. Piscator maintains that the grayling "is a Fish that lurks close all winter, but is very pleasant and jolly after mid-*April*, and in *May*, and in the hot months" (273), whereas the roach can be caught throughout the year with seasonally adjusted baits: "you shall fish for this *Roach* in Winter with Paste or Gentles [maggots], in *April* with worms or Caddis; in the very hot months with little white snails, or with flies under-water, . . . [i]n many of the hot months . . . [with] a *May-flie* or *Ant-flie*," and in August "with a Paste made only of the crumbs of Bread" (341). In his discussion of the perch, Piscator evokes an entire georgic ecology that likewise undergoes cyclical change: the perch, Piscator contends, "will not bite at all seasons of the year; he is very abstemious in Winter, yet will bite then in the midst of the day if it be warm: . . . [A]nd he hath been observed by some not usually to bite till the *Mulberry-tree* buds; that is to say, till extreme frosts be past that Spring; for when the *Mulberry-tree* blossoms, many Gardners observe their forward [early] fruit to be past the danger of Frosts, and some have made the like observation of the *Pearches* biting" (311). In all these accounts of fishes' behavior, Piscator preaches the same ecological sermon: the successful angler must understand, respect, and adapt to the cyclical changes that govern the natural world. In Walton's fishing treatise, seasonality thus places firm limits on humanity's ability to control the environment.

As we might expect, if Walton's emphasis on seasonal change poses an implicit challenge to traditional views of humanity's relationship to the environment, he also uses his evocation of the seasons to challenge interregnum religious and political orthodoxy. Steven N. Zwicker observes that "the cyclical and the seasonal are sharply at odds with the millenarian time of puritan eschatology,"[126] and so the georgic rhythms of the countryside that Walton repeatedly brings to our attention in *The Compleat Angler* tacitly deny the deepest underlying structure of the parliamentarian worldview. But Walton's politicized use of seasonality takes even more transgressive form when he provocatively designates phases of the angling year by reference to the holy days of the church calendar that had been banned in the wake of the civil wars. Piscator advises anglers to gather grubs to use as bait in the winter "[a]bout *All-hollantide*" (152), that is, around All Hallows' Day (November 1); he argues that one can rear maggots using an animal's liver as a growing medium "til after *Michaelmas*" (153), meaning September 29, the feast of St. Michael the Archangel; and in a passage added in 1655, he suggests that the best time to fish for carp occurs from "St. *James* Tide until *Bartholomew* Tide," that is, from the Feast of St. James on July 25 through to the Feast of St. Bartholomew the Apostle on August 24 (305).[127] In his commendatory poem to Edward Sparke's *Scintulla Altaris* published in 1652, Walton pointedly remarks that "Each Saints day / Stands as a Land-mark in an erring age / to guide fraile mortals in their pilgrimage."[128] Similarly, by mapping the quotidian georgic tasks of the angler onto the verboten Stuart ecclesiastical calendar, Piscator suggests an enduring consonance between the rhythms of the natural world and those of the prewar English church.

Walton's depiction of inclement weather provides another important aspect of georgic seasonality in *The Compleat Angler*. The rain may not raineth every day in Walton's book, but Piscator and his friends must nonetheless contend with frequent, severe, and prolonged spells of precipitation. In the chronology of the 1653 narrative that would remain unchanged in all Walton's later editions of his treatise, Piscator and his angling disciple spend a total of five days away from London. On the two separate days that Walton's sportsmen travel either from or back to the city, the weather is fair; likewise, during the second day of their time together (when they go otter hunting), they encounter no rain. But as soon as Piscator and his companion begin to fish full-time, it begins to rain—a meteorological phenomenon many twenty-first-century anglers will ruefully recognize. On their third day away from London, immediately after Piscator catches "a great logger-headed *Chub*," he and Viator must dodge a brief shower (88). The weather the two men face on day four proves much more problematic: after breakfast-time, the anglers' attempts to go trout-fishing are interrupted by periodic, and often torrential, rainfall that continues through the evening. Walton uses these downpours to integrate the georgic materials of his angling treatise within a realistic narrative framework: every time the heavens open, Piscator takes yet another opportunity to share his angling wisdom with his disciple, and because it rains so often and for such prolonged periods of time, Piscator has ample time to share lengthy, detailed tutorials on fish and fishing with his captive audience, Viator/Venator, and the eavesdropping reader.

Walton added some witty metanarrative about this structural feature of his book. Beginning with the second edition of *The Compleat Angler*, as Auceps, Venator, and Piscator takes turns praising the merits of their respective sports, both the falconer and the hunter treat Piscator disparagingly. First Auceps says he has heard "many grave, serious men" damn angling as "a heavy, contemptible, dull recreation" (176). Then Venator passes the conversational baton to Piscator only after remarking to Auceps that they need to give the angler time to defend his calling "which he calls an Art; but doubtless 'tis an easie one: and Mr. *Auceps*, I doubt [am afraid] we shall hear a watry discourse of it, but I hope 'twill not be a long one"; Auceps replies snarkily, "And I hope so too, though I fear it will" (185). As he deploys the term "watry discourse," Venator first insults Piscator by suggesting that the fisherman's defense of angling will not only be full of references to water (the physical habitat of fish) but will also be vapid in quality and then preemptively complains about the length of Piscator's remarks.[129] But as a text that is simultaneously a treatise, a narrative, and a series of conversations—all relevant seventeenth-century meanings of the word "discourse"—that not only discusses aquatic ecosystems but is also cleverly structured by precipitation, *The Compleat Angler* proves Venator's words to be both prophetic and laudatory.[130] Walton's book truly is a "watry discourse" in design as well as subject matter, a waterlogged text in both form and substance.

Walton depicts rainfall as a component of the natural world that creates both environmental challenges and opportunities for his anglers. In the first edition of Walton's book, after Piscator catches a chub and the sportsmen prepare to head back to their lodging for dinner on the third day of their trip, they have to pause for a precipitation break and hunker under a "high hedg... whilst this showr falls so gently upon the teeming earth," thus allowing Piscator to recount his meditative experience "under that broad *Beech tree*" when he had previously visited the same "Primrose hil" (88). This econarrative device of rainfall providing an opportunity for environmental discourse also structures the anglers' experience throughout day four in Walton's story. When Piscator and Viator must take shelter from a "smoaking showre"—a violent downpour of rain—under a sycamore tree shortly after breakfast, Piscator opportunistically gives his acolyte "more observations of flie-fishing for a *Trout*" (109), a lesson that concludes when the pelting rain ceases: "And now, Scholer, my direction for fly-fishing is ended with this showre, for it has done raining" (111).[131] The weather clears long enough for Viator to hook and lose a trout, but soon "it rains again, and [the two anglers] wil ev'n retire to the *Sycamore* tree," Piscator once more taking the opportunity, as he tells Viator, to "give you more directions concerning fishing" (114). It then rains for so long that Piscator has ample time to lecture about salmon, pike, carp, and bream, at which point Viator provides a weather update combined with a program note: "but I pray Sir, since you see it still rains *May* butter, give me some observations and directions concerning the *Pearch*" (135). Walton here reminds us that unlike the gentle shower his anglers had encountered the previous day, Piscator and Viator now face rainfall so heavy that the air seems filled by thick, opaque, bleached butter.[132] As the torrential downpour continues, Piscator obliges Viator by sharing his disquisition on perch but then proposes, "And now I think best to rest my selfe, for I have almost spent my spirits with talking so long" (137). Viator, however, invokes the continued bad weather as necessitating further tutelage: "Nay, good Master, one fish more, for you see it rains still" (137). After Viator, prompted by Piscator, briefly pulls his weight in the conversation by reciting a poem, the older man resumes his instructional role, yet again enabled by the continued precipitation: "Well, being I have now rested my self a little, I will make you some requital, by telling you some observations of the *Eele*, for it rains still" (138). As the anglers' time under the sycamore draws to a close, Piscator continues to benchmark his teaching against the rain: "And thus much for this present time concerning the *Eele*: I will next tel you a little of the *Barbell*, and hope with a little discourse of him, to have an end of this showr, and fal to fishing, for the weather clears up a little" (142); "And now, my honest Scholer, the long showre, and my tedious discourse are both ended together" (145). Piscator and Viator then return to their lodging just in time, for they no sooner meet their fellow anglers Peter and Coridon at the door than "it rains and blows" again (147).

Within the framework of Walton's narrative, Piscator's presentation of much of the "usefull part" (59) of *The Compleat Angler* is thus structured by repeated bouts of torrential rain. Rather than frustrating the master angler and his disciple, the "smoking showers" that repeatedly send the two men back to the shelter of the sycamore tree enable Piscator's program of outdoor education. So, if the term "watry discourse" describes both the instructional content of *The Compleat Angler* and the environmental conditions that foster Piscator's tutorials, what should we make of the rainstorms that give Piscator so much time to present his waterlogged insights about fish and the ecosystems they inhabit?

We can certainly derive a politically symbolic meaning from the adverse weather conditions that Walton portrays in *The Compleat Angler*. In his essay "Upon the Sight of a Rain in the Sunshine," Joseph Hall, using his typically emblematic mode of contemplative hermeneutics, observes that "if the sun of God's countenance shine upon me, I may well be content to be wet with some rain of affliction. How oft have I seen the heaven overcast with clouds and tempest, no sun appearing to comfort me! Yet even those gloomy and stormy seasons have I rid out patiently; only with the help of the common light of day, at last those beams have broken forth happily and cheered my soul.... Let me never hope, while I am in this vale, to see the clear face of that sun without a shower" (131). Such a moralized equation of tempestuous weather and the devout Christian's endurance of "affliction" gained new currency during the aftermath of the British Civil Wars as a metaphor of the material and spiritual state of defeated royalist Anglicans. In this vein, Lord Clarendon recounted how William Juxon, deprived of his post as the bishop of London in 1649, "wisely withdrew from the storm, and enjoyed the greatest tranquillity of any man in the three kingdoms throughout the whole boisterous time that followed" by devoting his time and energy to country pursuits in the Cotswolds until he was named archbishop of Canterbury at the Restoration.[133] Similarly, when stranded in Antwerp while his wife tried to compound for their estates in England, the former royalist military commander William Cavendish wrote in 1653 that his "tears converted to a shower of hail."[134] Walton's descriptions of tempestuous weather are sometimes designed to evoke the same political context. As we have already noted, in the poem he recites at the very end of *The Compleat Angler*, Piscator says, "*I would be high, but see the proudest Oak / Most subject to the rending Thunder-stroke*" (162): with the image of the majestic but storm-threatened oak, Piscator clearly alludes to the fate of the executed Charles I, the association of oak trees with the English monarchy having been cemented when the future Charles II hid from his pursuers in an oak at Boscobel after the Battle of Worcester in 1651.[135] From this perspective, when they are afflicted by bad weather, Piscator and his friends display the resourceful tenacity of royalists like Izaak Walton himself as they patiently endure the political storms of the interregnum.

But we can now also recognize that Walton structures Piscator's "watry discourse" with realistic observations of the severe and unpredictable weather that frequently battered seventeenth-century Hertfordshire during the Little Ice Age. From roughly 1300 until 1850, the annual mean temperature in Europe was about two degrees Fahrenheit colder than would be the case between 1920 and 1960, and during the middle of the seventeenth century, southern England was afflicted by especially volatile and violent weather that often generated periods of heavy rainfall throughout the spring and early summer.[136] Thus in *The Compleat Angler*, Walton's depiction of "smoking showers" that repeatedly douse the Hertfordshire countryside with torrential rain provides us with a closely observed experience of the English environment during the Little Ice Age. Such tumultuous weather devastated the subsistence agriculture on which the English population depended, and the adverse impact of bad weather had been especially acute in the years immediately preceding the initial publication of *The Compleat Angler*. Between 1646 and 1651, in addition to the trauma of the civil wars, Walton and his contemporaries had endured "a fearful experience ... when disastrous weather conditions had ruined harvests and spread sickness among livestock," resulting in "years of food shortages and high prices."[137] This unpredictable, tempestuous weather also affected all the inhabitants of the aquatic ecosystems of early modern England. "Extreame winde or extreame colde" and "raine that is great, heavy, and beating," Gervase Markham observed, "taketh from Fish all manner of appetite," and Walton himself first noted in 1655 that "*those very flies that use to appear about and on the water in one month of the year, may the following year come almost a month sooner or later; as the same year proves colder or hotter*" (171–72).[138] Yet as both a fisherman and a proponent of angling, Piscator shows us how to adapt: leaving his baited rod unattended to fish for him while he takes shelter from the deluge, Piscator transforms rain breaks into teachable moments of environmental education. And over the centuries, as they have eavesdropped on these conversations, many of Walton's readers have followed Viator's lead and "turned angler" themselves. What we now might categorize as the dynamics of nonequilibrium ecology—the recognition that nature (and thus human life) are "*fundamentally* erratic, discontinuous, and unpredictable"—thus structure the core of Walton's narrative.[139] Walton was by no means the first early modern writer to explore what can happen to human lives and psyches when they are "entangled with a hostile world."[140] But whereas storms in works of literature such as *King Lear* fracture both individual identities and social roles, in *The Compleat Angler*, by contrast, Piscator opportunistically uses the threatening weather of the Little Ice Age to foster both knowledge of the natural environment and innovative modes of selfhood and community.[141]

The environmental vision Walton presents in *The Compleat Angler* is thus finally notable for its interwoven combination of idealism, pragmatism, and resilience. The English countryside, always understood as the handiwork of a beneficent God who created the earth and saw that it was good, challenges humanity—spiritually, intellectually, and physically—yet supports the well-being of those who constructively adapt to local conditions. Walton's anglers both exploit and care for the environment as part of their remit to hold dominion over the earth, but they also recognize that there are powerful forces of nature beyond their control. Piscator and his companions inhabit a world that is numinous, beautiful, and sustaining even though it is also riven by political force fields, studded with dung, and frequently lashed by rain.

Just as the environmental complexities of seventeenth-century England shape *The Compleat Angler*, so they also structured the final chapter of Izaak Walton's life. Thanks to the research of climatologists, we now recognize that as the Little Ice Age approached its most severe phase in the later seventeenth century, English winters often became unusually cold for prolonged periods of time: the Thames froze over in 1648–49, snow blanketed the south of England for more than three months during 1657–58, and ice destroyed the Trent Bridge at Nottingham during a five-month-long freeze in the winter of 1682–83.[142] But the coldest winter in English history—the Great Frost—was yet to come.[143] Intermittently freezing weather in November 1683 turned "unsufferably cold" in December, and by early January 1684 the Thames was frozen solid.[144] Although the "intollerably severe" cold "clench[ed]" London "in its bitter fist" until early February, many residents of the capital regarded the Great Frost as a marvelous recreational and business opportunity rather than a natural disaster.[145] A miniature city devoted to "Continual faire" soon mushroomed on the ice-covered Thames, and thousands of Londoners thronged to booths selling food and drink (plum cakes, "hot pudding-pies," roasted meat, and brandy), bought wildly expensive souvenirs, and enjoyed a dizzying array of entertainment options including "Bull-baiting, Horse & Coach races, Pupet-plays & interludes."[146]

Yet as John Evelyn noted, even though the Great Frost "seem'd to be a bacchanalia, Triumph or Carnoval on the Water, . . . it was a severe Judgement upon the Land."[147] Thomas Tryon lamented the "sad Effects" of the unprecedentedly cold weather "whereof so many Thousands of Poor Creatures Shiver and Pine, and Languish."[148] As the bitter cold persisted, "deare universaly perished in most of the parks thro-out England, & very much Cattell"; fish and birds died in droves; and "after having many years escaped the severest Winter," Evelyn's garden tortoise—"which by his constant burying himself in the Earth at approach of Winter" Evelyn regarded as "a kind of *Plant-Animal*"—was unable to burrow to safety beneath the frost line and froze to death.[149] The frigid temperatures likewise devastated plants, not only killing "exotique" species but also causing mature native trees—especially oaks—to split "as if lightning-strock," and in Needwood Forest, the "*cleaving* or *splitting of Trees* in the time of the hard Frost" generated such loud explosions that "the *Keepers* there thought that the *Deer* were shot by the people of the Country."[150] Forest officials may well have been expecting raids by starving poachers, for the Great Frost "pinch'd, and almost famish'd many poor" as the cost of food and fuel skyrocketed and the human mortality rate surged: "the sharpeness of the season tooke off the moste parte of them that was aged and of them that was under infirmities, the people did die so fast that it was the greatest parte of their work (which was appointed to doe that worke) to burie the dead."[151] It was during this period of dangerous cold, several months after his ninetieth birthday, that Izaak Walton died.

When Walton made his will, he had the frigid winters of the Little Ice Age on his mind. Among his bequests, Walton left money for the mayor of his hometown of Stafford to "buie coles for some pore people, that shall most neide them in the said towne," stipulating that the coal must be "delivered the last weike in Janeway, or in every first weike in Febrewary ... because I take that time to be the hardest and most pinching times with pore people."[152] As occurred during the Great Frost, severely cold winters caused English coal prices to spike repeatedly during the latter half of the seventeenth century, and altruistic individuals began to help local officials purchase fuel for their impoverished neighbors.[153] Walton's bequest of coal to the poorest inhabitants of Stafford was thus typical of a mode of philanthropy that developed in early modern England to alleviate the human suffering caused by climate change. When he wrote his will—a text, like *The Compleat Angler*, indelibly shaped by his fraught personal experience of the Little Ice Age—Izaak Walton could never have imagined that he was inadvertently helping to launch an era of fossil-fuel consumption that centuries later would inflict a new environmental crisis of global heating on all the inhabitants, human and nonhuman, of his beloved English countryside.

CHAPTER 2

Creating the Brotherhood of the Angle

Before the publication of *The Compleat Angler*, the recreational fisherman was a loner. In Walton's book, by contrast, an angler's life-altering experiences in the natural world are always shared with others. We thus cannot fully understand Walton's environmental vision in *The Compleat Angler* until we examine how it shapes and is shaped by his portrayal of human relationships.

A passage from Francis Bacon's *Advancement of Learning* helps us to identify the organizational precursors of Walton's Brotherhood of the Angle:

> For there are, as we see, many Orders and Societies, which, though they be divided under severall Soveraignties & spacious Territories, yet they doe contract and maintain a Society and a kind of *Fraternity* one with another; in so much that they have their *Provincialls* and *Generalls*, to whom all the rest yeeld obedience. And surely as nature creates *Brother-hoods* in *Families*; and Arts Mechanicall contract *Brother-hoods in Communalties*; the Anointment of God super-induceth a *brother-hood in Kings and Bishops*; Vowes and Canonicall rules unite a *Brotherhood in Orders*. [I]n like manner there cannot but intervene *a Noble and Generous Fraternity between*

men by Learning and Illuminations; reflecting upon that relation which is attributed to God, who himselfe is called, *The Father of Illuminations or Lights*.[1]

We find strands of the cultural DNA of these religious, craft, and learned associations in both the structure and the culture of Walton's community of gregarious fishermen. But the group identity of the Brotherhood of the Angle emerges, first and foremost, from its members' shared pursuit of an environmental activity. Walton thus creates in *The Compleat Angler* a new kind of voluntary association that transforms men's shared leisure-time experiences of the natural world into the basis of their self-definition.[2] Moreover, by drawing on familiar models of evangelism and education, Walton created a text that remains to this day "conversional in both its content and its function."[3] Although early modern concepts of rank and gender finally limit the demographic scope of Piscator's recruitment drive, we nonetheless catch vivid glimpses of other modes of ecosocial relationships in Walton's text even as Piscator excludes some elite men—and all women—from his innovative, environmentally focused fraternity of anglers.

THE SOCIABLE ANGLER

When Walton created a brotherhood of sociable fishermen as the main characters of *The Compleat Angler*, he knowingly defied his culture's long-established view of angling as a solitary pastime. From its earliest existence in manuscript, the *Treatyse of Fysshynge wyth an Angle*—the first text about recreational fishing to be printed in English—portrayed the fisherman as a recluse.[4] Like Walton in the post-1653 editions of *The Compleat Angler*, the unknown author of the *Treatyse* argues that recreational fishing is preferable to other sports such as hunting and hawking.[5] Unlike Walton's book, however, the fifteenth-century *Treatyse* ascribes angling's superiority to its practitioner's solitude: being entirely self-sufficient, the angler "may have no colde nor no dysease nor angre but yf he be causer hymself."[6] If he has the right gear, the author of the *Treatyse* enthuses, an angler can travel through the countryside undetected by others: "And thus shall ye make you a rodde soo prevy that ye maye walke therwyth: and there shall noo man wyte where abowte ye goo" (192–93). And like Walton's contemplative fishermen who would stop and smell the cowslips more than a century and a half later, the angler in the *Treatyse*, even if he doesn't catch any fish, "atte the leest he hath his holsom walke and mery at his ease. A swete ayre of the swete savoure of the meede floures. . . . He hereth the melodyous armony of fowles. He seeth the yonge swannes: heerons: duckes: cotes and many other foules wyth theyr brodes" (188–89). Such experiences, the author of the *Treatyse* concludes, "me semyth better than alle the noyse of honndys: the blastes of hornys and the scrye of foulis that hunters[,] fawkeners & foulers can make" (188–91). Near the end of the *Treatyse*, the antisocial nature of the fifteenth-century angler becomes even more explicit as the author advises against conviviality: "whan ye purpoos to goo on your disportes in fysshyng ye woll not desyre gretly many persones wyth you. whiche myghte lette you of your game [hinder you in your pastime]. And thenne ye maye serve god devowtly in sayenge affectuously youre custumable prayer" (226–27).[7] The author of the *Treatyse* here anticipates Walton's emphasis on angling as an opportunity for religious devotion—but unlike Walton, the *Treatyse* associates this salutary by-product of recreational fishing with the angler's fundamentally unsociable character.

The woodcut that heads the text of the 1496 *Treatyse* portrays the idealized solitude of the fifteenth-century angler even more explicitly (see fig. 3). The image vividly depicts a male angler in action on the banks of a river. The fisherman's feet are planted firmly apart for optimal stability, and as he leans forward slightly from the waist with his right hand outstretched, a fishing rod with its attached line and float arches high in his left hand: the angler is working to land the speckled fish (a trout?) that has gorged his hook, and a pair of fish that the angler has already caught are stashed nearby in a tub on the riverbank. The angler is not far from human habitation—the tightly packed buildings of a town are visible in the distance on the far side of the river—but other than the struggling fish, the reader of the *Treatyse* is the only witness of the fisherman's prowess: the angler is alone on a peninsula, separated from the other members of his society by the bountiful river. Thus, as depicted by both the author and the illustrator of the *Treatyse of Fysshynge wyth an Angle*, this forebear of Walton's Piscator enjoys enhanced health and happiness because he pursues a pastime that allows him to experience the natural world in blissful solitude.

Compared to the fisherman-protagonist of William Samuel's *The Arte of Angling* (1577), however, the angler of the *Treatyse* seems like a social butterfly. Walton certainly knew and drew on some version of the *Treatyse*

FIGURE 3 | Image of the fisherman from the *Treatyse of Fysshynge wyth an Angle* in the *Boke of Saint Albans*, 2nd ed. (1496). RB 82008, detail, The Huntington Library, San Marino, California.

as he wrote *The Compleat Angler*—most obviously in his instructions for dyeing horsehair fishing line (158–59) and the list of "twelve kinds of Artificial made Flies to Angle with upon the top of the water" that Walton added to the second edition of his treatise (254)—but even though he never acknowledges the existence of Samuel's text, Walton was much more deeply indebted to *The Arte of Angling*.[8] Most obviously, Walton borrows from Samuel's book the dialogue format that structures *The Compleat Angler* as well as the names of his main characters, Piscator and Viator; and like Walton's later version of this duo, Samuel's Piscator is an experienced master angler who agrees to tutor the nonfisherman Viator in "the Art of angling."[9] William Samuel was a clergyman, and so we might expect his character Piscator to display a benevolent disposition similar to that of his namesake in *The Compleat Angler*; Samuel, however, depicts his angler-protagonist as a short-tempered, acerbic curmudgeon who loves fish far more than his fellow men.[10] Thus we find in *The Arte of Angling* a disjunction between the inherent sociability of the book's dialogue structure and Piscator's desire for solitude—a gap that William Samuel deftly exploits to comic effect. The opening exchanges between the Piscator and Viator of *The Arte of Angling* and their doppelgängers in *The Compleat Angler* contrast strikingly: whereas Walton's Piscator speaks first as he strives to introduce himself to a stranger, Samuel's Piscator speaks only after being queried by Viator, who has discovered the master angler fishing by himself early on a "whisteling cold morning" (A1v). Viator greets the fisherman with the epithet "friende" in the very first words of Samuel's text (A1r), but Piscator does not seem to reciprocate the warmth of Viator's view of their relationship, and the comedy of manners that unfolds in the ensuing conversation between the two characters arises from the social tension that develops between the misanthropic angler and his unwelcome sidekick.

In the opening pages of *The Arte of Angling*, Piscator responds tersely to Viator's questions and pointedly does not invite the other man to join him. When the obtuse Viator finally asks if he might "sit down on the ground by you," Piscator brusquely replies, "Yea, so that you sitte not over neere the water" (A2r). Self-indulgently assuming that this reaction indicates Piscator's concern for his well-being, Viator assures the angler, "I trow, I will sitte farre inough off for [to avoid] slipping in" (A2r). Piscator, however, quickly disabuses Viator of his presumptuousness: "I do not meane therefore [i.e., not for the reason you think], but I wold not have you sit, so that the fishe may see either your shaddowe, your face, or any part of you" since "with the least moving, they shun straight" (A2r). First and foremost, Piscator cares about the sensibilities of the fish he is trying to catch, not Viator's feelings or welfare. Historians argue that rather than designating a close acquaintance, the term "friend" was most commonly used in sixteenth-century England to refer to kinsfolk or "someone whose interests were tied to your own":[11] whatever the basis of Viator's claiming Piscator as his "friende" at the beginning of *The Arte of Angling*, Piscator certainly seems to regard the company of fish as preferable to that of Viator.

The comedy of *The Arte of Angling* intensifies as Piscator becomes increasingly irritated by his doltish companion. After Viator obediently settles himself at a distance so as not to spook any fish, he asks if Piscator will allow him to talk. In response, Piscator warns him that he must not speak too loudly. Viator assumes that fish must be frightened by the sound as well as the sight of human beings, but Piscator again corrects him: "No, you may talke, [w]hoope or hollowe, and never stirre them, but I woulde not gladly by your loude talking, that either some bungler, idle person, or jester, might thereby, resort unto us, and also I know not what you have to say, for freends as they seldome meete, so spare they not to utter secretes, which loude talke doth oftentimes hurt, and the truth is, the water hathe an Eccho, more than the land, and therefore easelier heard" (A2v). Rather than appreciate the natural beauty of his rural surroundings as Izaak Walton's Piscator would do three-quarters of a century later, William Samuel's master angler paranoically regards the countryside as the potential site of social pitfalls: undesirable lowlifes, lurking near the riverbanks, will either be attracted by the sound of Viator's "loude" voice and bother Piscator or eavesdrop on conversations in which Viator will inevitably reveal harmful secrets since he and Piscator "seldome meete." As far as Piscator is concerned, a riverside companion can easily ruin an angler's "pleasure" (B6r).

And indeed, as the dialogue between Piscator and Viator continues, Viator plays all the roles in the unholy trinity of "bungler," "idle person," and "jester" dreaded by Piscator. Viator's barrage of unsolicited advice, inane questions, and color commentary provokes increasing sarcasm from Piscator until the exasperated angler finally exclaims, "I could be wel content to have lesse talk now, my messe of fishe beeing so litle, that I might the more attentively take heede, for I have lost a bite or two that you saw not, and some that I did not see, nor you neither, until it was past, besides some practises that belongeth to this science, that nowe I woulde put in use if you were not here, to make up my dish of fishe withall or ever I went, or else it shoulde goe hard" (A7v–A8r). In response to this outburst, it finally dawns on Viator that he has been imposing on "friende Piscator": "Why then I perceive I am now a let [hindrance] unto you, but I hope you be not angrie, for surely I ment nothing but mirth, notwithstanding, I will trouble you no longer, but leave you where I founde you" (A1r, A8r). Piscator, with the delightful vision of a Viator-free river now dancing in his head, tries to recalibrate the men's strained relationship by moving their future interactions out of the countryside and into a domestic setting: "Yet assure your self, as you came my frend, so shall you go on my behalfe, and that shall ye well knowe, if you will come to me soone to supper, and then shall ye be a partaker, not onely at my table of my dayes worke, but also, if you intreat me faire, and bring a quart of sacke with you, and minde [wish] in deed to be acquainted in our ministerie, and to know the mysteries of it, you shal be welcome" (A8r–A8v). And so later the same day, Viator, having retreated from the river, arrives at Piscator's house for supper bearing a bottle of sack, and while the two men dine on plentiful gudgeons, perch, ruffe, chub, and roaches, Piscator gives Viator an extended tutorial about angling. As they begin their meal together, however, Piscator can't resist another dig at Viator: angling, Piscator declares, "is moste meetest for a solitary man" (B6r).[12]

After the only surviving copy of *The Arte of Angling* was discovered and reprinted in the 1950s, readers immediately recognized its formative influence on Walton's conception of *The Compleat Angler*. Indeed, the extent to which Walton's unacknowledged use of William Samuel's work constitutes plagiarism was hotly debated.[13] For our purposes here, however, it is more enlightening to consider the ways in which Walton chose to diverge from the model of human relationships that he found so vividly depicted in *The Arte of Angling*. While Walton appropriated the inherently sociable structural framework as well as the identities of the main characters that he found in Samuel's work, his departure from Samuel's depiction of a misanthropic angler revolutionizes the interpersonal dynamics that Walton depicts and promotes in *The Compleat Angler*. Walton certainly copied the name of his protagonist from *The Arte of Angling*, but he gave William Samuel's Piscator a temperament transplant before setting him loose in rural Hertfordshire. And by doing so, Walton transformed the practice of early modern angling from a solitary to a sociable activity.

FISHERS OF MEN

As Walton turned William Samuel's misanthropic Piscator into the Dale Carnegie of recreational fishermen, he self-consciously drew on familiar models of Christian evangelism. The 1653 title page of *The Compleat Angler* lacks Walton's own name but instead features a quotation from the Geneva Bible translation of the New Testament: "Simon Peter *said, I go a fishing: and they said, We also wil go with thee*" (56). Walton's citation of John 21:3 as the epigraph of his book firmly links his anglers with the fishermen-disciples portrayed in the Gospels, hardworking men who had been plying their trade in the Sea of Galilee when Christ recruited them. Jesus famously greets the fishermen he seeks to convert to his cause as protoevangelists who will redirect their fish-capturing skills toward their own species: "Follow me, and I will make you fishers of men" (Matt. 4:19). Walton thus frames *The Compleat Angler* as an extension of the foundational Christian conversion narrative that underwrites what Bacon would term "*Brotherhood[s] in Orders.*"[14] Piscator is not only a master fisherman: he is also a masterful fisher of men.

Throughout *The Compleat Angler*, Walton encourages us to view Piscator and his "Fraternitie" within this Christian tradition of angler-discipleship. The name of Piscator's angling friend and fellow lodger at Bleak Hall, Peter, evokes the fisherman who became the leader of Christ's followers, and as Piscator tries to impress Viator with his "Commendation" of angling while they walk from Tottenham to Hoddesdon (69), the master angler notes that of the followers of Christ, not only did Jesus choose "four that were Fishermen," but this quartet—Peter, Andrew, James, and John—also became an elite, earning "a prioritie of nomination in the catalogue of his twelve Apostles" (74). Piscator later stresses this same point again in lyrics he sings after dinner one night: "*The first men that our Saviour dear / Did chuse to wait upon him here, / Blest Fishers were*" (97). Walton's repeated evocation of Christ's fishermen-followers thus establishes a charged religiopolitical context within which to understand Piscator's Brotherhood of the Angle: Walton's anglers follow the example of St. Peter, the fisherman-turned-disciple who became the founding bishop of the Christian church. And like Peter and his followers who went fishing in the dark days after the crucifixion of Jesus, Piscator and his angling friends find sustenance together when the episcopacy of the English church has been abolished.

Seventeenth-century clergymen with evangelical interests delighted in teasing out the implications of the fishers-of-men metaphor. The same year that Walton first published *The Compleat Angler*, John Evelyn reported hearing a sermon "comparing this troublesome world to the Sea, the Ministers to the fishers, & Saints to the Fish."[15] Twenty years earlier, in one of his *Piscatorie Eclogs*, Phineas Fletcher depicted St. Peter and his fellow angler-disciples as being transformed by Christ into the very creatures they had previously sought to capture:

> Those fisher-swains, from whom our trade doth flow,
> That by the King of seas their skill were taught;
> As they their boats on *Jordan* wave did row,
> And catching fish, were by a Fisher caught;
> (Ah blessed chance! much better was the trade,
> That being fishers, thus were fishes made).[16]

Samuel Gardiner extensively developed the same "fishers of men" metaphor as a model for seventeenth-century Christian ministry. "It is preaching that ingendreth and encreaseth faith," Gardiner asserts in *A Booke of Angling, or Fishing*, and thus "if wee lay the properties of them both togeather, wee shall see how fitly such as are preachers are compared unto fishers."[17] Recreational fishing and ministry make similar stringent demands on the practitioner, Gardiner argues, and he explains how the master fisherman's repertoire of angling techniques provides a template for "the sacred ministrie to fish for mens soules": "Ordinarie Fisher-men have many observations, having excellent correspondencie with the Office of the ministerie. . . . They observe the qualities of Fishes in their kinds, and fit themselves to their severall natures. Whether they float higher, or swimme neere the ground, or keepe themselves in holes, or runne into the mud, they have meanes and wayes to come by them. The spirituall Fisherman learneth from this schoole, to frame himselfe to the capacitie of his auditorie, and to use all the policies he may, to withdraw them from their errors or redundant manners" (71–72, 81). The angler's calculating attempts to deceive hungry fish exemplify the effective preacher's focus on his spiritually famished audience, according to Gardiner: "Wee that are spirituall fishermen, have our severall baites sutable to the stomackes we angle for. If we observe not the natures of our auditors, & fit our selves to them, we shall not do wisely" (95). Gardiner thus analyzes the angler and his fish-catching techniques with an unrelentingly emblematic mode of hermeneutics.

Gardiner's depiction of "spirituall fishermen" as scheming but morally upright anglers illuminates Piscator's recruitment techniques in *The Compleat Angler*. When we first meet him at the very beginning of *The Compleat Angler*, Walton's protagonist is not attempting to catch a fish—instead, he is trying to catch up with a man. Piscator sees a stranger walking ahead of him on the public highway and deliberately accelerates so he can strike up a conversation: "You are wel overtaken Sir; a good morning to you; I have stretch'd my legs up *Totnam Hil* to overtake you, hoping your businesse may occasion you towards *Ware*, this fine pleasant fresh *May day* in the Morning" (63). Thus the first words and actions in *The Compleat Angler* are designed to allow one man (the master angler Piscator) to accost another man (Viator) as both characters turn their backs on London and walk north into the countryside.[18]

Walton seems to have modeled the opening of his book on the first sentence of *A Treatise of the Nature of God* by Thomas Morton of Berwick.[19] As Morton's theological dialogue commences, a "Gentleman" catches up with a "Scholer, or some Minister" and greets him with the salutation that Walton would redeploy more than a half century later: "Well overtaken Syr."[20] Suffering from a crisis of faith, Morton's gentleman seeks the scholar-minister's "helpe in some poynts of divinitie,"[21] and as the two men ride through Northumberland toward Newcastle, it is the scholar who dominates their discussion about the existence and nature of God. But just as he revolutionizes the relationship between Piscator and Viator depicted in William Samuel's *Arte of Angling*, so Walton also upends the social dynamics that shape Morton's text. Although Morton's gentleman initiates the (painfully attenuated) plot of the *Treatise of the Nature of God*, he otherwise plays a minor role in Morton's dialogue. Walton, by contrast, transforms the first character who speaks into the commanding presence of his narrative, a role reversal that commences with Piscator's reiterated use of the verb "overtake": "You are wel overtaken Sir; . . . I have stretch'd my legs up *Totnam Hil* to overtake you." In Walton's day, "overtake" could mean "to encounter . . . a person travelling in the same direction," but it could also connote aggression ("to reach with a blow," "to capture or seize"), deception and, in the passive form that Piscator first uses, an overpowering by emotion.[22] The implication of predatory domination hardwired into the name of Walton's protagonist combined with the diction of Piscator's greeting make it clear from the very beginning of *The Compleat Angler* that we are in the company of an opportunistic, highly skilled fisher of men.

Walton's fascination with the scenario of an evangelist "angling" for prospective converts while walking in the countryside would later reappear in his *Life* of George Herbert (first published in 1670). Walton recounts how Herbert, while a priest at Bemerton, would walk twice a week to Salisbury. On one of these journeys, Walton reports, Herbert assumed the role of Piscator when he "overtook a Gentleman that is still living in that City" and began quizzing him about his faith, asking that the gentleman excuse his forwardness "*because I know there be some Sermon-hearers, that be like those Fishes, that always live in salt water, and yet are always fresh*"; after Herbert thus "overtook" and catechized his new companion, "the Gentleman did so fall in love with him, and his discourse, that he would often contrive to meet him in his walk to Salisbury."[23] We find in this brief narrative the same dynamics of "overtaking," teaching, and conversion central to Piscator's relationship with Viator, and after listing other examples of Herbert helping men while en route between Bemerton and Salisbury, Walton provides a theological gloss that also illuminates Piscator's behavior: "Thus, as our blessed Saviour after his Resurrection did take occasion to interpret the Scripture to *Cleopas*, and that other Disciple which he met with and accompanied in their journey to *Emmaus*; so Mr. *Herbert*, in his path toward Heaven, did daily take any fair occasion to instruct the ignorant, or comfort any that were in affliction; and did alwaies confirm his precepts, by shewing humility and mercy, and ministring grace to the hearers" (305–6). Walton here alludes to the story of how Christ, resurrected but incognito, joined two of his followers while they were traveling to the village of Emmaus; it was only when Cleopas and his fellow disciple invited their companion to lodge and eat with them that they recognized his true identity as their risen Lord. After Christ had vanished, Cleopas and his comrade marveled, "Did not our heart burn within us, while he talked with us by the way, and while he opened to us the scriptures?" (Luke 24:32).

At the beginning of *The Compleat Angler*, Piscator's "overtaking" of Viator combines the providential dynamics of Christ's post-Resurrection road trip to Emmaus with the fishers-of-men strategies promoted by Samuel Gardiner. Within moments of meeting Viator, Piscator invites himself to walk with his new acquaintance to the Thatched House, an inn at Hoddesdon:

"and to that house I shall by your favour accompany you," he announces to Viator, "and either abate of my pace, or mend it, to enjoy such a companion as you seem to be" (63). To stay close to Viator, Piscator is willing to change his own plans and behavior, a demonstration of the angler's adaptability that would have earned Samuel Gardiner's approval: "Some fishes may bee pulled up sooner then other some, according to the proportion of them, and the holde wee have of them. Strangers are more favourably to bee handled than our ordinary hearers: Such as are but *Catechumen* and *Neophites* in the faith of the first planting, are to bee ordered more tenderly, than such as have made furder progresse in the same" (Gardiner, 91). After synchronizing his walking speed with the "pace" of his target, Piscator embarks on a purely verbal phase of his recruitment campaign: in order to entice Viator to become his "Scholer," Piscator must first "convince" the nonfisherman through conversation that angling is "an Art, and an Art worth learning" (67). Walton's veteran angler rises to this challenge by razzle-dazzling Viator with a lengthy encomium of the history, Christian virtues, and natural wonders of angling, and by the time they reach Hoddesdon, Viator describes himself as a fish that has been securely hooked by the evangelist-angler Piscator: "Sir, You have Angled me on with much pleasure to the *thatcht House*, and I now find your words true, *That good company makes the way seem short*; for, trust me, Sir, I thought we had wanted three miles of the *thatcht House*, till you shewed it me: but now we are at it, we'l turn into it, and refresh our selves with a cup of Ale and a little rest" (79). Piscator goes along with this plan, exemplifying Gardiner's advice that successful fishers of men will "gently entertain such as are coming on, and have taken downe the hooke they have layde for them, and by the coales of kindnesse heaped upon their heades, worke their full conversion" (Gardiner, 90). As the travelers' first day together draws to a close, Viator affirms that Piscator has begun to convert him: Viator now numbers himself among "the lovers of Angling" and has "put on new thoughts both of the Art of Angling, and of all that profess it" (79). By the end of the opening chapter of Walton's book, Piscator thus displays his opportunistic ability to adapt to—and dominate—not trout but what Samuel Gardiner termed "men-fish" (Gardiner, 150). And Viator, like his New Testament prototype Cleopas, comes to recognize his loquacious traveling companion as his lord and master. During the ensuing course of the narrative, as Piscator teaches his new companion about angling and the natural environment, Viator's relationship with Piscator deepens to the point that when the men return to Tottenham and say their goodbyes at the end of *The Compleat Angler*, Viator testifies that he has been born again: "I thank you for your many instructions, which I will not forget; your company and discourse have been so pleasant, that I may truly say, I have only lived, since I enjoyed you and them, and turned Angler" (163).

Walton may have modeled his brotherhood of apostolic anglers on a group of dispossessed Church of England clergymen. Since the fourth century, clerics had been prohibited from hunting for pleasure, but recreational fishing was regarded as a suitable activity for men of the cloth, as Piscator notes in a passage added to the 1655 edition of *The Compleat Angler*: "he that views the ancient Ecclesiastical Canons, shall find *Hunting* to be forbidden to *Church-men*, as being a turbulent, toilsom, perplexing Recreation; and shall find *Angling* allowed to *Clergy-men*, as being a harmless Recreation, a recreation that invites them to *contemplation* and *quietness*" (202–3). This long-standing association between angling and the clergy took on enhanced significance in England during the middle decades of the seventeenth century. Between 1641 and 1646, the Church of England "was dismantled piecemeal," and by the interregnum, many of the clergymen whom Walton knew "had been ejected from their livings and from their colleges; they were forbidden to use the Book of Common Prayer, were spied on in their correspondence, restricted in their movements, were often short of money and might be liable to imprisonment at any time."[24] With no choice but to seek refuge in the households of family or friends, some of these expellees took up angling to while away the time during their years of abjection. In the early 1650s, Robert Payne, an ejected Church of England cleric and natural philosopher, wrote a series of letters to Gilbert Sheldon, another dispossessed clergyman who was a friend of Walton and, according to Piscator, an expert angler "whose skill is above others" (325).[25] In his correspondence, Payne characterizes himself as a "disciple" and "scholar" to his angling "master," Gilbert Sheldon, and on one occasion Payne mentions a shared acquaintance who is "a brother of the Angle, practising his art on our scaly cattle."[26] Given Walton's relationship with Sheldon—a fellow Staffordshire man who would later help persuade Walton to write his biography of Richard Hooker—it seems plausible that Walton knew of and was inspired by Sheldon's interregnum circle of angler-clergymen.

Yet the ecosocial context within which Walton portrays Piscator and his recruitment techniques finally diverges from such early modern reworkings of the fishers-of-men tradition. In one of his letters to Gilbert Sheldon, Robert Payne describes himself wanting to become "an Apostle reversd," that is, a fisher of men who has been transformed by circumstances beyond his control into a fisher of fish.[27] This description does not capture the complexity of Piscator's own position: Piscator's identities as a fisher of men and an angler of fish are consubstantial rather than serial. And unlike clergymen such as Samuel Gardiner who used angling emblematically to think about the challenges of ministry, Walton, through Piscator, literalizes the fishers-of-men analogy to recruit his brotherhood of anglers. By conceiving of recreational fishing as a pursuit through which an angler must capture both fish and men simultaneously, Walton collapses the division between the vehicle and tenor of the fishers-of-men metaphor. Walton thus refashions Christian evangelism into an environmental mode of conversion—and everything Piscator catches, whether a trout or a man-fish, he will never release.

MASTER AND SCHOLAR

By reworking the dynamics of Christian conversion, Walton develops a model of recruitment that allows the Brotherhood of the Angle to grow far beyond the boundaries of its members' preexisting personal and professional relationships. At the very beginning of the first edition of his book, Walton replaces the testy familiarity between the main characters he found in William Samuel's *Arte of Angling* with the more formal interaction of two strangers. As Piscator and Viator begin to converse on the road between Tottenham Hill and their first night's lodging at the Thatched House in Hoddesdon, they decorously address each other as "Sir."[28] When Piscator rises to the challenge of convincing his new acquaintance that angling is "an Art, and an Art worth learning" (67), however, he begins to refer to Viator as "my worthy Friend," and Viator responds in kind (68–69). As the second day of the narrative opens on the crest of Amwell Hill, Viator greets his companion even more familiarly as "My friend *Piscator*" (80), and after the otter hunt is over, Viator continues to address Walton's protagonist warmly as "my friend" and "*Piscator*" (81–82). This mode of social intimacy is short-lived, however, for at the beginning of their third day in each other's company, relations between the two men suddenly turn frosty when Piscator, invited to agree with Viator that the Host of the Thatched House is "a witty man," instead expresses his disapproval of what Piscator regards as the Host's blasphemous and "lascivious jests" (82). An uncomfortable gap in values suddenly divides the two men, and the characters' ensuing dialogue immediately becomes studded with "Sirs" once again.

It takes a fish to salvage the frayed relationship between Walton's Piscator and Viator. After he eats a chub that Piscator catches and then has cooked to exacting standards, Viator's attitude toward the moralistic angler changes dramatically, and he earnestly asks Piscator if "from henceforth you wil allow me to call you Master, and that really I may be your Scholer" (84). Piscator replies with words and gestures that transform the men's interaction into a ritual of commitment: "Give me your hand: from this time forward I wil be your Master, and teach you as much of this Art as I am able; . . . and I am sure I shal tel you more then every Angler yet knows" (84). The next time Viator speaks, he addresses Piscator as "Master," an honorific with which Viator will address Piscator for the duration of the narrative, often adding an epithet, a possessive, or both—"good Master," "my loving Master" (85–86)—to enhance Viator's expression of regard. After several pages of such displays of Viator's newly deferential respect for him, Piscator begins to reciprocate and address Viator as "Scholer" (87), likewise soon adding the variations "good Scholer" and "honest Scholer" to his new repertoire of affectionate titles for Viator (88, 93).[29]

By the middle of Viator's stint as an angler-in-training, Walton has thus introduced the full lexicon of relationships that structure his society of fishermen in *The Compleat Angler*. As he travels into the Hertfordshire countryside, Walton's protagonist Piscator enters a social world of "friends" and "brothers" who have created a group identity as a "Fraternitie" and "Brotherhood" of angling enthusiasts. The members of this group of anglers usually address one another as fraternal equals: when they meet at Bleak Hall, the rural alehouse that provides their meals and lodging, Piscator greets his "brother *Peter*," who responds in kind to his "Brother *Piscator*" (92). Walton provides Viator's full name in the list of dramatis personae that appears at the beginning of the 1653 dialogue and appends an abbreviated version of Viator's moniker before every statement the character makes within the text, but Viator's name is never actually uttered by any of the characters in Walton's narrative, including Viator himself. Piscator, as we have seen, initially addresses Viator as "Sir," and Piscator's angling friend Peter refers to Viator as "my young brother" (92); but for most of the 1653 narrative, Viator is instead repeatedly addressed as Piscator's "Scholer." Viator's lack of autonomous identity becomes especially pronounced near the end of *The Compleat Angler* when Peter takes his leave of the two Londoners and directly addresses only Piscator: "And now brother *Piscator*, I wish you and my brother your Scholer a fair day, and good fortune" (151). Viator thus comes to be defined entirely by his subordinate relationship to his "Master," a dynamic that helps to prepare Viator for membership in Piscator's Brotherhood of the Angle.

In some ways, Walton's educational dialogue between two characters who address each other as "Master" and "Scholer" evokes early modern English catechisms. With roots stretching back into the Middle Ages, the "manual of belief" structured as questions and answers was a familiar genre during Walton's lifetime, and catechisms were an integral component of the grammar school curriculum when Walton was a student.[30] Edmund Allen's *Catechisme* (first published in 1548) featured a dialogue between a "Master" and a "Scholar"; but more importantly for Walton, the English translations of the catechism written by Alexander Nowell were likewise structured as a conversation between "The Maister" and "The Scholar."[31] Between 1570 and 1645, six different versions of Nowell's catechism (in Latin, English, and Greek) appeared in dozens of editions, and the Church of England canons mandated that Nowell's catechism be taught in English schools. Ian Green argues that if early modern English grammar-school students were required to study a more complex treatise after learning the brief catechism included in the Prayer Book, they would have read a "condensed" version of Nowell's work that was explicitly designed to cater to the student market.[32] Early in *The Compleat Angler*, Piscator praises Nowell as an exemplar of the tradition of Christ's angler-disciples. During the reign of Elizabeth I, according to Piscator's version of ecclesiastical history, Nowell "was so noted for his meek spirit, deep Learning, Prudence and Piety, that the then Parliament and Convocation, both chose, injoyned, and trusted him to be the man to make a Catechism for publick use, such a one as should stand as a rule for faith and manners to their posteritie: And the good man (though he was very learned, yet knowing that God leads us not to heaven by hard questions) made that good, plain, unperplext Catechism, that is printed with the old Service Book" (75–76).[33] Although Nowell did not actually compose the brief English catechism that appeared in the 1549 Book of Common Prayer—the mention of which underlines Piscator's transgressive sympathies at a time when the Prayer Book was verboten—this attribution underscores the extent to which Nowell's work was closely associated with Walton's beloved "old Service Book," a connection explicitly emphasized in the editions of Nowell's catechism aimed at students.[34] For Piscator, Nowell's "plain, unperplext" catechetical prose indicates his intertwined spiritual and literary descent from Christ's angler-disciples. A "humble, lowly, plain" writing style, Piscator declares immediately before praising Nowell, is a hallmark of "a good natured, plaine Fisher-man. Which I do the rather believe, by comparing the affectionate, lowly, humble Epistles of S. *Peter*, S. *James* and S. *John*, whom we know were Fishers, with the glorious language and high Metaphors of S. *Paul*, whom we know was not" (75).[35] Piscator's discussion of Nowell's writing thus introduces a metatextual quality to our understanding of the brotherhood that Walton creates in *The Compleat Angler*. Through Piscator's foray into literary criticism, Walton links his own "affectionate, lowly, humble" dialogue of instruction with that of Nowell's catechism, establishing Walton's claim of literary descent from both Nowell and the angling saints of the Gospels.

But the structure, activities, and nomenclature of Piscator's group of anglers also evoke what Francis Bacon called the "*Brother-hoods in Communalties*" forged by "Arts Mechanicall."[36] Trade guilds were important components of urban life in early modern England. Metonymically called "livery companies" in London, these organizations—each of which had a characteristic uniform or "livery"—regulated the practice of trades by limiting the number of individuals admitted into each occupation and controlling members' training, wages, standards of workmanship, and prices.[37] Each livery company also fulfilled charitable roles (such as providing sustenance for the households of ailing or deceased members) and held regular feasts for its membership in its own hall. In such ways, a livery company equitably promoted the welfare of each member, a dynamic that likewise shaped the egalitarian diction of fellowship by which company members—the vast majority of whom were men—referred to themselves as "brothers" and "brethren." Despite their egalitarian activities and discourse, however, trade guilds in early modern England were fundamentally hierarchical. To become a "free brother" of a company, an individual first had to complete an apprenticeship (usually begun as a teenager) that would generally last for seven years. During this time, the apprentice paid tuition and lived in the same household as his "master," who taught the apprentice the skills necessary for competence in his chosen trade. When this training period was successfully completed, the apprentice could enter and then begin to try to rise through the ranks of the "freemen" of his company by paying entry fines, demonstrating his skills, and earning the votes of his higher-ranking "brothers."

Neither Walton nor any of the authors who wrote commendatory verses for his works ever mentions Walton's occupation, but scholars have discovered that Walton was a member of the Ironmongers' Company.[38] Walton served his apprenticeship under the supervision of his brother-in-law (who lived in the London parish of St. Dunstan-in-the-West), and the Ironmongers' records note that in 1618, "Isaack Walton, late apprentice to Thomas Grinsell 'was now admitted and sworne a free brother of this Companie, and payd for his admittance,'" thus gaining the right to trade within the City and indenture his own apprentices.[39] A "free brother" neither had to practice nor train his apprentices in the trade of his livery company, however, and it seems that Walton, like his brother-in-law, actually worked as a linen-draper and sempster.[40] Walton thus functioned professionally as a "brother" in a trade guild long before he wrote *The Compleat Angler*, and the fraternal language with which Piscator and Peter describe their group of anglers duplicates the terminology showcased decades earlier in pageants for the Lord Mayor sponsored by the Ironmongers' Company that hail an individual member as "a worthy Brother" and describe the guild itself as a "much to be honored Brother-hood" and a "worthy Brotherhood."[41]

In Walton's angling treatise, the interactions among Viator, Piscator, and Peter often resemble the relationship of an apprentice with his master and another "free brother" of the same guild. When Piscator takes Viator's hand and declares that "from this time forward I wil be your Master, and teach you as much of this Art as I am able" (84), he echoes the language of the Elizabethan statute that granted adult householders who worked at "any Arte Misterie or Manuell Occupacion" the right to take on apprentices.[42] Beginning with the second edition of his book in 1655, Walton further enhances our sense of his main characters' master-apprentice relationship when Piscator tells his student (now named Venator), "I am glad to enter you into the Art of fishing by catching a *Chub*, for there is no Fish better to enter a young Angler" (219): the locution "enter . . . into" suggests that Piscator has initiated his apprentice's admission into both a skilled occupation and the guild that controls it.[43] In all editions of *The Compleat Angler*, Peter regards the training of Viator/Venator as a project in which he can assist his "brother"

Piscator. Upon meeting Piscator and Viator at their shared place of lodging in the first edition of 1653, Peter learns that Viator "is one that would faine be a brother of the *Angle*: he has been an *Angler* but this day" (92), and Peter immediately offers to provide material assistance to Piscator's training program: "I wil furnish him [Viator] with a rod, if you wil furnish him with the rest of the tackling, we wil set him up and make him a fisher" (92). In this context, the formulation "set him up" means "to establish or start (a person) in a business or profession," and the *Oxford English Dictionary* presents as its first example of this usage the bequest in a sixteenth-century will providing funds for the Mercers' Company to "deliver yerlie ... to one poore yong man to sett hym up that hathe nother father nor mother."[44] Remarking that he must "look [for] a Line to fit the Rod that our brother *Peter* has lent you" (105), Piscator emphasizes the significance of Peter's generous help in "setting up" Viator's angling apprenticeship. As a London tradesman, Walton functioned very successfully within the guild system, and his own experience as the "master" of apprentices whom he instructed until they became "free brothers" of the Ironmongers' Company underpins his portrayal of Piscator's pedagogical relationship with Viator.[45] Thus in his imagined community of the Brotherhood of the Angle, Walton extends to the pastime of recreational fishing the organizational structure of apprenticeship that he knew so well in his professional life.

PISCATOR AND THE VIRTUOSOS

The cultural impact of the seventeenth-century enthusiasm for Baconian science also shapes Walton's portrayal of the Brotherhood of the Angle. Francis Bacon was especially interested in the final category of his list of "Orders and Societies" that he provides in the *Advancement of Learning*: the "*Noble and Generous Fraternity between men by Learning and Illuminations.*"[46] In both his scientific works and his utopian narrative *New Atlantis*, Bacon championed a visionary (and self-serving) program to reform natural philosophy by collecting the particulars of natural history, an endeavor that would, in Bacon's scheme, also require the creation of new groups of scientific investigators that Bacon imagined himself overseeing.[47] Fostered in part by the millenarian utopianism of the 1640s and 1650s, Bacon's methodology—"a concerted collective program of observational and experimental fact collecting"—came to dominate the practice of natural philosophy in seventeenth-century England, and the ideas and activities of the interconnected scientific circles that developed around such influential figures as Robert Boyle, Samuel Hartlib, and John Wilkins paved the way for the foundation of the Royal Society in 1660.[48] As part of this zeitgeist, it became fashionable for an English gentleman to cultivate and display his *virtù*—his intellectual vitality and leadership—by pursuing Bacon's inductive mode of scientific research and thus earning a reputation as a "*virtuoso*."[49] The twinned fascination with novelty and genteel disdain for practicality that were hallmarks of this version of Baconianism led seventeenth-century English virtuosos to become avid collectors not only of "curiosities"—breathtakingly anomalous physical objects—but also of "secrets," nuggets of specialized technical knowledge gleaned from artisans and householders that could be extracted from their lowly sites of origin and savored instead as rarities by elite connoisseurs. In *The Compleat Angler*, Piscator's angling Brotherhood sometimes overlaps—uncomfortably—with both the membership and the attitudes of this new social formation.[50]

Whenever Piscator introduces the topic of bait oils, the Brotherhood of the Angle crosses into the cultural territory of England's seventeenth-century virtuosos. Near the end of his tutorial about pike, for example, Piscator says he will share with Viator some information "that was told me for a secret" and then immediately provides this formula: "*Dissolve Gum of Ivie in Oyle of Spike, and therewith annoint your dead bait for a Pike; and then cast it into a likely place, and when it has layen a short time at the bottom, draw it towards the top of the water, and so up the stream; and it is more then likely that you have a Pike follow you with more then common eagerness*" (127). The value of this "secret" seems dubious, however, because Piscator admits in the very next sentence that "this has not been tryed by me, but told me by a friend of note, that pretended to do me a courtesie" (127). Piscator's failure to test his own bait-oil formula (a situation that would persist through the final edition of 1676) seems odd,[51] and ambiguity about the motives of Piscator's "friend of note" hovers unresolved in Walton's use of the word "pretended," which could, in this context, mean both "intended" and "feigned." Why does Piscator share this information when he seems so skeptical about its veracity?

Piscator's pike-bait "secret" establishes a pattern that recurs throughout *The Compleat Angler*. Walton's master angler, navigating a rigidly stratified social world, has obtained closely guarded "secrets" from virtuosos (men "of note") who trade in rare chemical formulae; he then shares these "secrets" with Viator but refuses to try them himself. In another passage of this type, we can imagine Piscator suddenly leaning closer to Viator and speaking sotto voce when, near the end of his tutorial about salmon, he shares with his "scholar" a tantalizing tale of mystery:

> And now I shall tell you, that which may be called a secret: I have been a fishing with old *Oliver Henly* (now with God) a noted Fisher, both for *Trout* and *Salmon*, and have observed that he would usually take three or four worms out of his bag and put them into a little box in his pocket, where he would usually let them continue half an hour or more, before he would bait his hook with them; I have ask'd him his reason, and he has replied, *He did but pick the best out to be in a readiness against he baited his hook the next time*: But he has been observed both by others, and my self, to catch more fish then I or any other body, that has ever gone a fishing with him, could do, especially *Salmons*; and I have been told lately by one of his most intimate and secret friends, that the box in which he put those worms was anointed with a drop, or two, or three of the Oil of *Ivy-berries*, made by expression or infusion, and that by the wormes remaining in that box an hour, or a like time, they had incorporated a kind of smel that was irresistibly attractive, enough to force any fish, within the smel of them, to bite. This I heard not long since from a friend, but have not tryed it; yet I grant it probable [...]: 'tis left for a lover of Angling, or any that desires to improve that Art, to try this conclusion. (120)

Other than Piscator's testimony that he was "a noted Fisher," we know virtually nothing about Oliver Henly;[52] what is most important for our purposes, however, is the arm's-length social tension that Walton portrays as having existed between Piscator and Henly. From the one sentence of Henly's own words that Piscator quotes, we learn that Henly deliberately obfuscated rather than truthfully answer Piscator's question about his mysterious spa treatment for worms: Piscator documents Henly's withholding of this "secret" even as he shares the same piece of information with Viator. Tellingly, the convivial Piscator never describes Henly as his "friend": Piscator has learned of Henly's use of ivy-berry oil as a worm perfume only through the intermediation of "a friend" who was also one of Henly's "most intimate and secret friends." Oliver Henly may now be with God, but during his lifetime he most certainly was not with Piscator as a member of the Brotherhood of the Angle.

After sharing Henly's bait-oil "secret" with Viator, Piscator immediately situates it within the context of seventeenth-century Baconianism. Citing related observations in Bacon's own *Sylva Sylvarum* and Gesner's *Historiae Animalium*, Piscator suggests that further investigation into the efficacy of ivy-berry oil as a salmon attractant could help to determine whether fish "can smell in the water" as otters do (120).[53] Piscator then ventures even further into the repertoire of the virtuoso by letting Viator in on an additional "secret": "I shall also impart another experiment (but not tryed by my selfe) which I wil deliver in the same words as it was by a friend, given me in writing. *Take the stinking oil drawn out of* Polypody *of the Oak* [a species of fern], *by a retort mixt with* Turpentine, *and Hive-honey, and annoint your bait therewith, and it will doubtlesse draw the fish to it*" (120). Beginning with the 1655 edition of *The Compleat Angler*, Piscator goes on to proffer a third bait-oil formula that he has "not tryed," this one written in Latin because, according to Piscator's source, it was "too good to be told, but in a learned language, lest it should be made common" (279).[54] Piscator, although slighted by Oliver Henly, has himself adopted the virtuosos' mode of elitist exclusion by using Latin, "the tribal language of educated men,"[55] to keep his recipe safe from the undeserving masses.

By sharing these secret bait-oil formulas with his angling acolyte, Piscator traffics in what the avid natural philosopher Sir John Hoskins dubbed "ingenious information."[56] Rooted in a genteel ethos that scorned labor, virtuoso culture sought to drain technical "secrets" of their use value. Like the snobbery of the untranslated Latin formula that he passes along to his scholar-apprentice, Piscator's failure to try using the "secret" bait oils himself even as he circulates their recipes bespeaks the virtuoso's extravagant denial of practicality—and perhaps, as a closeted tradesman, Walton also scrupulously avoids any suggestion that his alter ego might be interested in the use value of "curious" information. As soon as Piscator behaves like a virtuoso, however, he begins to dither: "But in these things I have no great faith, yet grant it probable, and have had from some chimical men (namely, from Sir *George Hastings* and others) an affirmation of them to be very advantageous: but no more of these, especially not in this place" (120). Piscator first undercuts everything he has just said—"in these things I have no great faith"—only to backtrack as he recalls the opinions of Sir George Hastings and his fellow "chimical men" (virtuosos who dabble in alchemy and/or chemistry). Yet again, Piscator seems unable to establish a productive relationship between his past experiences with virtuosos and his current leadership role in the Brotherhood of the Angle.

Near the end of *The Compleat Angler*, Piscator's thoughts turn once more to fish attractants and "chimical men." As Walton's two main characters begin to walk back to London, Piscator's disquisition on roach and dace suddenly opens up a vista onto both the mysteries of bait oils and Piscator's personal history as a tangential member of a group of virtuosos: "There be several Oiles of a strong smel that I have been told of, and to be excellent to tempt fish to bite, of which I could say much, but I remember I once carried a small bottle from Sir *George Hastings* to Sir *Henry Wotton* (they were both chimical men) as a great present; but upon enquiry, I found it did not answer the expectation of Sir *Henry*, which with the help of other circumstances, makes me have little belief in such things as many men talk of" (154). Piscator functions in this autobiographical narrative as the lackey of higher-status men: he is sufficiently trusted to be used as a courier between the two socially elite virtuosos, but Piscator serves as the bearer—not the recipient—of Hastings's gift, and thus, as in Piscator's earlier anecdotes about bait oils, the master angler never actually tries to use such a substance himself.

This episode also suggests another rationale for Piscator's consistent failure to provide his own firsthand reports about the efficacy of bait oils. Piscator has received word from Wotton that Hastings's gift was disappointingly ineffective, and Wotton's assessment, along "with the help of other circumstances" that Piscator will not specify, makes Walton's master angler doubt the effectiveness of bait-oils altogether. What "other circumstances" could allow Piscator to support Wotton's appraisal of Hastings's gift? Has Piscator, despite his protestations otherwise, been conducting his own tests of bait oils? In early modern England, only the testimony of "gentlemen"—landed members of an hereditary elite who did not have to labor for a living— was considered trustworthy; merchants and tradesmen, by contrast, were regarded as inherently unreliable because of their overriding professional concern with money.[57] So Piscator, as a nongentleman, faces an impossible situation when he obtains virtuosos' "secrets." If he tries to test a "secret," Piscator reveals a nongenteel interest in the practical application of rare knowledge: Wotton's elite status protects him from being sullied if he shows interest in the use value of arcana, but Piscator has no such social capital to spend. And even if he were to risk testing the efficacy of a bait-oil formula obtained from a "chimical man," Piscator's lowly status ensures that his testimony would earn little credence. Piscator's fraught relationships with secret-loving virtuosos is thus symptomatic of the extent to which he can never truly be part of their social milieu.

Piscator's display of ambivalence about "chimical men" is especially charged whenever he is in the textual vicinity of Sir Henry Wotton. The identity of Sir George Hastings is uncertain,[58] but Wotton—who became both an ambassador to Italy and the provost of Eton College before his death in 1639—was a nationally known figure who played a pivotal role in Walton's literary career. Walton insists more than once that he became an author in deference to Sir Henry Wotton. In his dedicatory letter to the first edition of *The Compleat Angler*, Walton depicts himself as Wotton's posthumous water boy, dutifully bringing to fruition Wotton's unrealized plans for an angling treatise: "*I remember Sir* Henry Wotton *(a dear lover of this Art) has told me, that his intentions were to write a discourse of the Art, and in the praise of* Angling, *and doubtless he had done so, if death had not prevented him; the remembrance of which hath often made me sorry; for, if he had lived to do it, then the unlearned* Angler *(of which I am one) had seen some Treatise of this Art worthy his perusal which (though some have undertaken it) I could never yet see in English*" (57). According to Walton's self-effacing etiology, *The Compleat Angler* thus owes its existence to Wotton. In his *Life* of John Donne that was first published in 1640, Walton had similarly credited Wotton with initiating the biography, attesting that he moved from his subsidiary role as Wotton's research assistant only when impelled to tell Donne's story with his own "*artless Pensil*" after Wotton died (*Lives*, 21)—although an extant letter from Wotton suggests it was actually Walton himself who had launched the project.[59] Walton's self-fashioning as Wotton's deferential literary assistant also led him to edit the *Reliquiae Wottonianae*, which was published in 1651 prefaced by Walton's biography of Wotton.[60] We know that Wotton went fishing with Walton—he wrote a letter in which he said he was "hoping shortly to enjoy [Walton's] own ever-welcome company in this approaching time of the fly and the cork"[61]—and Wotton appears in the body of *The Compleat Angler* as an exemplar of angling virtue. During his first day's walk into the Hertfordshire countryside, Piscator describes Wotton as a "most dear lover, and a frequent practicer of the Art of Angling" and "a man with whom I have often fish'd and convers'd," and he then recites a bucolic poem that Wotton ostensibly composed "as he sate quietly in a Summers evening on a bank a fishing" (76). Although Piscator thus approvingly depicts Wotton as an inheritor of the New Testament angler-disciple tradition, it is striking that he never calls Wotton his "friend":[62] there always seems to be a social barrier between Piscator and an elite virtuoso, even someone whom Piscator apparently knows well.

Wotton's appearance late in *The Compleat Angler* as a virtuoso complicates even further our understanding of Piscator's equivocal relationship to the "chimical men." On the one hand, as an exemplar of angling Christian virtue known personally to Walton, Wotton both lends legitimacy to England's virtuosos as a social formation and confirms Walton's own proximity to such a group. Yet in Walton's narrative, Wotton's participation in the activities of a circle of virtuosos only confirms Piscator's outsider status. Thus in *The Compleat Angler*, the appearance of Sir Henry Wotton as a "chimical man" marks the social boundary that finally separates elite virtuosos like Wotton from Piscator and his fellow members of the Brotherhood of the Angle—despite the fact that Piscator and his comrades populate the very book, now authored by a tradesman, that Wotton himself ostensibly wanted to write. In the final analysis, then, Walton seems deeply ambivalent about angler-virtuosos: on the one hand, the virtuosos' cherry-picking perspective on both nature and society can never be fully reconciled with the much more expansive ecosocial boundaries of the worldview that shapes *The Compleat Angler*; but on the other hand, Walton cannot resist including their "secrets" (and thus his own personal connections with the elite sources of such "curious" information) in his book.

ENGENDERING THE BROTHERHOOD OF THE ANGLE

Women, by contrast, inspire no such ambivalence in Walton: Piscator's community of anglers exists as a club that only men can join.[63] Women do appear from time to time in Walton's narrative. Beginning with the second edition of *The Compleat Angler* (1655), Piscator makes a couple of derogatory comments about women anglers (who, like "young Anglers, or boys," enjoy catching small, low-status fish like minnows and sticklebacks), notes that Cleopatra "used Angling as a principal recreation," and mentions "a handsom Woman that had a fine hand" who used embroidered cloth to fashion an effective trout lure that she modeled on "a live *Minnow* lying by her" (349, 202, 247–48). Otherwise, however, female anglers are absent from the world of Walton's treatise, and they do not exist at all in the first edition of 1653.[64] Even more strikingly, the personal lives of the members of the Brotherhood of the Angle also seem to be entirely devoid of female companionship. Walton's depiction of gender in *The Compleat Angler* has received virtually no scholarly attention, perhaps because Walton's imagined community of sociable anglers has proven so popular and influential that the exclusively male membership of the Brotherhood of the Angle now seems unremarkable. Arising in a culture whose fault lines "ran along the axis of male-female relations, not homosexual or homosocial ones," voluntary associations in early modern England were "nearly always restricted to men": both formal associations (like the Society of Antiquaries) and more informal groups (like the Order of the Fancy or the Great Tew circle) had all-male memberships, and the fellows of the Royal Society had never admitted a woman to one of their meetings before Margaret Cavendish paid a visit to Arundel House in 1667.[65] Nonetheless, as Walton wrote *The Compleat Angler*, he chose to ignore other precedents that he knew very well as he created a scrupulously female-free Brotherhood of the Angle. Although most of the traditional "Orders and Societies" that shape Walton's depiction of the Brotherhood were exclusively male, during Walton's lifetime the London livery companies did include women as members.[66] Even more importantly, Walton must radically rewrite both his most influential source text and his own life story to portray in *The Compleat Angler* an all-male "Brotherhood" that is also a "Bachelorhood" of the Angle.

An unmistakable leitmotif of antifeminism recurs throughout Walton's fishing treatise. Positive but fleeting depictions of the relationships between men and women occasionally appear in *The Compleat Angler*, most notably in Piscator's recitation of "certain Verses in praise of a mean estate" from Phineas Fletcher's *The Purple Island*, which Walton added to his text in 1655:

His bed, more safe than soft, yields quiet sleeps,
While by his side his faithful Spouse hath place,
His little son, into his bosom creeps,
The lively picture of his fathers face. (335)

This stanza's pivot in focus from the married man's wife to his "*little son*" suggests, of course, that the "*faithful*" woman has value only as a conduit of her husband's bloodline. But Walton more often quotes writers who warn men against becoming involved with women at all. As Piscator sings William Basse's "Anglers Song" during the fishermen's after-supper entertainment one evening, he lists the hazards of hunting, hawking, and games but warns that even greater dangers confront the man "*who falls in love*" because he "*Is fettered in fond* Cupids *snare*"; by contrast, Piscator concludes, "*My Angle breeds me no such care*" (242). The reader encounters similar sentiments in the dedicatory poem by Thomas Weaver that Walton added to *The Compleat Angler* in 1655:

> His fate's foretold, who fondly places
> His bliss in womans soft embraces.
> All pleasures, but the Anglers, bring
> I'th'tail repentance like a sting. (430)

In another passage original to *The Compleat Angler*, Piscator rates the beauty of fish more highly than the physical attractions of women: "the *Trout* or *Salmon* being in season, have at their first taking out of the water . . . their bodies adorned, the one with such red spots, and the other with such black or blackish spots, as give them such an addition of natural beauty, as I think, was never given to any woman by the Artificial Paint or Patches in which they so much pride themselves in this Age" (280). And a lengthy passage added to the final edition of 1676 indicts, as examples of female vanity, "*a Woman, that broke her* Looking-glass *because it would not shew her face to be as young and handsom as her next Neighbours was*" and a querulous woman who dragged her husband into lawsuits against a neighbor—whose wife was equally "*peevish and* Purse-proud"—because both wives claimed the right to "*sit in the highest Pew in the Church*" (364). The stereotypical misogyny expressed in such passages is undeniable, but given the pervasive sexism of seventeenth-century English culture[67] and the sheer length of *The Compleat Angler*, one might feel that such nuggets of antifeminism are both unremarkable and negligible.

But the discomfort with women that appears explicitly in such passages also shapes *The Compleat Angler* both formally and thematically. As we have already seen, although he borrowed the dialogue structure and main characters of his fishing treatise from William Samuel's *Arte of Angling*, Walton diverged from his Elizabethan source text by changing Samuel's short-tempered, misanthropic Piscator into a model organization man. As Walton thus transformed both Piscator and recreational fishing into inherently sociable entities, however, he also removed his title character from the domestic relationships that William Samuel had depicted with great verve and humor. In Samuel's *Arte of Angling*, Piscator's education of Viator occurs in the master angler's home over a "supper" of multiple species of fish, freshly caught by Piscator, and the quart of sack that Viator has supplied to fulfill his host's BYOB requirements for the meal (*Arte of Angling*, B3r–B3v). In comparing *The Compleat Angler* to *The Arte of Angling*, Jonquil Bevan comments that "versions of a domestic scene at evening, when the day's catch is eaten, appear in both books,"[68] thus downplaying Walton's significant—and significantly gendered—revisions to Samuel's work. Most importantly, by reincarnating Samuel's Elizabethan anglers as interregnum Londoners who lodge at a Hertfordshire alehouse, Walton eliminates the one character from *The Arte of Angling* who can stand up to William Samuel's irascible master fisherman: Piscator's spirited, sharp-tongued wife, Cisley.

While the hapless Viator in *The Arte of Angling* is ultimately dominated by Piscator, Cisley springs to life in Samuel's dialogue as a forceful personality whom even Piscator must respect. The narrative's shift in setting from waterside to the interior of Piscator's home is signaled in the text by a centered phrase that seems like a stage direction: "Piscator and his wife Cisley" (B2r). The ensuing exchange between these characters immediately establishes the cheerful sparring of two feisty people who have lived with each other for years. "Good Lord husbande where have you beene all this daye," exclaims Cisley when Piscator returns to the house, and as Piscator shows off the fish he has caught, Cisley preempts any boasting by suggesting that she and good luck are solely responsible for her husband's success: "I am gladde now that I did throw an olde shooe after you in the morning" (B2v). Piscator responds in kind, making it clear that both he and Cisley are engaged in a long-running game of trash talking: "Your old shooe was fit for an old foolish woman to have throwen, that hathe more confidence in such dismole toies than in the providence of God, who guideth aswel the fishes in the sea, as the foules in the ayre, but I knowe you speake merrily as I did when I bad[e] you do it" (B2v–B3r).

Cisley not only prepares the fish for Piscator and Viator's supper, but she and one of the couple's children, Anne, also join the men at the table. Although Anne, an exemplary daughter of the Tudor era, speaks only when directed to do so by her father—fetching her mother after Viator arrives and saying grace at the end of the meal—her mother is neither silent nor obedient. Like his namesake in Walton's book, Samuel's Piscator waxes loquacious on the subject of fishing techniques, but whereas the anglers' technical conversations in *The Compleat Angler* are structured by environmental features (the geography of the River Lea and the stormy weather of the Little Ice Age), Piscator's tutorial in *The Arte of Angling* is shaped instead by Cisley, who strives to keep her husband's discourse within the bounds of social propriety. As supper and Piscator's lecture drag on, Cisley tries to make her husband treat their guest Viator more hospitably. "You eate no meate nowe, therfore it may be taken away," Cisley declares when Piscator stops briefly to take a breath, and Viator, trapped at the table as Piscator's captive audience, seconds the motion: "Well, then, if it please you let us have a cup of sack, and an apple, or a peare, and then let us rise a Gods name" (D2v). True to his socially inept nature, however, Piscator refuses to take these hints and opts instead to delay the dessert course and continue droning at the table. He later allows Viator to retreat to a chair in front of the fire, at which point Piscator launches into an extended lecture about carp, bream, dace, and roach. After her husband berates Viator for asking what Piscator regards as a stupid question, Cisley suddenly intervenes to bring a halt to Piscator's conversational death march, and we realize she has stayed in the room to monitor her husband's behavior: "But I pray you good sirs when wil ye to bedde, the night is farre spent" (E5v). Not allowing Piscator to utter a syllable in response, Viator immediately seizes the lifeline that Cisley has just thrown him and rushes for the exit: "Well then God be with you, untill an other time" (E5v). William Samuel's Piscator certainly perpetuates antifeminist stereotypes—when Cisley chides him for talking ad nauseam about the minutiae of bait-fishing, he retorts that "all is nothing with you and your kinde, unlesse it be about pinnes and laces, frindge and gards, fine linnen and wollen, hats and hat bandes, gloves, and scarffes" (C6v–C7r)—but Cisley's witty levelheadedness and her husband's social ineptitude undercut Piscator's authority. Samuel thus uses the character of Cisley both to structure the main body of his dialogue and to heighten his characterization of Piscator's zeal for angling as an index of the fisherman's misanthropy.

As he adapted Samuel's text, however, Walton eliminated all traces of his protagonist's domestic life. Walton relocates William Samuel's vividly portrayed scene of mealtime dialogue chez Piscator to the commercialized premises of an alehouse in rural Hertfordshire. Thus at Bleak Hall, Cisley's roles as cook and food server are played by the deferential Hostess, and Piscator's daughter Anne and her unseen siblings are replaced by the angling "brothers" who congregate around Walton's convivial reincarnation of Samuel's crotchety master fisherman. And in *The Compleat Angler*, Piscator never mentions having a wife or family, an aspect of Walton's revision of William Samuel's narrative that complicates our understanding of the relationship between the protagonist of Walton's treatise and the author himself. Because Walton's friends are Piscator's friends, Walton repeatedly invites us to interpret Piscator as his own alter ego. Yet by the time he published the final edition of his angling treatise in 1676, Walton was a widower twice over, his second wife, whom he married in 1647, having died in 1662. A pair of dedicatory poems written by the brothers of Walton's first wife, Rachel Floud, were added to *The Compleat Angler* in 1655 and thus implicitly identify the book's author as a onetime husband, but Piscator never explicitly mentions either of Walton's wives.[69] The closest Piscator ever comes to claiming Walton's domestic life as his own occurs in Walton's poem "The Anglers Wish," first added to *The Compleat Angler* in 1661. The poem, as we have seen, celebrates the beauties of nature that an angler can enjoy while he fishes in "*Christall streams*" that flow through "*flowery Medes*," and the speaker includes in his catalog of delightful waterside experiences the opportunity to "*heare my* Clora *sing a song*":[70] in the final edition of 1676, however, Walton revised the text so Piscator instead listens to a musical performance by "*my* Kenna" (262), a name that evokes Walton's long-dead second wife, Anne Ken. Thus more than twenty years after he first extricated William Samuel's Piscator from his domestic setting, Walton provides only an oblique, three-syllable suggestion that his master angler shares Walton's marital history.

By rewriting *The Arte of Angling*—and his own life story—to portray Piscator as a happy and successful man who is both surrounded by male friends and unencumbered by a wife, Walton aligns *The Compleat Angler* with his biographies of prominent Anglican men. Early in his account of John Donne's courtship of Anne More, Walton steps up onto his soapbox to condemn amatory relationships in general: "Love is a flattering mischief, that hath denied aged and wise men a foresight of those evils that too often prove to be the children of that blind father, a passion! that carries us to commit *Errors* with as much ease as whirlwinds remove feathers, and begets in us an unwearied industry to the attainment of what we desire."[71]

Despite his personal admiration for Donne (who had served as vicar of St. Dunstan-in-the-West when Walton was a parishioner), Walton cannot restrain himself from berating his former priest for imprudently deciding to marry for love: "His marriage was the remarkable error of his life; an error which though he had a wit able and very apt to maintain Paradoxes, yet he was very far from justifying it" (60). Of Walton's censorious account of Donne's relationship with Anne More, George Saintsbury dryly observes, "I doubt whether he in the least understood Donne's attitude to the matter."[72]

By contrast, Walton understood—and praised—men who intentionally created passionless marriages. According to Walton, Charles Danvers "so much commended" George Herbert to Danvers's daughter Jane that she "became so much a Platonick, as to fall in love with Mr. *Herbert* unseen" and then married Herbert within three days of first meeting him (*Lives*, 286). Walton insists we should interpret Herbert's swift courtship of Jane Danvers as an entirely unromantic, rational process: "This haste might in others be thought a *Love-phrensie*, or worse: but it was not; for they had wooed so like Princes, as to have select Proxies: such, as were true friends to both parties" (286).[73] The arm's-length quality of Herbert's marriage becomes highlighted again in Walton's account of Herbert's last hours. Shooing his "weeping" wife and nieces away into an adjacent room, Herbert insists that he wants to die with only two male friends in attendance, a decision Walton regards favorably: "Thus [Herbert] liv'd, and thus he dy'd like a Saint, unspotted of the World, full of . . . all the examples of a vertuous life" (318–19). Walton likewise approves of Robert Sanderson's reasoned and therefore lukewarm attitude toward marriage. Leaving behind the social life he had enjoyed as a fellow at Oxford, Sanderson took up a career as a country parson in rural Lincolnshire, where the "want of conversation" led him to "put on some faint purposes to marry" (*Lives*, 363). Even though he felt that "marriage be cumbred with more worldly care than a single life," Walton says, Sanderson recognized the biological reality that men can beget "little Images of themselves" only with the assistance of women, and so he "turn'd his faint purpose into a positive resolution to marry" (363–64). Walton further reports that Sanderson's decision to secure a reproductive resource also capable of "conversation" led him to find "a Wife, that demonstrated her affection by a chearful obedience to all his desires" (363–64). As George Saintsbury notes about Walton's *Lives*, "there is always a touch of oddity in Walton's accounts of courtships and marriages."[74] Having banned his wife from his deathbed,

Herbert draws his last breath in the company of men, while Robert Sanderson accepts the "worldly care" of marriage in order to be surrounded by "little Images" of himself: in Walton's biographies of both Herbert and Sanderson, we find an abiding discomfort with women and a simultaneous search for emotional fulfillment in an all-male community.

But Walton depicts women and marriage most scathingly in his biography of Richard Hooker. According to Walton's narrative (which historians now regard as wildly inaccurate),[75] Hooker lived happily in Oxford as a fellow of Corpus Christi College until he traveled to London one day in order to preach at St. Paul's Cross and had the misfortune to lodge at the home of an impoverished draper ironically surnamed "Churchman." When Hooker, exhausted and drenched by rain, arrived at his host's residence, Churchman's scheming wife saw an easy mark: after earning Hooker's gratitude by caring for him attentively, Mrs. Churchman persuaded the naive scholar not only "*that it was best for him to have a Wife, that might prove a Nurse to him*," but also that her daughter Joan, despite possessing "neither Beauty nor Portion," would be his ideal helpmate (*Lives*, 177–78). In Walton's vivid but apocryphal account, having thus been duped into marriage with the unappealing and unprofitable Joan Churchman, Hooker was forced to leave Oxford and take up residence in rural Buckinghamshire as rector of St. Mary the Virgin in the village of Drayton Beauchamp. When two of Hooker's former pupils came to visit their beloved tutor, they found him trying to read the odes of Horace while "tending his small allotment of sheep in a common field" because Joan had conscripted their servant to perform "houshold business" instead of watching over the family's livestock. When the servant finally resumed his proper role as a shepherd, the two visitors accompanied Hooker into his home, "where their best entertainment was his quiet company, which was presently denied them: for, *Richard was call'd to rock the Cradle*" (179). Unable to endure any further proof of Hooker's degrading uxoriousness, the two visitors headed back to Oxford the next morning, one of them uttering the valediction, "*Good Tutor, I am sorry your lot is fall'n in no better ground as to your Parsonage; and more sorry that your Wife proves not a more comfortable Companion after you have wearied your self in your restless studies*" (179–80).[76] For Walton, Hooker's life story reenacts the fall of Adam: "And by this marriage the good man was drawn from the tranquillity of his Colledge, from that Garden of Piety, of Pleasure, of Peace, and a sweet Conversation, into the thorny Wilderness of a busie World; into those corroding cares that attend a married Priest, and a Countrey Parsonage" (178–79). Thus in Walton's estimation, Richard Hooker's life as a bachelor in an all-male community, where he had earned the role of "master" to an appreciative group of scholars, was the paradise that Hooker lost the day he married Joan Churchman.

Walton's habitual unease about male-female relationships likewise shapes his depiction of female characters in *The Compleat Angler*. If expert mastery of angling is a goal achievable only by men in *The Compleat Angler*, it seems that the leisure necessary to pursue this "recreation" is likewise a uniquely male privilege, for we encounter all the female characters in Walton's book while they are working. Here again, we see strong parallels with William Samuel's *Arte of Angling*. In Samuel's sixteenth-century text, his protagonist's first words to Cisley are "How nowe wife, is the brothe ready" (B2r): while Samuel's master angler was out fishing, Cisley was at home preparing to cook her husband's catch of the day. Walton, however, removes his anglers' reliance on women's labor from the domestic sphere and instead portrays his female characters as engaged in commercial activities.[77]

Cisley's role as the protagonist's personal chef in *The Arte of Angling* is performed in *The Compleat Angler* by the Hostess of Bleak Hall, the alehouse at which the anglers lodge for the final two nights of their Hertfordshire vacation. Bleak Hall is apparently operated by a husband-and-wife team—although the Host never speaks, he participates in the fishermen's second evening of after-dinner festivities (151)—but we otherwise are privy only to the anglers' interactions with the establishment's "Hostess" (who, unlike William Samuel's Cisley, is always designated by her professional role rather than her name). Often run out of their proprietors' homes, many seventeenth-century English alehouses were licensed to married men whose wives functioned as the establishments' managers, and it seems that Bleak Hall fits this pattern. Although the role of alewife was "one of the most significant female occupations in early modern times," women who worked at small or unlicensed alehouses were often suspected of prostitution, and alewives who wanted to be viewed as morally righteous had to guard their reputations carefully.[78] As a space of monetized hospitality, the early modern alehouse thus straddled a fraught, gendered boundary between respectable domesticity and an ethically dubious commercial sphere, and this sexually charged tension between probity and licentiousness shapes Walton's depiction of the Hostess of Bleak Hall.

When he first tells Viator about Bleak Hall, Piscator commends it as "an honest Alehouse" (83). The seventeenth-century resonances of the word "honest" encompass all the virtues that Piscator expects from his holiday accommodation: delicious food, respectability, and female chastity.[79] Yet Piscator's description of the Hostess of Bleak Hall encodes a more equivocal attitude toward the woman's character. Unlike the smutty and sacrilegious Host of the establishment where Piscator and Viator lodged the night after their otter hunt, the Hostess of Bleak Hall is "both cleanly and conveniently handsome" (83). "Cleanly," a term of approbation that Piscator also uses to describe the condition of his room at Bleak Hall (83), conveys a sense of the Hostess's combined physical and spiritual purity.[80] Although Piscator's description of the Hostess does not convey the explicitly erotic tension of Robert Herrick's compound "cleanly-*Wantonnesse*," the basis of Piscator's regard for the Hostess remains ambiguous: "handsome" could mean "courteous" but could also mean physically "attractive," and the word "conveniently" does not clearly indicate which of the Hostess's characteristics—her decorous manners or her good looks—Piscator deems pleasingly suitable.[81] Piscator thus implicitly portrays the Hostess of Bleak Hall as an alluring woman, obliquely evoking the stereotype of the promiscuous alewife even as he proclaims the Hostess's "honesty" and "cleanliness."

In other ways, however, the Hostess embodies a more decorous mode of gendered subordination than the female behavior on display in William Samuel's *Arte of Angling*. The hierarchy structuring the commercialized relationship between Walton's Piscator and the Hostess is much more rigidly stratified than the chain of command within the household of Samuel's protagonist Piscator and his wife, Cisley. Whereas Cisley decides for herself what cooking method is "best" for each species of fish that her husband brings home with him for supper (*Arte of Angling*, B3r), Walton's alter ego triumphantly micromanages the Hostess of Bleak Hall: in *The Compleat Angler*, the Hostess has not only learned how to dress fish "after [Piscator's] fashion," but she is also prepared to do so "instantly" when Piscator crosses the threshold of her alehouse (*Compleat Angler*, 83–84). And as he presents Viator with his first shore lunch, Piscator takes the opportunity to praise his twinned mastery of both the Hostess and the fine art of fish cookery: "Now Sir, has not my Hostis made haste? and does not the fish look lovely?" (84). Unlike William Samuel's Cisley, whose sparring matches with her husband reveal that she has a mind and a voice of her own, Walton's Hostess speaks just twice—and both times in brief response to a command or question from Piscator (84, 91). Otherwise, the Hostess enters the narrative only when called and then silently executes the fishermen's orders: "Come Hostis, where are you? is Supper ready? come, first give us drink, and be as quick as you can"; "Come Hostis, give us more Ale, and our Supper with what haste you may"; "Come Hostis, give us a little more drink, and lay a few more sticks on the fire" (147–48). Even the Hostess's accounting of the anglers' bill is communicated through the voice of Piscator: "come, my Hostis sayes there is seven shillings to pay, lets each man drink a pot for his mornings draught, and lay down his two shillings" (151). Thus the "cleanly" Hostess of Bleak Hall, despite her potentially disreputable line of work and possible physical charms, exists as a stereotypically virtuous early modern woman: the anglers' Hostess is unfailingly obedient, habitually silent, and therefore, we can assume, unquestionably chaste as well.[82]

The tensions pervading Walton's depictions of women become even more acute when his anglers leave the confines of Bleak Hall. Whereas the female characters portrayed by William Samuel speak only within domestic spaces, women's voices are heard almost exclusively outdoors in *The Compleat Angler*. Walton's anglers converse twice with a milkwoman and her daughter, a milkmaid named Maudlin, while the two dairyworkers tend their cows in a field near Bleak Hall through which the fishermen pass on their way to and from the River Lea. Walton ominously shapes our interpretation of these dairywomen and their voices. Piscator recalls that shortly before he first encountered Maudlin and her mother, he was sitting under a tree enjoying the surrounding meadows when "the birds in the adjoining Grove seemed to have a friendly contention with an Echo, whose dead voice seemed to live in a hollow cave, near to the brow of that Primrose hil" (88).[83] According to Ovid, Echo was a talkative young woman who used her gift of gab to prevent Juno from catching the goddess's philandering husband Jove in flagrante; as punishment, Juno rendered Echo unable to initiate speech, granting her only the capacity to repeat the final words of other people's utterances. After being rejected by the young man Narcissus, Echo retreated into the woods and "sculk[ed] in desert Caves," wasting away until only her "voyce remayne[d]."[84] By thus framing our experience of the dairyworkers' utterances with the myth of Echo, Walton implicitly portrays female agency as an illusion and associates the sound of the female voice with sexual trauma and death. As part of the long-standing scholarly inattention to Walton's representation of women, the Hertfordshire milkwoman and her daughter have occasioned very little critical comment. But if we move beyond a cursory pigeonholing of these characters as stereotypes from "the never-never-land of sophisticated pastoral,"[85] we can better appreciate the gendered complexity of social relations in *The Compleat Angler*.

Rather than fanciful arcadianism, the realities of the seventeenth-century dairy shape Walton's depiction of Maudlin and her mother. Indeed, G. E. Fussell includes *The Compleat Angler* in his history of English dairy farming and finds Piscator's encounters with Maudlin and her mother so plausible that he assumes they reflect Walton's personal experience.[86] The verisimilitude of Walton's portrayal of these rural laborers begins with the calendar that structures Piscator's interactions with the two women. In the first edition of *The Compleat Angler*, Walton's anglers initially encounter the milkwoman and her daughter on May 3, 1653, but Piscator says he had seen and heard the two women when he "was last this way a fishing . . . about eight or nine dayes since" (89), thus fixing his previous sighting of Maudlin and her mother on April 24 or April 25.[87] In southeastern England during the early modern period, cows were traditionally fed winter fodder from the end of September through April 23, when the new grass had grown long enough to support grazing, and May Day celebrations throughout the country often included indulgence in dairy products to herald the beginning of the peak season of milk production, a time of year especially meaningful "for people perhaps short on protein in their diet throughout the cold months."[88] Walton's female dairyworkers thus exist not in a timeless pastoral idyll but rather inhabit a recognizably English countryside in which the arrival of spring necessitates their increased labor.

Dairying in early modern England was not the stuff of bucolic *otium*: it required unrelenting hard work and long hours, and during Walton's lifetime the difficult tasks involved in "*Dayrying, or raising . . . Cheese and Butter*" were performed almost exclusively by women.[89] Because milk could not be refrigerated, it had to be quickly and carefully transformed into "white meats," that is, more stable sources of dairy protein such as butter and cheese.[90] A farmer's wife was expected to supervise her daughters (and, if the dairy operation were large, the family's hired milkmaids) as this all-female workforce milked the household's cows, churned butter, and made cheese. Milkmaids thus necessarily spent much of their working lives outdoors. Cows were usually milked in the meadows in which they grazed, and a milkmaid was expected to begin her first milking between 4:00 and 6:00 a.m.; upon completion, she would carry her milk back to the dairy. The early modern English dairyworker was highly skilled: to milk cows, she needed to handle the animals gently, while successful food production required knowledge, experience, and painstaking cleanliness. After making butter and cheese, the milkmaid would return to the pasture at 6:00 or 7:00 p.m. for the evening milking, carry her pail back to the dairy, and then "set" the milk for the next day's processing.[91] If a farm produced more dairy products than were needed for the household's own consumption, the farmer's wife might assume the role of milkwoman and sell the excess. Because dairying could thus provide a socially acceptable means of financial survival for unmarried or widowed women, "the practice of marketing small quantities of milk, cheese and butter was so well established in rural communities that overseers of the poor on occasion aided poor women through the purchase of a cow, so that with rights of common they might be self-sufficient."[92] Yet a milkwoman, despite working as a producer and vendor of high-protein food, might well be chronically hungry: as Sara Mendelson and Patricia Crawford note, "In the poorest households, dairy products were probably sold to pay for rent, fuel, clothing, and miscellaneous expenses. . . . This [situation] left indigent families with little nourishing food for themselves."[93] In *The Compleat Angler*, Piscator's interactions with Maudlin and her mother suggest precisely this scenario.

Piscator's detailed knowledge of the rural environment of Hertfordshire extends to its human inhabitants. And since Piscator had observed the female dairyworkers on a previous fishing trip, his response to the women within the narrative of *The Compleat Angler* reflects his considered assessment of their plight. When Piscator first meets the women while he is fishing with Viator, Walton's master angler offers Maudlin and her mother a freshly caught chub for their dinner (89). In the wake of Walton's account of how the sixteenth-century clergyman Alexander Nowell gave all his catch to "the poor" who lived near the rivers that Nowell frequented (76), we assume that Piscator likewise practices charity by offering his extra fish to Maudlin and her mother.[94] Despite the notorious unpalatability of chub, the milkwoman immediately accepts the fish—she and Maudlin must be hungry—but the milkwoman refuses to treat the chub as a gift and offers Piscator "a draught of red Cows milk" (an especially high-quality beverage) in exchange (89).[95] Piscator declines the milk and asks instead for a "Ditty" he had heard the women perform previously in which Maudlin sang "that smooth Song which was made by *Kit Marlow*, now at least fifty years ago," and her mother "sung an answer to it, which was made by Sir *Walter Raleigh* in his yonger dayes" (89). The milkwoman accepts Piscator's revised offer, and Maudlin sings Marlowe's "Come live with me, and be my Love" followed by her mother's rendition of Raleigh's response.[96] These interactions ally the female dairyworkers with the Brotherhood of the Angle in some ways. Like Piscator's male companions, Maudlin and the milkwoman become the beneficiaries of the master angler's skill when they accept his freshly caught fish, and their lyrics become part of the collection of poems that Walton de facto anthologizes during the course of *The Compleat Angler*.[97] Moreover, the milkmaid and her mother provide the first songs performed in Walton's narrative, establishing a model for the exchanges of vocal music that will later structure the fishermen's postprandial sociability at Bleak Hall. Nonetheless, Maudlin and her mother always remain firmly outside the bounds of Piscator's community of fishermen.

In part, disparity in economic resources creates an unbridgeable gap between the dairyworkers and the anglers. Whereas Piscator and his followers share songs as part of their leisure-time activities, the women's musical performances are products of their labor that they reiterate in exchange for food. Many people sang or whistled as they labored during the seventeenth century, and what Walton depicts as the customary singing of the Hertfordshire milkwoman and her daughter reflects common practice among early modern dairyworkers.[98] Milkmaids habitually sang to improve their herds' yield since a cow could be trained to "let downe her milke" in response to a familiar song.[99] Indeed, Milton's statement in "L'Allegro" that "the milkmaid singeth blithe" puns on the tendency of elite observers to interpret dairyworkers' vocal music as expressions of joy rather than a pragmatic technique for increasing output, since the word "blithe" could be interpreted in this context to mean both "merry" and "yielding milk."[100] Contemporaries remarked on groups of seventeenth-century milkmaids "singing of Ballads" in the fields and noted that songs circulating as broadsides in rural areas became part of the repertoire of local dairyworkers, and decades before Piscator encountered Maudlin, Nicholas Breton depicted a milkmaid "under the side of the pied Cowe" who was singing Christopher Marlowe's "Come live with mee & be my love."[101] So rather than pastoral fantasy, the musicality of Maudlin and her mother originates in the daily routines of the women's work. Although, as we have seen, Walton's anglers regularly choose to enter the territory of georgic in pursuit of their sport, the female dairyworkers are too impoverished ever to leave that realm.

Finally, however, both the anglers and the milkwomen find it safer to remain within their separate, same-sex spheres. As Walton's narrative unfolds, we come to recognize that the well-being of both the dairyworkers and Piscator's brotherhood can barely withstand interaction between the two groups. Contradictory cultural traditions—both idealizing and menacing—suffuse Walton's portrayal of Maudlin. In early modern England, "dairymaids' pristine cleanliness, early rising, ample fresh air and a clear skin, naturally inoculated by cowpox from the devastation of smallpox, gave them a seemingly idyllic appearance and lifestyle."[102] Beginning in the second edition of *The Compleat Angler*, this concept of the milkmaid as a feminine ideal shapes Venator's reaction to Maudlin: "I now see it was not without cause, that our good Queen *Elizabeth* did so often wish her self a Milkmaid all the month of *May*, because they [milkmaids] are not troubled with fears and cares, but sing sweetly all the day, and sleep securely all the night: and without doubt, honest, innocent, pretty *Maudlin* does so" (234). At multiple times during her life, Queen Elizabeth I said that she yearned to escape from Tudor high politics by assuming the identity of a milkmaid, and Venator's reference to Elizabeth calls to mind a narrative that had first been presented in Foxe's *Book of Martyrs* and was later recounted both in Holinshed's *Chronicles* and the works of Thomas Heywood.[103] According to Holinshed's version of the story, after Mary I had placed her under house arrest, the Princess Elizabeth, "hearing upon a time out of hir garden at Woodstocke, a certeine milkmaid singing pleasantlie, wished hir selfe to be a milkemaid . . . saieng that hir case was better, and life more merier than was hirs in that state as she was."[104] As queen, Elizabeth likewise presented the milkmaid as an enviable (and, for a monarch, unattainable) ideal of female autonomy: in a 1576 speech to Parliament, Elizabeth declared that "if [she] were a milkmaid with a pail on [her] arm, whereby [her] private person might be little set by, [she] would not forsake that single state to match [her]self with the greatest monarch," and when, a decade later, she answered petitions urging the execution of her cousin Mary, Queen of Scots, Elizabeth imagined an alternative autobiography in which "it had pleased God to have made us both milkmaids with pails on our arms."[105] Venator's reference to the late queen of famous memory as an aspiring milkmaid was politically charged: claimed as a "propagandistic icon" by both royalists and parliamentarians, Elizabeth I functioned as a contentious symbol throughout the civil wars and interregnum, and while the queen was a potentially "counter-revolutionary" figure during the 1650s, the Woodstock narrative's emphasis on the Princess Elizabeth's lack of agency had made the story popular among parliamentarians before the regicide.[106] Thus, despite his royalist sympathies, Walton's evocation of Elizabeth in 1655 as a wannabe milkmaid seems ideologically ambiguous, serving to highlight female helplessness as much as self-determination.[107]

Other contradictions with even deeper cultural roots further complicate Walton's depiction of the two female dairyworkers in his angling treatise. By the eighteenth century, the milkmaid would become the female epitome "of a wholesome, natural, and vigorous sexuality,"[108] and as this stereotype gained currency during Walton's lifetime, the milkmaid was often portrayed as an eroticized figure. In early modern England, milkmaids were so closely associated with amatory dalliance that the term "*Cream-pot* love" referred to what "young fellows pretend to dairy-maids, to get cream and other good things of them."[109] In such scenarios, the milkmaid's presence outdoors both enables and emblematizes her sexual availability: "The maide shee went a milking, all in a misty morning, downe fell her milking pale, up went her diddle diddle tayle."[110] Walton was certainly aware of the cream-pot milkmaid, as such a figure appears a poem by Sir Henry Wotton that Piscator quotes early in *The Compleat Angler*:

> Jone *takes her neat rubb'd pail, and now*
> She *trips to milk the sand-red* Cow;
> *Where, for some sturdy foot-ball Swain,*
> Jone *strokes a* Sillibub *or twaine.* (77)

In his portrayal of "pretty *Maudlin*" (145), however, Walton evokes the figure of the sexy milkmaid only to imperil it. By linking the young woman with the Virgin Queen, of course, Walton implicitly suggests that the "handsome Milk-maid" (89) is destined for celibacy—or, at least, a love life free from men.[111] This hint that Maudlin will lead an anomalous existence becomes even more foreboding when Piscator's apprentice angler insists he will "bestow Sir *Thomas Overbury's* Milk maids wish upon [Maudlin], *That she may dye in the Spring, and have good store of flowers stuck round about her winding sheet*" (90).¹¹² By quoting this passage, Viator deliberately evokes the garlands of flowers traditionally gathered by young women on May Day: normally "emblematic of the nubile virgin," garlands were also displayed in early modern English churches during funeral services for unmarried young women.¹¹³ This symbolism may have further reminded seventeenth-century readers that the word "Maudlin" could refer both to flowering aromatic plants and to Mary Magdalene, the reformed sex-worker who discovered that the crucified Jesus had risen from the dead when she went to tend his body in the tomb.¹¹⁴ But Walton transposes the intertwined suggestions of illicit female sexuality and death that surround Maudlin into an even darker key: as Piscator describes how he had previously observed the young woman, he remarks that he overheard her singing "like a *Nightingale*" (89), and Maudlin's mother recapitulates this image in yet more sinister form two pages later when, as she sings Raleigh's response to Marlowe's poem, she describes an inhospitable winter landscape in which "Philomel *becometh dumb*" (91).

These allusions to the horrific myth of Philomela—who was transformed into a nightingale after being raped and then mutilated by her brother-in-law so she could not speak¹¹⁵—link Walton's depiction of Maudlin to the oldest and most disturbing portrayals of milkmaids in English literature. Although milkmaids in most eighteenth-century songs "were not depicted as passive victims of male sexual aggression or desire,"¹¹⁶ their forebears in earlier texts often did not lead such charmed lives. Helen Cooper suggests that the figure of the milkmaid accosted by a man seeking sexual favors commonly appeared in medieval English folksongs and shaped Sir Thomas Malory's account of the begetting of Sir Torre, the illegitimate son of King Pellinore: "When [Torre's mother] was a mayde *and wente to mylke hir kyne*, ther mette with me a sterne knyght, and half be force he had my maydynhed."¹¹⁷ Decades later, the sexually victimized milkmaid reappeared in a song known at the court of Henry VIII. In this text, a male speaker with the seemingly benign opening gambit "Hey troly loly lo! / Mayde, whether go you?" accosts a milkmaid who is heading "to the medowe" to milk her cow.¹¹⁸ When the man malevolently declares that, like Pluto stalking Proserpina, he will meet the young woman "to gather the flowres both fayer and swete," the milkmaid tries to dissuade her pursuer: "Nay, God forbede! That may not be— / I wysse [I know] my mother then shall us se!" (424). Undeterred, the man tries to entice the milkmaid into compliance:

> Now yn this medow fayer and grene
> We may us sport and not be sene;
> And yf ye wyll, I shall consent;
> How sey ye, mayde? Be ye content? (424–25)

But the milkmaid firmly replies, "I wyll not melle [have sex with] you; / I pray you, sir, lett me go mylke my cow!" (425). Despite the woman's repeated blunt rejections of his advances, the male speaker persists with increasing menace:

> Ye have my hert; sey what ye wyll.
> Wherefore ye muste my mynde fulfyll,
> And graunte me here your maydynhed,
> Or elles I shall for you be ded. (425)

And in his sinister final words in the song, the man drops all pretense of courtship and openly reveals himself as a sexual predator:

> Then for this onse I shal you spare,
> But the nexte tyme ye must beware
> How in the medow ye mylke your cow.
> Adew, farewell and kysse me now! (425)

Although the text ends with the milkmaid refusing him yet once more, one readily imagines the male speaker again trying to force himself on the young woman when she returns to the same field, as she must, for her cows' next milking.

This song reflects the grim cultural reality that in early modern England, "sexual harassment and coercion were probably . . . routine aspects of everyday life for many, perhaps most, women."[119] The scenario of a man sexually assaulting a milkmaid while she worked outdoors was painfully credible when Walton wrote *The Compleat Angler*: in 1647, Jane Bingley stated in a deposition that she was raped "while she was milking," and in 1653, Isabel Moorhouse was attacked "about eight or nine of the clock in the evening as she was coming from milking kine."[120] As Sara Mendelson and Patricia Crawford observe, although "indoor and outdoor space were equally hazardous environments" for women in the sixteenth and seventeenth centuries, "their susceptibility to male violence helps explain why women often went about in pairs or groups during the daytime, for they were vulnerable to opportunistic forms of bodily harm when they ventured into outdoor or male-dominated space."[121] Thus in *The Compleat Angler*, the inseparability of Maudlin and her mother suggests they inhabit the same dangerous social world as Jane Bingley and Isabel Moorhouse—and for the sake of her daughter's safety, the milkwoman will not let Maudlin out of her sight.

Nonetheless, Maudlin is assailed by a man even as we read Walton's narrative. When Piscator and Viator end their first conversation with the milkwoman and her daughter, the master angler sharply orders his companion, "Come Scholer, let *Maudlin* alone, do not you offer to spoil her voice" (91). Piscator's imperative statement, the word "spoil" resonating with suggestions of plunder and rape, serves as a stage direction that forces the reader to imagine what has just happened.[122] Commenting on this passage late in the eighteenth century, one of Walton's most influential editors, Sir John Hawkins, argues that Viator, "charmed perhaps with the maidenly innocence and probably beauty, of the young woman, for we are told that she is handsome, offers to kiss her; and that *Piscator*, an elder and more discreet man, checks him, lest he should offend her by too great familiarity."[123] As readers, we thus suddenly realize we have been privy to an attempted sexual assault on Maudlin: only Piscator's effective bystander intervention has prevented Walton's book from replicating the characteristically violent trajectory of the milkmaid narrative. And Maudlin's mother, we now recognize, insists on transforming the anglers' offer of charity into barter so she can control what the men might demand as recompense from her sexually vulnerable daughter.

Viator behaves very differently when he next encounters Maudlin. As he and Piscator head back to Bleak Hall for their final evening in Hertfordshire, they seek out the dairyworkers once again, this time bearing two extra trout for the women's "supper" (145). Now more sensitive to the milkwoman's refusal to become an object of the anglers' charity, Piscator preemptively couches his gift of freshly caught protein as an exchange: "we resolve to give you and *Maudlin* a brace of *Trouts* for supper, and we will now taste a draught of your *Red Cows milk*" (145). Yet again, the milkwoman instantly accepts the fish, but since Piscator's new offer is more generous than the previous day's chub in both quality and quantity, the milkwoman insists that she owes the anglers more than a drink of milk, promising them in addition "a good *Sillabub*" and another ballad sung by Maudlin "when you come next this way" (145).[124] It is Viator who accepts this offer and says farewell on behalf of both anglers, thanking the milkwoman and politely saying "good night" to her daughter (145). In response to this man who had attempted to "spoil" her only the day before, Maudlin says nothing.

We are prepared for this salutary change in Viator's attitude toward Maudlin when we overhear him recite a poem several pages earlier. Toward the end of the prolonged spells of torrential rain that structure Piscator's angling tutorials on the fourth day of his fishing trip, Walton's protagonist asks Viator to contribute something to their educational "Discourse" (137), and Viator obliges by reciting John Donne's "The Baite." Like the text of Raleigh's verses sung the previous day by Maudlin's mother, "The Baite" responds parodically to Marlowe's "Come live with me, and be my Love"— the pastoral poem that, when performed by Maudlin, Viator interpreted as an invitation to sexual assault. But sandwiched between Piscator's rain-induced discussions of perch and eel, Viator's recitation of Donne's poem transforms the social dynamics of both the milkwomen's songs and Walton's narrative.

With "The Baite," Donne simultaneously joined and interrogated the time-honored portrayal of seduction as fishing. Since classical antiquity, writers had styled the angler's baited hook as a metaphor of sensual temptation, and by the early modern period, "the image of woman as sexual bait and the male lover as the hooked fish" had become a literary commonplace.[125] Emulating Petrarch, who lamented that Laura was a "sweetly baited hook" he could not resist, sixteenth- and seventeenth-century English poets conjured up schools of abject fish men captivated by unattainable bait women, the sadomasochism of this scenario emphasized by Spenser in *Amoretti* 47, which showcases the fearsome angling skills of a bloody-handed woman who deploys her "smyling lookes" as "bayts" that allow her to catch, kill, and consume hordes of "foolish fish" that "take pleasure in her cruell play, / and dying doe them selves of payne beguyle."[126]

In responding to Marlowe's passionate shepherd, Donne deconstructs both this piscine variant of Petrarchan love and the pastoral mode—a dynamic that Walton's narrative intensifies. At the beginning of Viator's version of "The Baite," Donne's speaker promises "*golden sands,*" "*Christal brooks,*" and obligingly suicidal "*inamel'd fish*" that can be decorously caught with "*silken lines and silver hooks*" (138). But several stanzas later, Donne borrows the hardheaded environmental realism of Raleigh's nymph to demolish this bucolic vision of a piscatory la-la land: Donne's speaker admits that other fishers must *"freeze with Angling Reeds, / And cut their legs with shels and weeds"* while either wrenching fish out of their *"slimy"* riparian bolt holes with *"coarse bold hands"* or *"treacherously"* capturing them with nets, fake flies, and *"strangling snares"* (138). And the untouchable Petrarchan bait woman likewise vanishes as Donne's speaker voyeuristically imagines the auditor of his poem as the skinny-dipping protagonist of an Ovidian fantasy that one might entitle "Leda and the Finny Drove": each phallic fish *"which every channel hath,"* Donne's speaker leers, *"Most amorously to thee will swim, / Gladder to catch thee, then thou him"* (138). *"Thou thy self art thine own bait,"* Donne's speaker concludes, claiming that he, too, has been *"catch'd"* by the physical charms of the recipient of his verses (138). The anti-Petrarchan eroticism of this text is enhanced by its place in Walton's narrative, for when Viator recites Donne's words to Piscator, "The Baite"— in which only the lascivious male fish are explicitly gendered—becomes a same-sex love poem spoken by one man to another. In his dedicatory verse that appears only in the 1655 edition of the *Angler*, Alexander Brome declares, "I could *unman* myself, and wish to be / A *fish*, so that I might be *took* by thee," Brome's own expression of loyalty to "his ingenuous Friend Mr. IZAAK WALTON" replicating the piscine homoeroticism of Viator's recitation of "The Baite" to Piscator (435). After reprimanding his lecherous behavior toward Maudlin, including him in the guys-only festivities at Bleak Hall, and then lecturing him for hours about the joys of recreational fishing, Piscator has finally corralled Viator (and the Western tradition of piscatorial love poetry) within the female-free confines of the Brotherhood of the Angle.

So by the end of Walton's narrative, thanks to Piscator's tutelage and the other fishermen's fraternal conviviality, Viator has successfully been "turned Angler" (163). As Piscator and Viator prepare to go their separate ways, they take a break in a "cleane and cool" arbor conveniently located near Tottenham High Cross and share a bottle of sweetened sack, milk, and oranges—a refreshing drink that is "too good for any body, but us Anglers," Viator claims proudly (159). Helen Wilcox observes that marriage is a "significant trope in conversion texts," and in a makeshift ceremony that combines betrothal with Holy Communion, Piscator and Viator pledge each other as they take turns reciting poems about "Country recreations" and "happy thoughts" written by "lover[s] of Angling" (160–61).[127] In later editions of *The Compleat Angler*, Walton heightens the emotional charge of this ritual: the fishermen's arbor becomes a tapestry of "*Woodbines, Sweetbrier, Jessamine,* and *Mirtle*" (366), the anglers' spiked Orange Julius becomes "a drink like *Nectar*" (367), and the novice angler laments that in the absence of Piscator, he will feel such anguish that he wants to be rendered unconscious by "some *somniferous potion*" until he can once again "enjoy [Piscator's] beloved company" (371). Taken as a whole, Piscator's conversion of Viator thus structures *The Compleat Angler* as a comedy: Piscator deliberately "overtakes" Viator as the two travelers leave the city, the men bond within a green world while Piscator tutors his new friend, and just before they must return to their workaday lives in London, master and scholar sacramentally plight their troth to celebrate Viator's rebirth as a member of Piscator's fraternity of anglers.[128]

From 1655 onward, Walton emphasizes that by remembering what he has learned from his master, Piscator's scholar—who compares himself to "St. *Austin* in his Confessions" (370)—will be able to sustain his new identity as a Brother of the Angle. The neophyte fisherman promises that even when he is physically separated from Piscator, his teacher's precepts will continue to govern his life: "I will not forget the doctrine which you told me *Socrates* taught his Scholars, *That they should not think to be honoured so much for being* Philosophers, *as to honour* Philosophy *by their vertuous lives.* You advised me to the like concerning *Angling*, and I will endeavour to do so, and to live like those many *worthy men*, of which you made mention in the former part of your discourse" (371). As readers of Walton's book, of course, we have audited the same angling tutorials that Piscator conducted for his "Scholer"—and we have, Walton hopes, likewise "turned Angler." "[N]o man is born an *Artist* nor an *Angler*" (60), Walton affirms in his epistle to the reader, and he suggests that his own task as our teacher is even more difficult than that of his fictionalized alter ego Piscator: "Now for the Art of catching fish; that is to say, how to make a man that was none, an Angler by a book: he that undertakes it, shall undertake a harder task then [George] Hales, that in his printed Book [*The Private Schoole of Defence* (London, 1614)] undertook by it to teach the Art of Fencing, and was laught at for his labour. Not but that something usefull might be observed out of that Book; but that Art was not to be taught by words; nor is the Art of Angling" (60). Yet Walton asserts that receptive readers will nonetheless find his book "not unworthy the time of their perusall" because they will take "so much *profit*" from it (59), and he later adds that most people who "love" angling "may here learn something that may be worth their money" (60). Walton's commercialized diction of profitability—which anticipates John Bunyan's language in his preface to *Grace Abounding*—underlines rather than contradicts the status of *The Compleat Angler* as a conversion narrative.[129] A tale of conversion, Geoffrey Galt Harpham suggests, "stabilizes the wandering subject by proposing a species of imitation with the power to convert, to bind the life of the reader into its own pattern. . . . Spiritual 'conversion' might simply be a strong form of reading."[130]

In *The Compleat Angler*, by synthesizing different models of group identity, Piscator creates a powerful new type of community—and community-building—rooted in its membership's shared experiences and stewardship of a beautiful, complex, and challenging natural world. And as the author of Piscator's story, Walton himself functions in tandem with his doppelgänger-protagonist as a fisher of men. Having written and published his book, Izaak Walton thus continues to recruit as his brethren all those (nonvirtuoso male) readers who, like the founders of the Izaak Walton League of America in the 1920s, seek to enhance the well-being of both themselves and the natural world by turning angler.

CHAPTER 3

The Great Chain of Eating

In *The Compleat Angler*, hunger makes the world go around. Even the book's subtitle, *The Contemplative Man's Recreation*, punningly indicates its focus on food, since in the seventeenth century the word "recreation" could designate a meal. "The Earth feeds man, and all those several beasts that both feed him, and afford him recreation" (183), Izaak Walton declares early in the second edition of his angling manual, and throughout the text, Walton portrays the countryside as an "edible environment."[1] As we've already seen, Piscator's philosophy and practice of conservation emerge from his omnipresent concern with food security, and the otter hunt violently establishes Piscator's monopoly of power over fish as a foodstuff. From a nonanthropocentric perspective, Piscator and his disciples—like the fish they seek to capture and consume—are hungry animals seeking a good meal, and by helping to kill otters, Piscator eliminates his competition in the food chain so he becomes the apex predator in the aquatic ecosystems of Hertfordshire. Thus in *The Compleat Angler*, Walton's narrative repeatedly celebrates the ability of Piscator to transform Hertfordshire's numinous Great Chain of Being into a Great Chain of Eating—a hierarchy over which Piscator himself presides.

This abiding preoccupation with food—and its potential scarcity—reflects some of the deepest fears of Walton's first readers. In the decade preceding the publication of *The Compleat Angler*, much of the population of England experienced food insecurity. The erratic severe weather typical of the Little Ice Age struck England with particular ferocity between 1646 and 1651, threatening the nation's food supply. During these years, spring frosts, torrential summer rains (reprised by the "smoking showers" that inundate Walton's fishermen), and drought took turns destroying crops and sickening livestock. People who went hungry were less able to endure cold temperatures—a problem made more acute by the weather conditions of the Little Ice Age—and became more susceptible to illness and disease. In the wake of recurrent failed harvests, a combination of "plague, food shortages, and high prices" left England "on the verge of anarchy" in the late 1640s, with food riots breaking out in in some areas and the price of bread more than doubling by the end of the decade.[2]

The depredations of warfare only heightened the misery inflicted on the population of England by this prolonged period of dearth. As Christopher Hill explains, the civil wars "simultaneously disrupted agriculture and increased the number of those who had to be fed whilst themselves producing nothing."[3] Shortages of bread occurred when "vast quantities of wheat" had to be shipped to Ireland to feed Cromwell's invading army, and whenever troops moved into an area, local food prices spiked.[4] But market forces were frequently and violently abandoned altogether when inadequately provisioned troops—roundheads and royalists alike—combed the countryside looking for food, plundering the parks, farms, and homes of civilians as they frantically searched for something to eat. The "foraging" of ravenous soldiers "became others' starvation," and terrorized farmers were loath to raise or sell crops.[5] Military prisoners were often famished and reduced to eating turnips, cabbage leaves, or chunks of raw offal.[6] During sieges, hunger-driven suffering and depravity metastasized. When parliamentary forces beleaguered Colchester in the summer of 1648, trapped townspeople and royalist troops desperately tried to stay alive by eating cats, dogs, and rotting horse's flesh; one eyewitness to these horrors grimly remarked that "there is noe death more terrible than starving."[7] The specter of hunger likewise haunted the increasingly destitute royalists who had escaped to the Continent, and many agonized whether they should abandon their principles and sign the Engagement—the required oath of loyalty to the republican commonwealth—so they could redeem their sequestrated estates or instead risk "starving in the Street."[8] Little wonder, then, if these years of privation catalyzed in Walton and his readers an omnipresent fascination with acts of feeding and eating.[9]

In *The Compleat Angler*, it is Piscator's superior knowledge of the dietary preferences of all the hungry creatures inhabiting the English countryside that allows him to flourish. Angling was regarded as a sport precisely because it pitted the fisherman, armed with his "angle" (a hook), against his quarry. Unlike the techniques of netting, trapping, or spearing fish, angling requires a fisherman to feed his would-be prey. An angler will succeed only if he can successfully disguise his piece of barbed steel with an irresistible piece of food that a hungry fish will try to swallow: as the author of the fifteenth-century *Treatyse of Fysshynge wyth an Angle* explains, "ye can not brynge an hoke in to a fyssh mouth wythout a bayte" (210–11). Hence to be successful, an angler must understand and exploit the appetite of his would-be prey. In *The Pleasures of Princes*, one of Walton's source texts, Gervase Markham writes that in angling, "baytes and inticements . . . are the agents and effecters of our desires": as Markham's diction implies, the angler uses food to lure fish into his own libidinal economy.[10] Piscator excels as an angler because he knows exactly how to provide fish with meals they cannot resist: he is a master at exploiting an animal's appetite so as to satisfy his own.

The logistics of how to catch fish by feeding them preoccupy all the angling writers who precede Walton. Markham identifies three categories of bait that may be utilized by the angler: "live baytes," that is, creatures in whose living (and thus dying) bodies the angler conceals hooks; "dead-baytes," including fruit, seeds, animal by-products, and amalgams of human foodstuffs; and artificial flies, which Markham calls "baytes living but in apparance onely."[11] Although he provides some basic information gleaned from previous treatises about artificial flies, Walton himself was not a fly fisherman, and so *The Compleat Angler* focuses instead on Walton's encyclopedic knowledge of live and dead baits. The commendatory poems added to the later editions of his book celebrate Walton's prowess at choosing and deploying what the author of the *Treatyse* called "quycke baytes" (222–23): Thomas Weaver marvels that "With hook hid in an insect," Walton can "fit the wish / O'th'Epicure and fill his dish," while James Duport lauds Walton as the "most expert fisherman" who can "capture the insatiable perch with a very small bleak [a species of fish], or a trout with a red worm or smooth mussel."[12] In *The Compleat Angler*, Walton's alter ego Piscator likewise displays an exhaustive knowledge of how to cater to—and exploit—the seasonally variable appetites of different species of freshwater English fish. As we join Piscator in the Hertfordshire countryside, we repeatedly forage for bait with him, harvesting a multitude of flies, worms, grubs, beetles, grasshoppers, snails, bees, minnows, frogs, and berries from different locales. Piscator consequently devotes a significant proportion of each tutorial session explaining how to deploy all of these diverse baits effectively: in his discussion of the chub alone, Piscator describes in careful detail the use of eleven different baits chosen for each of the four seasons of the year (222).

Some of the commendatory poems in *The Compleat Angler* complicate our view of Piscator's prowess as a fish feeder, however. When Thomas Weaver's versified catalog of Walton's angling triumphs becomes increasingly disturbing—the fisherman's "treacherous Quill [a float made from a feather] . . . / Betrays the hunger of a *Bream*" and his "false flie cheats a speckled *Trout*"—the poet shifts gears and instead tries to affirm the probity of Walton's behavior:

> When you these creatures wisely chuse
> To practise on, which to your use
> Owe their creation, and when
> Fish from your arts do rescue men;
> To plot, delude, and circumvent,
> Ensnare and spoil, is innocent.
> Here by these crystal streams you may
> Preserve a Conscience clear as they. (429)

The diction of deceit and violence that marks this passage—"plot," "delude," "circumvent," "Ensnare," "spoil"—overwhelms the anthropocentric logic of Weaver's stilted apologia. The poet inadvertently reveals the angler's hungry victims, not the duplicitous fisherman himself, to be "innocent": it seems that the successful angler must "delude" himself along with the fish he catches if he wishes to remain morally complacent. Likewise, the commendatory poem written for *The Compleat Angler* by Alexander Brome initially portrays masochistic fish that "leap for joy when they are *caught*" by Walton, yet the poet soon acknowledges that "Thou'rt *killing* them [the fish]," and the final line of the poem begins with the blunt and unsettling statement "By *Thee Fish die*" (435). Thus even as the commendatory poems prefacing *The Compleat Angler* extol Piscator's cunning use of bait, they also imply that we should regard Piscator's angling triumphs as the morally reprehensible acts of a dissembler who offers food to hungry fellow creatures in order to catch and kill them.

This ethical ambiguity complicates our interpretation of the social dynamics of Walton's book because Piscator is also skilled at providing irresistible food for hungry fishermen. As the head of his angling fraternity, Piscator both increases the group's ranks and secures the personal loyalty of its members by carefully controlling what his "brothers" eat. Throughout the days that Viator and Piscator fish together, the activities and interactions of Walton's anglers are shaped, above all, by the men's appetite for fresh fish—a foodstuff that was neither easy nor cheap to obtain in early modern England. Because it spoils quickly without refrigeration, fresh fish was very difficult to handle in the seventeenth century, and London fishmongers were prohibited from selling unsalted fish that was more than two days old: one writer lamented that trout and salmon "are fish that waste / In time of travel, besides they lose their taste / And sweet complexion," and John Evelyn bluntly advised that "all fish in generall is best dressed alive."[13] Roger Manning notes that "the supply of freshwater fish never quite caught up with the demand in Tudor and Stuart England, and the excess demand had to be satisfied with the cured products of deep-sea fishing," most commonly the salted and air-dried cod known as "stockfish."[14] Since stockfish were, in Peter Brears's memorable description, "more like slabs of oak than any food," they had to be bludgeoned and stewed into edibility before being doused with mustard and melted butter.[15] Despite such elaborate efforts to make salted fish palatable, few people ate it with any enthusiasm, and Walton's anglers will have nothing to do with such unappealing fare: instead, as urban foodies with a taste for freshly caught fish, Piscator and his pupil leave both London and salt fish behind so they can become rural locavores.[16] During their vacation in Hertfordshire, Walton's characters do not practice catch-and-release angling but instead avidly fish for food, and as the narrative of Walton's book unfolds, we realize that Piscator possesses not only extraordinary angling skills but also an unparalleled knowledge of how to transform his catch of the day into a delicious meal.

THE CATCH-AND-COOK ANGLER

Piscator's achievements as the seventeenth-century Iron Chef of fish cookery secure his status as the leader of the Brotherhood of the Angle. We have already noted that the relationship between Piscator and the novice angler Viator is transformed after the elder man catches a chub. If we analyze *The Compleat Angler* as an ecosocial conversion narrative, we discover that the chub episode functions as Viator's road-to-Damascus moment. On the morning of their third day in Hertfordshire, after the two Londoners have parted company with the otter hunters, Piscator promises Viator an angling demonstration that will conclude with a midday meal of fresh fish: "I doubt not but at yonder tree I shall catch a *Chub*, and then we'll turn to an honest cleanly Ale house that I know right well, rest our selves, and dress it for our dinner" (82–83).[17] Viator, however, blurts out a comically ungracious response to this offer: "Oh, Sir, a *Chub* is the worst fish that swims, I hoped for a *Trout* for my dinner" (83). Walton's first readers would have sympathized with Viator. Early modern English gastronomes, like their twenty-first-century counterparts, regarded the chub as a trash fish, and whereas a creative chef might nowadays try to salvage a chub by preparing it as ceviche,[18] many anglers of Walton's era agreed with the fifteenth-century author of the *Treatyse* that only the head of a chub was worth eating (214–15), an opinion likewise shared by the protagonist of William Samuel's *Arte of Angling* (D3v).

By establishing chub cookery as a crucial test of Piscator's leadership, Walton deliberately responds to Samuel's narrative. Walton's master angler remarks that the chub is unwelcome at most dinner tables since "as he is usually drest, . . . he is objected against, not only for being full of small forked bones, disperst through all his body, but that he eats watrish, and that the flesh of him is not firm, but short [crumbling] and tastless" (218).[19] In this passage, Walton evokes the mealtime experience depicted by William Samuel in *The Arte of Angling*. Samuel's protagonist cannot overcome the inherent unpalatability of chub: the chub served late at Piscator's supper table "is a sweete fish, but he eateth somewhat flashly [insipidly], and is full of bones," a verdict supported in damning detail by the master angler's long-suffering wife, Cisley: "I dare not lette my children eate of that fishe, or else I give them great charge to take heed of bones. . . . But for this fishe my husband hathe no greate pleasure in them, and if he doe bring any home, he will not eat of them if hee have any other fishe" (*Arte of Angling*, D3r). Thus in *The Compleat Angler*, by choosing to test Piscator's culinary prowess with a chub, Walton sets up an intratextual trial for his master angler that is also intertextual: Walton's Piscator must simultaneously convert his prospective new angling disciple Viator and demonstrate his superiority to his predecessor in William Samuel's *Arte of Angling* by preparing chub to an unprecedented new level of palatability.

As always in *The Compleat Angler*, Walton's protagonist proves himself adaptable to an ever-changing natural world that he must continually master. Piscator knows a trout would be a much easier fish to prepare than a chub, but as he explains rather testily to the querulous Viator, he is constrained by environmental conditions: "Trust me, Sir, there is not a likely place for a *Trout* hereabout, and we staid so long to take our leave of your Huntsmen this morning, that the Sun is got so high, and shines so clear, that I will not undertake the catching of a *Trout* till evening" (83). Piscator realizes that he faces a double challenge: he must both catch a chub and transform the infamously unappealing fish into a gourmet delicacy that will satisfy the dubious Viator. "Though a *Chub* be by you and many others reckoned the worst of all fish," Piscator declares, "yet you shall see I'll make it a good fish by dressing it" (83). "Why, how will you dress him?" queries the novice angler in response, greeting Piscator's culinary bravado with undisguised skepticism (83). Thus in the chub episode, Piscator's credibility as a leader among (fisher)men is at stake: to win Viator's fealty, Piscator must prove himself to be an angling prodigy both streamside and in the kitchen.

Although Piscator intentionally structures his pursuit of the chub as a display of angling virtuosity, "a tryal of [his] skill" (216),[20] it is finally Piscator's culinary prowess that converts Viator. Walton builds narrative suspense as Piscator, trying to impress his companion, hubristically ratchets up the technical difficulty of his feat of chub fishing. "There lye upon the top of the water twenty *Chubs*: I'll catch only one, and that shall be the biggest of them all: and that I will do so, I'll hold you twenty to one" (83), Piscator brags to Viator. The younger man remains skeptical and coolly replies, "I marry, Sir, now you talk like an Artist, and I'll say, you are one, when I shall see you perform what you say you can do; but I yet doubt it" (83). As Viator watches him from a patch of shade, Piscator targets a jumbo-sized chub (conveniently identifiable by the white spot on its tail), deftly pulls it from the water, and immediately acknowledges that he must also "be as certain to make [the chub] a good dish of meat, as I was to catch him" (83). Churlish Viator, his mind still focused firmly on his stomach, does not applaud his companion's angling triumph but instead seconds Piscator's suggestion that they take the chub to Bleak Hall, the nearby alehouse whose hostess had previously been tutored by Piscator in the fine art of chub cookery. The Hostess, as we have already seen, obeys Piscator's instructions to "instantly" prepare the chub "after [Piscator's] fashion" (83), and her compliance ensures that the chub is cooked as quickly as possible—a culinary necessity since, as Piscator observes in the second edition of Walton's book, a chub will be highly palatable only if it is "newly taken and newly drest" (218). Viator is favorably impressed by the quality of the food Piscator provides for him, and he proclaims that "'tis as good meat as ever I tasted" (84). Thus, despite Piscator's ostentatious display of fish-catching genius, it is only after Viator has eaten the chub that his opinion of the master angler is transformed: "You are such a companion, and have so quickly caught, and so excellently cook'd this fish, as makes me ambitious to be your scholer," Viator declares (84). Likewise, when he accepts Viator as his new disciple, Piscator acknowledges the importance of fish cookery in the curriculum that Viator will study with him: as the two men clasp hands and pronounce themselves "Master" and "Scholer," Piscator promises that he first will teach Viator "how you shall catch such a *Chub* as this way; and then how to cook him as this was" (84).[21]

Piscator, it seems, has become supremely adept at dressing his freshly caught fish because he operates as a serial recruiter for the Brotherhood of the Angle. We learn that the chub episode replays the master angler's previous visit to Bleak Hall, since Piscator asks the Hostess to prepare the fish "as you drest my last" about ten days earlier (84). Piscator's talent for opportunism and his ability to exploit aquatic ecosystems also appear in his feats of food preparation that he must perform as the Brotherhood's headhunter-in-chief. Shortly after Viator pledges his loyalty to his new angling "Master," Piscator takes charge of another homosocial relationship that is similarly structured around catching and eating fish. As we have already noted, when Piscator and his newly enlisted disciple return to Bleak Hall for the night, they meet Piscator's angling "brother" Peter and his "friend" Coridon (92). After Piscator urges Peter to introduce his companion, Peter observes that Coridon has "met me here purposely to eat a *Trout* and be pleasant," and Peter vows that in response to Coridon's wishes, "I wil fit him tomorrow with a *Trout* for his breakfast, if the weather be any thing like" (92). Piscator immediately takes over this project to feed Coridon: "Nay brother," Piscator replies to Peter, "you shall not delay him so long, for look you here is a *Trout* . . . will fill six reasonable bellies" (92). Piscator thus proves himself a better provider of fish than Peter, and Peter responds by heralding Piscator's status as a master angler, telling Viator that he is fortunate to be schooled by someone who not only has an encyclopedic knowledge of the natural history of fish but who "can also tell him as well how to catch and cook them, from the *Minow* to the *Sammon*, as any that I ever met withall" (93). Thanks to his shrewd knowledge of the early modern English palate and his extraordinary skills as a catch-and-cook angler, every time he lands and dresses fish, Piscator also captures the hearts of men.

Piscator's dual roles as both master and manciple of his fish-loving brotherhood is suggested by the epigraph that Walton included on the 1653 title page of *The Compleat Angler*. As Paul Hartle observes, "the culinary and the spiritual intertwine throughout early modern culture,"[22] and Walton's epigraph signals the extent to which this dynamic shapes his angling manual. As we have already seen, the title-page motto based on the Geneva Bible translation of John 21:3—"Simon Peter *said, I go a* fishing: *and they said, We also wil go with thee*" (56)—places Walton's book firmly within the Christian fishers-of-men tradition; however, the epigraph also roots *The Compleat Angler* within a narrower subset of stories in the New Testament that celebrate miracles involving fish and feeding. As the final chapter of John's Gospel begins, a group of Christ's disciples, headed by Peter, decide that in response to the crucifixion and resurrection of Jesus, they will return to their old occupation of fishing. The text immediately following the passage quoted in Walton's epigraph recounts how the fishermen-disciples catch nothing until a man standing on the shore commands them, "Cast out the net on the right side of the ship"; when Peter and his companions obey, they immediately capture so many fish that they cannot pull up their net (John 21:3–6, Geneva Bible). As they struggle to draw in "the multitude of fishes," the disciples realize that the man on the shore is the resurrected Jesus, and Peter dives into the water and swims to meet him (John 21:6–7, Geneva Bible). Until this point, the narrative in John 21 strongly resembles the story told in the fifth chapter of Luke about the miraculous, net-breaking "draught" of fish that caused Peter and his fellow fishermen to abandon their boats and follow Jesus instead (Luke 5:1–11, Geneva Bible). John diverges from this earlier story, however, for the disciples' net miraculously does not disintegrate, thus allowing the resurrected Christ to prepare a shore lunch of charcoal-roasted fish for his friends:

> As soone then as they were come to land, they saw hote coales, and fish layed thereon, and bread.

> Jesus sayd unto them, Bring of the fishes, which ye have now caught.
>
> Simon Peter stepped foorth and drew the net to land, full of great fishes, an hundreth, fiftie and three: and albeit there were so many, yet was not the net broken.
>
> Jesus sayde unto them, Come, *and* dine. And none of the disciples durst aske him, Who art thou, seeing they knewe that hee was the Lord.
>
> Jesus then came and tooke bread and gave them, and fish likewise. (John 21:9–13, Geneva Bible)

The postprandial narrative in John 21 similarly emphasizes food: after the disciples have eaten their fill of fish and bread, Jesus asks Peter three times if he truly loves him, and after each of Peter's affirmations of his love, Christ commands him to become a pastor and provide food for his followers: "Feede my lambes," "Feede my sheepe," "Feede my sheepe" (John 21:15–17, Geneva Bible).[23]

Walton thus deliberately chose as the epigraph for his book a passage of scripture that depicts Jesus as a feeder of men. Early modern commentators on John 21 emphasize how the meal that Christ provides for his disciples makes this episode far more miraculous than a simple replay of the astonishing haul of fish reported in Luke 5. Calvin observes, "Firste of all, Christe shewed one token of his power in such a plentifull draught of fish: and hee shewed another, in that he kept the net whole by his hidden power.... Now hereunto are added other circumstances, that the disciples find hot coales upon the banke, that there are fishes, that there is also breade layed ready there."[24] Analyzing the New Testament during his forced interregnum retirement, the Church of England clergyman Henry Hammond similarly emphasizes that the disciples' meal in John 21 is of much more theological importance than the catch of fish that precedes it: Hammond argues that Christ's provision of food constitutes "a greater miracle then the former, a fire of coals, and a fish laid on it, and bread, all created or produced out of nothing, by the power of Christ."[25] Seventeenth-century commentators also underline the importance of Christ's partaking of the same fish and bread that he offers to Peter and his fellow fishermen: the resurrected Jesus chooses to eat alongside his followers "not that he now wanted food, but ... to assure them of the truth of his manhood then present, that they might not think it to be only a dream or *phantasme*."[26] The opening gloss to John 21 in the Geneva Bible asserts that the fish dinner portrayed in the text provides conclusive evidence of Jesus's triumph over death: "that Christ here is not onely present but also eateth with his disciples, he giveth a most full assurance of his resurrection." Christ's final meal of fish thus provided Walton and his contemporaries with a theologically resonant model of self-fashioning. In 1647, the prophetic teenager Sarah Wight modeled the breaking of her miraculous fast on this event,[27] and after dining on trout with his companions at Bleak Hall, Piscator shares song lyrics that place the anglers' meal within this same scriptural context: not only did Christ choose fishermen as his first disciples, Piscator sings, but *"fish the last / Food was, that he on earth did taste"* (97). The parallel between the experience of Christ's fishermen-followers and Walton's anglers is further strengthened by the argument that in John 21, the disciples must have been catching and eating "Trouts, Pikes, Chevins [chubs] and Tenches"—the same species that Piscator and his Brotherhood pursue and consume.[28] The epigraph on the 1653 title page of *The Compleat Angler* thus evokes the resurrected Christ who displayed his power over the grave, the natural world, and the hearts of men by providing and sharing in a meal of freshly caught fish similar to those enjoyed by Walton's own fishermen.

These food-focused group dynamics are highly politicized in both the New Testament and Walton's angling manual. The miraculous meal beside the Sea of Galilee not only functions as the last of the risen Christ's three appearances to his disciples but also calls to mind the pre-Crucifixion miracle of the loaves and fishes, when Jesus transformed five barley loaves and two fishes into enough food for the thousands of people who had gathered around him (John 6:1–14).[29] In this earlier narrative, the presence of such a large group of followers suggests "the possibility of militant insurrection,"[30] an outcome of his miraculous feeding of the multitude that Jesus himself anticipates and rejects: "When Jesus therefore perceived that they [the multitude] would come and take him by force, to make him a king, he departed again into a mountain himself alone" (John 6:15). According to the Gospel of John, after the Crucifixion the followers of Jesus faced an even more dangerous situation and huddled together "for fear of the Jews" (John 20:19). As Anne McIlhaney observes, "John 21:3 marks a complete reversal of Jesus' calling in Matthew: the disciples are in a time of persecution, unable to (or unsure how to) pursue their ministry."[31] Their renewed occupation of fishing thus serves as a defensive fallback position for the disciples, a way for them to survive dangerous times far from centers of political and religious power.

In 1653, readers of *The Compleat Angler* would have recognized the beleaguered, anxious fishermen of John 21 as archetypes of the abject supporters of the murdered King Charles I and his dismantled episcopal church. In the second edition of his book, published in 1655, Walton enhanced this politicized connection by switching to the King James translation of John 21:3 for his title-page epigraph and providing commentary on John 21 within the body of his revised text.[32] As we have already seen, from the first edition of Walton's text, Piscator recounts how Jesus favored the four fishermen among his disciples, but in a passage new to the 1655 edition, Piscator goes on to argue that John 21 proves the rest of the surviving disciples became fishermen as well: "And it is to be believed, that all the other Apostles, after they betook themselves to follow Christ, betook themselves to be Fishermen too; for it is certain that the greater number of them were found together Fishing by Jesus after his Resurrection, as it is recorded in the 21. Chapter of St. *Johns* Gospel" (201). Thus according to Walton, John 21 warrants us to regard as fishermen all the leaders of the Primitive Church who struggled to survive—both physically and spiritually—in the traumatic aftermath of the Crucifixion. And at the same time, Walton's piscatory midrash also encourages readers of his fishing manual to recognize the apostolic lineage of the Brotherhood of the Angle.

Yet the distinctive emphasis on food in both John 21 and *The Compleat Angler* makes Walton's evocation of the Gospel text politically ambivalent. As we have already seen, it is not Peter but Piscator who provides fish for the anglers' meal on the first night that the four men dine together at Bleak Hall. Peter pulls his weight more effectively the next day since he catches five trout that he presumably contributes toward the evening's repast (147). We learn, however, that while Piscator was conducting angling tutorials for Viator during downpours of rain, Peter and Coridon were in retreat: "for indeed we went to a good honest Ale-house," Peter reports, "and there we plaid at shovel-board half the day; all the time that it rained we were there" (147). Because of his greater perseverance in the face of bad weather, not only does Piscator land more trout in total than Peter,[33] but Piscator's tutelage also allows Viator to catch three trout himself, thus enhancing both the size of the group's overall catch and the younger man's allegiance to the Brotherhood; Coridon, by contrast, never seems to land any fish. Moreover, having caught ten trout between them, Piscator and Viator can afford to be charitable and give a brace of fish to Maudlin and her mother as well as provide plentiful food for themselves and their friends. Thus it is Piscator, not Peter, who more closely emulates the risen Christ of John 21 by feeding his followers. And by extending his altruism beyond the membership of the Brotherhood to feed the laboring poor who frequent the meadows near the River Lea, it is likewise Piscator, not Peter, who obeys Christ's reiterated command to "Feed my sheep." John Morrill observes that during the interregnum, "the Church leaders lost their nerve. The bishops fled, hid, or remained silent. They were not replaced as they died. By 1660 the survivors were all over 70 years of age, and Church of England bishops were an endangered species."[34] When we analyze the narrative of *The Compleat Angler* from this perspective, Peter's self-indulgent lassitude—his decision to shelter indoors and play games rather than endure the adverse weather of the Little Ice Age—mirrors the lack of leadership that afflicted adherents of the prewar church throughout the 1650s. Adapting to a new political and environmental reality, Walton's master angler Piscator thus also fills an ecclesiastical leadership vacuum and combines in one person the apostolic roles of fisherman, fisher of men, and feeder of Christ's hungry followers.

FISH AND DIET IN EARLY MODERN ENGLAND

Long-standing ideas about fish made them complex creatures to "think with" in an early modern culture obsessed with food, and the title-page epigraph indicates only one of multiple contexts that illuminate Walton's depictions of eating in *The Compleat Angler*. Even as they evoke scenes from the Gospels, the meals of fish that Walton's anglers enjoy at Bleak Hall also stage a transgressive revival of preinterregnum "fish days," the dates on which healthy laypeople were prohibited from processing, selling, and eating meat.[35] The observation of fish days reflected an ancient Judeo-Christian aversion to the human consumption of animals. Many commentators on the Bible argued that humankind was initially vegetarian: "Certain it is," John Evelyn declared, that "Almighty God ordaining herbs and fruit for the food of men, speaks not a word concerning flesh for two thousand years."[36] God finally permitted Noah and his children to eat meat after the Flood—"Every moving thing that liveth shall be meat for you; even as the green herb have I given you all things" (Gen. 9:3)—yet the deity's attitude toward meat-eating seems contradictory, since in the very next verse of Genesis, God commands, "But flesh with the life thereof, *which is* the blood thereof, shall ye not eat" (Gen. 9:4). Multiple echoes of this latter passage in the New Testament made it difficult for Christians to regard God's blood ban as an outmoded feature of Jewish ceremonial law, and many patristic writers argued that men and women could approach humankind's prelapsarian perfection only by refusing to eat the flesh of animals.[37] And because the consumption of fish was believed to "reduce carnal passions" in human beings, fish was regarded as an especially appropriate food for penitent Christians who were prohibited from eating meat.[38]

A shifting set of religious and economic concerns shaped the English experience of fish days. In medieval England, fish days were observed on all Wednesdays, Fridays, and Saturdays; important saints' days; a three-day period at each "quarter day"; and during the entire season of Lent except Sundays.[39] As part of his break with Rome, Henry VIII abolished fish days, but Edward VI reinstated the officially mandated fasts on Fridays and Saturdays, and in 1563, Elizabeth I followed her half brother's lead and added "every Wednesdaye in every Weeke through the whole yere" to the kingdom's schedule of fish days.[40] The population of England was thus expected to abstain from eating meat two or three days per week throughout the year, as well as during the "Vigils" (the days preceding church festivals or holy days), the "Ember Days" (four three-day periods of fasting distributed throughout the year), and the forty days of Lent.[41] The physician Thomas Cogan reckoned that thanks to Elizabeth's policies, "one halfe of the yeare is ord[a]yned to eat fish in."[42] Faced with penalties for noncompliance, people substituted fish (usually dried or salted sea fish) for meat on these days of dietary restriction.[43] Although Edward VI's "Acte for Abstinence from Fleshe" notes that "due and godlye abstynence ys a meane to vertue,"[44] fish days were reimposed in the sixteenth century not for the sake of religious piety but as a tool of realpolitik. By forcing the population of England to consume fish for six months per year, the Tudor fish-days statutes regulated demand for meat, promoted fisheries, encouraged shipbuilding, and ensured that experienced sailors were always available for military service.[45] Yet as the influence of radical Protestantism grew, dietary abstinence became an increasingly contested practice in early modern England. Elizabeth's government tried to eradicate the traditional religious significance of fish days: after frankly declaring that these mandatory fasts were designed "politikely for thincrease of Fishermen & Mariners" and "not for any Supersticion," one statute threatened to punish any person who suggested that "eating of Fishe [and] forbearing of Fleshe" on fish days "ys of any necessitee for the saving of the Soule of Man, or that yt ys the Service of God," and a contemporary observer agreed that fish days were imposed "not for any religion or holinesse supposed to be in the eating of fish rather then of flesh, but only for a civill policy."[46]

But the centuries-old association between the consumption of fish and Christian piety could not be legislatively erased from cultural memory. As Alec Ryrie observes of fish days, "This uniquely deritualized ritual became both a site of and an accelerator of confessional conflict, a marker of identity and difference."[47] In 1626, the Church of England clergyman Daniel Featley judiciously described Lenten fasting in England as having "a mixed constitution; partly civill, appointed by the King or State, to preserve young cattell, spend fish, and encourage fishermen: partly Ecclesiasticall ordered by the Church for religious ends."[48] Unsatisfied with such hybridity, godly English Protestants, who scorned the Catholic nature of regularly scheduled fish days, instead championed public fasts and accompanying sermons, organized ad hoc in response to crises, that were designed to foster repentant "humiliation," and by the time Walton published the first edition of *The Compleat Angler* in 1653, fish days had been banned as a popish superstition.[49] The *Directory of Public Worship*, which replaced the Prayer Book in 1645, deemed that fasts were appropriate "when some great and notable Judgements are either inflicted upon a People, or apparently imminent, or by some extraordinary provocations notoriously deserved," and the *Directory* specified that "a Religious Fast requires total abstinence ... from all food": not only was the old schedule of fasting verboten, but fish was also no longer regarded as a penitential foodstuff.[50] So the meals of Hertfordshire chub and trout enjoyed by Walton's anglers at Bleak Hall subversively recall a preinterregnum era when, in Piscator's deliberately provocative words, "the Church kept Fasting-days" (273).[51] And this prohibited association between fish and rituals of Christian repentance likewise obliquely underpins Piscator's recipe for "excellent *Minnow-Tansies*" (349), omelets made with the herb *Tanacetum vulgare* that were considered appropriate Lenten fare since they evoked the Passover tradition of eating "bitter herbs."[52] Piscator's advocacy of a fish-centric diet thus carries a defiantly conservative religious charge throughout *The Compleat Angler*.

Yet Walton also explicitly—and problematically—justifies the consumption of fish on the basis of physical rather than spiritual health. In a highly charged passage added to the second edition of *The Compleat Angler*, Piscator warns that the abolition of fish days has precipitated a national health crisis: "'tis observed by the most learned Physicians, that the casting off of Lent and other Fish-daies, (which hath not only given the Lie to so many learned, pious, wise Founders of Colledges, for which we should be ashamed) hath doubtless been the chief cause of those many putrid, shaking, intermitting Agues, unto which this Nation of ours is now more subject than those wiser Countries that feed on Herbs, Sallets, and plenty of Fish; of which it is observed in Story [historical writings], that the greatest part of the world now do" (186–87). Piscator thus denounces the republican government's prohibition of fish days for causing repeated national epidemics of "Agues"—fevers—that were "one of the most frequently diagnosed and mentioned causes of death and sickness" in early modern England.[53] "Each yeare," the poet Abraham Holland remarked grimly, "New troupes of raging Fevers domineere," and epidemics of fever-causing illnesses recurred during the fraught middle decades of the seventeenth century: as the civil war raged in 1643, royalist soldiers spread typhus through the Thames Valley; in the wake of the ruinously bad harvest of 1647, another epidemic of typhus struck, causing Ralph Josselin to lament the "agues abounding more than in all my remembrance"; and mortality rates spiked during both the late 1630s and the interregnum in response to "epidemic waves" of "enteric fevers."[54] Piscator blames the abandonment of fish days for these health catastrophes and implicitly recommends a piscivorous diet to protect the nation from future onslaughts of such febrile diseases.

Piscator's comments both draw on and challenge early modern concepts of health. According to Galenic physiological theory, the human body, as a microcosm of the creation, was constituted of the four elements (earth, water, fire, air) and their qualities (dryness, moisture, heat, coldness) via the four "humors."[55] Each humor was a fluid that combined two different elements and thus exhibited a distinctive "complexion": black bile was cold and dry, phlegm was cold and moist, yellow bile was hot and dry, and blood was hot and moist. Environmental and demographic factors established an individual's baseline humoral constitution, which always tended toward one of the four complexions (melancholic, phlegmatic, choleric, or sanguine). Healthfulness resulted from a relative balance of the humors within an individual's body, whereas disease was caused by an excess of one or more humors.[56] Hence fever was an abnormal heating of the body caused by the decomposition of superfluous humors—"when there is abundance of humours in the body," explained the physician Levinus Leminius, "Agues must needs be engendred of that continuall obstruction and putrefaction"—and the temporal patterns characteristic of "intermittent" fevers (that inflicted paroxysms of hot and cold upon sufferers at regular intervals) indicated the movement of such "putrid" humors through the body.[57]

Within this theoretical framework, fevers were regarded as a consequence of misguided eating. Like all other entities of natural origin in the Galenic paradigm, food was composed of varying proportions of the four elements. Because "cooking and digestion were understood to be the same sort of heat-driven process," early modern medical theorists believed that food was "concocted" within the stomach into humors that were then converted into blood in the liver and subsequently circulated throughout the body, with other organs further refining the nutriment: in Thomas Cogan's formulation, "there be three concoctions, the first, in the Stomacke, the second, in the Liver, the third, in every part of the body."[58] Since the Galenic body thus functioned as "a giant stomach, a torus through which food passes," a foodstuff's complexion directly affected the humoral balance of the consumer's entire physiology: "meates and drinkes doe alter our bodies, and either temper them or distemper them greatly," noted Cogan, "and no marvaile, seeing that such as the food is, such is the blood: and such as the blood is, such is the flesh."[59] Health and diet were thus inextricably connected: foods, John Evelyn explained, "being converted into the substances of our bodies, they become aliment; so in regard of their change and alteration, we may allow them medicinal."[60] Given the direct relationship between one's food and the nature of one's own flesh, a person would find it easiest to "concoct" foods that shared his or her bodily complexion: Cogan counseled that when "in health," one ought to consume "such meates [solid foods] . . . as be like in temperature to the body."[61] Conversely, dietary treatment for illness sought to counter superfluous humors with their opposites: for "bodies untemperate and in sicknesse," instructed Cogan, "such meates or drinks are to be given, which bee in power contrary to the distemperance."[62] Because humoral bodies were what they ate, diet was crucial to the maintenance of health—and fish was thus a problematic food for human beings.

Even without considering the tendency of fresh fish to spoil easily, most medical authorities in the early modern period regarded fish as nonnutritious at best and a health hazard at worst. According to Galenic physiology, the aquatic origin of fish was the basis of its drawbacks for hungry humans. Dietary theorists maintained that a food's texture was crucial to its nutritional profile, and because the human body could most easily assimilate food that was similar to its own substance, meat—animal "flesh"—was regarded as the most nutritious form of aliment.[63] Fish, by contrast, like their aquatic habitats, were predominantly of a watery texture and hence "of little nourishment, engendring watrish and thinn blood" in human consumers.[64] Indeed, as Thomas Cogan explained, its poor nutritional profile enhanced fish's appropriateness as a penitential food: "if a man would refraine from such meats, as do most nourish and cherish his body, (which indeed is the exercise of fasting) he should rather forgoe the eating of flesh than fish."[65] And as a cold and moist foodstuff, fish could also make its consumer—especially someone who was naturally phlegmatic in complexion—susceptible to a host of serious ailments, including fevers. Tobias Venner warned that "fish increaseth much grosse, slimy, and superfluous flegme, which residing and corrupting in the body, causeth difficulty of breathing, the Gowt, the Stone, the Leaprie [leprosy], the Scurvy, and other foul and troublesome affects of the skin,"[66] and the fifteenth-century *Treatyse of Fysshynge with an Angle* cautioned against eating barbel since "comynly he [gi]vyth an introduxion to the Fe[v]res" (212–13). George Herbert, who had, in Walton's words, "a body apt to a *Consumption*, and to *Fevers*," was "forbid utterly to eat any Fish" during Lent while he was a student at Cambridge, exemplifying how the preservation of human health in seventeenth-century England often entailed the avoidance of fish.[67]

Given the problematic nature of fish as a human foodstuff in the early modern period, "those men that [were] much delighted with the use of fish" needed to "be very carefull in the choise of it."[68] Health-conscious diners were advised to consider multiple factors about a fish—including its morphology, habitat, and behavior—before deciding whether they should consume it. Scaly fish were safer to eat than unscaled fish since scales, created through the excretion of bodily moisture, indicated that a fish's substance was dryer and thus more digestible for humans.[69] Environmental conditions also affected the edibility of a fish. Salt moderated a fish's phlegmatic complexion, and thus sea fish were "of better nourishment, th[a]n fresh water fish of the same sort"; since its substance was even more difficult for humans to digest, however, salted fish, while not "amiss for" the robust digestive systems of "Sailers and Ploughmen," was "most hurtful and dangerous for other persons."[70] Their inherently cold and moist quality could be counteracted if fish were eaten when the weather was warm and dry, and since motion characterized both healthy air and water according to humoral theory, fish that lived "in a pure water, tossed to and fro with waves," were safer for human consumption than those that inhabited stagnant ponds and marshes.[71] A fish's diet also affected its quality as a foodstuff for human beings: fish that ate either live creatures or "wholsom roots, herbs, and weeds" were most healthful, but bottom-feeding species were to be avoided, especially those that "feed and fat themselves neer to the common-sewers, sincks, chanels and draughts of great Cities; whose chiefest meat is either carrion or dung."[72] For people concerned about their health in seventeenth-century England, the decision to eat fish entailed a multifaceted process of risk assessment.

THE COMPLEAT ANGLER AS RECIPE BOOK

Given the "fear of fish" that pervaded early modern medical thought,[73] Walton's championing of a piscivorous diet was unorthodox. Even the protagonist in William Samuel's *Arte of Angling* treats fish as a second-rate foodstuff: "I do not much passe of [care to have] any fishe to eate,"[74] Samuel's master angler declares, "but that hunger forceth mee sometimes and want of other things, and when I am wearie (as it were) of flesh [meat]" (D3r–D3v). Englishmen were proverbially regarded as beef-eaters,[75] so Piscator's provocative comment that his compatriots should emulate "those wiser Countries that feed on Herbs, Sallets, and plenty of Fish" (187) suggests that his risky dietary advice reflects political rather than health concerns. Although the cuisine of the Stuart elite—and recipes by early Stuart food writers like Gervase Markham—had been influenced by European cookery, the English vogue for continental cuisine intensified later in the seventeenth century when royalists who had escaped across the Channel adopted the foodways of their hosts; indeed, the English translation of François Pierre de La Varenne's monumental work *Le Cuisinier François* was published the same year as the first edition of *The Compleat Angler*.[76] Both herbs and salads were characteristic of the cuisine that English exiles discovered on their grand tours of the Continent: John Evelyn observed that "the more frugal Italians and French, to this day, accept and gather *ogni verdura*, any thing almost that's green and tender, to the very tops of nettles; so as every hedge affords a sallet (not unagreeable) season'd with . . . vinegar, salt, oyl, &c."[77] Unlike royalist chef-authors such as William Rabisha and Robert May, however, Walton never depicts Piscator's cosmopolitan cookery as a remnant of an aristocratic tradition of "*Liberality and Hospitality*," nor do Piscator's simple alehouse meals of chub or trout resemble the opulence of the forty-dish fish dinners enjoyed by the "honourable Families" of the Stuart elite.[78] Nonetheless, a royalist-continental mode of cuisine informs many of the fish recipes that Walton provides in *The Compleat Angler*: Piscator makes liberal use of herbs, and his recipe for minnow tansies exemplifies an explicitly continental genre of cooking, what Markham had decades earlier called "the compound Fricases" that were "of great request and estimation in *Fraunce, Spaine*, and *Italy*."[79] Piscator's broiled chub recipes likewise suggest French influence, since "Charbonados or Carbonados, which is meate broil'd upon the coales," were an "invention ... first brought out of *Fraunce*."[80] And in his recipe for roasted pike, Piscator says that one can opt to use garlic, either in the mixture placed in the pike's belly or to rub the dripping pan / serving dish, so as "*to give the sawce a hogoe*" (128), the word "hogoe" being an anglicized version of the French term *haut goût* (high flavor).[81] Walton thus links the fish-centric diet he promotes in *The Compleat Angler* with the continental cuisine embraced by exiled royalists, a style of food preparation that would return to England full-bore—along with the court of Charles II—at the Restoration.

Yet Walton seems to recognize that he is promoting a controversial stance, and he attempts to further buttress his case for eating lots of fish by invoking yet another foodway. Beginning in 1655, Piscator immediately follows his assessment of the deleterious state of England's fish-lite diet with an appeal to biblical authority: "And it may be fit to remember that Moses (*Lev.* 11.9. *Deut.* 14.9.) appointed Fish to be the chief diet for the best Common-wealth that ever yet was" (187). Piscator's citation of Hebrew scripture as the precedent for the ichthyophagy that he champions would have resonated provocatively for readers in the 1650s. As Achsah Guibbory explains, throughout the early modern period, English Protestants of all religiopolitical stripes "looked to the Jews to define, confirm, or legitimate their Christian identity" by fashioning themselves as "the true Israel" and their opponents as the Jews' biblical oppressors.[82] During the civil wars and interregnum, royalist supporters of the prewar Church of England viewed themselves as reliving the Jews' experience of exile in Babylon.[83] Like his evocation of Psalm 137,[84] Walton's reference to Jewish dietary laws is thus politically charged because it portrays Piscator and his disciples as latter-day Israelites—who, despite their current state of dispossession, will one day return to Jerusalem and rebuild their Temple. Yet Piscator misrepresents the scripture that he portentously cites. Although Leviticus 11:9 and Deuteronomy 14:9 permit the Children of Israel to eat water creatures that have fins and scales, these passages do not suggest that fish should be a mainstay of the Israelites' diet: Piscator's citation of biblical precedent can be allied with his argument for a piscivorous diet only through overstatement. The tenuous quality of Piscator's analysis thus suggests both the aberrancy of the fish-centric diet that Piscator advocates and the master angler's nervous desire to provide himself with a scriptural bodyguard as he ventures into medically hazardous terrain.

At the same time, Piscator mitigates the risks of his dietary advice by including relatively healthful recipes in his text, a feature that Walton enhanced as he revised his book. According to the precepts of Galenic humoralism, different methods of preparation could alter—and ameliorate—the impact of fish on human physiology: Thomas Cogan assured his readers that "as it is said, a good Cooke can make you good meat of a whetstone, even so it may bee that such fish and flesh as is of it[s] owne nature unwholesome and unpleasant, by the skill of dressing may bee made both wholesome and pleasant."[85] Salting transformed dried fish into a hot and dry foodstuff, but health-conscious cooking methods and recipes were necessary to amend both the watery substance and the phlegmatic humoral complexion of fresh fish. Although boiling could serve as an appropriate preparation technique for fresh fish that were relatively dry and tough, consumption of boiled fish needed to be carefully controlled: one writer warned that eating boiled salmon more than three times per week "suffers the body to be hurried into a flux, and sometimes into a fever, as pernicious as death."[86] Frying did not allow excess moisture (and phlegmatic humors) to drain off during the cooking process, whereas roasting and grilling were optimal ways to prepare moist species of fish: Tobias Venner advised that "the roasted or broiled Eele is far wholesomer, than the boiled, because the fire exhausteth, and consumeth much of the slimie, and excrementall moisture that is in it."[87] Additional ingredients could further correct the harmful properties of fresh fish: mustard and acidic liquids (such as vinegar and citrus juice) would make the substance of fish more digestible, while condiments that had a hot and dry complexion (like pepper and parsley) counteracted a fish's naturally phlegmatic quality.

And the health-conscious diner also needed to consider that the consumption of wine greatly improved one's ability to digest fish.[88]

These medical principles underlie the recipes that Piscator promotes in *The Compleat Angler*. Walton provides two recipes for cooking chub in the 1653 edition of his book. In the first recipe, Piscator explains how to "dresse" a chub using the same delectable method that so impressed Viator (86–87): the chub must be broiled over charcoal and basted with a mixture of butter, salt, and thyme (an herb that was regarded as "hot and dry" and thus a corrective for phlegmatic complexions). Not only does this method of preparation maximize the chub's palatability and healthfulness, but it also further aligns Piscator's cookery with Christian precedent: in Luke 24, when the resurrected Christ appears to his followers for the final time and asks for "meate," his disciples give him "a piece of a broiled fish," which Christ then eats in front of them (Luke 24:41–43, Geneva Bible). Just as Christ and his followers shared a meal of broiled fish "for the greater confirmation of his disciples faith,"[89] so a broiled chub cements the relationship between Piscator and Viator. And the reader of *The Compleat Angler* can likewise bond with Walton's master angler over a freshly grilled chub, thanks to Piscator's detailed instructions. By contrast with this narratively freighted recipe for broiled chub, the second recipe that appears in the 1653 edition of *The Compleat Angler* entails boiling the chub in a salt-and-thyme-seasoned broth of either white wine or a mixture of vinegar and water (87).[90] In 1655, however, Walton replaced this formula with a new recipe in which the chub is not boiled but instead roasted on a spit and basted with vinegar or verjuice (an acidic fruit juice), butter, and salt (219). This technique for fire-roasting chub is more closely aligned both with scriptural precedent and with Galenic medical advice about fish cookery, an impression that Piscator himself emphasizes: "Being thus drest," the master angler assures his disciple, "you will find [the chub] a much better dish of meat than you, or most folk, even than Anglers themselves do imagine; for this dries up the fluid watry humor with which all *Chubs* do abound" (218). In addition to this more wholesome recipe for chub, beginning with the second edition of his book Walton also provided new recipes for eel, carp, and minnows. Thus, as Walton revised the text of *The Compleat Angler*, he sought to enhance its value as both a spiritually and physically nourishing "recreation" for his readers.

From 1655 onward, Piscator's concern with the healthfulness of the fish that he encourages his disciples to eat also becomes an aesthetic principle of

Piscator's discourse as a whole. Early in the post-1653 versions of *The Compleat Angler*, the three characters who meet on the road leading north out of London (Piscator, Venator, and Auceps) agree to take turns commending their eponymous sports. Auceps goes first, followed by Venator, and just as Auceps begins his praise of falconry by praising its related natural "Element" (air), so Venator commences his panegyric to hunting with a tribute to "the Earth" (179, 183), leading us to anticipate that Piscator will similarly preface his remarks about angling with an appreciation of water.[91] Before Piscator can take up the conversational baton, however, the tone of Walton's text suddenly sharpens. When Venator concludes his encomium of hunting, he sneeringly declares that he'll truncate his remarks to avoid "be[ing] so uncivil to Mr. *Piscator*, as not to allow him a time for the commendation of *Angling*, which he calls an Art; but doubtless 'tis an easie one: and Mr. *Auceps*, I doubt [fear] we shall hear a watry discourse of it, but I hope 'twill not be a long one" (185). As we noted earlier, Venator intends his phrase "watry discourse" to play on the "Element" of Piscator's sport (water) and preemptively damn the vapidity of Piscator's praise of angling. But given fish's dubious value as a foodstuff, Venator's derogatory description also ascribes the insipidity of the angler's "discourse" to the phlegmatic humoral complexion of fish—a quality shared by men like Piscator (and Izaak Walton) who consume a piscivorous diet.

As Piscator embarks on his celebration of angling, Walton has thus increased the narrative tension: Piscator, we realize, must win over an unabashedly hostile audience. Piscator clearly recognizes the implications of Venator's insult. After decorously but firmly calling out his two companions for their rudeness ("Gentlemen; let not prejudice prepossess you"), Piscator shifts into culinary metaphor to refute Venator: "for as I would not make a *watry* discourse, so I would not put too much *vinegar* into it" (185). Vinegar, the corrosive bite of the truth-teller, was traditionally a weapon of the satirist: Piscator's words, the master fisherman admits in response to Venator, will be "*calm* and *quiet*" (185) like angling itself yet laced with enough acid to obliquely criticize those in power—an accurate characterization of the ideological complexity of Walton's book.[92] Just as Galenic physicians recommended dressing fish with vinegar to counteract its glutinous texture, so Piscator will carefully balance his irenic praise of angling with the beneficially tart corrective of social and political critique. In his authorial epistle to the reader, Walton promises that in the text of *The Compleat Angler* he has "*in several places mixt (not any scurrility, but) some innocent, harmless mirth*" (169) for the reader's delectation, but as he responds to Venator, Piscator transforms this principle of generic mixture into the carefully considered preparation of healthful meals of freshwater fish.

By focusing so much attention on food preparation, however, Walton was venturing into a minefield of gender stereotypes, for cookery was normatively understood as women's work in early modern England. Gervase Markham typified this attitude, arguing that wives should regard as their "first and most principall" competency "a perfect skill and knowledge in Cookery, together with all the secrets belonging to the same; because it is a duety really belonging to the woman."[93] Even though guilds of professional male cooks had existed in English cities (including London) since the Middle Ages, cooking was nonetheless regarded in the seventeenth century as a demeaning activity for a man: "Those Trades are of least use and benefit, which are called Huswives Trades (as *Brewer*, *Baker*, *Cooke*, and the like)," Thomas Powell declared in 1631, "because they be the skill of Women as well as of men, and common to both," and decades later, John Evelyn defensively promoted the falsehood that he had "received" the recipes he published in his treatise on salads "from an experienc'd housewife."[94] The shameful specter of the housewife that haunted the male practice of cookery in early modern England likewise threatened to emasculate Walton, a vulnerability exploited by the fly fisherman Richard Franck in his book *Northern Memoirs*. While describing the arduous journey he made in Scotland during the 1650s as a Cromwellian soldier,[95] Franck provides both a series of explanations of angling technique and a volley of potshots directed at Izaak Walton—and in his attacks on Walton, Frank repeatedly mocks the importance of food in *The Compleat Angler*. Franck scoffs that Walton "prefers the trencher before the troling-rod" and habitually "dress[es] fish before [he] catch[es] them," and in multiple taunts, Franck also lambasts Walton's emphasis on food preparation in explicitly gendered terms, scoffing that Walton "industriously has taken care to provide a good cook, (supposing his wife had a finger in the py)."[96] In Richard Franck's estimation, Walton must be tied to his wife's apron strings since real men don't cook fish.

As we have already noted, however, Walton and his fishermen seem to exist as bachelors in *The Compleat Angler*, and the striking contrast in marital status between Walton's anglers and William Samuel's Piscator becomes especially pronounced at mealtimes. Much of the narrative in *The Arte of*

Angling unfolds while Samuel's characters eat the fish that Piscator had earlier caught and brought home with him. In *The Arte of Angling*, Samuel emphasizes that Piscator's wife, Cisley, is responsible for preparing the meal: the moment Piscator crosses the threshold of his house, he calls out, "How nowe wife, is the brothe ready[?]"—thus providing a realistic glimpse into sixteenth-century English cuisine, since Elizabethan cooks often boiled fish in highly seasoned broths[97]—and he then orders Cisley to "let my supper bee readie as soone as may be" (*Arte of Angling*, B2r–B2v). *The Compleat Angler* maintains this brusquely patriarchal dynamic of food preparation, as Walton's Piscator officiously commands the Hostess of Bleak Hall to feed him and his friends on the double: "Come Hostis, where are you? is Supper ready? come, first give us drink, and be as quick as you can, for I believe wee are all very hungry" (147). And whenever Walton's Piscator utters a command about food preparation, the Hostess of Bleak Hall immediately leaps into deferential action and never talks back, unlike William Samuel's irrepressible Cisley.

Although Walton's Piscator emulates Samuel's protagonist by overtly controlling the female labor responsible for feeding him and his friends, he also possesses knowledge about fish preparation that allows him to dictate cooking methodology in much greater detail than his sixteenth-century predecessor. In *The Arte of Angling*, William Samuel's master angler vaguely orders his wife to prepare all the different species of fish he's brought home with him "after the best manner" (*Arte of Angling*, B3r). But as we've seen, the chub that converts Viator into an angling enthusiast in *The Compleat Angler* has been prepared by the Hostess of Bleak Hall "after [Piscator's] fashion" (83), a description implying that Walton's alter ego, unlike Samuel's protagonist, has provided his female subordinate with a recipe that she now follows upon command. As we read *The Compleat Angler*, we never actually witness or hear an account of Piscator giving cookery lessons to the Hostess: such tutoring apparently occurred sometime in the past, for the Hostess has now "drest many a [fish]" in accordance with Piscator's "fashion" (83). Instead, we experience cookery instruction as part of the homosocial student-teacher dynamic that structures the relationship between Piscator and his angling disciples. In the first edition of Walton's book, after Viator declares that he wants to "learn [Piscator's] direction," Walton's protagonist initially explains "how to dresse" a chub in the way that so captivated his new disciple and then provides another "perfect direction" for cooking chub that, Piscator hopes, will likewise help to restore chub's culinary reputation previously "lost by ill Cookery"—that is, preparation methods not executed under the "direction" of Piscator (86–87). Rather than "receipt" (the term most commonly used in the early modern period), Walton repeatedly uses the word "direction" to describe the cookery instructions that Piscator shares with his acolyte, a term Viator also uses to describe Piscator's angling advice.[98] The word "receipt" (derived from the Latin verb *recipere*, which implies actions of taking back, receiving, or accepting) emphasizes the agency of the recipient of a set of instructions;[99] the term "direction," by contrast, transforms a recipe into a precept or command imposed by an authority figure. Thus, unlike most English recipe books published during the interregnum—which were attributed to women and nostalgically invoked the domestic sphere of aristocratic Stuart patriarchy—Walton's narrative instead presents culinary excellence as a male prerogative that reinforces the homosocial teacher-scholar relationship central to Piscator's identity as a master angler.[100]

By incorporating recipes into *The Compleat Angler*, Walton both adopts and distances himself from the representation of cookery that he found in an earlier fishing treatise. Thomas Barker, a native of Shrewsbury, was living in a Westminster almshouse when he published his *Art of Angling* in 1651 and became the first author to include recipes for dressing fish in an English book about angling.[101] Barker apparently patched together a meager living as both a cook and an angler in seventeenth-century London's gig economy, and Barker hoped that his treatise would help him gain additional employment as a fishing tutor.[102] Walton certainly knew and admired Barker's book: from the first edition of *The Compleat Angler*, Piscator speaks approvingly of Barker and passes along his advice about fly-fishing for trout (107–8).[103] Yet while Walton also tacitly follows Baker's example by providing fish recipes in his text, he diverges significantly from Barker's depiction of the social context from which his recipes have emerged.

The first-person narrative that intermittently structures Barker's treatise presents the author as the hireling of aristocratic men. In his 1651 text, Barker portrays himself going fishing not for recreation but for the sake of employment: "A Lord lately sent to me at Sun going down to provide him a good dish of Trouts against the next morning by six of the clock," Barker recalls before detailing what bait, tackle, and techniques he used to fulfill this charge (8). Barker's innovative inclusion of recipes in his angling treatise likewise emerges from this relationship of paid service. "And now I am waiting on my Lord, with a great dish of Trouts, who meeting with company, commanded me to turn Scullion and dresse a Dinner of the Trouts we had taken; whereupon I gave my Lord this bill of fare, which I did furnish his Table with, according as it was furnished with Flesh," Barker recounts (16–17), and he subsequently describes an elite extravaganza of more than a dozen dishes of trout prepared in different ways, of which Barker provides instructions for only a sample. Yet Barker betrays the status anxiety of the seventeenth-century male food-worker by describing his role in his employer's kitchen as "Scullion," the title of a menial domestic servant that was often used in early modern England as a more generalized term of contempt.[104]

Barker clearly reconceived his text after reading *The Compleat Angler*. In his revised book—issued under the new title *Barker's Delight* by Walton's own publisher, Richard Marriot, in 1656—Barker not only developed his range of topics to encompass all the species of fish covered in Piscator's tutorials, but he also added a series of his own verses to emulate the hybrid texture of Walton's treatise. (The influence of *The Compleat Angler* as well as the quality of Barker's poetic craftsmanship may be seen in a couplet that advises fly fishermen, "*A Brother of the Angle must alwaies be sped / With three black Palmers, & also two red*.")[105] At the same time, in *Barker's Delight* the author enhances both the place of recipes in his work and his self-portrayal as a cook employed in elite kitchens. Barker expands his 1651 subtitle to advertise that his revised treatise contains "many rare secrets" about the "dressing" of fish, and Barker further develops this theme in his new Epistle Dedicatory, in which he promises that his book will demonstrate how he can "furnish any Lords table, onely with trouts, as it is furnished with flesh, for 16 or 20 dishes" (A3v). In *Barker's Delight*, poetry serves as a medium through which the author relentlessly promotes his expertise as a cook: in verses about trout fishing that Barker added to his 1656 text, he declares, "*But the chief point of all is the cookery*" (13); Barker similarly concludes another poem about pike fishing with the punch line "*When the Pike is at home minde the cookery*" (38); and later in the treatise, he commands his reader that "*when of all sorts thou hast thy wish, / Follow* Barker's *advice to cook the fish*" (50). Reflecting this heightened emphasis on cooking, *Barker's Delight* also abounds with new recipes: although the author's instructions for chub "baked in a pot" (40) resemble one of the recipes that Piscator presents in the first edition of *The Compleat Angler*, most of Barker's new recipes—such as his sections on trout pies and a "black sauce" for carp—have no counterparts in Walton's book (20–21, 48). With such additions, Barker seems intent on winning the fish-recipes arms race that Walton had begun by emulating the first edition of Barker's treatise.

But the angler-cook in *Barker's Delight* also seeks to elevate his social status as a food worker. Barker had addressed the epistle of the first edition of his book to "*the Right Honourable, and Gentlemen Anglers of the Citie of London, and else where within the Realm of* England," but he ups the social ante (and explicitly sets his book in political opposition to Walton's project) by instead dedicating *Barker's Delight* to "Edward *Lord* Montague" (A2r). This dedication anchors Barker and his book within the ruling elite of the Protectorate, for Edward Montagu belonged to Oliver Cromwell's council and held multiple high-level posts, including (as Barker specifies in his epistle) treasury commissioner and general at sea.[106] Barker develops this implicit claim of status and Cromwellian political allegiance later in his book. As he did in the first edition of his treatise, Barker at one point provides a primer on different national styles of fish cookery, explaining how English, Italian, and French cooks diverge in their preparation of stewed fish. In 1651, Barker said he acquired this knowledge because he had "been admitted into the Kitchins, to furnish men of most Nations, when they have been in England" (*Art of Angling*, 18), but in his revised treatise, Barker goes much further and establishes his identity as a cook on the payroll of Cromwell himself: "Though I have been no traveller I may speak it, for I have been admitted into the most Ambassadors Kitchens that have come into England this forty years, and do wait on them still at the Lord Protector's charge, and I am paid duly for it" (19–20). Significantly, Barker adds a final clause to this sentence to distinguish his status as Cromwell's knowledgeable and respected cook from the lowly rank of a menial servant, writing disdainfully that "sometimes I see slovenly scullions abuse good fish most grosly" (20). Emboldened by his enhanced fortunes under the Protectorate (and perhaps by Walton's flattering imitation of his book), Barker in 1656 portrays himself as socially superior to the mere "Scullion" who had published *The Art of Angling* five years previously.

By contrast, in *The Compleat Angler* Walton sometimes depicts Piscator's recipes as curiosities that have been circulating among elite men. Of the four new fish recipes that Walton added to the second edition of his book, two are identified as gifts—"S.F." provided the recipe for roasted eel (319), while "Dr. T." gave Piscator the instructions for transforming a carp into a "curious dish of meat" (298–99)—and beginning in 1655, Piscator ascribes his recipe for pike (which he calls a "secret") to "M.B." (290).[107] By portraying his recipes as technical "secrets" that yield "curious" results, Piscator implies that he shares with his student-disciple the rare information beloved of seventeenth-century virtuosos and relocates cookery from the kitchen, a space dominated either by women or socially suspect "money-getting-men" like Thomas Barker, to the homes and commonplace books of high-ranking connoisseurs such as John Evelyn and Sir Kenelm Digby.[108] Thus, despite his evident discomfort with the social dynamics of virtuoso culture, Walton sometimes depicts Piscator's knowledge of cookery as the by-product of his association with a rarefied circle of learned and influential men.

Yet one mode of cookery in *The Compleat Angler* does not occasion any social defensiveness. As we have seen, in contrast to Thomas Barker's increasingly confident self-portrayal as a food worker, Walton always distances Piscator from the preparation of fish for human consumption even as he follows Barker's example by including recipes in *The Compleat Angler*. Yet Walton never exhibits any qualms about Piscator preparing different types of bait with which to feed (and thus catch) fish. Some of the bait recipes that Walton presents seem like nauseating parodies of human cookery. Piscator teaches us that mixtures of grain, blood, cow dung, or bran attract carp, as do balls of sweetened bean flour that has been mixed with "the flesh of a Rabbet or Cat cut small" (297); gelatinous cubes of sheep's blood, "half dried on a Trencher" and salted, appeal to dace and roach; and the larvae of wasps or bees, first dipped in blood and then "baked or hardned in their husks in an Oven, after the bread is taken out of it," become an "especially good" bait for bream (344). By transforming the tools, equipment, and techniques of the kitchen into substances that are delectable to fish (but revolting to humans), Walton's angler both emulates and parodies the cookery of the seventeenth-century English housewife.

Given Walton's sensitivity to the emasculating potential of kitchen work, the bait recipes that resemble human cuisine potentially endanger Piscator's standing as a male authority figure. One recipe uses the ingredients and cooking techniques of traditional pottage: "Take a handful or two of the best and biggest *Wheat* you can get, boil it in a little milk . . . till it be soft, and then fry it very leasurely with Honey and a little beaten Saffron dissolved in milk," instructs Piscator, comparing the texture of the cooked grain to

"*Frumity,*" a dish made of spiced and sweetened wheat berries cooked in milk (346).[109] But it seems that the freshwater fish of early modern England prefer Piscator's many recipes for "pastes" (297), soft mixtures of ingredients that a fish would normally never encounter in its aquatic habitat. Rather than hunting streamside for worms and insects, Piscator as a paste-bait chef instead forages in his household's pantry. The simplest paste recipe in *The Compleat Angler* consists only of bread crumbs (preferably of high-quality wheaten "Manchet") moistened with water and worked into a dough that can conceal a "small hook" with which the angler can catch roach and dace in late summer (341). Carp, by contrast, cannot resist "sweet pastes," so the addition of honey to white bread crumbs will yield "a good bait" for that species (297–98). At one point, Piscator turns to the brewhouse for the ingredients of a "ground-bait" of boiled and strained barley malt that, sprinkled liberally over a stream bed, will lure carp or bream to an area so they can be caught with worm-baited hooks (303–4). By contrast, the dairy provides the main ingredients for pastes beloved by chub in the autumn and winter: one of these recipes seems like an appealing spread for canapés—a lemon-yellow mixture of cheese, butter, and saffron—but another formula crosses into the less palatable territory of early modern medical receipts by combining cheese with turpentine, a tree resin widely used to treat human ailments because of its "curative" properties (222).[110] All of Piscator's recipes for pastes thus require the angler to "turn Scullion" so he can transform human comestibles into piscatory amuse-bouches.

Generations of English anglers before Walton had developed similar baits. Indeed, versions of most of Walton's bait-cookery instructions can be found in earlier angling manuals. Framed within the food-centric narrative of *The Compleat Angler*, however, these recycled bait recipes gain a distinctive new thematic resonance. In the fifteenth-century *Treatyse of Fysshynge with an Angle*, we learn that to catch a barbel in August, we should "take the talowe of a shepe & softe chese: of eche ylyke moche: and a lytyll hony & grynde or stampe theym togyder longe. and tempre it tyll it be tough. And put therto floure a lytyll & make it on smalle pellettys. And that is a good bayte to angle wyth at the grounde" (214–15). The author of the *Treatyse* has no specialized way to classify the mixture he describes: he refers to the substance only as "it" or the generalized term "bayte." In the version of the same recipe that he includes in *The Compleat Angler*, by contrast, Walton writes that "some advise to fish for the *Barbel* with Sheeps tallow and soft cheese beaten or work'd into a Paste" (324): unlike the author of the *Treatyse*, Walton describes this homemade barbel-chow as an example of the subgenre of "Paste" baits. This subtle change in diction registers a considerable shift in perspective. The word "paste" was first used in the late thirteenth century to designate a soft dough used in cookery, and it retained this meaning throughout the early modern period. As a foodstuff, paste played an important role in seventeenth-century cuisine: in his popular recipe book *The English Huswife*, Gervase Markham insists that a married woman "must be skilfull in the pastrie, and know how and in what manner to bake all sorts of meate, and what paste is fit for every meate, and how to handle and compound such pastes."[111] Although the *Oxford English Dictionary* suggests that Walton and Thomas Barker were the first authors to use the word "paste" to refer to bait, earlier angling writers were in fact responsible for this innovation: Leonard Mascall explained how to catch carp with a "paste made with hony and wheate flower" in the angling treatise he published in 1590, and Markham described a category of "made baites, which are Pastes," in *The Pleasures of Princes* in 1614.[112] Thus during the century and a half separating the *Treatyse* from *The Compleat Angler*, the word "paste" migrated from the kitchen into the realm of recreational fishing, this transition both reflecting and creating a gradual blurring of the conceptual demarcation between human food (normatively prepared by women) and "made baites" (created by men).

Rather than trap Walton's Piscator in the effeminizing role of the housewife, the angler's paste-bait cookery instead transforms the kitchen into a georgic space in which men prepare to feed animals before slaughtering them. In a passage that first appears in the second edition of *The Compleat Angler*, Piscator himself links his bait-cookery activities with animal husbandry when he describes how to make a ground bait for bream: after boiling and straining a couple of gallons of malted barley, Piscator reports that he gives the "liquor" resulting from this process to his horse (303).[113] As we have already seen, the georgic mode pervades *The Compleat Angler*, and Walton regularly depicts his anglers opportunistically exploiting agricultural landscapes where live bait can be foraged beneath cowpats and in the furrows of freshly ploughed fields (342). Such invertebrate-focused georgic activities likewise appear in Piscator's instructions about the care and feeding of worms that temporarily become the angler's pets: the unfortunate creatures must be initially "well scowred"—starved—so that they will be "clean and sweet" and thus delectable to fish such as barbel, but if kept in captivity for an extended time, the languishing worms will need to be fed with a "little milke or cream," preferably fortified with an egg, that the angler dribbles onto the moss in which he keeps his live bait (324, 245). And Piscator's recommendations for raising and feeding "Gentles" in captivity are downright stomach-churning: maggots drop into a pot from a suspended piece of festering "Beasts liver" or lie buried in cold storage over the winter, awaiting the angler's just-in-time harvesting, as they consume the fly-blown carcass of "a dead Cat or Kite" (343). Like Walton's recipes for bait pastes, these grotesque parodies of cookery and feeding confuse the boundaries between what Walton's culture regarded as divided and distinguished worlds: the human and the animal, the edible and the inedible, the domesticated and the wild, women's work and men's recreation.[114]

THE FOODFUL EARTH

This strand of georgic food-preparation exists in tension with a leitmotif of mystical feeding that likewise recurs, in different guises, throughout *The Compleat Angler*. As Maudlin and her mother sing songs in exchange for the fish that Piscator gives to them, the pastoral mode of Christopher Marlowe's "Passionate Shepherd" briefly provides a glimpse of an English land of Cockaigne. In the first edition of Walton's book, Maudlin sings a five-stanza version of Marlowe's poem to which her mother responds with a five-stanza version of Sir Walter Raleigh's "The Nymph's Reply"; beginning in 1655, however, Walton adds a sixth stanza to each poem and thus opposes two different visions of the relationship between hungry humanity and the natural world. As she sings the expanded version of Marlowe's lyric, Maudlin presents a fantasy of luxurious alfresco dining in a perpetually sunny green world—

> *Thy silver dishes for thy meat,*
> *As precious as the Gods do eat,*
> *Shall on an Ivory Table be*
> *Prepar'd each day for thee and me.* (234)

—but Maudlin's mother promptly attacks such delusion:

> *What should we talk of dainties then,*
> *Of better meat than's fit for men?*

> *These are but vain: that's only good*
> *Which God hath blest, and sent for food.* (235)

In the previous stanzas of her response to Marlowe's poem, as we have already noted, Maudlin's mother skewers the falsity of the shepherd's pastoral vision of nature, countering the speaker's promises of endless leisure, cute clothes, and a Club Med climate with a grimly realistic vision of a harsh world afflicted by winter, decay, and predatory men. The milkwoman's response to Marlowe's portrayal of gastronomic excess is not simply georgic, however, but theological, a smackdown of the shepherd's hedonistic classical "Gods" by the Judeo-Christian deity who unflashily but unfailingly provides appropriate food for humankind.

Throughout his angling treatise, Walton is fascinated by the ways through which God ensures that his myriad creatures do not go hungry. In one recurrent variation on this theme, Walton's master angler posits that thanks to God's providential design, some animals live as anorexics. Every August, Piscator asserts, a frog's lips naturally grow together, "and he continues so for at least six moneths without eating, but is sustained, none but he whose name is Wonderful, knows how" (287–88).[115] Similarly, Piscator reports that the metamorphosis of the puss moth caterpillar entails a prolonged, mysterious abstinence from food: "at a fixed age this *Caterpillar* gives over to eat, and towards Winter comes to be covered over with a strange shell or crust called an *Aurelia*, and so lives a kind of dead life, without eating all the Winter; and . . . so this *Caterpillar* then turns to be a *painted Butter-fly*" (250). Walton suggests that he draws on Bacon's *Sylva Sylvarum* in this passage,[116] but all the details and the reiterated emphasis on the caterpillar's self-starvation are entirely Walton's own additions.

Piscator develops this theme of anorexia at searching length in his account of a species of fish—probably sea trout—found near the town of Fordwich in Kent.[117] The "*Fordidge Trout*" enters Walton's narrative as a nugget of information provided by the virtuoso Sir George Hastings, who reported that "he thought that *Trout* bit not for hunger but wantonness" since "both he then, and many others before him, have been curious to search into their bellies, what the food was by which they lived; and have found out nothing by which they might satisfie their curiosity" (225). Piscator then embarks on an extended riff (expanded by Walton in later editions of his book) in which he catalogs other examples of animals that miraculously survive without food. The anorexia of the Fordwich trout, Piscator says,

> may be the better believed, because it is well known, that *Swallows* and *Bats* and *Wagtails*, which are call'd half year birds, and not seen to flie in *England* for six months in the Year (but about *Michaelmas* leave us for a hotter Climate); yet some of them that have been left behind their fellows, have been found (many thousands at a time) in hollow trees, or clay-Caves, where they have been observed, to live and sleep out the whole Winter without meat; and so *Albertus* observes that there is one kind of *Frog* that hath her mouth naturally shut up about the end of *August*, and that she lives so all the Winter: and though it be strange to some, yet it is known to too many among us to be doubted. (227)

Drawing on books by Francis Bacon and Edward Topsell,[118] Walton merges the mysteries of migration and hibernation and then transforms both phenomena into miracles of survival without food. The idea that birds, rather than migrating, hibernate without eating complements Walton's food-obsessed worldview, and Piscator returns to the same imaginative territory when he discusses the behavior of eels: "It is granted by all, or most men, that *Eels*, for about six months (that is to say, the six cold months of the year) stir not up and down, neither in the Rivers, nor in the Pools in which they usually are, but get into the soft earth or mud, and there many of them together bed themselves, and live without feeding upon any thing (as I have told you some *Swallows* have been observed to do in hollow trees for those six cold months): and this the *Eel* and *Swallow* do, as not being able to endure winter weather" (316–17). And in a song that he sings for his companions after dinner one night, Piscator recounts that "*yet though while I fish I fast, / I make good fortune my repast*" (242): the angler himself experiences the providential anorexia that structures the lives of the wondrous amphibians, insects, birds, and fish that flourish for long periods in the English countryside without eating.

Walton's fascination with anorexia is the flip side to the stories of miraculous feeding that occur even more frequently in *The Compleat Angler*. The concept of a "foodful earth" designed and overseen by a beneficent deity captivates Walton, and the appearance of the new character Auceps in the second edition of *The Compleat Angler* allows Piscator to remind us that "when God would feed the Prophet *Elijah* . . . after a kind of miraculous manner he did it by *Ravens*, who brought him meat morning and evening" (181).[119] In Walton's natural world, some animals can consume the most basic elements of the creation—"the birds of *Paradise*, and the *Camelion* are said to live by the *Sun* and the *Air*" (227), Piscator says—and we further learn that "it is reported by good Authors, that *grass-hoppers* and some Fish have no mouths, but are nourisht and take breath by the porousness of their Guills, Man knows not how; And this may be believed, if we consider that when the *Raven* has hatcht her eggs, she takes no further care, but, leaves her young ones, to the care of the God of Nature, who is said in the *Psalms, To feed the young Ravens that call upon him*. And they be kept alive, and fed by a *dew*, or *worms* that breed in their nests, or some other ways that we Mortals know not" (225–27). Although he begins with a mash-up of images from natural history (Thomas Moffett's comments about grasshoppers in his *Theater of Insects*)[120] and scripture (Ps. 147:9) that he has gleaned elsewhere, Walton embroiders his sources to portray a numinous natural world that miraculously sustains both mouthless fish and motherless baby birds.

The final image in Walton's allusion to Psalm 147—the baby ravens' nest that, in the absence of a nurturing parent, can itself as a physical structure provide food for the juvenile birds—has no precedent in Walton's biblical source but shows instead Walton's abiding belief in providentially designed ecological niches in which God's creatures are both born and fed. It is this concept that underpins Walton's recurrent depictions of spontaneous generation in *The Compleat Angler*. Like many of his contemporaries, Walton thought that God had devised both sexual and nonsexual processes of biological reproduction, and he thus regarded "spontaneous" or "equivocal" generation as a mode of propagation common in many species. Quoting a passage from Du Bartas's *Divine Weeks*, Piscator explains that "*God not contented to each kind to give, / And to infuse the vertue generative, / By his wise power made many creatures breed / Of liveless bodies without* Venus deed" (251). Like Du Bartas, Walton accepted the ancient theory that some organisms were generated, without parents, from mud, warm water, dew, or putrefying matter. Since spontaneously generated creatures, "lacking father or mother and children, . . . refuse family orders," the theory of spontaneous generation tacitly promoted what we now might term a "queer ecology" in which the natural world fosters "non-heterosexual forms of relationship, experience, and imagination."[121] Aristotle believed that plants, invertebrates, and fish originated spontaneously, and in later eras theologians aligned Aristotle's ideas about spontaneous generation with Christian interpretations of the book of Genesis. According to St. Augustine, God's commands that the land and waters should "bring forth" plants and animals continued to govern the spontaneous generation of living things on earth; moreover, Augustine argued, the existence of spontaneous generation explained how "the tiniest of creatures" were saved during Noah's Flood, since "it was not necessary for there to be in the Ark those creatures which can be generated from certain things, or from the corruption of such things, without sexual intercourse."[122] Although some early modern theorists fretted that spontaneous generation also seemed to occur without divine intention and oversight, many others, like the seventeenth-century jurist Sir Matthew Hale, believed that only "a knowing and perfectly intelligent Being" could control the earth's astonishing capacity for spontaneous generation.[123] Sir Thomas Browne—combining Augustine's account of Noah's adventures in zoo-keeping with Aristotle's argument that solar heat was a crucial component in the process of spontaneous generation—declared that "the most imperfect creatures, and such as were not preserved in the Arke, but having their seeds and principles in the wombe of nature, are every-where where the power of the Sun is; in these is the wisedome of [God's] hand discovered," and early modern works of natural history are filled with reports of caterpillars generated from dew, fleas bred from mixtures of dust and urine, and bedbugs produced by sweat.[124]

In *The Compleat Angler*, Walton is enthralled by what he depicts as spontaneous generation's bioecology of breeding and feeding. Many trout, Walton reports, "have sticking on them Sugs, or *Trout lice* [parasitic crustaceans], which is a kind of a worm, in shape like a clove or pin with a big head, and sticks close to him and sucks his moisture; those, I think, the *Trout* breeds himself, and never thrives till he free himself from them" (229). Most caterpillars, Walton observes in another passage, "content themselves to feed on particular herbs or leaves, (for most think those very leaves that gave them life and shape, give them a particular feeding and nourishment, and that upon them they usually abide)" (250). This vision of an ecology—of "relationships between living organisms and their environment"[125]—that generates parent-free animals enchants Walton repeatedly. Piscator reports that some frogs, as Topsell and Pliny suggest, breed "by laying eggs: and others to breed of the slime and dust of the earth, and . . . in winter they turn to slime again, and . . . the next Summer that very slime returns to be a living creature" (287), and elsewhere he discusses at length how "others say, that as *Pearls* are made of glutinous dew-drops, which are condensed by the Suns heat in those Countries, so *Eels* are bred of a particular dew falling in the months of *May* or *June* on the banks of some particular Ponds or Rivers (apted by nature for that end) which in a few dayes are by the Suns heat turned into *Eels*" (315). In another passage that he elaborated in two separate revisions, Walton develops his theme "that every plant has his particular flie or Caterpillar, which it breeds and feeds": "*Pliny* holds an opinion, that many [caterpillars] have their birth or being from a dew that in the Spring falls upon the leaves of trees; and that some kinds of them are from a dew left upon herbs or flowers; and others from a dew left upon Coleworts or Cabbages: All which kinds of dews being thickned and condensed, are by the Suns generative heat most of them hatch'd, and in three days made living creatures; and these of several shapes and colours" (249).[126] And in a passage he added to the conclusion of *The Compleat Angler* in 1655, Walton evocatively locates the scriptural lilies of the field within a sacred ecology of spontaneous generation: "So when I would beget *content*, and increase confidence in the *Power*, and *Wisdom*, and *Providence* of Almighty God, I will walk the *Meadows* by some gliding stream, and there contemplate the *Lillies* that take no care, and those very many other various little living *creatures*, that are not only created but fed (man knows not how) by the goodness of the God of *Nature*, and therefore trust in him" (371).

Walton's enthusiasm for spontaneous generation increased over the years he wrote and revised *The Compleat Angler*, and he came to make some daring—and controversial—claims about the genesis of fish. Walton believed that pike breed both through the sexual process of spawning and by spontaneous generation. "'Tis not to be doubted," Piscator declares, "but that they are bred, some by generation, and some not: as namely, of a Weed called *Pickerel-weed*, unless learned *Gesner* be much mistaken, for he says, this weed and other glutinous matter, with the help of the Suns heat in some particular Months, and some Ponds apted for it by nature, do become *Pikes*" (281). Although Walton credits Gesner for his account of pike spontaneously generating from pickerel weed, this narrative was, in fact, entirely Walton's own invention since neither Gesner nor any of Walton's other sources ever suggests such a phenomenon. Walton does follow William Samuel's *Arte of Angling* when he maintains that pike eat pickerel weed,[127] but Walton then makes his habitual connection between food and spontaneous generation and goes far beyond any of his sources to claim that pike not only consume but are generated by the plant. A pike's "feeding," Piscator states in a later passage, "is usually of *fish* or *frogs*, and sometimes a weed of his own called *Pickrell-weed*. Of which I told you some think some *Pikes* are bred; for they have observed, that where none have been put into Ponds, yet they have there found many: and that there has been plenty of that weed in those Ponds, and that that weed both breeds and feeds them; but whether those *Pikes* so bred will ever breed by generation as the others do, I shall leave to the disquisitions of men of more curiosity and leasure than I profess my self to have" (286).

Walton maintained his belief in the spontaneous generation of pike despite forceful opposition. One day in the 1650s, Walton was accosted in his hometown of Stafford by none other than Richard Franck who, true to his name, pulled no punches when he had the opportunity to confront Walton in person. "I remember," Franck recounts,

> I urged his own argument upon him, that pickerel weed of it self breeds pickerel [young pike]. Which question was no sooner stated, but he transmits himself to his authority, viz. Gesner, Dubravius, and Androvanus [Aldrovandus]. Which I readily opposed, and offered my reasons to prove the contrary; asserting, that pickerels have been fished out of pools and ponds where that weed (for ought I knew) never grew since the nonage of time, nor pickerel ever known to have shed their spawn there. This I propounded from a rational conjecture of the heronshaw [a small or young heron], who to commode her self with the fry of fish . . . probably might lap some spawn about her legs, in regard adhering to the se[dge]s and bull-rushes, near the shallows, where the fish shed their spawn, as my self and others without curiosity have observed. And this slimy substance adhering to her legs . . . and she mounting the air for another station, in probability [it] mounts with her. Where note, the next pond she happily arrives at, possibly she may leave the spawn behind her, which my Compleat Angler no sooner deliberated, but drop'd his argument, and leaves Gesner to defend it; so huff'd away: which rendred him rather a formal opinionist, than a

reform'd and practical artist, because to celebrate such antiquated records, whereby to maintain such an improbable assertion.[128]

Though we might cringe at his tactlessness, Richard Franck was, in fact, correct that water birds can transfer fertilized fish eggs from one body of water to another.[129] Walton published multiple editions of *The Compleat Angler* after his encounter with Franck, and when he revised each subsequent version of the text Walton never qualified or removed his account of the spontaneous generation of pike. Indeed, Walton utterly ignored Franck's critique, and his enthusiasm for spontaneous generation appears throughout the final edition of his fishing treatise that Walton published in 1676.

Walton's natural world is, first and foremost, an *edible* world for all the creatures who inhabit it. And in Walton's portrayal of spontaneous generation, foodstuffs rather than parents give rise to new creatures within a riparian environment. In *The Compleat Angler*, Walton's fish thus exist both as sources of food that generate a new breed of fishermen—Piscator's Brotherhood of the Angle—and as biological models of how groups of organisms—like schools of fish—might arise nonsexually through an ecosocial process akin to spontaneous generation. After Viator signifies his new allegiance to the female-free Brotherhood of the Angle by reciting Donne's amatory poem "The Baite" to Piscator, the thoughts of Walton's doppelgänger-protagonist turn at length to the equivocal generation of eels (139–41), thus emphasizing the parallels between the anglers' recruitment techniques and the dynamics of spontaneous generation.[130] Although Richard Franck sneered that the food-centrism of *The Compleat Angler* indicates that Walton's wife must have "had a finger in the [textual] py," Walton *per ipsum* creates a new, all-male social formation by harnessing the generative potential of food: Piscator's angling "sons" come into existence not through relationships with women but rather through the men's shared activities of catching and eating fish. Piscator and his angling brethren-sons are thus both created and sustained by the wondrous "foodful earth" of early modern England that spontaneously breeds and feeds fishermen as well as pike and eels.

Walton's transformation of equivocal generation into an ecosocial model for his Brotherhood of the Angle provides an important case study of the "historicity" of early modern ecology.[131] Rather than "project a prefabricated set of ethical and epistemological concerns onto the past," Peter Remien argues, we should instead examine "the constellation of ideas involved in ecology's early development."[132] To fulfill this mandate, Remien analyzes how the concept of "the oeconomy of nature" formulated by the seventeenth-century natural philosopher Sir Kenelm Digby posits "a protoecological world" in which nonhuman creatures, behaving like manorial householders, function within "a vast network of exchange" while "exerting dominion over [their] surroundings."[133] We discover in *The Compleat Angler* another seventeenth-century model of protoecology, but unlike the genteel Digby (and, as we shall see, Charles Cotton), who found the dynamics of the landed patrilineal household governing the natural environment, the linendraper Izaak Walton instead explores how the process of spontaneous generation could create a new kind of social order freed from the biological constraints of conjugal reproduction.

The ease with which pike are spontaneously produced by pickerel weed—and Piscator's angler-sons are generated from their delighted experiences of catching and then consuming fish in rural Hertfordshire—contrasts with the tenuousness of Izaak Walton's personal track record as a father. All seven children born to Walton and his first wife, Rachel Floud, died in early childhood, including six sons of whom the eldest had been named Izaak. Two children from Walton's second marriage to Anne Ken survived to adulthood—his daughter Ann, born in 1648, and a son named Izaak, who arrived in 1651—but in 1650, Walton had lost yet another infant son yet again named Izaak. So in *The Compleat Angler*, written after he had lost seven sons (including two namesakes), Izaak Walton explores a model of "equivocal" filiation that is much more successful (and much less heartbreaking) than Walton's own experience of biological paternity. The breeding-and-feeding dynamic of spontaneous generation that fosters the perpetually hungry Brotherhood of the Angle thus transforms the foodful earth of early modern England into a new and improved source of patriarchal identity for Piscator—and his own literary progenitor, Izaak Walton.

CHAPTER 4

Charles Cotton and the Properties of Angling

Near the end of February in 1676, an urgent message arrived at the home of the Staffordshire country gentleman Charles Cotton. Would Cotton please write a treatise on fly-fishing—and complete the manuscript in less than two weeks? Because this last-minute request came from Cotton's dear friend Izaak Walton, Cotton dropped everything and "*upon the instant*" began "*to scribble*" what would become the first specialized fly-fishing manual ever published.[1] Thus when Walton issued the fifth and final edition of *The Compleat Angler* later that year, it was accompanied by Cotton's innovative new angling treatise as Part II of Walton's revised text.[2]

Cotton's ability to throw together such an accomplished work testifies to his unsurpassed knowledge and love of his subject. Born in 1630 on his family's estate in Beresford Dale beside the River Dove, Cotton grew up with a fishing rod in his hand: in his angling manual, Cotton's alter ego says he can provide "better directions" about fly-fishing "having from my Childhood pursued the recreation of angling in very clear Rivers" (185). Cotton had long promised Walton that one day he would write "*particular Directions for the taking of a* Trout" with artificial flies (169), and in response to Walton's eleventh-hour request, he finally fulfilled this commitment. Cotton lamented that given more time, he could have presented his directions in "*neater dress*" (169), but modern anglers nonetheless still regard Charles Cotton's "Instructions How to Angle for a TROUT or GRAYLING in a Clear Stream" (167) as one of the most "seminal and definitive" books ever written about fly-fishing.³

As he decided how to frame his angling treatise, Cotton "*endeavour'd to accommodate*" his new text "*to* [Walton's] *own Method*" (169). Mirroring Walton's original narrative, Cotton thus structures Part II of *The Compleat Angler* as a series of conversations between two travelers who meet by chance: Piscator Junior (Cotton himself) and Viator, the man who "turned angler" in Walton's book after being accosted by Piscator on the road to Ware in 1653. In a crucial departure from Walton's narrative, however, Cotton sets his story far from Hertfordshire in the Peak District, with most of the action occurring at Cotton's childhood home, Beresford Hall. So even as Cotton recycles both the narrative "*Method*" and a major character from *The Compleat Angler*, the conceptual primacy of Cotton's country house in his fishing treatise contrasts starkly with the disdain for elite landownership that pervades Walton's book. And at the same time, Cotton's emphasis on genteel values likewise shapes his material practice of fly-fishing, thus further distancing Cotton's angling manual from the modes of bait-fishing central to the ecosocial dynamics of Walton's *Angler*.

PISCATOR AND THEOBALDS: THE ROAD NOT TAKEN

To fully appreciate how Charles Cotton's angling manual both honors and critiques its model, we must first understand how Izaak Walton's treatise had earlier rejected the aristocratic modes of environmental, social, and legal domination symbolized and perpetuated by landed property like Cotton's own estate in Beresford Dale. Beginning in the second edition of his angling manual, Walton not only changed Viator's name to "Venator" and added the character Auceps, but he also included new topographic detail about the route that Piscator and his companions take as they walk north from Tottenham Hill toward Ware. In Walton's revised narrative, Auceps responds to Piscator's opening salutation by naming his destination: "Sir, I shall by your favour bear you company as far as *Theobalds*, and there leave you, for then I turn up to a friends house who mews a Hawk for me, which I now long to see" (174). Accordingly, after the three travelers have each competed in their impromptu brag-fest about their respective sports, Piscator cuts short his encomium of water when he catches sight of "*Theobalds* house," at which point Auceps hives off from the Ware road, telling the other two sportsmen, "I must part with you at this Park-wall, for which I am very sorry" (188–89).

As Auceps strikes out on his own, he enters an ideologically complex landscape that Piscator and Venator choose to bypass.[4] Built between 1564 and 1584 by William Cecil, Lord Burghley, Theobalds was a magnificent country house surrounded by parklands and astonishing gardens (the latter including hidden water features that would squirt unsuspecting passersby) located about twelve miles from London in Hertfordshire.[5] As part of his construction program, Burghley replaced a circuitous lane that approached the house from the north with a straight driveway, guarded by portals at each end, that ran west from the London–Ware road.[6] It is at this grand entrance to Theobalds where, decades later, Auceps would part ways with Piscator and Venator. A prodigy house designed to showcase the political and cultural power of Burghley and his family, Theobalds ostentatiously flaunted William Cecil's aristocratic credentials and loyalty to the Tudor dynasty: the painted walls of one gallery were decorated with a "pictorial atlas" of England consisting of fifty-two trees—"one tree for every county in England"—from the boughs of which hung "the arms of those earls, barons, and nobles who live[d] in that particular county"; portraits and ornamentation in another gallery celebrated the families of both Queen Elizabeth I and William Cecil; and a loggia facing the Great Garden was decorated with painted genealogies of Burghley, the English monarchs, and "divers other antient families."[7] Staying in the royal suites that Burghley had designed specifically for her, Elizabeth I visited Theobalds more than a dozen times, each visit reputedly costing Burghley between two and three thousand pounds.[8] Theobalds thus originally functioned as William Cecil's theater of dynastic display.

During the early Stuart period, Theobalds became even more prominent as a site infused with aristocratic values. King James I, an avid hunter and falconer, was hosted frequently at Theobalds by William Cecil's son Robert, and the king became so enamored of Theobalds that in 1607 he persuaded Robert Cecil to swap it for seventeen royal manors, including the palace and park at Hatfield.[9] As a house, Theobalds had to be renovated to befit its new status as a royal palace, and at the same time, James also upgraded the estate's blood-sport infrastructure: in addition to constructing new stables, kennels, deer houses, pheasant pens, and a lodge for his keeper, James expanded the park at Theobalds until it encompassed more than 2,500 acres.[10] To thus supersize the estate's fenced-in game preserve, James continued the unpopular enlargement of Theobalds Park begun by Robert Cecil and enclosed hundreds of acres despite vehement—and sometimes violent—opposition from local people, many of whom depended on access to common lands for their subsistence.[11] Other aspects of James's tenure of Theobalds created further hardship for his non-elite neighbors: James imposed draconian punishments for poaching on the grounds of Theobalds, and nearby inhabitants complained not only about their loss of common lands but also about their enforced provision of meat for the king's hawks.[12] The social unrest that James thus fomented led to vandalism. The enlarged park at Theobalds was initially surrounded by palings—a fence made of wooden stakes designed to keep deer in the park and poachers out—but after this fence was repeatedly damaged by local people foraging for wood, it was replaced by an eighteen-inch-thick, nine-foot-tall brick wall more than nine miles long.[13] The resources required to build this structure were so extraordinary—and far beyond the willing participation of local inhabitants in the project—that master bricklayers were allowed to impress laborers and requisition horses and carts to construct the monumental barrier.[14] By 1637, nearly forty buttresses had been installed to keep the wall upright, the structure's deterioration surely hastened by the numerous trespassers who scaled it to break into the grounds of Theobalds.[15] In *The Compleat Angler*, it is this controversial "Park-wall"—both an instrument and a symbol of the Stuart monarchy's domination of the countryside—that marks the limit of Auceps's interaction with Piscator and the Brotherhood of the Angle.

James I died at Theobalds in 1625, and until the Restoration the estate's history was intertwined with the demise of the Stuart monarchy. Although it remained a royal palace, King Charles I spent much less time at Theobalds than his father; nonetheless, the king sometimes visited Theobalds as his political fortunes waned, and Charles supposedly planned his *Eikon Basilike* at Theobalds.[16] During the civil wars, Theobalds Palace was ransacked and vandalized, and much of the Theobalds estate "appears to have been parcelled out among the officers of the Parliamentary army."[17] Perhaps the "friend" mewing a hawk for Auceps was one of these roundheads.

Theobalds suffered further devastation during the interregnum. By 1650, more than 15,600 trees on the estate had been cut down or marked for felling to supply the navy's insatiable appetite for timber, and even though the palace was still structurally sound, most of it was soon razed and its materials sold, with the funds thus generated being funneled to the army.[18] Religious meetings were held in the park at Theobalds during the 1650s, and Presbyterians continued to use a chapel—one of the few components of the palace that had not been destroyed—long after the Restoration.[19] Piscator's remark that he sees "*Theobalds* house" suggests that the building's "central tower, with its turrets and cupola," which was visible from the highway, still stood in 1655, a forlorn and isolated fragment of the once-glorious royal palace.[20] So as Walton's anglers walk away from Theobalds, their trajectory resonates ideologically. On the one hand, Piscator skirts a landscape that has been seized and devastated by men whose beliefs Izaak Walton abhorred. From this perspective, Piscator escorts Venator away from a site of contaminating religiopolitical influences to ensure the younger man can be recruited to join the resistance movement embodied by the Brotherhood of the Angle. Yet if Walton's narrative thus seems to take a politically reactionary direction at the moment that Auceps exits from the book, it also simultaneously rejects Theobalds's identity as a showcase of elite landed power.

The transformation of William Cecil's prodigy house into James I's blood-sport headquarters had both furthered and represented the king's program of environmental medievalism. Rather than a hunger-driven quest for food, royal hunting functioned as a purely symbolic exercise: an elite man performed his "natural" domination of lesser beings by ritualistically pursuing and killing wild creatures, activities that showcased the hunter's preeminent knowledge of animals' behavior and habitat alongside his theatrically violent ability to exterminate his inferiors.[21] Early in the second edition of *The Compleat Angler*, as Venator argues for the supremacy of his eponymous recreation, he calls hunting "a game for Princes and noble persons" (184), reiterating the traditional English view of venery as a patrician symbol. Since the medieval designation of vast tracts of England as *forests*—game preserves, administered by their own legal code, that were set aside for the exclusive use of the monarch—English hunting had created a "political ecology" that emblematized royal power.[22] By selectively granting hunting privileges to members of the landed elite, the Crown displayed its own mystified prerogative while allying itself with the aristocracy through shared rites of environmental mastery. Upon ascending the throne, James I aggressively sought to intensify and expand this archaic representation of the English monarch as "lord of the beasts."[23] Even as he argued that the king could hunt anywhere he chose (and behaved accordingly), James also increased the financial qualifications for other men to participate in hunting, thus ensuring that venery became even more socially restricted during the early Stuart era.[24] But the enhanced imbrication of hunting, royal authority, and elite privilege that James sought to impose on the English countryside was violently rejected during the civil wars and interregnum as forests, parks, and herds of deer were destroyed.[25] Thus the devastation of Theobalds was symptomatic of widespread attempts by hungry soldiers and alienated local residents to eradicate Stuart modes of environmental sovereignty.

By introducing Theobalds as a landmark in the second edition of *The Compleat Angler*, Walton greatly complicates the political resonance of his opening narrative. When Auceps bids farewell to Piscator and Venator and turns up the drive that leads to Theobalds, he necessarily evokes memories of James I's tenure of the estate. Yet the fact that his falcon is being "mewed" transforms the symbolism of Auceps's journey to the heart of Stuart environmental mystique. During the molting season—which commenced at the beginning of Lent and lasted until August—early modern English falconers kept their adult hawks in specially designed aviaries called "mews." While they were mewed, the molting hawks could not be used to hunt and were confined so they would not damage their new plumage.[26] So like his mewed hawk, Auceps is grounded and unable to hunt: the fruitlessness of Auceps's journey to Theobalds in 1655 only underlines how the estate now symbolizes the demise of Stuart blood-sport privilege. In his revised version of *The Compleat Angler*, Walton thus tacitly depicts falconry as a recreation for losers and the social order represented by Theobalds as a dead end. And as Piscator and his companion turn their backs on Theobalds, they head into a landscape that is no longer congruent with the traditional values of the English monarchy and landed elite.

The symbolism of Theobalds likewise complicates the ecosocial dynamics of Walton's depiction of hunting. At the very beginning of Walton's narrative, we learn that both Piscator and Viator/Venator are heading into Hertfordshire to hunt otters. Since the early twelfth century, otter hunting had been pursued in England not as a mode of vermin control but as a blood sport. Nonetheless, otters held a lowly position in the caste system of early modern prey species: unlike deer, which were hunted on horseback in the noblest modes of venery, otters were pursued by groups of hunters that included pedestrians.[27] Following scent hounds, unmounted otter hunters would take up their positions on the banks of a stream or river and alert the hunt master when they spotted the quarry trying to escape into the water.[28] The morning after they part ways with Auceps, Piscator and Venator perform exactly these roles during an otter hunt arranged by the country gentleman Ralph Sadler, and the accuracy of Walton's depiction suggests that he himself had participated in such events.[29] When Walton's anglers appear on Amwell Hill at daybreak, the hunters and their packs of otter hounds have been "busie" for an hour (210). Venator provides color commentary as the dogs and mounted men first dispatch the exhausted otter and then discover the dead animal's holt containing her five juvenile offspring (210–12). Their work completed, Piscator and Venator join the other otter hunters at "an honest Ale-house" (212) and spend the rest of their second day in Hertfordshire sharing in the men's post-kill drinking, singing, and revelry.

The references to Theobalds that first appear in the 1655 edition of *The Compleat Angler* subtly align Walton's otter hunt with the early Stuart program of environmental mastery. As it had originated in the Middle Ages, otter hunting "was very much a sport of kings," and James I exercised the royal pack of otter hounds much more often than his early modern predecessors.[30] And to further demonstrate his control over the natural world, James used otters as more than a prey species. In *The Compleat Angler*, after the adult otter has been killed by the hunters, Piscator saves one of her five babies from extermination so he can "tame" it and teach it to "catch Fish, and do many other things of much pleasure" (212). Although Piscator says he thus hopes to emulate "an ingenuous Gentleman in *Leicester-shire*," he also follows the example of James I, who kept otters and other piscivorous creatures that were trained to catch fish for him under the watchful eye of the "Keeper of His Majesty's Cormorants, Ospreys, and Otters."[31] Thus, as both a hunter and a would-be otter tamer, Piscator's activities on Amwell Hill recall aspects of James I's own career as England's lord of beasts.

Yet as the equivocal symbolism of Theobalds suggests, Piscator does not fully embrace elite Stuart attitudes toward hunting. When Walton's master angler takes his leave of the hunters, he cheerfully declares, "God keep you all, Gentlemen, and send you meet this day with another bitch *Otter*, and kill her merrily, and all her young ones too" (82), but from 1655 onward, Piscator immediately elaborates on this sentiment by declaring to Venator that for the sake of "the preservation of *fish*," he is "glad these *Otters* were killed" and "sorry there are no more *Otter-killers*" (213). Although Piscator seems to be a strong proponent of hunting, he praises it only insofar as hunting advances his ultimate agenda of conserving fish and thus enhancing his opportunities for angling—a sport never mythologized as a performance of chivalric masculinity.

Indeed, Piscator's narrowly fish-centric rationale for hunting ultimately rejects the ecosocial worldview promoted by the Stuart monarchs. Whereas Viator/Venator seeks the "pleasure" of hunting otters for the first time, Piscator joins the same hunting party only because he wants to help protect fish from the predations of "those villanous vermin" (175).[32] Piscator thus frames the otter hunt as a necessary evil rather than an appealing recreation, and having been invited by Venator to continue his apotheosis of angling after Auceps heads to Theobalds, the master angler cannot resist casting aspersions on his traveling companion's favorite sport. In a passage that first appears in Walton's revised text of 1655, Piscator establishes the doctrinal basis of his generalized disapproval of hunting. "Angling is always taken in the best sense" in Scripture, Piscator argues, "and that though hunting may be sometimes so taken, yet it is but seldom to be so understood"; moreover, Piscator adds, "he that views the ancient Ecclesiastical Canons, shall find *Hunting* to be forbidden to *Church-men*, as being a turbulent, toilsom, perplexing Recreation; and shall find *Angling* allowed to *Clergy-men*, as being a harmless Recreation, a recreation that invites them to *contemplation* and *quietness*" (202–3).[33]

Although Piscator's moralistic disdain for venery vanishes during the otter hunt itself, it resurfaces shortly thereafter. On the morning of their third day in Hertfordshire, when the anglers leave the "honest ale-house" and the otter hunters behind, Viator/Venator asks his companion, "How do you like your lodging and mine Hoste and the company? is not mine Hoste a witty man?" Piscator delays answering for a while to lessen the blunt-force social trauma of his response: their "Hoste," Piscator finally declares, "is not to me a good companion: for most of his conceits were either Scripture jests, or lascivious jests; for which I count no man witty" (213–14).[34] Having climbed onto moralistic high ground, Piscator next takes aim at one of the elite otter hunters, complaining that "a Gentleman" of the company was as smutty and blasphemous as the Host of the (apparently not-so-honest) alehouse. Royalists were notorious for meeting at alehouses during the 1650s to indulge in heavy drinking, bawdiness, plotting, and the politically transgressive pledging of healths, but Piscator's scathing indictment of scurrilous alehouse behavior suggests he shares puritans' visceral disapproval of such cavalier debauchery.[35] And Piscator's association of hunting with immorality and elite decadence aligns him with the anti-blood-sport sentiments that became increasingly widespread—especially among puritans—during the seventeenth century.[36] Despite his numinous view of the natural world, however, Walton never depicts hunting as an immoral abuse of animals: although he condemns hunting in general, Piscator zealously champions the extermination of otters for the sake of fish conservation. By thus advocating hunting only as a form of vermin control, Walton severs the connection between blood sports and aristocratic social authority—and thus rejects the foundation of the Stuart program of environmental mastery symbolized by the park wall of Theobalds.

A related critique of aristocratic values likewise pervades Walton's book. As indicated by Piscator's uneasy, defensive relationships with virtuosos like Sir Henry Wotton,[37] a tension between ascribed and achieved status shapes the social order that Walton portrays in *The Compleat Angler*. After Auceps leaves the narrative in the second edition onward, Piscator begins to bolster his case for the superiority of angling by bragging to Venator about the sport's "*antiquity*" (190). Building on his earlier disquisition about water as the "eldest daughter of the Creation" (185), Piscator riffs on a passage from Gervase Markham's *Pleasures of Princes* to establish angling's bona fides as a time-honored recreation. Markham had buttressed the legitimacy of this line of argument by appealing to the social sphere, briefly noting that "all pleasures, like Gentry, are held to be most excellent which is most auncient."[38] Markham's glib acceptance of early modern truisms about lineage seems to irritate Piscator, however, and Walton's doppelgänger spends less time enumerating anglers in myth and scripture than he does questioning the value of pedigrees:

> I would rather prove my self a *Gentleman* by being *learned* and *humble, valiant,* and *inoffensive, vertuous,* and *communicable,* than by any fond ostentation of riches, or wanting those vertues my self, boast that these were in my Ancestors. . . . So if this Antiquity of *Angling* (which for my part I have not forced) shall like an ancient family, be either an honour or an ornament to this vertuous Art which I profess to love and practice, I shall be the gladder that I

made an accidental mention of the antiquity of it; of which I shall say no more. (191–92)

In the midst of this mini-rant, Piscator does briefly try to find a reason to praise ancestry—"I grant that where a noble and ancient descent and such merits meet in any man, it is a double dignification of that person" (191)—but he cannot bring himself to portray the happenstance of one's birth as laudable in and of itself. Likewise, Piscator has apparently stocked his commonplace book with poems that question the value of lineage: "*Blood Ally'd to Greatness is alone / Inherited, not purchas'd, nor our own. / Fame, Honour, Beauty, State, Train, Blood and Birth / Are but the fading Blossoms of the earth*," Piscator counsels Venator near the end of their journey together (369), and other passages in *The Compleat Angler* similarly stress that a man's stature as a recreational fisherman reflects his own endeavor, not his birth. In his epistle to the reader, Walton declares that "*as no man is born an artist, so no man is born an Angler*" (172), and Piscator later suggests that true anglers embrace an alternative social hierarchy that disregards conventional markers of "noble" status: "I will tell you, Scholar, I once heard one say, *I envy not him that eats better* meat *than I do, nor him that is* richer, *or that wears better* clothes *than I do. I envy no body but him, and him only, that catches more* fish *than I do. And such a man is like to prove an Angler, and this noble emulation I wish to you and all young Anglers*" (348). *The Compleat Angler* thus repeatedly celebrates anglers as a distinctive group of self-made men whose merit cannot be measured by traditional norms of social status.

Even more transgressively, the sui generis social identity of Walton's anglers shapes their alarmingly unorthodox relationship to property. Much of the seventeenth-century English countryside had been rendered off-limits to commoners by enclosure, a legal process through which pieces of land were converted from communal to individual ownership, access, and control.[39] The wildlife inhabiting enclosed land de facto became private property, as both symbolized and enforced by the nine-foot-high walls that King James had erected around the deer park at Theobalds.[40] Bodies of fresh water— and the fish that populated them—could also be owned, and the likes of Piscator could not legally fish in a pond or in running fresh water that had been rendered still—such as part of a river that had been dammed—without permission.[41] Most importantly for our understanding of *The Compleat Angler*, seventeenth-century English anglers were allowed to catch fish in the flowing water of a nontidal river only if they could gain access to that water on unenclosed land—and Walton's anglers spend virtually all their time fishing above the tidal portion of the River Lea.[42]

Just as the georgic meadows in Walton's world are dotted with cowpats, so too *The Compleat Angler* unfolds in rural settings marked by unmistakable signs of landownership. As R. A. Houston argues, during Walton's lifetime "the English controlled people by organizing space . . . onto which they mapped law," and the countryside depicted in Walton's text thus consists of "legally bounded spaces"—experienced both mentally and physically—that were characteristic of the early modern English landscape.[43] At the beginning of the otter hunt, Piscator excitedly urges his traveling companion, "Lets be gone, lets make haste, I long to be doing; no reasonable hedge or ditch shall hold me" (80). English deer parks were traditionally surrounded by a barrier comprising an interior ditch backed by a mound topped with pales or a hedge, so Piscator locates the Amwell Hill otter hunt within an elite enclosed landscape.[44] But even as Piscator evokes a geography that renders property law "legible in space," he also envisions himself transgressing its legal restrictions in a culturally equivocal way.[45] The physical demarcation of property boundaries triggered strong, disruptive "psychic resonances" in the population of early modern England: commoners whose subsistence was threatened by enclosure regularly "turned their anger upon the hedge and the ditch," yet elite hunters were also prone to harming their neighbors' property by "treading and breaking down" their hedges.[46] Does Piscator's vision of trespassing in the name of otter extermination ally him with dispossessed commoners or irresponsible gentlemen? Earlier angling writers staked out their attitudes toward private landownership much more clearly: the fifteenth-century author of the *Treatyse of Fysshynge wyth an Angle* commanded readers to "breke noo mannys heggys in goynge abowte your dysportes" (226–27), and William Samuel's Elizabethan angler-protagonist—despite describing the perch as a "ravenous fish" that "liveth . . . by eating up of his fellowes, as the covetous inclosers do"—declares that a recreational fisherman must have "Love to the owner of the game" and therefore not poach on someone else's land (*Arte of Angling*, C7v–C8r, B7r). In striking contrast, just as Walton's stance toward inherited status cannot be clearly defined, so his anglers' relationship to landed property seems ambiguous.

After Walton's characters decide to "turn Angler" and leave the landmarks of Theobalds, Hoddesdon, and Amwell Hill behind,[47] it is never clear exactly where they are geographically until they reach Tottenham High Cross at the end of the narrative. Nonetheless, their experience of the environs of the River Lea is realistically structured by the legally and symbolically freighted presence of hedges. As Walton revised *The Compleat Angler*, the image of a hedge engulfed by honeysuckle appeared in his text with increasing frequency. In the 1676 edition of Walton's treatise, we initially encounter such a hedgerow late on the first day the anglers dedicate to fishing: as they head back to the alehouse Bleak Hall to enjoy Venator's freshly caught trout for dinner, it begins to rain, and Piscator suggests they take shelter under a "high *honysuckle* hedg" (231). The alliterative descriptor "*honysuckle*"—which Walton added to this passage only in the final version of his text—simultaneously romanticizes the hedge and downplays its function as a boundary marker. The native honeysuckle *Lonicera periclymenum*, often called "woodbine" in the early modern period, was—and still is—a common English hedgerow plant with fragrant yellow flowers and a rampant climbing habit that enables it to transform trees into "over-canopied" arbors, to borrow an image from *A Midsummer Night's Dream*.[48] Walton's anglers wait out the rain in such a bower, and later in the narrative, as Piscator catches fish and gives angling tutorials, he takes advantage of other hedgerows similarly enveloped by honeysuckle: after spending their first night at Bleak Hall, Walton's protagonists set off to go angling the next morning, and when they reach the river, Piscator invites his pupil to "sit down under this *Honey-suckle* hedg" while he prepares Venator's rod (250), and later the same day, in a passage Walton added to his book in 1655, Piscator tells his companion that since it is raining, "we'l sit still and enjoy our selves a little longer under this *honey-suckle-hedg*" (314). Likewise, in a section that first appeared in 1676, as the two main characters make their return journey to Tottenham High Cross, Piscator remarks that he and Venator are walking "*in the cool shade of this sweet* Hony-suckle-Hedg" (362): the bond forged between the two men in the hedgerow bowers of Hertfordshire continues to be fostered by similar botanical structures as the anglers return to the city. The image of Piscator and his pupil sheltering within a natural honeysuckle arbor—a haven that bespeaks intimacy and lasting friendship—focuses our attention on the setting's beauty and interpersonal symbolism rather than the hedge's function to demarcate (and protect) private property.[49]

We should not, however, become so entranced by Walton's evocative— and increasingly ubiquitous—bowers of honeysuckle that we fail to ask a pivotal question: Given the anglers' repeated proximity to hedges, have Walton's characters been fishing on enclosed land? And if so, have they sought and been granted the (invisible and unnamed) landowners' permission—or have Walton's anglers been trespassing and poaching? As Andrew McRae argues in an important essay, *The Compleat Angler* seems strangely "unconcerned with owned places."[50] At the same time as Walton's anglers transform honeysuckle-ridden portions of hedgerow into impromptu fishing huts, they also exhibit a distinctive proprietary attitude toward the land they traverse. Late in the narrative, on the anglers' final evening in Hertfordshire, Piscator's pupil recounts how earlier that day he sat alone beneath a waterside willow tree in a "pleasant Meadow" whose owner—apparently a royalist whose property has been sequestrated—"had a plentiful estate, and not a heart to think so; that he had at this time many Law-suits depending, and that they both damp'd his mirth, and took up . . . much of his time and thoughts" (333).[51] To this point, Walton provides a conventional lament for the hardships endured by royalist landowners, and even after the Restoration, readers would have regarded this passage as social realism since magnates like William Cavendish endured years of legal wrangling when they tried to recover the land they had lost during the interregnum.[52] But Walton's novice angler abruptly abandons this cavalier script when he observes that the beleaguered owner of the meadow had become so preoccupied with his legal problems

> that he himself had not leisure to take the sweet content that I (who pretended no title to them), took in his fields; for I could there sit quietly, and looking on the water, see some Fishes sport themselves in the silver streams, others, leaping at Flies of several shapes and colours; looking on the Hills, I could behold them spotted with Woods and Groves. . . . I say, as I thus sate joying in my own happy condition, and pitying this poor rich man, that own'd this and many other pleasant Groves and Meadows about me, I did thankfully remember what my Saviour said, that the *meek possess the Earth*; or rather, they enjoy what the other possess and enjoy not, for Anglers and meek quiet-spirited-men, are free from those high, those restless thoughts which corrode the sweets of life. (333–34)

Walton cites the Sermon on the Mount in the final sentence of this passage but makes important alterations to his biblical source text. In both the

Geneva and King James translations of the Bible, rather than "*possess the Earth*," the "meek" in Matthew 5:5 "shall inherit the earth": Walton's substitution of "possess" for "inherit" and his use of present rather than future tense transform Christ's beatitude into a description of the angler's unorthodox but divinely authorized relationship to landed property.[53] Giving the reader a preview of this passage, Edward Powell's commendatory poem, which first prefaced the 1655 edition of Walton's text, praises Walton because "whilst some vex they from their lands are thrown, / He joys to think the waters are his own" (431). And in a long section added near the end of the 1676 edition of his book, Walton again misquotes the third beatitude and suggests that humble men like his anglers enjoy a superior kind of "possession" of the earth that is unrelated to social rank: "Blessed be the meek; for they shall possess the earth. . . . [H]e *(and he only) possesses the earth as he goes towards that Kingdom of Heaven, by being humble and cheerful, and content with what his good God has allotted him: he has no turbulent, repining, vexatious thoughts that he deserves better: nor is vext when he sees others possest of more honour or more riches than his wise God has allotted for his share; but he possesses what he has with a meek and contented quietness*" (365). Piscator and his band of angling brothers seem to lead the paradisal existence depicted in Thomas Traherne's mystical poem "Wonder" in which the speaker recounts how, as a child, he "wander'd over all men's grounds / And found repose" in a world freed from "curs'd and devis'd proprieties," but unlike Traherne's speaker, for whom "hedges, ditches, limits, bounds" did not exist,"[54] Walton's anglers simply ignore—or make their own use of—such property markers as they traverse (and fish on) land that does not belong to them, seeming to share the subversive outlook expressed in the beggars' song that Piscator sings at one point—"*The world is ours and ours alone, / For we alone have world at will; / We purchase not, all is our own*" (265). As they wander through Hertfordshire, Walton's anglers thus forge a radically new, superior relationship to the countryside that is unavailable to its landowners: the fishermen "enjoy" and "possess" the rural environment in a way that rejects traditional concepts of landed property. Although Piscator criticizes "pertinacious Schismatick[s]" (264), he behaves as if he shares the Diggers' belief that the earth is "a Common Treasury . . . Free and Common for all."[55]

Walton's transgressive disregard for property law did not go unnoticed—or unchallenged. Just as the Restoration reestablished hereditary monarchy, so it also unleashed a zeitgeist that sought to bolster the traditional interests of English landowners. And thus a decade before the Game Act of 1671 would restrict sporting rights to members of the landed gentry, an explicit rebuttal of Walton's radical reenvisioning of landownership appeared in the "Short Discourse by Way of Post-Script, Touching the Lawes of Angling" that was first added to the third edition of *The Compleat Angler* in 1661.[56] As Andrew McRae observes, this anonymous mini-treatise confronts and attempts to remedy Walton's failure to depict the legal implications of his anglers' sojourn in Hertfordshire.[57] The author of the "Lawes of Angling" provides his readers with pragmatic knowledge of what legal historians would now term early modern English "law-in-space."[58] He cannot, the author acknowledges, improve on his "good Friend" Walton's vindication of the "Legality" of his "Apostolical Recreation" in "Divine" terms; nonetheless, the author insists, fishing in Restoration England is also governed by "the known Laws" that the author proceeds to explicate.[59] Laws of landownership constrain the angler's access to freshwater fish in "Running Streams," the author briskly explains: "No man can go upon another mans ground to fish, without his license, but that he is a Trespasser; but if a man have license to enter into a Close or Ground for such a space of time, there, though he practise Angling all that time, he is not a Trespasser" (S1v–S2r). "If the Angler take care that he offend not with his feet," the author summarizes encouragingly, "there is no great danger of his hands" (S3r). Apparently assuming that his reader's feet will inevitably offend, however, the author goes on to describe the rights of a fisherman who is caught trespassing, explaining when and to what extent property owners can legally use force against a trespasser and his fishing rod. Anticipating even more trouble, the author concludes his "Lawes of Angling" by outlining the limits placed on financial damages should a property owner sue a trespassing angler. Walton's book, this little treatise trenchantly demonstrates, is far from "compleat" in its depiction of the angler's relationship to English property law.

As a coda to *The Compleat Angler*, the "Lawes of Angling" thus presents alternative narratives that suggest the countryside celebrated in Walton's "*Arcadia*" (S4r) is actually a legal minefield that Piscator and his acolyte have somehow traversed unscathed since they veered away from Theobalds. The jarring thematic otherness of the "Lawes of Angling" is further highlighted by the printer's decision to set the text in black-letter typeface rather than the roman typeface used in Walton's own treatise. Whereas roman typeface predominated in English books printed after 1550, black letter (also known as

"English letter") had been widely used in books produced before that date, and by Walton's era the customary use of black letter had become limited to popular secular works (like jest books and broadside ballads) and "texts designed to enforce conformity," including the Bible, the Book of Common Prayer, catechisms, psalters, legal works, and government documents.[60] So as the reader's gaze shifts from *The Compleat Angler* to the "Lawes of Angling," the ostentatiously old-fashioned typeface of the latter text functions as a "bibliographical code"—the typographic equivalent of a hedge or park wall—that portrays the text as a realm of authoritative respect for the English legal system.[61] This polemically conservative stance is replicated by the treatise's contents, which seek to warn Walton's readers that the saga of Piscator and his friends must not serve as a blueprint for their own disregard of English property law.

PISCATOR JUNIOR AND BERESFORD HALL

By setting Part II of *The Compleat Angler* on his estate in Beresford Dale, Charles Cotton further attempts "to correct the waywardness of Walton's anglers"[62] even as he creates an emotionally charged monument to Walton himself. In his fly-fishing manual, Cotton—who, as we shall see, proudly styled himself in real life as Walton's adopted "Son" (169)—becomes his book's protagonist, Piscator Junior. One day in early March 1676, while returning to his home in the rugged area of the English Midlands known as "the Peak," Piscator Junior encounters the apprentice angler from Walton's narrative—now aptly reverted to his original name of "Viator" ("Traveler")—near the village of Brailsford in Derbyshire.[63] "You are happily overtaken Sir" (171), Piscator Junior greets the stranger on the road: by deliberately echoing the first line of Walton's text, Cotton imbues his fly-fishing treatise with similarly complex dynamics of fellowship and domination.[64] Viator—who is journeying on horseback from his home in Essex to Lancashire—has been struggling to navigate the muddy road northwest of Derby, and he asks if he may join Piscator Junior as far as the town of Ashbourne, where Viator intends to spend the night at an inn. Piscator Junior obligingly slows down "out of complacency to a Traveller utterly a Stranger in these parts" (172), and the two men talk as they ride along together. Inspired by the myriad "little Brooks" that interlace the countryside (172), their conversation soon turns to angling, whereupon Piscator Junior and Viator discover they are both members of the Brotherhood of the Angle—and thus enthusiastic fans of Piscator himself, Izaak Walton. Any friend of Walton is a friend of Piscator Junior, who immediately lobbies Viator to change his itinerary and join him at Beresford Hall so Viator may take tutorials—complete with engaged-learning activities on the River Dove—to supplement the angling education he received years earlier from Piscator "under the *Sycamore* Tree" in Hertfordshire (174).

Cotton further emulates the "*Method*" of Walton's book by framing his own angling manual as a conversion narrative. From the very beginning of Cotton's treatise, Viator embodies the long-term transformative power of Walton's philosophy and teaching: nearly a quarter century after he first met Piscator on Tottenham Hill, Viator—who previously was, he confesses, "wholly addicted to the Chace"—still lives happily as a born-again angler thanks to his relationship with his "Master," Izaak Walton (174). Although this new storyline compliments Cotton's beloved friend, it also eradicates the social tension between student and teacher that shaped the arc of Walton's *Compleat Angler* plot: Cotton must find a new source of interpersonal conflict to propel his narrative. So in Cotton's text, his two main characters diverge not in their attitudes toward angling but rather in their responses to the geography of their surroundings. Instead of persuading Viator to join the Brotherhood of the Angle, Piscator Junior must convert him into appreciation of the inhospitable natural environment of the region of England that Cotton elsewhere calls "the scorn'd *Peak*."[65]

As both a physical place and a cultural construct, the Peak has resisted human mastery for centuries. Located at the southern end of the Pennine Hills, not regarded as "northern" England yet distinctly nonsouthern, the Peak straddles a geographic threshold where southeastern lowlands meet northwestern uplands.[66] Since the Middle Ages, the region's ambiguity has been reflected and compounded by the Peak's shifting boundaries and proliferating names: the High Peak—also called the "Dark Peak"—which is an area of moorlands and ravines with elevations reaching two thousand feet in northern Derbyshire (and often understood to encompass parts of Cheshire and Staffordshire as well); the more southerly White Peak (also known as the "Low Peak" and the "Derbyshire Dales"), a limestone plateau etched by river valleys; and the Moorlands (or "South West Peak"), an upland strip stretching from Leek north to Stockport and from Buxton west to Macclesfield.[67] A lifelong denizen of the region where the White Peak meets the

Moorlands,[68] Charles Cotton possessed a profound understanding and love of the area's rugged liminality. Yet as Cotton later admitted in *The Wonders of the Peake*, his versified "review of early outdoor ecotourism" first published in 1681,[69] the region seemed to outsiders "A *Country* so deform'd, the *Traveller* / Would swear those parts Natures *pudenda* were" (2:323, lines 7–8). Cotton's obscene pun on "*Country*" develops Michael Drayton's earlier depiction of the Peak as "A withered Beldam long, with bleared watrish eyes, / With many a bleake storme dim'd," both poets misogynistically transforming the mountainous terrain of the Peak into a revoltingly grotesque female body.[70] Other seventeenth-century authors likewise constructed the region as simultaneously uncanny and dangerous: Edward Browne called the Peak a "strange mountainous, misty, moorish, rocky, wild, country"; Celia Fiennes warned that the district "is full of steep hills, and nothing but the peaks of hills as thick one by another . . . which are very steepe which makes travelling tedious, and the miles long"; and Robert Plot observed that in the area near Cotton's home, "many of the *Mountains* of that part of the *Country* . . . are hardly passable, some of them being of so vast a height, that in rainy weather I have frequently seen the *tops* of them above the *Clouds*."[71] Unlike the setting of his first fishing trip in 1653, Viator would find no pleasant pastoral landscapes awaiting him as he headed into unfamiliar territory in 1676.

As Part II of *The Compleat Angler* opens, it is thus not angling but the harsh, unsettling topography of the Peak that takes center stage. Rooted in Charles Cotton's detailed knowledge of the region's landscape and its demands—both physical and psychological—on travelers, the first two chapters of his fly-fishing manual stage a comic debate between the chronically whinging Viator and his new companion Piscator Junior, who seems to be moonlighting as a spokesman for the Peak District Development Commission.[72] Whereas at the beginning of Walton's narrative, it was Viator's identity as a nonangler that rendered him an ecosocial Other, in Cotton's text, by contrast, Viator is alienated from his surroundings—and hence often testily at odds with his traveling companion as well—because he is "a Stranger in these parts" (171). As they ride together toward Ashbourne and then further north to Beresford Dale,[73] the two men perceive the landscape they traverse in markedly different ways. At the very beginning of the narrative, Viator feels that he has somehow entered a foreign (and highly unpleasant) space-time continuum. When Piscator Junior tells him that he is nearly five miles from his intended destination for the day, Viator is incredulous: he gripes that he had been told that Ashbourne lies only ten miles from Derby, "and methinks I have rode almost so far already" (171). Viator, we realize, has not yet learned how to gauge distances in "Peakish miles," which were much longer than the statute miles observed in the south of England.[74] Piscator Junior tries to deflect Viator's complaint by comparing their surroundings favorably to the rest of the country—"O Sir, find no fault with large measure of good Land, which *Derby-shire* abounds in, as much as most Counties of *England*" (171)—but Viator, refusing to take this hint, instead grouses about the condition of the roads: "Good Land I confess affords a pleasant prospect," Viator agrees, "but . . . large measure of foul way is not altogether so acceptable" (171). Piscator Junior parries this new attack by cheerfully declaring that muddy roads are proverbial indicators of "the fertility of the soyl" since they are created by the "continual Travel, and Traffick" of "loaden Horses" going to market (171). Yet Piscator Junior's bonhomie has begun to wear thin, and when he learns that Viator hails from Essex, he cannot forbear chiding Viator's lack of fortitude—and warning ominously that this softy from the south will soon need to toughen up: "I do not then wonder you should appear dissatisfied with the length of the Miles, and the foulness of the way: though I am sorry you should begin to quarrel with them so soon; for, believe me Sir, you will find the Miles much longer, and the way much worse before you come to your Journies end" (172). This rebuke chastens Viator back into courteousness, and as the men continue their conversation, they realize they are both angling disciples of Izaak Walton. When Piscator Junior discovers their shared relationship with Walton, he cajoles Viator into staying at Cotton's country house, Beresford Hall (apparently using "Peakish" measurement to shave three miles off the distance between Ashbourne and his estate as he tries to persuade Viator to revise his itinerary).[75] After Viator accepts Piscator Junior's invitation, he remains civil for a while longer, only to be jolted back into churlishness at the sight of the landscape of the White Peak northwest of Ashbourne: "What Mountains are here! are we not in *Wales*?" Viator exclaims (176). Piscator Junior once again tries to accentuate the positive—"yet these Hills though high, bleak, and craggy, breed and feed good Beef, and Mutton above ground, and afford good store of Lead within"—but he is countered by Viator's default negativity: "They had need of all those commodities to make amends for the ill Land-schape" (176–77).

At this point in the narrative, however, heart-pounding fear suddenly replaces the sarcasm in Viator's voice.[76] Surveying the "Mountains" in front of him, Viator confesses, "I hope our way does not lye over any of these; for I dread a *precipice*," and he proposes to dismount from his horse so he can "entrust [his] neck to the fidelity of [his] own feet" (177). The narrative tension builds as Piscator Junior takes charge: although their route may "appear a little terrible to a Stranger," Piscator Junior concedes, he and Viator must keep up their pace by staying mounted for as long as possible so they can traverse "the formidable Hill" known as Hanson Toot before nightfall (177, 179). Viator's status as a "Forraigner" in the Peak (177), which so far has made him comically antisocial, now threatens his survival. Viator stifles his panic and obeys his host for a spell, but as the two men approach the River Dove, the steep descent becomes too frightening for Viator to endure any longer on horseback. Although Piscator Junior usually rides the entire route—Celia Fiennes marveled that native Peakrils "will climbe up and down with their horses those steep precipices"[77]—he agrees that Viator's horse, "not acquainted with these slippery stones" (179), has now become a liability, and he considerately joins Viator on foot for the last stage of their journey over Hanson Toot. Nevertheless, as the men lead their horses down the precipitous incline, Viator exclaims that he fears "breaking [his] neck" since the hill is "as steep as a penthouse": "Hoist thee! there's one fair scape! these stones are so slippery I cannot stand! yet again! I think I were best lay my heeles in my neck, and tumble down" (180). The panic-stricken traveler seems destined to fall.

But just as Viator begins to slip-slide away, Piscator Junior intervenes and literally takes Viator in hand to ensure his guest's safety. "Give me your hand at this broad stone," Piscator Junior orders Viator, "and then the worst is past" (180). The imperative "give me your hand" echoes the command uttered by Piscator twenty-three years earlier in *The Compleat Angler* (84) after his astonishingly delectable chub convinced Viator that he should become Piscator's "Scholer." But in Cotton's text, the bond established by his characters' handclasp proves short-lived. No sooner have Viator and Piscator Junior descended Hanson Toot unscathed than Viator recovers sufficiently to give vent to a new series of Peakophobic complaints: griping that he is so bathed in sweat that his shirt sticks to his back, Viator says he hopes "we have no more of these Alpes to pass over" and declares that he would "go twenty Miles about" Hanson Toot rather than negotiate the hill ever again (181).[78] After the two men cross the River Dove into Staffordshire at Milldale—on a packhorse bridge so narrow that "a mouse can hardly go over it" (180)—Piscator Junior promises his companion that "wee'l reconcile you to our

Country before we part with you; if shewing you good sport with Angling will do't" (181). Viator, no longer frightened out of his habitual surliness, replies ungraciously that "to be plain with you, I do not find my self much inclin'd that way" (181). When the two men finally catch sight of Beresford Hall in the twilight, we detect an unmistakable edge of exasperation to Piscator Junior's voice: "Well Sir, your raillery upon our Mountains has brought us almost home" (181).[79] Thus, as the travelers near the end of their fraught journey, it seems impossible that anyone could "reconcile" Viator to the Peak. Piscator Junior has his work cut out for him.

But as the travelers approach Charles Cotton's estate, they leave behind the aberrant "Country" hostile to human existence and instead enter the controlled space of landed property.[80] A beneficent environmental force field seems to emanate from Beresford Hall: before Viator sees the house itself, he notices that the River Dove now seems "a much finer River" than it did at the foot of Hanson Toot. Given Viator's innate tactlessness, we take his first remarks about Cotton's country house as truthful rather than flattering: "it stands prettily, and here's wood about it too, but so young, as appears to be of your own planting" (181). Built early in the seventeenth century, Beresford Hall was not an opulent grand home like William Cecil's Theobalds or that celebrated architectural "wonder" of the Peak, Chatsworth, but rather was a modest L-shaped stone house that Cotton had inherited when his father died in 1658.[81] As an improvement-minded landowner, Cotton was interested in arboriculture, and he had published a treatise about fruit trees the year before Viator arrived in Beresford Dale.[82] In the early 1660s, Philip Kinder had ruefully observed that trees "are soe few, in ye Peake espetially, that had Judas been there, he would have repented, before he could have found one to act his execution": by establishing a wooded vista on the grounds of his estate, Cotton was—both literally and symbolically—attempting to tame the landscape of the Peak.[83] Cotton's cousin Sir Aston Cokain celebrated the new plantings at Beresford Hall and urged Cotton to likewise improve the grounds of the manor of Bentley, another of his family's properties:

> Your *Basford* [Beresford] house you have adorned much;
> And *Bently* hopes it shortly shall be such:
> Think on't; and set but *Bentley* in repair,
> To both those *Basfords* you will show y'are Heir.[84]

In these lines, Cokain explicitly links Cotton's "adorn[ment]" of the grounds of Beresford with his identity as the lineal "Heir" of his father's estates: Cotton's nascent woodland exists as both a fashionable exercise in landscape gardening and as a symbol of Cotton's stewardship of his family tree. Extending this project of elite display, Piscator Junior draws Viator's attention to the bowling green that Cotton had created on his property, a carefully contrived expanse of level ground and good turf that likewise exhibits Cotton's genteel "improvement" of the natural condition of the Peak's landscape.[85]

Piscator Junior's exertion of control within the boundaries of his estate also shapes his interactions with his new guest at Beresford Hall. When the travelers reach the front door of Cotton's country house, Piscator Junior tries to reset their strained relationship by again taking charge of Viator. This time, however, instead of serving as Viator's local guide through the wilds of the Peak,[86] Piscator Junior now performs his role as magnanimous lord of the manor and ceremoniously greets his guest: "Now permit me after all your pains and dangers to take you in my arms, and to assure you, that you are infinitely welcome" (182). Viator initially seems to respond with equal courtesy—"I thank you Sir, and am glad with all my heart I am here"—but then impolitely qualifies his response by noting that he is delighted to arrive at Beresford Hall only because "in down right truth, I am exceeding weary" (182). Still traumatized by his experience of the topography of the Peak, Viator cannot dutifully behave as a courteous guest at Piscator Junior's home.

Cotton's alter ego initially remains gracious in response to Viator's discourtesy. His guest has, Piscator Junior remarks sympathetically, "take[n] a troublesom Journey into an ill Country" only to humor his host, but Viator will now be rewarded by living like Piscator Junior himself—as a gentleman (182). When Viator first caught sight of Beresford Hall, Piscator Junior introduced the house as his guest's "Inn, for want of a better" (181)—an especially self-deprecating comment given the notoriously miserable conditions at commercial accommodation in the Peak—but it immediately becomes apparent that Beresford Hall affords a much more civilized existence than any seventeenth-century inn. Suddenly we realize that an invisible retinue of servants has leapt into action. Glasses of "good Sack" instantly materialize when the travelers arrive at Beresford Hall, and Piscator Junior directs some of his men to set the table and give Viator "a light supper" while others make up the bed in Beresford Hall's VIP suite, "my Father *Waltons* Chamber"

(182): Viator will have the honor of staying in the same room always occupied by Izaak Walton when he visits Cotton's home. Decades previously, we recall, as a customer at a Hertfordshire alehouse with more guests than beds, Viator had bunked with Piscator;[87] now, as a guest staying at Piscator Junior's country house in the Peak, Viator sleeps alone in Walton's own bed. Viator thus relives the pattern of the life-changing fishing trip he took during the interregnum—but as the guest of a landed gentleman, Viator enjoys a much more luxurious existence at Beresford Hall in 1676 than he had experienced as a paying customer at Bleak Hall in 1653.

The service at Bleak Hall likewise pales by comparison with Viator's experience at Cotton's country house. Whereas Viator's first meal at Bleak Hall had revealed Piscator's prowess at chub cookery, his first meal at Beresford Hall is notable for the quality of service that Piscator Junior commands. No sooner have the travelers drunk their revivifying sack than their food appears. Piscator Junior urges his guest, "Come Sir fall to then, you see my little supper is always ready when I come home," to which invitation Viator replies, "That your Meal is so soon ready is a sign your Servants know your certain hours, Sir; I confess I did not expect it so soon" (182). The next morning, Piscator Junior again draws attention to his servants' expert anticipation of his needs. After Piscator Junior asks Viator what he'd like to eat and drink, Viator replies, "For Breakfast I never eat any, and for Drink am very indifferent; but if you please to call for a Glass of Ale, I'm for you" (183). No summons is necessary, however: a servant has already appeared bearing Viator's liquid breakfast (183).[88] Piscator Junior quickly explains that his servants only seem to be telepathic: "Well *Sir*, You see the Ale is come without Calling; for though I do not know yours, my people know my diet, which is always one Glass so soon as I am drest, and no more till Dinner [at midday], and so my Servants have served you" (183). Although in Walton's text Piscator commands the skills of the Hostess of Bleak Hall, the members of Piscator Junior's attentive, unobtrusive entourage provide an inarguably higher quality of service to their master and his guest.

Servants were "important accoutrements of rank" in seventeenth-century England, and the quality of a gentleman was reflected by the behavior of his retinue, the members of which ideally should "[yield] him a blind obedience."[89] By emphasizing that he commands such exemplary attendants, Piscator Junior underscores his elite social status—and the first readers of Cotton's treatise would have found the excellence of Piscator Junior's household staff all the more admirable since residents of the Peak were stereotypically regarded as "uncouth semi-barbarians."[90] Even the pattern of Piscator Junior's meals reflects a patrician identity that transcends the regional setting of Beresford Hall: Philip Kinder observed that in the Peak, whereas a "Peasant" would eat four meals daily and "Moorelanders" would dine seven times per day (both schedules always including breakfast), "For Diett the Gentrie [take] after the southern mode, two state meales a day, with a bitt in the Buttery to a morneings draught."[91] Thus like the wooded approach to his house and bowling green, Piscator Junior's highly skilled, well-trained servants—and the schedule of the meals they provide for their master and his guest—display Charles Cotton's genteel ability to civilize the "naturel rudeness" of the Peak's hoi polloi within the boundaries of his family's estate.[92]

The elite social relations underpinning life at Beresford Hall likewise structure the fishing lessons that Piscator Junior conducts for his guest. After Viator drinks the glass of ale that has appeared as if by magic, he and Piscator Junior walk for the first time to the site of their angling tutorials. As we have already seen, in Izaak Walton's treatise the timing and location of Viator's halieutic lessons were largely determined by environmental happenstance: Piscator, ever the opportunist, took advantage of intermittent rainfall (and the shelter conveniently provided by a tall hedge or a sycamore tree) to instruct his pupil at length about the art of angling.[93] At Beresford Hall, by contrast, it never rains during the course of Cotton's narrative; indeed, the weather is so "delicate" on Viator's first morning at Piscator Junior's home that he has to agree with his host that "the Sun shine[s] as bright" in the Peak as in the "Southern Countries" of England (184, 183). Cotton, yet again following Walton's "*own Method*" (169), certainly capitalizes on the weather in his narrative but not as a structuring principle of his characters' angling tutorials; instead, Cotton uses the unexpected sunshine to compel Viator to reconsider his opinion of the Peak. Continuing the comedy of manners with which Cotton's narrative begins, Piscator Junior deliberately exploits the hierarchy of the host-guest relationship to make Viator squirm a bit: "I expect you should raise all the exceptions against our Country you can," he says, causing Viator to fib abashedly, "Nay *Sir*, do not think me so ill natur'd, nor so uncivil, I only made a little bold with it last night to divert you, and was only in jest" (183). Piscator Junior, giving Viator a dose of his own tactless medicine, briskly corrects his guest: "You were then in as good earnest as I am now with you: but had you been really angry at it, I could not blame you: For, to say the truth, it is not very taking at first sight" (183). This project of forcing Viator to look again at the Peak and reassess his "first sight" of the region will continue in tandem with the official curriculum of Piscator Junior's angling tutorials.

Whereas in Walton's narrative, Viator learned about fishing *en plein air*, his tuition at Beresford Hall takes place indoors. Moreover, Piscator Junior chooses the perfect classroom space for Viator's continuing education course: the fishing house that Charles Cotton recently built beside the River Dove. Early in Cotton's narrative, when Piscator Junior was trying to persuade Viator to visit him, it was Piscator Junior's description of the fishing house that convinced Viator to change his itinerary: "I will tell you that my House stands upon the margin of one of the finest Rivers for Trouts, and grayling in *England*; that I have lately built a little Fishing House upon it, dedicated to Anglers, over the door of which you will see the two first Letters of my Father *Walton's* name and mine twisted in *Cypher*" (175). Thus on his first full day at Beresford Hall, Viator bounces out of bed early in the morning, impatient to begin his angling "Lesson" because, as he tells Piscator Junior, "I long to see the little Fishing-house you spoke of" (183). Cotton's charming fishing lodge consisted of one square room, the "finely wainscoted" interior space of which was dominated in the 1670s by a "Marble Table" (184). The facade of the fishing house featured two windows on either side of a rounded doorway flanked by Tuscan pilasters, and the entire structure was topped by a pyramidal slate roof. The intertwined initials of Charles Cotton and Izaak Walton were engraved on the doorway's keystone, and above this ornament was inscribed the date "1674" and the motto "PISCATORIBUS SACRVM" (Dedicated to Fishermen). This inscription, along with the building's classicism, suggests that Cotton wittily designed the structure as a temple, a self-consciously erudite display of genteel conspicuous consumption anticipating the outbreak of follies on English estates in the eighteenth century.[94]

In Part II of *The Compleat Angler*, as Viator and his host prepare to descend the path that leads from Beresford Hall to the fishing house for the first time, Piscator Junior pauses so his guest can appreciate the prospect. "But look you *Sir*, now you are at the brink of the Hill, how do you like my River, the Vale it winds through like a Snake, and the scituation of my little Fishing-house?" Cotton's alter ego queries his guest (184).[95] Here again, Piscator Junior insists that Viator re-view his surroundings to appreciate the amenities of the Beresford estate, and his repeated first-person possessive pronouns emphasize Piscator Junior's status as the owner of the property that the men are admiring. The parity that Cotton's reiterated "my" establishes between the outbuilding ("my little Fishing-House") and the Dove ("my River") emphasizes that Piscator Junior's rights as a property owner encompass both the man-made and natural features of the scene, since his ownership of the riverbank gave Cotton property and fishing rights in the adjacent river as well.[96] Viator demonstrates that he is learning how to behave like a courteous houseguest by praising his host's estate as "all very fine" and his fishing lodge as "a neat building" before contemplating the Latin inscription that surmounts the doorway: "*Piscatoribus sacrum*. Why then I perceive I have some Title here, for I am one of them [i.e., fishermen], though one of the worst" (184). Viator's humorously self-deprecating claim of having "Title"—legal right of possession[97]—to the fishing house further flatters Piscator Junior by using the lens of property ownership through which Cotton's alter ego regards and describes the landscape. Adopting his host's elite perspective on the grounds of Beresford Hall, Viator demonstrates that he is beginning to correct his "first sight" of the Peak.

As we survey the fishing house with Piscator Junior and his guest, we approach the emotional core of Cotton's treatise, and the social dynamics of the work become even more complex. The name "Piscator Junior" styles Cotton's protagonist as the son of Piscator,[98] but Piscator Junior ignores his fictional namesake in *The Compleat Angler* and instead refers repeatedly to "my Father *Walton*" (174). Viator, while likewise abandoning Walton's pseudonym in Cotton's text, instead uses the honorific "my Master *Walton*" (175): as Viator thus revives the title of "Master" with which he had referred to Piscator in *The Compleat Angler*, he also highlights the uniquely filial nature of Piscator Junior's relationship with Walton. Early in Cotton's narrative, when Viator first asks his opinion of Walton's angling manual, Piscator Junior cannot resist praising the author even more fulsomely than his book: "I must tell you further, that I have the happiness to know his person, and to be intimately acquainted with him, and in him to know the worthiest Man, and to enjoy the best, and the truest Friend any Man ever had: nay, I shall yet acquaint you further, that he gives me leave to call him Father, and I hope is not yet asham'd to own me for his adopted Son" (173). This passage develops the discourse of filiation with which Cotton frames his book: in his prefatory epistle, Cotton addresses Walton as "My most Worthy FATHER and FRIEND" and designates himself as Walton's "most affectionate Son and

Servant" (169), and in his own letter that he appended to the conclusion of Cotton's treatise, Walton responds in kind by declaring himself "*Your most affectionate Father and Friend*" (223). The Christian resonances of the figure of the fisherman that permeate *The Compleat Angler* are extended in these descriptions of Cotton as the master angler's "adopted Son," a title that evokes the discourse of male adoption in the epistles of St. Paul: "For as many as are led by the Spirit of God, they are the sons of God.... Ye have received the Spirit of adoption, whereby we cry, Abba, Father" (Rom. 8:14–15).[99] The discourse of father-son relationships in Cotton's treatise thus richly develops the trope of filiation central to the social bonds depicted by Walton in *The Compleat Angler*.

Charles Cotton first documented his friendship with Izaak Walton in the commendatory verse he wrote in 1672–73 for Walton's *Lives*. In this poem, Cotton repeatedly calls Walton his "friend": the poem's title refers to "my Old, and most Worthy Friend, Mr. IZAAK WALTON," and later in the body of the poem, Cotton replaces the neutral possessive "*my Friend*" with more emotive noun phrases so that Walton becomes "*my dear friend*" and "*the best friend, I now, or ever knew.*"[100] As the poem unfolds, Cotton's friendship with Walton thus seems to intensify; nonetheless, throughout the text Cotton reserves the name "father" for his biological sire, Charles Cotton the Elder. Cotton depicts his father, John Donne, Sir Henry Wotton, and Walton as linked by intertwined ties of friendship that will transcend the grave, thanks to the commemorative power of Walton's biographies:

> *How happy was my Father then! to see*
> *Those men he lov'd, by him he lov'd, to be*
> *Rescu'd from frailties, and mortality.*
> ....
> *And, even, in their flowry Characters,*
> *My Fathers grave, part of your Friendship shares:*
> *For, you have honour'd his in strewing theirs.* (25–27, 37–39)

Like Beresford Hall, Cotton inherited his friendship with Izaak Walton from his father, and Cotton here honors his father by praising Walton. Yet at the end of the poem, Cotton pivots decisively away from his identity as his father's son to consider only his relationship with Walton, declaring that "*I ask no more of Fame, / Nor, other Monument of Honour claim, / Then that, of your* true Friend, *t'advance my name*" (121–23). The end point of the affective arc that structures this text—the shift in the poet's focus from Charles Cotton père to Izaak Walton—becomes the emotional foundation of Cotton's angling treatise: despite his status as a hereditary landowner in a patrilineal society, Piscator Junior never mentions his father.[101] Developing Walton's complex portrayal of the Brotherhood of the Angle as a voluntary, nonbiological patriarchy, Cotton thus explores how he could transform his patrimony—the Beresford estate—into the basis of a new mode of identity as the adopted son of Izaak Walton.[102]

The anglers' transgressive discourse of filiation is most powerfully displayed on the keystone of Cotton's fishing temple. It is the "Cifer" over the door of the little building that particularly appeals to Viator. This graphic representation of the shared affection—for each other and for angling—that binds a retired artisan with a landed gentleman transforms Cotton's fishing temple into an enduring monument to the men's unlikely friendship. Piscator Junior earlier suggested the psychological symbolism of this lapidary sculpture when he explained to Viator how a man could gauge his standing with Walton: "my Father *Walton* will be seen twice in no Man's company he does not like, and likes none but such as he believes to be very honest men, which is one of the best Arguments, or at least of the best Testimonies I have, that I either am, or that he thinks me one of those, seeing I have not yet found him weary of me" (174). The disdain for ascribed status that shaped Walton's angling treatise also underwrote his personal relationships: rather than offer up knee-jerk deference to Cotton as his social superior, Walton esteems Cotton because he's a "very honest" man, and as Walton and Cotton embrace calligraphically over the door of the fishing temple, the cipher allows Cotton to exist forever in the approving "company" of his adopted father. Studying the little fishing house, Viator asks if "my Master *Walton*" has seen the engraved keystone, and in Piscator Junior's reply to his guest we hear Charles Cotton's heartfelt disappointment: "Yes he saw it cut in the stone before it was set up; but never in the posture it now stands: for the house was but building when he was last here, and not rais'd so high as the Arch of the dore, and I am afraid he will not see it yet; for he has lately writ me word he doubts his coming down this Summer, which I do assure you was the worst news he could possibly have sent me" (184). The tone of Piscator Junior's voice becomes increasingly anguished in this passage. We now realize it has been at least two years since Cotton's adopted "father" last visited Beresford Hall. Probably the letter that Walton "lately writ" to Cotton asking him to compose a fly-fishing treatise also contained the bad news that Walton would not be able to journey to the Peak in the summer of 1676. Did Walton's extended absence from Beresford Dale indicate a change in his attitude toward Piscator Junior? Had Izaak Walton become "weary" of Charles Cotton—best known for writing risqué poems[103]—because he no longer regarded him as a "very honest" man?

Walton himself registered the depth of emotion that pervades this part of Cotton's narrative. In a letter dated April 29, 1676, published with Part II of *The Compleat Angler*, Walton assures Cotton "that, though I be more than a hundred Miles from you, and in the eighty third Year of my Age, yet I will forget both, and next Month begin a Pilgrimage to beg your pardon, for, I would dye in your favour" (223). We do not know if Izaak Walton ever again visited Cotton's fishing house beside the River Dove. But as he prepared the final edition of his angling manual for publication in 1676, Walton transformed Cotton's lovingly designed cipher into the ornament that dominates the title page of Part II of *The Compleat Angler* (see fig. 4). Thus, like the experience of crossing the threshold of the little fishing temple in Beresford Dale, as we begin to read Cotton's fly-fishing treatise we enter a realm indelibly shaped by the author's friendship with Izaak Walton.

Charles Cotton's fishing lodge and its decorated keystone embody rival modes of identity, a contest between the imperatives of rank and the power of affect. Cotton himself called the fishing house "my Seat's best grace," aligning the little building unthreateningly with an elite worldview in which "property was the sole basis of identity."[104] Yet the libidinal economy represented by Cotton's angling lodge seems antithetical to the ideology symbolized by Beresford Hall itself. Viator finds the fishing temple—an architectural monument to Cotton's relationship with Walton—much more admirable than Beresford Hall: "I am the most pleased with this little house of any thing I ever saw," Viator declares to his host (184). The word "house" in the early modern period was richly multivalent, referring to lineage as well as human habitation,[105] and in Cotton's angling treatise Piscator Junior seems much more emotionally invested in his relationship with Izaak Walton, as symbolized by his fishing temple, than in his lineal "house" as embodied by Beresford Hall.

THE COMPLEAT ANGLER.

Being Inſtructions how to angle for a TROUT or GRAYLING in a clear Stream.

PART. II.

Qui mihi non credit, faciat licet ipſe periclum: Et fuerit ſcriptis æquior ille meis.

LONDON,
Printed for *Richard Marriott*, and *Henry Brome* in St. *Paul's* Church-yard. MDCLXXVI.

FIGURE 4 | Title page of Charles Cotton, *The Compleat Angler, Part II* (1676). RB 120897, The Huntington Library, San Marino, California.

In seventeenth-century England, the conjugal family was understood as the foundation of society. Genealogy and rank were, in theory, inextricably linked, and lineage was thus vitally important in establishing a man's social identity. A responsible gentleman regarded himself as "a trustee for the handing on of blood, property and tradition" and strove to perpetuate his bloodline by procreating within marriage.[106] Although Charles Cotton's biography suggests he embraced this social code, in Cotton's angling manual, by contrast, his alter ego Piscator Junior apparently ignores his role as the steward of his family's pedigree. Like Walton's fishermen in *The Compleat Angler*, Piscator Junior seems to be a bachelor, and the dramatis personae of Cotton's treatise is even more scrupulously female-free than the social world of Walton's book: whereas Piscator conversed with both the Hostess of Bleak Hall and the two Hertfordshire milkwomen, Piscator Junior interacts solely with his all-male entourage of servants.[107] The makeup of Piscator Junior's fictional household thus diverges markedly from the real-life demographics of Beresford Hall. When Cotton wrote his fly-fishing treatise, five of his nine children were still alive: legal documents suggest that his four daughters were unmarried and thus still living at home, and Cotton's only surviving son, Beresford, would have been a teenager when Viator arrived in the Peak.[108] Cotton's first wife, Isabella Hutchinson (who was the mother of all his children) had died in 1669, and Cotton subsequently married his neighbor Mary Cromwell, dowager countess of Ardglass, in 1671.[109] Cotton, like his father, was perpetually skint—by the time Isabella died, he had twice been forced to sell some of his lands and often hid from his "Obstrep'rous Creditors" in caves near Beresford Hall—so Mary Cromwell's jointure of £1,500 per year must have provided Charles Cotton with a welcome new source of income.[110] Given his chronic money problems, Cotton's decision to build the fishing temple as a tribute to Walton was daring financially as well as ideologically, and the timing of the little building's construction suggests that Mary Cromwell's jointure bankrolled the project. Nonetheless, Cotton had to sell land yet again in 1675: it seems that Cotton's architectural celebration of his relationship with Izaak Walton (rather than with his new wife) was not only maritally insensitive but also financially ill-advised. In his fishing temple, as in his angling treatise, Charles Cotton thus uses (and risks) the Beresford estate to honor not the members of his own family but rather his "adopted" father Izaak Walton.

Yet from this point forward in Part II of *The Compleat Angler*, Cotton reasserts the social code of the landed estate to circumscribe the transgressive power of his relationship with Walton. Having registered his host's dismay that Walton has never seen the completed fishing temple, Viator, thoroughly shaken out of his self-absorbed social ineptitude by Piscator Junior's distress, attempts to comfort his host. "Men must sometimes mind their affairs to make more room for their pleasures," Viator advises his companion, "and 'tis odds [Walton] is as much displeas'd with the business, that keeps him from you, as you are that he comes not" (184). As he reassures Piscator Junior that Walton's absence does not indicate any waning of affection for his "son" at Beresford Hall, Viator forbears pointing out that no octogenarian could reasonably be expected to traverse the treacherous roads north of Ashbourne, much less Hanson Toot: such a line of thought would only provoke an even more upsetting acknowledgment of Walton's mortality. Viator then pivots to a less emotionally fraught topic and tries to give Piscator Junior time to compose himself by enthusing at detailed length about the fishing house. Viator's host, still struggling to contain his grief at Walton's long absence, finally pulls himself together: "Enough, *Sir*, enough, I have laid open to you the part where I can worst defend my self, and now you attaque me there. Come Boy set two Chairs, and whilst I am taking a Pipe of Tobacco, which is alwaies my Breakfast, we will, if you please, talk of some other Subject" (184–85). As he issues a command to a heretofore invisible servant, Piscator Junior masters his emotions by resuming his role as the lord of Beresford Hall.

This process of reframing Cotton's house and its environs as genteel property also catalyzes a transformation in Viator's attitude toward the Peak. In response to his host's request that they change the subject of their conversation, Viator drops his encomium of the transgressive little fishing lodge and instead recasts his relationship with both his host and his physical setting as homage to elite landownership: "I will not conceal from you," Viator declares to Piscator Junior, "that I am so far in love with you, your courtesie, and pretty Moreland Seat, as to resolve to stay with you long enough by Intervals (for I will not oppress you) to hear all you can say upon that Subject" (185). From this point forward in the narrative, Viator becomes an enthusiast of the Peak as experienced on the Beresford estate. At the end of his first tutorial in Cotton's fishing temple, Viator declares to his host that "in good earnest, if business would give me leave, and that if it were fit, I could find in my heart to stay with you for ever" (192). Aided by a servant whom Piscator Junior has armed with a landing net,[111] Viator's thoughts of eternal devotion become even more ardent after he catches his first fish in the River Dove. Gazing at the dusky, sixteen-inch-long grayling, Viator enthuses to Piscator Junior that he now likes the Dove "so well, that I am afraid you will be troubled with me once a year, so long as we two live" (196). Viator's concluding echo of the marriage ceremony in the Book of Common Prayer indicates the sincerity of his new, appreciative relationship with both his host and the landscape of the Peak.

We soon see further evidence of his transformed attitude when Viator, in a reprise of his previous day's journey to Beresford Dale, once again must navigate the region's slick, vertiginous terrain. As the two men continue to make their way along the banks of the Dove, Piscator Junior advises his guest that he "must venture over these slippery cobling stones" and then commends Viator's uncomplaining surefootedness: "believe me, Sir, there you were nimble or else you had been down" (197). A few moments later, after a servant calls the men to their midday meal, Piscator Junior explains that his guest can choose one of two paths back to Beresford Hall: Viator can either "climb this steep Hill before [him]" or take a relatively unchallenging but longer route (197). Viator—who less than a day earlier had been terrified by Hanson Toot—now breezily tells his host, "Nay, sure the nearest way is best; at least my stomach tells me so; and I am now so well acquainted with your Rocks, that I fear them not" (197). The next day, as Piscator Junior concludes his tutorials, he says that he hopes Viator will reside with him "a good while longer"; Viator replies that he cannot stay more than one additional day but promises to return to Beresford Dale as soon as possible: "if I live till *May* come twelve Month, you are sure of me again, either with my Master *Walton*, or without him" (222). Thanks to the amenities of Beresford Hall and its grounds, Piscator Junior has successfully "reconciled" Viator to the "Country" of the Peak. Although two decades earlier, Walton's master angler had steered him away from Theobalds and turned him into a poacher, Viator now embraces his new identity as a guest sportsman on Cotton's Beresford estate—an elite landscape to which Viator will happily return in the future regardless of Walton's own travel plans.

GENTLEMEN PREFER FLY-FISHING

By revising the ecosocial dynamics of Walton's treatise, Cotton innovatively portrays angling as an inextricable component of genteel life and identity.

Since the medieval period, private ponds had provided religious orders and landed households with fresh fish, and its rarity and cost ensured that pond-reared bream and pike functioned as status symbols in elite cuisine and gift-giving rituals.[112] Unlike falconry and the chase, however, angling had never been viewed as a sport fit for a king and his nobles. So while it was a truism in the early modern period that a man "cannot be a gentleman whyche loveth not hawkyng and hunting," he might not really be a gentleman if he loved recreational fishing.[113]

Prior to Cotton's fly-fishing treatise, English angling manuals were thus often suffused with status anxiety. The author of an early work in the genre deemed his fifteenth-century manuscript "a gentlymanly tretyse,"[114] a defensive claim both reiterated and challenged in 1496 when Wynkyn de Worde published the second edition of the *Boke of Saint Albans*, a compendium of guidebooks for gentlemen. Like the first edition published a decade earlier, the revised *Boke of Saint Albans* discusses hawking, hunting, and heraldry, but in the second edition, placed awkwardly between two halves of the *Boke*'s treatise on heraldry (which promises to explain "how gentylmen shall be knowen from ungentylmen"), de Worde inserted the first version of the *Treatyse of Fysshynge wyth an Angle* ever to appear in print.[115] As a transition from the first portion of the bisected heraldry manual, de Worde or his assistant added an editorial segue to the fishing treatise that boldly calls angling "one of the dysportes that gentylmen use."[116] The author of the *Treatyse* itself, however, addresses the issue of social rank circumspectly by making a novel argument about the superior mental-health benefits of angling as compared to other field sports. After trenchantly describing the unpleasant frustrations of venery, falconry, and fowling, the author of the *Treatyse* concludes that unlike angling, these recreations "ben so laborous and grevous that none of theym maye perfourme nor bi very meane that enduce a man to a merry spyryte: whyche is cause of his longe lyfe acordynge unto the sayd parable of Salamon" (188–89). By thus elevating the status of angling above traditionally elite blood sports, the *Treatyse* implicitly questions the tenets of a social hierarchy that promotes such deleterious activities.

But the text and physical structure of the *Boke of Saint Albans* soon undermines the *Treatyse*'s challenge to the sporting status quo. As the angling manual concludes, the editor of the *Boke* reenters the text. He explains that instead of publishing the *Treatyse* as a brief, standalone booklet, he has deliberately packaged it within a much larger (and thus much more expensive) volume to repel the wrong sort of reader: "And for by cause that this present treatyse sholde not come to the hondys of eche ydle persone whyche wolde desire it yf it were enpryntyd allone by itself & put in a lytyll plaunflet therfore I have compylyd it in a greter volume of dyverse bokys concernynge to gentyll & noble men. to the entent that the forsayd ydle persones whyche sholde have but lytyll mesure in the sayd dysporte of fysshyng sholde not by this meane utterly dystroye it."[117] By carefully barricading the *Treatyse* with manuals on purely genteel topics, the publisher of the *Boke of Saint Albans* will keep the text out of the hands of down-market riffraff who would certainly use the knowledge they gleaned from the *Treatyse* to devastate the sport of angling. Such defensive concern with the social standing of the angler would continue to shape early modern English discussions of recreational fishing for nearly two centuries: John Dennys fretted that his social superiors believed angling "is no pastime for a gentleman" and foresaw that his versified fishing manual could be accused of sharing "the hidden secrets of this Art" with "the vulgar sort," Piscator got heartburn from his uneasy relationships with virtuosos in *The Compleat Angler*, and Robert Venables observed that angling still had a bad reputation in Restoration England because of its "cheapnesse" since "nothing pass[es] for noble or delightful which is not costly."[118]

By ostentatiously rooting his practice of fly-fishing in his identity as a genteel landowner, Cotton transforms the ambiguous social status of early modern English angling. While they fish in the River Dove on the Beresford estate, Piscator Junior and Viator inhabit a world far from "the vulgar sort" that is governed by the same aristocratic values showcased at Theobalds in its heyday. Yet as Cotton thus eradicates the conflicted social dynamics of Walton's treatise, he also portrays a much less complex vision of the natural world. We do not find in Cotton's fly-fishing manual the numinous riparian ecosystems in which Walton's trespassing anglers taught us to search for both God and fish bait. As he approaches Beresford Dale, Viator is reassured to learn he is still in "*Christendom*" when he catches sight of a church (181), but St. Peter's in the Staffordshire village of Alstonefield—Cotton's parish church containing his family's pew—functions symbolically as an outpost of the Beresford estate, and Cotton's characters never again speak of religion.[119] And as a fly fisherman who does not need to continually ransack the landscape for invertebrates, Piscator Junior pays little attention to the interwoven communities of plants and animals adjacent to the River Dove. Instead, Cotton's alter-ego protagonist controls national and international networks of trade so he can magically dominate the natural world by using artificial flies—a method of angling that is much more "Gentile" (genteel) than any of Walton's modes of bait-fishing (215).

The tradition of fabricating flies that Charles Cotton would revolutionize in Part II of *The Compleat Angler* began with the publication of the *Treatyse* in 1496.[120] The author of the *Treatyse* explains how an angler can create a dozen different fake insects—each one fashioned around the shank of a steel fishing hook—that will entice trout and grayling.[121] Every artificial fly described in the *Treatyse* is intended to represent a particular species of insect, and the list of counterfeits is organized by the month, March through August, in which each fabricated fly will be most effective because its living prototype is active and abundant. Like all English angling authors before Cotton, Walton's own brief discussion of artificial flies was deeply indebted to the *Treatyse*, and Walton characterized the items in this influential catalog as "a Jury . . . likely to betray and condemn all the Trouts in the River" (255).

The man-made flies profiled in the *Treatyse* are ingenious miniature sculptures created with fibers and feathers. All twelve have "bodies" fashioned from wools—some probably natural in color, others certainly dyed—of various hues: "donne" (dun or greyish-brown), "blacke," "roddyd" (ruddy), "yelow," "dolke" (a misprint of "doske" meaning "dusky"), "tandy" (tawny), and "grene."[122] Six of the bodies are multicolor, an effect achieved either with contrasting overlays of fibers of various materials or through a technique later called "dubbing" in which filaments of wool or fur are dressed onto a waxed silk thread as a fly is tied.[123] The "wings" of the artificial flies in the *Treatyse* are crafted with feathers, and to make all twelve counterfeits a fly-tying angler would need plumage from multiple types of birds, both domesticated and wild: rooster, capon (a castrated cock), partridge, male mallard duck, Eurasian jay (*Garrulus glandarius*), peacock, and the common buzzard (*Buteo buteo*, a kind of hawk).[124] Using materials harvested from the bodies of mammals and birds to fashion replica insects with which to capture fish, the creator of fake flies exploits animals of the earth, air, and water alike.

From beginning to end, the *Treatyse*'s calendar of artificial flies repeatedly confuses the manufactured and the natural. Whereas later writers who recycle the catalog clearly specify that the flies are fabricated—Leonard

Mascall uses the term "made Flies," while Gervase Markham calls such lures "dead *Flyes*" and "*Baytes* living but in apparance onely"[125]—the *Treatyse* itself does not initially distinguish artificial lures from living insects: the author simply introduces the list of counterfeits by announcing, "Thyse ben the .xii. flyes wyth whyche ye shall angle" (222–23). The twelve human-made flies in the *Treatyse* thus initially seem as natural to the reader as to the fish they deceive. Moreover, the terse descriptions of the lures—which simply provide short lists of the materials used to fabricate each counterfeit and do not explain how to tie any of the flies—regularly confuse the bodies of creatures that have been scavenged for their feathers and fur with the artificial insects fabricated from these materials. For example, the author of the *Treatyse* describes a good fly for angling in March as having "the body of blacke woll: the wynges of the blackyst [mallard] drake: and the Jay under the wynge & under the tayle" (224–25). As soon as the jay enters this picture, perceptual confusion reigns: Are we to imagine the jay's body or the woolen body of the fabricated insect? Are the artificial fly's wings fashioned from both mallard plumage and feathers plucked from beneath a jay's wing and tail, or are jay feathers placed under the wing and tail of the fake fly?[126] The syntax of the description of the Black Leaper, an artificial fly effective in May, is likewise ambiguous: "the body of blacke wull & lappyd abowte wyth the herle [fiber of the shaft] of the pecok tayle: & the wynges of the redde capon w[ith] a blewe heed" (224–35). Does the "blewe he[a]d" belong to the fake fly or to the red capon from whose feathers the artificial insect's wings have been fashioned? And the *Treatyse*'s description of the artificial Drake Fly—"the body of blacke wull & lappyd abowte wyth blacke sylke: wynges of the mayle of the blacke drake wyth a blacke heed" (224–25)—similarly confounds the reader: the "blacke he[a]d" with which the description concludes could belong either to the fabricated insect or to the mallard drake that has also (unwillingly, of course) contributed some breast feathers ("mayle") to the angler's diminutive craft project. Thus the tortuous syntax of the *Treatyse*'s catalog of fake flies often refuses to privilege the products of human artifice over the nonhuman creatures whose bodies have been stripped for parts to fabricate the lures.

In Part II of *The Compleat Angler*, Charles Cotton changes many features of the catalog of artificial flies showcased in the *Treatyse*. Cotton was certainly not the first English angling writer to break with this influential precedent. In their discussions of artificial flies, both Thomas Barker (whose angling manual, as we have already noted, was initially published in 1651) and Robert Venables (a disgraced roundhead whose treatise *The Experienc'd Angler* first appeared in 1662) diverge significantly from the model that had been established in the *Treatyse* and copied by Mascall, Markham, and Walton. Barker provides the first detailed instructions about fly-tying published in English and essentially abandons the catalog format; nonetheless, Barker's brief discussion of different artificial flies introduces a new range of materials unmentioned in the *Treatyse*: gold thread, silver thread, fine crewel yarns, feathers from a plover's crest, and the wools (short hairs growing next to the skin) of the hog, the bullock, and the bear.[127] Venables likewise disregards the *Treatyse*'s catalog and instead presents extended, cogent directions for "How to make the artificial fl[i]e several wayes," including the first printed guidelines for "dubbing" a fly's body.[128] Venables concludes his advice by exhorting the Restoration angler to obtain a wide range of fly-tying supplies:

> That you the better counterfeit all sorts of flies, get furs of all sorts and colours you can possibly procure, as of Bears hair, Foxes, Cows, Hogs, Dogs, who next their bodies have a fine soft hair or fur, Moccado ends [warp (lengthwise) threads of a velvety wool or silk fabric], Crewels, and dyed wooll of all colours, with feathers of Cocks, Capons, Hens, Teals, Mallards, Widgeons, Pheasants, Partridges, the feather under the Mallard, Teal or Widgeons wings, and about their tails, about a Cock or Capons neck and tail, of all colours; and generally of all birds, Kite, Hickwall [European green woodpecker, *Picus viridis*], &c. that you may make yours exactly of the colour with the natural flie.[129]

Venables thus depicts the fly fisherman, equipped with "furs of all sorts" and the feathers "of all birds," as a kind of angling Noah.

Charles Cotton seems to have heeded Venables's counsel, for the technical core of his treatise resides in Cotton's meticulous instructions for creating artificial flies from a panoply of materials.[130] Unlike Barker and Venables, Cotton arranges the descriptions of his fake flies as a calendar, thus reviving the organizational template first used in the *Treatyse*. At the same time, however, Cotton demolishes the seasonal limitations the *Treatyse* had imposed on English fly-fishing: because grayling and trout can be caught in the River Dove with artificial flies during the six months that the

Treatyse (and Izaak Walton) had regarded as "dead," Cotton's fictionalized alter ego structures his list of counterfeit insects as a twelve-month calendar that begins in January (198). Piscator Junior thus frames his tutorials with Viator as a rejection of the authority of the *Treatyse*'s catalog of artificial flies—but in so doing, he must also reject Walton's restatement of that same list in *The Compleat Angler*. Piscator Junior acknowledges upfront that "my Father *Walton* tells us but of 12 Artificial flies only" and tactfully suggests that biogeographical difference explains this deficiency in his beloved friend's book: "And it may be in the Rivers about *London*, which I presume he has most frequented, and where 'tis likely he has done most execution, there is not much notice taken of many more: but we are acquainted with several others here (though perhaps I may reckon some of his by other names too) but if I do, I shall make you amends by an addition to his Catalogue" (198). Piscator Junior's remark that he will add "several" new items to the catalog that Walton derived from the *Treatyse* is a disingenuous understatement: by discussing a total of sixty-five artificial flies—"at one stroke exceeding" the total number of artificial flies previously described in English—Cotton renders the *Treatyse*'s catalog (and thus Walton's reiteration of it) obsolete.[131]

In the name of regionalism, Cotton also rejects the southern style of fly-dressing that Walton promotes. Piscator Junior asserts he will not fabricate flies "either of the same Dubbing, or fashion" as London-based anglers, who make fly bodies "both much bigger and longer" than does Cotton (198, 193). Fishermen (and, more importantly, trout) in the Peak regard London-style flies as "very unhandsom, and, in plain *English* . . . very unnatural and shapeless" (191). Piscator Junior tells Viator that he once "had one of those Flies given me by an honest Gentleman, who came with my Father *Walton* to give me a Visit, which (to tell you the truth) I hung in my parlour Window to laugh at: but *Sir*, you know the Proverb, *They who go to* Rome, *must do as they at* Rome *do*; and believe me you must here make your Flies after this fashion, or you will take no Fish" (193). Cotton thus softens his implicit criticism of Walton by portraying him as only an accessory to the crime of bringing a chunky London fly into Beresford Hall.[132]

Elsewhere, Cotton pays homage to the *Treatyse* and its influence so as to highlight the superiority of his own landmark work on fly-fishing. Like the author of the *Treatyse*, Cotton provides a separate description for every item in his list of artificial flies. And as in the *Treatyse*, each entry in Cotton's catalog includes information about the materials needed to fabricate a fake insect on the shank of a fishing hook. But Cotton goes far beyond his precursors by greatly expanding the variety of animals whose bodies provide his fly-tying materials. Despite this throng of creatures, however, Cotton's treatise depicts animals very differently than Walton's how-to manual. In *The Compleat Angler*, Walton often portrays animals that possess language, thoughts, and feelings: "*Cats talk and reason with one another*" (177), domesticated fish appear when called by their human owners (269), hounds understand "the language and meaning of one another . . . perfectly" (184–85), eels are "greedy" (318), frogs exhibit "*anger*" (284), pike are "melancholy" (283), and barbel "love" very swift and shallow streams (322). Cotton certainly could perceive such qualities of mind in animals—in a charming, deeply felt poem about his pet pine marten, Cotton writes that "my *Matty* does not want / Heart t'attack an Elephant. / Yet his Nature is so sweet, / Mice may nibble at his feet"[133]—but in his fly-fishing treatise, Piscator Junior pays unwavering attention only to the exploitable materiality of animals' bodies.

The menagerie present in Piscator Junior's catalog of fake flies includes a badger, bears, camels, cats, a coot, multiple types of dogs, a fox, hares, hogs, martens, ostriches, a polecat, a rabbit, a sable, squirrels, and a weasel. As we progress through his extensive roster of artificial flies, we come to regard Cotton as the Arcimboldo of fly-tying, an artistic genius who assembles tiny chimeras from an amazing array of natural materials. The first entry establishes many of the distinctive qualities of Cotton's catalog: "A red brown with wings of the Male [breast feathers] of a Malard almost white: the dubbing of the tail of a black long coated Cur, such as they commonly make muffs of; for the hair on the tail of such a Dog dyes, and turns to a red Brown, but the hair of a smoth coated Dog of the same colour will not do, because it will not dye, but retains its natural colour, and this flie is taken in a warm sun, this whole Month thorough" (199). As he does throughout his profiles of fabricated insects, Cotton here replaces the laconic vagueness of the *Treatyse*'s catalog entries with nuanced detail. Descriptors proliferate: the angler needs mallard feathers that are "almost white" and fur for the fly's body that is "red brown"; grayling and trout will find this fly especially enticing on a January day when there is "a warm sun." But in this entry, as in many of Piscator Junior's descriptions of artificial flies, it is fur that especially captures Cotton's imagination. As Cotton considers the optimal material with which to dub the fly's body, animals, types of fur, and narratives proliferate.[134]

Whereas Venables recommends that the fly-tying angler should stock up on the fur of "Dogs," Cotton is much more precise. Piscator Junior not only distinguishes between different dogs on the basis of the color and texture of their coats—the "black long coated Cur" as opposed to a "smoth coated Dog of the same colour"—but he also specifies the portion of the dog's body from which fur should be harvested (in this case, the animal's tail). And other stories about humans exploiting dogs' fur appear, partially submerged, in Cotton's description: artisans chemically alter the natural hue of canine fur while a cheap hand-warmer is fashioned from a dog's pelt, the latent pun of "dye/die" reminding us sotto voce how a dog becomes a muff.[135]

"No dog was safe from Cotton," remarks the angling historian Andrew Herd, noting how often canine fur appears in Piscator Junior's catalog of artificial flies.[136] A half dozen of Piscator Junior's dressings call for either brown or black "Spaniels furr," and it is only fitting that the spaniel—the quintessential hunting companion of the English landed elite—seems to have been Cotton's go-to dog when he was tying flies on his Beresford estate (199, 201, 203, 206, 209).[137] The greyhound—long regarded as "the best of the gentle kinde of houndes"—provides even more scope for Cotton to exercise his connoisseurship of dog fur.[138] As he describes how to create a "blew Dun," Piscator Junior provides painstakingly precise fur-harvesting instructions: "Take a small tooth comb, and with it comb the neck of a black Grey hound, and the down that sticks in the teeth, will be the finest blew, that ever you saw" (201).[139] The obsessive particularity that permeates this statement—the fineness of the comb, the mapping of the dog's body according to subtle variations in the hue and texture of its coat—reveals Cotton's powerful imaginative response to fur. In another catalog entry, similar dynamics bring Cotton's instructions to a narrative halt so Piscator Junior can deliver a mini-disquisition about hogs' hair: "the dubbing that should make this Flie, and that is the truest colour, is to be got of the black spot of a Hogs ear: not that a black spot in any part of the Hog will not afford the same colour; but that the hair in that place is by many degrees softer, and more fit for the purpose" (199). Cotton's fascination with the highly localized color and texture of an animal's coat likewise informs his descriptions of "the down of a Fox Cub, which is of an Ash colour at the roots, next the skin" and "the fur of a Hares neck, that is of the colour of Fearn, or Brackin" (202, 211). One fly for March requires "dubbing . . . of the bottom fur of a Squirrels tail," whereas another is "made of the roots of Camels hair" (201). His enthusiasm for distinctive textures and colors of fur also leads Cotton to forage in unlikely places for fly-tying materials: the body of the "Camel-brown Flie" is made with ox, cow, or goat hair that has been "pull'd out of the lime of a Wall," while the dubbing for a fly effective in the latter half of March "is to be had out of a Skinners Lime-pits, and of the hair of an abortive Calf, which the lime will turn to be so bright, as to shine like Gold" (211, 201).[140]

In other entries in his catalog, Cotton explains how one kind of fur must be combined with other materials to create multicolored fly bodies. Sometimes a desired coloration can be achieved by mixing fur with an animal-derived fabric: a "Flesh-flie" requires "the dubbing of a black Spaniels furre, and blew wool mixt" (209), the dubbing for "the great blew Dun" consists of "the bottom of Bears hair next to the roots, mixt with a little blew Camlet" (200),[141] the fly fisherman creates a "shel-flie" used in July with "the dubbing of yellow-green Jersey Wool, and a little white Hoggs hair mixt" (210), and the body of "a Harry-long-leggs" (a large crane fly) is "made of Bears dun [dull brown fur], and blew Wool mixt" (211). Piscator Junior fashions some fly bodies from the tail feathers of peacocks or ostriches (203, 199), while other dressings blend the fur of different species of animals: one fly used in September is "made of the black hair of a Badgers skin mixt with the yellow softest down of a sanded [sandy colored] Hog" (211), whereas a minute "Dun Gnat . . . is to be made of a mixt dubbing of Martins fur, and the white of a Hares scut [tail]" (199).[142] Sometimes the physical mixing of the bodies of different animals that Cotton regularly demands takes the form of surprising cross-species substitutions: the dubbing of a "bright brown" fly can be created "either of the brown of a Spaniel, or that of a Cows flanck" (201), whereas the black body of another tiny fly may be fashioned "either of the fur of a black water-Dog, or the down of a young black water-Coot" (201). All of Cotton's artificial flies sport "wings" made of feathers, and his most elaborate creations combine birds' plumage with fabrics, different furs, and decorative silk or metallic threads. The "Grey-Drake" (modeled on the adult female mayfly) entails "the Dubbing of the down of a Hogs bristles, and black Spaniels fur mixt, and ribb'd down the body with black silk, the whisks of the hairs of the beard of a black Cat, and the wings of the black grey feather of a Mallard" (206). Even more complicated, the dubbing of the "Artificial Green-Drake" requires "Camels hair, bright Bears hair, the soft down that is comb'd from a Hogs bristles, and yellow Camlet well mixt together . . . and ribb'd about with green silk, or rather yellow waxt with green-wax, the whisks of the tail of the long hairs of sables, or fitchet [the polecat, *Mustela putorius*], and the wings of the white grey feather of a Mallard dyed yellow" (206).

Repurposing pelage and plumage harvested from a dizzying variety of creatures, Charles Cotton thus creates tiny masterpieces of assemblage art. Piscator Junior sometimes foregrounds the elaborate artifice of his fake flies by naming them after the materials from which they are fabricated: a fly effective in May is "call'd the Peacock-flie" since its body is "made of a whirl of a Peacocks feather" (203), and Piscator Junior designates an entire group of his creations as "Hackles" (201) because their bodies are enwrapped with spirals of shiny feathers ("hackles") from the necks of cocks and capons.[143] But each of Cotton's diminutive composites is designed to represent a real insect, and like the author of the *Treatyse*, Piscator Junior usually refers to his fabricated flies as if they were living invertebrates instead of tiny sculptures of fur, feathers, and fibers carefully constructed on shafts of barbed steel. Cotton's alter ego thus styles himself as the creator of a diverse swarm of insects, including "the Thorn Tree Flie," "a little black Gnat," "the Horse-flesh Flie," "a white Gnat," "the Cow-Lady" (a ladybird beetle), "the Cow-turd flie," the "Stone-Flie," "the Owl-Flie," a "little flesh-flie," "the flying Ant, or Ant-flie," "a brown Gnat," "a green Grashopper," "a little dun Grashopper," "a Wasp-flie," "the Palm-flie" (an insect named for its resemblance to the spring-flowering willows colloquially called "palms"), and "a Harry-long-leggs" or crane fly (201–3, 207, 208–11). As Piscator Junior thus blurs the boundaries between his fabricated simulacra and the live insects they imitate, Cotton's angler assumes the roles of both God and Adam by simultaneously creating and naming his new pieces of handiwork.

Contrasting dynamics of rank and gender further distinguish Cotton's depiction of fly-tying from Walton's. In *The Compleat Angler*, Walton—a dyed-in-the-wool bait fisherman—portrays Piscator's knowledge of fly-fishing as secondhand information gleaned from other low-born men. Piscator says that in addition to Thomas Barker, he has obtained much of his information about fly-fishing from "an ingenuous brother of the Angle, an honest man, and a most excellent *Flie-fisher*" (255, 254): Walton thus transforms Leonard Mascall (the how-to-manual author who had died before Walton was born and from whose angling treatise Walton cribbed the catalog of artificial flies that had originated in the *Treatyse*) into a personal acquaintance. Although Walton, as we have seen, does not hesitate to portray his alter ego as a georgic fish-bait chef, he steadfastly avoids depicting Piscator as an artisan, and the only lure Piscator claims to use was fabricated not by himself but by a woman:

> I have (which I will shew to you) an *artificial Minnow*, that will catch a Trout as well as an *artificial Flie*, and it was made by a handsom Woman that had a fine hand, and a live *Minnow* lying by her: *the mould or body of the Minnow was cloth, and wrought upon or over it thus with a needle: the back of it with very sad French green silk, and paler green silk towards the belly, shadowed as perfectly as you can imagine, just as you see a Minnow; the belly was wrought also with a needle, and it was a part of it white silk, and another part of it with silver thred; the tail and fins were of a quill, which was shaven thin, the eyes were of two little black beads, and the head was so shadowed, and all of it so curiously wrought, and so exactly dissembled, that it would beguile any sharpe sighted Trout in a swift stream. And this Minnow I will now shew you,* (look here it is) *and if you like it, lend it you, to have two or three made by it, for they be easily carryed about an Angler, and be of excellent use; for note, that a large Trout will come as fiercely at a Minnow, as the highest mettled Hawk doth seize on a Partridg, or a Grey-hound on a Hare.* (247–48)

In this lengthy ekphrasis, Piscator celebrates his ability to transform the labor of "a handsom Woman" into his personal ownership of an object of breathtaking skill, artistry, and effectiveness. But just as Piscator supervises the Hostess's fish cookery rather than prepare meals himself at Bleak Hall, so too he will not risk his patriarchal standing by doing needlework, a normatively feminine activity in early modern England.[144] Piscator then further elevates his possession of this soft-sculpture minnow by comparing its use with the elite sports of hawking and hunting—and thus further dissociates the fabricated lure from any hint of Walton's own plebeian professional activities in the cloth trades.

By contrast, Charles Cotton's demiurgic fly-tying is an all-male activity that springs from and reinforces his identity as the squire of Beresford Hall. In Part II of *The Compleat Angler*, Piscator Junior tells Viator that he learned how to create artificial flies from "the best Flie maker" he has ever met, his "Kinsman" Henry Jackson of the Stanshope estate near Alstonefield (191):

although he cherishes and honors Walton as his angling "Father," Cotton traces his lineage as a fabricator of artificial flies not to the low-born Walton but to a genteel male blood-relative.[145] Cotton likewise structures his narrative to ascribe elite status to the practice of fly-tying. Angling writers previous to Cotton had paid little attention to the material infrastructure needed to fabricate flies. Markham gives advice about storage, observing that when you have followed his instructions (recycled from the *Treatyse*) to craft a bevy of flies, "you may keepe them in close boxes uncrushed, and they will serve you many yeeres."[146] But it is Cotton's foster father Izaak Walton who first describes a special flytier's man purse, a "*Magazin bag*" that contains different types of fur, feathers, and fibers (*Compleat Angler*, 111, 109)—an innovation perhaps reflecting Walton's personal knowledge of Cotton's own fly-tying kit. Having this receptacle "alwaies with him," Walton advises, the angler can "repair [to it] upon any occasion" and manufacture new flies most appropriate for the weather conditions he finds streamside at any given moment (109, 111).[147] In Cotton's fly-fishing treatise, Piscator Junior uses a similar holdall, but Cotton ensures that his alter ego's angling bag functions as a socially symbolic prop that proclaims his elite identity every time it appears.

Like food and drink at Beresford Hall, Piscator Junior's fly-tying pouch always enters Cotton's narrative accompanied by a manservant. Lecturing to Viator within the fishing temple, Piscator Junior opens the sixth chapter of Cotton's treatise with a command addressed to a previously invisible attendant: "Boy, come give me my dubbing bagg here presently" (192). Cotton's protagonist then addresses Viator: "and now Sir, since I find you so honest a man, I will make no scruple to lay open my Treasure before you" (192). Rather than a storehouse of merchandise, as implied by Walton's term "*Magazine-bag*,"[148] Piscator Junior instead describes the contents of his dubbing bag as "Treasure," evoking a more generalized vision of wealth, and a passage in Cotton's poem "The Angler's Ballad" suggests that Viator gazes into a "pouch" that is "stuft . . . / with wax, crewells, silks, hair, furs and feathers."[149] Despite the elite social force field of the fishing temple (further enhanced by the presence of Piscator Junior's servant), his host's huge trove of fly-tying materials shocks Viator into oafish incredulity: "Did ever any one see the like! What a heap of Trumpery is here! certainly never an Angler in *Europe* has his shop half so well furnisht, as you have" (192). Viator's derogatory, commercialized diction—"a heap of Trumpery" and a "shop"—portrays the lord of Beresford Hall as a dishonest retailer rather than the genteel custodian of wonderful "Treasure." In response, Piscator Junior deploys the language of connoisseurship to reestablish the elite aura of his cache of fly-tying materials: "You perhaps may think now, that I rake together this Trumpery, as you call it, for shew only, to the end that such as see it (which are not many I assure you) may think me a great Master in the Art of angling: but let me tell you here are some colours (as contemptible as they seem here) that are very hard to be got" (192). Churlish Viator has yet again forgotten that he is the guest of a landed gentleman: like a visitor to an aristocratic curiosity cabinet, he has been given privileged access to a display of rarities that signifies Piscator Junior's status as an angling virtuoso. But after he discovers that trout in the River Dove swarm to the lures his host has created, Viator belatedly gets with the patrician fly-tying program. Insisting that Viator must try his own hand at fabricating a fly, Piscator Junior yet again addresses the ever-present but usually invisible manservant who carries his fly-tying pouch: "Give me that Bag again, *Sirrah*" (193). Cotton thus emphasizes that Piscator Junior's possession and use of fly-tying materials are inextricable from his social role as the master of Beresford Hall.

A godlike creator of dozens of different artificial flies, Piscator Junior commands the natural resources of the entire globe. Taken together, the entries of Cotton's catalog of flies function as a synecdochic menagerie, a grouping of exotic creatures that symbolized elite power during the seventeenth century. Both before and after the civil wars, the Stuarts displayed their princely command of the natural world by collecting rare birds and animals: whereas Oliver Cromwell's wife pastured cows in St. James's Park during the interregnum, Charles II restored not only the monarchy but also his grandfather's aviaries and menagerie.[150] John Evelyn marveled after the Restoration that St. James's Park was once again "stored with infinite flocks of severall sorts of ordinary, & extraordinary Wild foule," and he argued that all princely gardens should likewise contain displays of "curious Birds," a model Evelyn himself emulated by installing an aviary on the grounds of his own home.[151] As a flytier, Charles Cotton extends such elite ownership and display of birds into the material culture of angling. The sheer variety of wild and exotic birds whose feathers Cotton has amassed suggests the ostentatious abundance of the aristocratic Restoration aviary, while the feathers of peacocks, ostriches, and roosters that adorn many of Piscator Junior's artificial flies embody aristocratic symbolism even more explicitly.

Six of Cotton's artificial flies feature peacock feathers, including two different simulacra that Cotton names "the Peacock-flie" (203, 209). Native to India, peacocks' shimmering tail feathers had long adorned genteel English accessories and curiosity cabinets, and Charles II's restored aviaries in St. James's Park predictably included this species.[152] Like his grandfather, Charles II also kept ostriches, which had become even more chic than peacocks: elaborate ladies' fans were made with ostrich feathers, and fashionable men (including the king) adorned their hats with expensive ostrich plumes, which could be dyed, combined with other types of feathers, or "encrusted in gold or silver spangles."[153] Cotton uses ostrich feathers to create two of his flies, including a "black Flie" whose ostrich-feather body is "rib'd with silver twist" (208), a pattern that demonstrates how Cotton's lures regularly combine zoological materials with opulent fibers of silk, gold, and silver. But it is the cock feathers featured in most of Cotton's artificial flies that would have been most personally emblematic, for each hackle feather stored in Cotton's dubbing bag evoked his blood relationship with the Cokain family, whose coat of arms featured three cocks.[154]

The sheer number of animals whose fur adorns Cotton's artificial flies likewise bespeaks the angler's genteel domination of the natural world. Piscator Junior's dubbing bag functions as the flytier's answer to King Charles I's "store" of furs from which the king's skinner would obtain pelts to line and decorate the monarch's clothes.[155] As with the birds that populate his fly-tying instructions, the appearance of certain mammals further enhances the patrician symbolism of Cotton's catalog of artificial flies. Piscator Junior's "black blew Dun," for example, requires "the dubbing of the furre of a black Rabbet mixt with a little yellow" (210): not only were rabbits regarded as a suitable quarry for elite hunters, but black rabbit fur was a luxury material used in aristocratic garments.[156] James I kept camels at his menagerie at Theobalds, and the pelts of sables (*Martes zibellina*), which were imported from Russia, yielded a very expensive fur favored by royals and members of the nobility.[157] The spaniel, greyhound, fox, and hare all evoke the hunt, as does the marten, which became an increasingly popular quarry for early modern hunters as deer populations dwindled.[158] But the most thematically freighted material in Cotton's catalog is the bear's fur with which Piscator Junior fabricates multiple flies. Extinct in Britain long before the seventeenth century, bears were imported from Europe to be baited for entertainment during the early modern period. Some English aristocrats kept their own bears, and James I added a new twist to the spectacle of animal-baiting by setting bears against lions from his menagerie in the Tower of London.[159] Charles Cotton's identity as a landed gentleman was symbolically rooted in this elite early modern practice of ursine torture. Cotton's maternal grandmother was a Beresford, and it was from their relationship with this family that Charles Cotton the Elder and his namesake son gained possession of the Beresford estate on the banks of the River Dove. The Beresford family's coat of arms featured a captive bear bridled for baiting—muzzled, collared, and chained—rearing up on its hind legs, and this lineal symbol was displayed both above the front door and in some of the windows of Beresford Hall.[160] Whereas Wynkyn de Worde had defensively sandwiched the down-market *Treatyse* and its list of artificial flies between two discussions of heraldry, Cotton instead hardwires the values, material culture, and representational codes of the landed elite into his own practice as a genteel fly fisherman.

Through Cotton's innovative mode of fly-tying georgic, a country grandee expands his domination of the creatures of the air and land into his conquest of the creatures of the aquatic realm as well. The multum in parvo materiality of Cotton's artificial flies—painstakingly fashioned composites of zoological fragments, luxurious textiles, and precious metals—positions them within a long English tradition of elite bricolage: the Earl of Leicester gave Queen Elizabeth I "a fanne of white fethers, sett in a handell of golde; the one side thearof garnished with dyamondes and rubyes[,] and the backe syde a white beare and twoe perles hanging, a lyon ramping with a white moseled beare at his foote"; Robert Peake's portrait of the teenaged Prince Henry features a beaver hat ornamented with ostrich feathers and a bejeweled hatband; and the inventories of Charles I's clothing compiled for the postmortem sale of his possessions included a gown made "of sad Coloured sattin lined with furre and edged with sable tayles."[161] In Alexander Pope's *Rape of the Lock*, this tradition of patrician luxuries fashioned from the bodily fragments of disparate animals famously reappears on Belinda's dressing table, where "The tortoise . . . and elephant unite, / Transformed to combs, the speckled, and the white."[162] The death of animals is occluded in all these hybrid objects, which simultaneously display and deny their owners' command of global networks of environmental exploitation, trade, and commerce. Before he and Viator arrive at Beresford Hall, Piscator Junior repeatedly brags about the Peak's imbrication in national and international economies even as he celebrates the region's unique geography. When the travelers have a drink at an Ashbourne inn, Piscator Junior assures Viator that "you may drink worse *French-wine* in many Taverns in *London*, than they have sometimes at this House" (176), and, as we have already noted, he suggests that roads in the Peak are so difficult to navigate because they are full of "loaden Horses" transporting "Malt, Wool, Lead, and Cole" (171, 173). Such explicit acknowledgment of trade, industry, and agriculture vanishes, however, when Cotton's characters reach the Beresford estate. In Part II of *The Compleat Angler*, Cotton thus replaces Walton's transgressive depiction of the plebeian angler as a trespassing poacher with a mystified display of the aristocratic power of the genteel fly fisherman who transforms Beresford Hall into angling's answer to Theobalds.

Charles Cotton's poem "The Retirement" functions as a coda to Part II of *The Compleat Angler*, and it concludes with Cotton hoping that he might "*Contented live*" to "*sixty full years old*" in Beresford Dale beside his "*beloved Nymph fair* Dove" (227, 226). Cotton's life as a country gentleman fishing on the banks of the River Dove was not to endure, however. In dire financial straits yet again, Cotton was forced to sell Beresford Hall in 1681, and he passed away in London half a dozen years later at the age of fifty-six. Cotton's only surviving son, Beresford, would later die unmarried and childless, and in 1856, Beresford Hall was demolished.[163] But Charles Cotton's diminutive fishing house still stands today at the north end of Beresford Dale on "a kind of *Peninsula*" in the River Dove (184), with Cotton and Izaak Walton still locked in a calligraphic embrace over the door, and this architectural monument to Cotton's relationship with his "most Worthy FATHER and FRIEND" (169) is now protected for posterity by the British government.[164] Modern-day Viators may still follow Piscator Junior's path to Beresford Dale on the narrow, winding, vertiginous roads of the Peak, and the current owner of the Beresford estate will allow fee-paying visitors to take a break from catching trout in the River Dove to eat a sack lunch, tie some flies, and read Cotton's angling treatise in his little fishing temple. We now remember Charles Cotton not as the seventeenth-century scion of an elite Staffordshire family but as the unlikely soulmate of an elderly linendraper who loved both angling and the fly-fishing squire of Beresford Hall in equal measure. Thomas Westwood's tribute to the authors of the final edition of *The Compleat Angler* has proven prophetic: "While rivers run, shall those twin names endure— / WALTON and COTTON linked for evermore."[165]

Epilogue

Haunted by Walton

"The bastard doesn't even know how to spell 'complete.'"[1] In the opening pages of Norman Maclean's autobiographical novella *A River Runs Through It*, the narrator's brother Paul thus hammers a nail into the coffin of Izaak Walton, putting an orthographic spin on the derogatory opinion of Walton previously expressed by his father, a Presbyterian minister and avid fly fisherman raising his two sons in early twentieth-century Montana. As Maclean observes in his fictionalized family memoir, the men in his household believed "there was no clear line between religion and fly fishing," so Reverend Maclean objected to Walton on purely theological grounds: "'Izaak Walton,' he told us when my brother was thirteen or fourteen, 'is not a respectable writer. He was an Episcopalian and a bait fisherman'" (1, 5). Although Paul was three years younger than his brother Norman, Maclean's narrator admits that Paul "was already far ahead of me in anything relating to fishing and it was he who first found a copy of *The Compleat Angler* and reported back to me" (5). Not only is the Episcopalian worm drowner a deficient speller, Paul complains, but Walton also "has songs to sing to dairymaids" (5).[2] After reading *The Compleat Angler* for himself, the teenaged Norman (who in real life would write his PhD dissertation on lyric poetry and spend his career as an English professor at the University of Chicago) dares to disagree with Paul: "Some of those songs are pretty good" (5). Dismissing his elder brother's appreciation of Walton's artistry, Paul scoffs, "Whoever saw a dairymaid on the Big Blackfoot River?" and then imagines punishing Walton for his sins:

> "I would like," he said, "to get him for a day's fishing on the Big Blackfoot—with a bet on the side."
> The boy was very angry, and there has never been a doubt in my mind that the boy would have taken the Episcopalian money. (5)

Paul and Norman's debate about Walton constitutes only the second time in the narrative that we hear the brothers' words directly. Several pages earlier, both youngsters respond in unison to their father's weekly catechism: "'What is the chief end of man?' And we answered together so one of us could carry on if the other forgot, 'Man's chief end is to glorify God, and to enjoy Him forever'" (1). Maclean thus differentiates the brothers' voices for the first time when Paul and Norman argue about *The Compleat Angler*.[3] Maclean's narrator underlines the thematic importance of this dialogic episode, emphasizing how the teenagers' disagreement over Walton reveals immutable truths about Paul's temperament and worldview that will forever mystify his elder brother:

> Since one of the earliest things brothers try to find out is how they differ from each other, one of the things I remember longest about Paul is this business about his liking to bet. He would go to county fairs to pretend that he was betting on horses, like the men, except that no betting booths would take his bets because they were too small and he was too young. When his bets were refused, he would say, as he said of Izaak Walton and any other he took as a rival, "I'd like to get that bastard on the Blackfoot for a day, with a bet on the side."
> By the time he was in his early twenties he was in the big stud poker games. (6)

These memories foretell the circumstances of Paul's demise that Maclean tersely chronicles near the end of his story. An astonishingly talented fly fisherman who was also addicted to gambling, fighting, alcohol, and stubborn self-reliance, Paul was murdered at the age of thirty-two.

In *A River Runs Through It*, Maclean counterpoints the tragic arc of Paul's life against the laughable misadventures of Norman's brother-in-law Neal. Like Paul, Neal is a prodigal son whose family strives but fails to understand and help him. When Neal, an aspiring professional tennis player now living in California, returns home to Montana for a visit, he insists that he wants to go fishing with the Maclean brothers—especially Paul. Norman breaks the bad news to his brother, and the final clause of Paul's response evokes their father's condemnation of Walton: "I won't fish with him. He comes from the West Coast and he fishes with worms" (9). As Paul continues to denounce Neal, he reiterates Reverend Maclean's damning description of Walton—"he's a bait fisherman"—and then scornfully predicts how Neal will behave: "All those Montana boys on the West Coast sit around the bars at night and lie to each other about their frontier childhood when they were hunters, trappers, and fly fishermen. But when they come back home they don't even kiss their mothers on the front porch before they're in the back garden with a red Hills Bros. coffee can digging for angleworms" (10). To appease Norman's mother-in-law, however, Paul agrees to take Neal fishing, and every time he tries to go fishing with the Macleans (even when he's forgotten to bring a rod), Neal enters the narrative clutching a Hills Brothers coffee can filled with nightcrawlers. His makeshift bait container, a scarlet letter denoting the moral turpitude of the bait fisherman, becomes "Neal's special badge of inadequacy," and Neal's sidekick, the local sex worker Old Rawhide, styles herself the keeper of Neal's bright red binky, protectively insisting that "Buster always likes to have it with him" (70).[4] His identity inextricably bound up with this transitional object, Neal ultimately assumes its physical form: his drunken nap au naturel on a sand bar in the Blackfoot River leaves Neal so badly sunburned from head to toe that he turns the same color as his shameful Hills Brothers coffee can.

Before Neal receives his just deserts, however, Maclean associates him even more closely with that degenerate patriarch of bait fishermen, Izaak Walton. Shortly after arriving at his family's home, Neal drinks "3-7-77" whiskey with Norman in Black Jack's Bar and tells his terrestrial version of a fish story:[5]

> Neal had trailed an otter and her pups up to Rogers Pass, where the thermometer officially recorded 69.7 degrees below zero. While he

trailed this otter, I tried to trace its lineage from his description of it. "I had a hard time following it," he said, "because it had turned white in the winter," so it must have been part ermine. After he treed her, he said, "She stretched out on the lower branch ready to pounce on the first deer that came along," so she had to have a strain of mountain lion in her. She also must have been part otter, because she was jokey and smiled at him. But mostly she was 3-7-77, because she was the only animal in western Montana besides man that had pups in the winter. "They snuggled up right in my shirt," he said, showing us a shirt under his two red-white-and-blue sweaters. (33)

Neal does exactly what Paul says expat Montanans do when they transmogrify into Californians: he stores angleworms in a coffee tin and tells outrageous lies about his youthful exploits as an outdoorsman. But under the influence of 3-7-77, Neal also relives the story told by his bait-fishing prototype Izaak Walton: the otter that Neal supposedly pursued across the Continental Divide in the Rocky Mountains is a twentieth-century American reincarnation of the female otter hunted by Piscator near Amwell Hill in seventeenth-century Hertfordshire, and the otter pups that curled up against Neal's chest—which allow Neal to draw attention to his effete tennis sweaters as he tells his whopper—are descendants of the baby otter that Piscator saved from the huntsmen so he could tame it.[6] Within the framework of intertextual allusion that Maclean has established, we can thus trace the lineage of Neal's otter back to *The Compleat Angler*.

But Neal's mythical otter also inhabits an intratextual ecosystem populated by comedic animals. Just as Neal functions as Paul's doppelgänger, so Neal's tall tale about a "jokey" otter parallels Paul's earlier story about an uncanny jackrabbit. Before Neal appears in Maclean's narrative, Paul tells Norman about a car wreck he had recently on his way home from a solitary day of fishing on the Blackfoot River:

> It was moonlight, he was tired and feeling in need of a friend to keep him awake, when suddenly a jackrabbit jumped on to the road and started running with the headlights. . . . He drove, he said, with his head outside the window so he could feel close to the rabbit. With his head in the moonlight, his account took on poetic touches. The

vague world of moonlight was pierced by the intense white triangle from the headlights. In the center of the penetrating isosceles was the jackrabbit, which, except for the length of his jumps, had become a snowshoe rabbit. The phosphorescent jackrabbit was doing his best to keep in the center of the isosceles. . . . My brother said, "I don't know how to explain what happened next, but there was a right-angle turn in this section-line road, and the rabbit saw it, and I didn't." (14)

The moment he abandons the jackrabbit, Paul runs off the road and nearly totals his car. Maclean's narrator is unsure how to interpret his brother's anecdote, "wondering whether I had been told a little human-interest story with hard luck turned into humor or whether I had been told he had taken too many drinks and smashed hell out of the front end of his car" (14).

The parallels between these two fanciful tales of communion with wild animals emphasize how Neal and Paul mirror each other. Not only are both otters and jackrabbits native to Montana, but the behavior and appearance of Neal's otter also underscore its kinship with Paul's jackrabbit. Both fictive animals are followed across rugged terrain by their drunken pursuers, and as they flee, both animals hybridize, losing their natural dark-brown coats and assuming instead the protective winter coloration of a different species: in addition to morphing into a cougar, Neal's otter becomes "part ermine" (a short-tailed weasel that turns white in the winter) so it can merge with its snow-covered surroundings in Rogers Pass, just as Paul's jackrabbit, bleached by his car's headlights, turns into "a snowshoe rabbit" (which, like the ermine, becomes white during the winter).[7] The fantastical whiteness of these two shape-shifting creatures—a sign of what Norman terms the fabulist's "poetic" mindset (14)—aligns them with another animal associated with comedy in *A River Runs Through It*: the mountain goat emblazoned on the Great Northern Railway box car that houses Black Jack's tavern, "the only goat that ever saw the bottom of his world constantly occupied by a bottle of bar whiskey labeled '3-7-77'" (30). The Great Northern—the most northerly transcontinental railroad in America—provided passenger service to Montana's Glacier National Park, and the company's famous logo displayed a white mountain goat against a solid backdrop that was as red as a Hills Brothers coffee can.[8] Contemplating the Great Northern sign that welcomed customers to Black Jack's Bar, Maclean's narrator describes this emblem of comic confusion as "a mountain goat gazing through a white beard on a world painted red" (30). When Neal reaches the end of his narrative career in *A River Runs Through It*, the iconic red-and-white color scheme of the Great Northern goat reappears: as he unwillingly submits to medical attention from the fearsome women in his family, the sunburned Neal becomes nothing more than "a red carcass on a white sheet" (74). Thus Black Jack's mountain goat, like Paul's jackrabbit and Neal's otter, functions as the heraldic emblem of misadventurers who may get drunk, run off the road, and suffer second-degree burns but nonetheless will live to tell their tales.

Earlier in Maclean's story, after listening—along with the Great Northern goat—to Neal's ludicrous account of otter hunting in Rogers Pass, Old Rawhide asks an important interpretive question: "Hey, Buster, what are otters doing on the top of the Continental Divide? I thought otters swam in creeks and played on mud slides?" (33). Maclean's totemic creatures of comedy, regardless of their species' normal ranges, are all denizens of the Continental Divide, the hydrological boundary running through the Rocky Mountains from which point rivers flow west to the Pacific rather than east to the Atlantic (or vice versa, depending on the viewer's perspective). Black Jack's mountain goat would have spent its working life traversing the Continental Divide via Marias Pass on the Great Northern's mainline through Montana,[9] while Neal's otter—an inhabitant of both Amwell Hill and Rogers Pass—straddles the "divide" between seventeenth-century Old World east and twentieth-century New World west. Paul and Norman's identities as fly fishermen originate in the same borderland, for their beloved Big Blackfoot River "runs straight and hard . . . from its headwaters at Rogers Pass on the Continental Divide" (12). Maclean's narrator recalls that whenever he and Paul drove west across Rogers Pass to go fishing, they "sat silently respectful until we passed the big Divide, but started talking the moment we thought we were draining into another ocean" (13). As the brothers began heading toward the Pacific like the Blackfoot, Paul would recount what Norman calls "Continental Divide stories" in which Paul "was the leading character but not the hero" (13). His tale of the albino jackrabbit exemplifies the characteristic ambiguity of Paul's "seemingly light-hearted" Continental Divide yarns: "Often I did not know what I had been told about him as we crossed the divide between our two worlds," Norman recalls (14). In *A River Runs Through It*, the Continental Divide functions as a topographical pun, a zone of fluctuating identity where stories and lives can take new directions.

This geography of the divide likewise structures "the patterns of a river," Maclean's narrator muses (63). Studying these patterns, the fisherman

> says he is "reading the water," and perhaps to tell his stories he has to do much the same thing. Then one of his biggest problems is to guess where and at what time of day life lies ready to be taken as a joke. And to guess whether it is going to be a little or a big joke.
> For all of us, though, it is much easier to read the waters of tragedy. (63–64)

In their twinned pursuits of Continental Divide animals, both Neal and Paul experience their lives as a joke. But the narrative trajectories (and fates) of the two young men diverge. According to Montana's code of masculinity, Neal will always be an inept figure of fun who's "painted red": as betokened by his trusty Hills Brothers bait tin, Neal was destined never to become a real (fisher)man, but after being burned in his attempt to emulate Paul, Neal learned his lesson and "was never to come back" to Montana (77). At the very same time that Neal roasts in the sun, Paul briefly considers emulating his comic foil. As Paul tells Norman that "some day . . . Neal is going to find out about himself and he won't come back to Montana. He doesn't like Montana," Paul suddenly declares, "I should leave Montana. . . . I should go to the West Coast" (57). When his brother asks why, Paul confesses that as a small-town reporter, he has nothing to do except fish, hunt, and "get into trouble," but as soon as Norman offers to help him get a job with an urban newspaper, Paul refuses to imagine himself leading a different kind of life: "I'll never leave Montana. . . . And I like the trouble that goes with it" (58). In *A River Runs Through It*, not only is it "much easier" for a superlative fly fisherman to "read the waters of tragedy," but it is also much more difficult for him to go with the flow of comedy. The Continental Divide holds these contrasting trajectories of existence in tension: although they function as comic doubles within its force field, Paul and Neal exit Maclean's narrative on opposite paths. Neal, wounded but wiser, retreats from Montana. Paul, by contrast, stands his ground, unable to abandon Montana's code of tough-guy manhood. The last time Maclean's narrator heads west through Rogers Pass, he is accompanied by a police officer: "Together we drove across the Continental Divide and down the length of the Big Blackfoot River . . . to tell my father and mother that my brother had been beaten to death by the butt of a revolver and his body dumped in an alley" (102).

In his pioneering work of environmental criticism *The Comedy of Survival*, Joseph Meeker argues that literary modes always assume and promote particular ecosocial models of human life. By focusing on the dynamics of "literary ecology," Meeker suggests, we can apprehend both the "biological themes and relationships which appear in literary works" and "what roles have been played by literature in the ecology of the human species."[10] According to Meeker, comedy depicts and celebrates contingency, adaptation, and biological survival. Comedy, Meeker observes, "illustrates that survival depends upon our ability to change ourselves rather than our environment, and upon our ability to accept limitations" (49). The comic protagonist is thus "respectful of the prerequisites for life" and seeks to restore "ecological balances," his story exemplifying Montaigne's adage that "our great and glorious masterpiece is to live appropriately" (156, 154). By contrast, Meeker contends, an anthropocentric worldview underpins tragedy: the tragic hero, who unflinchingly lives his life according to abstract ideals, always "exists in a state of conflict with powers that are greater than he is" and attempts to bend both nature and society to his will—until he inevitably perishes (38).

In *A River Runs Through It*, Paul pursues the glory and pays the price of the tragic hero. Paul's brilliance as a fly fisherman allows him to master the most challenging canyon of the Blackfoot, "no place for small fish or small fishermen," and the narrator describes his brother's demiurgic "shadow-casting" through which Paul conjures up a swarm of hatching insects with his circling line, a technique Norman confesses he could never develop (15, 20–21). When Paul catches his last fish, Maclean depicts the angler's deathblow as the coup de grâce inflicted by an ancient warrior during brutal hand-to-hand combat: "Then the shoulder shot straight out, and my brother stood up, faced us, and, with uplifted arm proclaimed himself the victor. Something giant dangled from his fist. Had Romans been watching they would have thought that what was dangling had a helmet on it" (99–100). When Maclean's narrator and his father later reminisce about Paul winning this final trophy, they realize they "never saw the fish but only the artistry of the fisherman" (100). Yet Paul's determination to live as a go-it-alone hero is finally, fatally limited. Maclean's narrator recalls that "when things got tough, my brother looked to himself to get himself out of trouble.... Though he was my brother, he was sometimes knot-headed. I pursued this line of thought back to the Greeks who believed that not wanting any help might even get you killed" (90). Paul, his right arm and wrist larger than his left through constant use in the solitary activities of both casting and punching, always fights as he will die: alone.

Yet in his Continental Divide story, Paul, like Neal, imagines himself instead as a figure of fun. As protagonists of comic narratives, both men treat the natural world with unusual restraint insofar as neither tries to harm the fantastical animal he pursues. From a mustelid's perspective, Neal transposes Walton's otter hunt into a much more salubrious comic key, since in Montana (unlike in Hertfordshire) the mother otter and all her offspring survive their close encounter with a bait fisherman, and unlike his eerily white jackrabbit, any fish that comes within striking distance of Paul is caught and killed. Moreover, both Neal and Paul modify their behavior to enhance their companionship with their shape-shifting totems of comedy: Neal cuddles the pups of his "jokey" otter, while Paul, "in need of a friend," sticks his head out of his car's window "so he could feel close to the rabbit" (14). Paul's story, however, concludes with him veering away from the jackrabbit and crashing—a foreshadowing of Paul's abrupt and solitary demise. Neal's story of the otter, by contrast, emphasizes his kinship with that literally and culturally long-lived patriarch of bait fishermen, Izaak Walton, an affiliation tacitly reiterated every time Neal appears with (or as) his red Hills Brothers coffee can. According to Paul, Montana is no place for "a bait-fishing bastard" like Neal or his seventeenth-century prototype (72). But in the cosmos of early twentieth-century Montana, the gods ultimately stand up for bastards: unlike the brilliant angler Paul, the hapless Neal survives—as does Paul's elder brother, an admittedly second-rate fly fisherman who cannot help but find artistry in *The Compleat Angler* despite his brother's scorn for everything the book represents.

In *A River Runs Through It*, Norman Maclean thus transforms his family history into a Continental Divide story, a tale that can at any moment head in either a comic or tragic direction. Remarking on its stark shifts in tone and mood, Wallace Stegner suggests that Maclean's powerful yet enigmatic narrative is characterized by "the same alternations of sunshine and shadow that a mountain stream has."[11] Within this fluctuating literary terrain, Izaak Walton and *The Compleat Angler* function as avatars of comedy. Castigated by Reverend Maclean and his talented but troubled younger son, Walton epitomizes a less domineering (and thus, for Paul, less manly) attitude toward the natural world and human society alike. Maclean first differentiates Paul—who lives to conquer both fish and his fellow men—from his more irenic brother through their divergent reactions to Walton, and each young man's response to Walton ultimately proves to be an index of his character and fate. And when *The Compleat Angler* reappears in Neal's ludicrous 3-7-77 tale, we must adopt the interpretive double vision demanded by the Continental Divide: even as Walton is mocked by his association with the drunken, soon-to-be-sunburned Neal, *The Compleat Angler* represents a pathway to survival that Neal traverses but Paul refuses to take. At the end of his novella, as Norman Maclean's elderly narrator looks back elegiacally over his life and tries to understand his long-lost brother, he is famously "haunted by waters" (104). But as readers alert to the intertextual dialogue that frames our experience of Paul's tragic death, we recognize that *A River Runs Through It* is also haunted by Walton.

In 1653, Izaak Walton dared to imagine how ordinary people might create new, more resilient forms of community and environmental stewardship by reconnecting with (and within) the natural world. Just as Viator was fortuitously "overtaken" by Piscator at the beginning of *The Compleat Angler*, so readers for more than three and a half centuries have likewise accepted Walton's invitation to accompany him on a springtime fishing trip. As generations of angling "scholars" have thus headed into the Hertfordshire countryside with their irrepressibly chatty, convivial tutor and traveling companion, they have chosen the path of comedy, turning their backs on tragic anthropocentrism so they can immerse themselves in—and be transformed by—a green world. Despite the adverse weather inflicted on them by climate change, generations of Walton's acolytes have bonded with one another, learned about ecology and environmental preservation as well as fishing, and discovered God (and great food) in a landscape of breathtaking beauty and complexity. And some have gone on to reprise this life-changing journey in even more adventurous surroundings by visiting Piscator Junior's diminutive fishing temple on the banks of the River Dove. In 1922, the founders of the Izaak Walton League of America turned their experiences with Piscator into the blueprint for an innovative mode of community-building environmental activism with which they would revolutionize the modern conservation movement. A century later, as humankind faces a new era of devastating ecological and political crises, Izaak Walton once again invites us to join him on his challenging yet hopeful journey: "I have neither a willingness nor leasure to say more, then wish thee a *rainy evening* to read this book in, and *that the east wind may never blow when thou goest a fishing*" (60).

NOTES

All references to the *Oxford English Dictionary* (*OED*) cite the OED Online database, last modified March 2022.

INTRODUCTION

1. Buckmann, *First 50*, 5.
2. Beatty, afterword to *Compleat Angler*, 182, 179. On Dilg, see Scarpino, *Great River*, 117–21.
3. Voigt, *Born with Fists Doubled*, 16.
4. Buckmann, *First 50*, vi.
5. *Outdoor America* 2, no. 3 (October 1923): title page.
6. The Sierra Club confined itself to mountains and national parks, the National Conservation Association focused on forestry, and the Audubon Association concentrated on birds and wildlife.
7. Fox, *John Muir*, 162.
8. Trefethen, *American Crusade for Wildlife*, 183; Fox, *John Muir*, 162. As of early 2022, the Izaak Walton League of America had more than forty thousand members nationwide ("About Us," Izaak Walton League of America, accessed March 26, 2022, https://www.iwla.org/about/about-us).
9. Fox, *John Muir*, 162.
10. Ibid.; Ruth Saari, "The Izaak Walton League of America: A Capsule History," Minnesota Division, Izaak Walton League of America, accessed August 9, 2022, https://www.minnesotaikes.org/Izaak/HistorySaari.html; Joe Penfold, "Izaak Walton League of America: 75 Years in Defense of the Boundary Waters," Walter J. Breckenridge Chapter, Izaak Walton League of America, accessed February 13, 2020, http://breckenridgeikes.org/bwca.penfold.html.
11. Quoted in Fox, *John Muir*, 163.
12. McCutcheon, "Battle."
13. Fox, *John Muir*, 124. Roosevelt died in 1919.
14. Although Walton expanded his text in subsequent editions, he did not change the original form of his book: see Bevan, introduction to *Compleat Angler*, 11–15, 33–51; and Horne, *Compleat Angler*, 1–20. I use the non-inclusive term "fisherman" here because, as I explain in chapter 2, Walton characterizes the audience of his work as male.
15. Guiver, *Izaak Walton's Literary Legacy*, 46. Douglas Bush's assessment that Walton's treatise "has been second only to the Bible in popular fame" is amplified by David Novarr, who reckons the *Angler* "has been reprinted more often than any book in English except the 1611 Bible" (Bush, *English Literature*, 238; Novarr, review of *Compleat Angler*, 122).
16. Contemporary "presentist" environmental scholarship seeks in early modern texts "an inclusive, non-anthropocentric conception of life" so as to foment "meaningful sociopolitical change" (Cefalu, Kuchar, and Reynolds, introduction to *Return of Theory*, 2; Jones, "Environmental Renaissance Studies," 4).
17. Scholarship that bucks this trend includes my introduction to the new Oxford World's Classics edition of the *Angler*—which outlines ideas I develop throughout this book—and Myra Wright's discussion of psychological and biological processes of transformation in Walton's treatise (*Poetics of Angling*, 134–55).
18. Guyer, "Izaak Walton's 'Holy War,'"

283; Zwicker, *Lines of Authority*, 88–89. Similar readings of Walton's treatise as a royalist polemic include Maltby, "From Temple to Synagogue," 92–93; Miner, *Cavalier Mode*, 44–45, 304–5; Smith, *Literature and Revolution*, 327–36; Tranter, "By the Rivers of Babylon"; and Theis, *Writing the Forest*, 235–36.

19. On Walton's work as a royalist agent, see Swann, introduction to *Compleat Angler*, ix–x. On the term "Prayer Book loyalist," see Maltby, "Suffering and Surviving," 159.

20. Boehrer, *Shakespeare Among the Animals*, 181; Williams, *Problems in Materialism*, 70. In using the term "ecosocial," I follow the example of Lance Newman ("Marxism and Ecocriticism," 11).

21. Richards, *Unending Frontier*, 11, 22, 618.

22. Parker, *Global Crisis*, xv.

23. Ibid., 324–76.

24. Gentles, *English Revolution*, 439–46; Beaver, *Hunting*; Trench, *Poacher and the Squire*, 106–8; Underdown, *Revel, Riot, and Rebellion*, 159–62.

25. Landry, *Invention of the Countryside*, 5–6; Carlton, *Going to the Wars*, 55.

26. Cavert, *Smoke of London*, 116–17; Evelyn, *Fumifugium*, 7.

27. Cavert, *Smoke of London*, 117.

28. Thomas, *Man and the Natural World*, 18, 89, 91. Other scholars characterize this dynamic as a conflict between a concept of nature as an organism and a theory of nature as a machine (Glacken, *Traces on the Rhodian Shore*, 378) or as a shift from a "system of resemblance" to categories of analysis conceived in "terms of identity and difference" (Foucault, *Order of Things*, 54). Robert Watson argues this transition sparked an epistemological crisis that caused Europeans to question whether they could ever achieve "authentic contact with the world of nature" (*Back to Nature*, 47).

29. Thomas, *Man and the Natural World*, 166; Boehrer, *Animal Characters*, 10. The questioning of anthropocentrism catalyzed in the early modern period continues to underpin the work of twenty-first-century "posthumanist" scholarship (Campana and Maisano, introduction to *Renaissance Posthumanism*, 2–11).

30. Marvell, "To His Coy Mistress," in *Poems of Andrew Marvell*, p. 81, line 11; Browne, *Religio Medici*, in *Works*, 1:83. On such botanical fantasies, see Swann, "Vegetable Love."

31. On early modern concepts of animal intellect and language, see Fudge, *Brutal Reasoning*; and Cummings, "Pliny's Literate Elephant." Myra Wright explores "the early modern fascination with the cognitive faculties of fish" in her analysis of John Dennys's versified Jacobean angling manual (*Poetics of Angling*, 76).

32. Edwards, *First and Second Part of Gangraena*, 17.

33. Bauthumley, *Light and Dark Sides of God*, 4.

34. Smith, "Bothumley, Jacob." Bauthumley—who was also dismissed from the parliamentary army, his sword having been broken over his head—was punished in accordance with the Blasphemy Act passed by the Rump Parliament in August 1650 (Smith, introduction to *A Collection of Ranter Writings*, 14–15).

35. Philip Major finds this paradoxical dynamic characteristic of many royalists during the interregnum (introduction to *Literatures of Exile*, 3).

36. Lawrence Buell argues that an "environmental text," by depicting the natural world as both a "presence" and a "process," "begins to suggest that human history is implicated in natural history," demonstrates that "the human interest is not . . . the only legitimate interest," and promotes "human accountability to the environment" (*Environmental Imagination*, 7–8; original italics removed).

37. As I am using the term, seventeenth-century "Anglican" thought entailed support for "a national episcopal Church, with a set liturgy defined in a Book of Common Prayer" (Hughes, "Cromwellian Church," 444).

38. Borlik, introduction to *Literature and Nature*, 12.

CHAPTER 1

1. "Compleat" instructional manuals published in England before Walton's fishing treatise include Henry Peacham's *The*

Compleat Gentleman (1622) and Thomas de Grey's *The Compleat Horseman and Expert Ferrier* (1639). Although the term "ecosystem" was not coined until the twentieth century, the concept it designates—"a biological system composed of all the organisms found in a particular physical environment, interacting with it and with each other" (*OED*, s.v. "ecosystem, *n*.")—was central to Walton's environmental vision.

2. Duckert, "Recreation," 80; *OED*, s.v. "recreation, *n*.1."

3. On the distinction between mode and genre, see Fowler, *Kinds of Literature*, 74, 107.

4. As translated by Ben Jonson, Horace advises that "Poets would either profit, or delight, / Or mixing sweet, and fit, teach life the right" (*Horace, of the Art of Poetry*, in *Ben Jonson: The Complete Poems*, p. 366, lines 477–78).

5. To the illustrations of the trout, pike, carp, tench, perch, and barbel that first appeared in the 1653 edition, Walton added images of the bream, eel, loach, and bullhead in the second edition, all of which remained in Walton's subsequent editions of the *Angler*. On Walton's illustrations, see Bevan, "Izaak Walton and His Publisher," 348–49; and Swann, "*Compleat Angler*," 103–5.

6. See Oliver, "Composition and Revisions," esp. 301–9. The scholarly apparatus of Jonquil Bevan's invaluable Clarendon Press edition of the *Angler* reveals how the text developed as Walton revised his book after 1653.

7. Floud thus also places Walton's book in the tradition of how-to manuals that copied the dialogue form of Erasmus's *Colloquies*.

8. Frye, *Anatomy of Criticism*, 311–12; Radcliffe, "'Study to Be Quiet,'" 100–101.

9. Browne, preface to *Compleat Angler*, 2nd ed. (1759), vi.

10. *Letters of Charles Lamb*, 1:21.

11. Buell, *Environmental Imagination*, 421, 126.

12. Park and Daston, introduction to *Early Modern Science*, 8; Buell, *Environmental Imagination*, 422.

13. I am applying Raymond Williams's model of cultural complexity as outlined in *Marxism and Literature*, 121–27.

14. The religiosity of this passage is further enhanced by Venator's reference to "the *Lillies* that take no care" (371), which evokes Matt. 6:28 and Luke 12:27.

15. Glacken, *Traces on the Rhodian Shore*, 379.

16. On the cultural genealogy of Natura, see Curtius, *European Literature*, 106–27. Raymond Williams places this figure within a wide range of the meanings of the term "nature" in *Keywords*, 215–21.

17. Coates, *Nature*, 59; *OED*, s.v. "nature, *n*."

18. Herbert, "Man," in *Complete English Poems*, p. 84, lines 27–30.

19. On Thomas Weaver, see Walton and Cotton, *Compleat Angler*, ed. Swann, 233.

20. Tillyard, *Elizabethan World Picture*, 26. On the development of this metaphor from classical antiquity through the seventeenth century, see Lovejoy, *Great Chain of Being*, 1–182.

21. Gabriel Egan emphasizes this theory holds in "tension" both hierarchy and similarity, differentiation and correspondence ("Gaia," 59); see also Carson, "Great Chain of Being."

22. The sixteenth-century physician and naturalist Guillaume Rondelet ("Rondeletius") provided illustrated accounts of fish that resembled clergymen in his *Libri de Piscibus Marinis*, 492–94.

23. Piscator's argument that the *vita contemplativa* and the *vita activa* productively coexist in the experience of the angler parallels the conceptualization of seventeenth-century Baconian natural philosophy, which "unexpectedly revived the medieval contemplative as a cultural analogue for the early modern scientist" (Summit, "Active and Contemplative Lives," 532).

24. Tranter, "By the Rivers of Babylon," 198. Paula Loscocco similarly argues that his evocation of Psalm 137 establishes Walton "as a key propagandist in the fully developed project of royalist psalmic poetics" ("Royalist Reclamation of Psalmic Song," 532). On Psalm 137 within royalists' broader appropriation of the narrative

of the Babylonian captivity, see Guibbory, *Christian Identity, Jews, and Israel*, 133–46.

25. Tranter, "By the Rivers of Babylon," 200.

26. Verses 24-25 of Psalm 104 proclaim, "O Lord, how manifold are thy works! in wisdom hast thou made them all: the earth is full of thy riches. / So is this great and wide sea, wherein are things creeping innumerable, both small and great beasts."

27. Browne, *Religio Medici*, in *Works*, 1:24–25. On early modern English Protestant concepts of the Book of Nature as a source of knowledge of the divine, see Harrison, *Bible*, 193–204; and Walsham, *Reformation of the Landscape*, 328–40.

28. On Ignatian meditation, see Martz, *Poetry of Meditation*, 25–27. On the relationship between early modern Roman Catholic and Protestant meditational practices, see Lewalski, *Protestant Poetics*, 147–62; and Green, *Print and Protestantism*, 277–88.

29. This and all future parenthetical references to the Geneva Bible cite the 1608 edition; Ambrose, *Media*, 193. In both the Geneva and King James translations of the Bible, the words "meditate" and "meditation" appear in the Psalms multiple times more than in all the other books of the Bible combined.

30. This wording indicates that Walton draws from the Geneva Bible's translation of Ps. 107:23–24: "They that goe downe to the sea in ships, and occupie by the great waters, / They see the workes of the Lorde, and his wonders in the deepe."

31. On the biblical Isaac as an evening meditator, see Ambrose, *Media*, 194. The Geneva Bible translation of Gen. 24:63 reads, "And Izhak went out to pray in the field toward the evening," but the word "pray" is glossed by a note that reads, "This was the exercise of the godly fathers, to meditate Gods promises, and to pray for the accomplishment thereof." On the blurring of the boundaries between meditation and prayer in early modern English translations of the Bible, see Lewalski, *Protestant Poetics*, 458n24.

32. Bush, *English Literature*, 209–11; McCabe, "Hall, Joseph."

33. On the publication history of these books, see Huntley, introduction to *Bishop Joseph Hall*, 58–61. On Hall's meditational method as distinctively "Anglican," see Radcliffe, *Forms of Reflection*, 8–10.

34. "Izaak Walton's Will," 607. In his *Life of Sir Henry Wotton*, first published in 1651, Walton notes that Joseph Hall's "many and useful Works speak his great Merit" (*Lives*, 136).

35. Hall, *Bishop Joseph Hall*, 73. Subsequent references to Hall's works in this edition appear parenthetically.

36. Hall, *Christian Moderation*, 47.

37. Walsham, *Reformation of the Landscape*, 5.

38. Hall also advocates and practices "deliberate" meditation, which he describes as being "wrought out of our own heart" rather than being "occasioned by outward occurrences offered to the mind" (72); this type of meditation corresponds to the anthropocentric, memory-based lamentation of the Children of Israel that Piscator mentions only to reject. On Hall's ideas and their influence, see Anselment, "Feminine Self-Reflection," 69–71. The seventeenth-century "use" of the natural world by the meditative outdoorsperson prefigures the post-Renaissance experience of the countryside walker, whose "instinct to gather" specimens or "picturesque views" is likewise the foundation of a type of environmental mastery (Landry, *Invention of the Countryside*, 22).

39. Hall, *Devout Soul*, 21–24.

40. We find an earlier, less explicitly theological example of this type of meditation in Jaques's "contemplation" (2.1.64) of a dying deer in Shakespeare's *As You Like It* (2.1.47–63).

41. The author of the first passage is unknown; the second, slightly altered by Walton, was written by George Herbert. Since the oak was a traditional symbol of English nobility, the moral of the image would have seemed especially poignant in the wake of the execution of Charles I.

42. This poem was added to the third edition of *The Compleat Angler* (1661), but Walton introduced the name "Kenna" (p. 262, line 22)—apparently a reference to his second wife, Anne Ken, who had died in 1662—in the fifth edition of 1676.

"Shawford-brook" (p. 262, line 31) probably refers to the River Sow as it flows through the small Staffordshire village of Shallowford, in the vicinity of which Walton bought property in the 1650s.

43. Lewalski, *Protestant Poetics*, 152.
44. Huntley, introduction to *Bishop Joseph Hall*, 9.
45. Hall, *Devout Soul*, 20.
46. Shapiro, *Probability and Certainty*, 92. On natural theology in early modern England, see also Glacken, *Traces on the Rhodian Shore*, 375–428.
47. Ray, *Wisdom of God*, Preface, n.p. On Ray as an environmental thinker, see Glacken, *Traces on the Rhodian Shore*, 379–80, 415–23.
48. Ray, *Wisdom of God*, preface, n.p.
49. Piscator here invokes Eccles. 3:11.
50. Glacken, *Traces on the Rhodian Shore*, 423.
51. On the role of "wonder" in Walton's treatise, see Swann, "Compleat Angler." On the contradictory dynamics of mastery and alterity that shaped the early modern experience of wonder, see Swann, *Curiosities and Texts*, 22–25.
52. From 1655 onward, Piscator adds two more species—"the *flag-flie*" and "the *vine-flie*"—to this catalog (248).
53. Herbert, "Providence," in *Complete English Poems*, p. 109, lines 31–32; emphasis added.
54. Byron's "Don Juan," 3:407.
55. Borlik, *Ecocriticism and Early Modern English Literature*, 141.
56. Gifford, "Pastoral," 19.
57. Puttenham, *Arte of English Poesie*, 53.
58. Ibid. On the development of piscatory pastoral, see Cooper, *Art of "The Compleat Angler*," 60–61; and Bevan, *Izaak Walton's "The Compleat Angler*," 82–86.
59. Quarles, *Shepheards Oracles*, A3v–A4v. The preface to *The Shepheards Oracles* is signed by the publisher John Marriot, who says he is passing along the account of the poems' genesis that he received from "*A friend of the Authours*" (A4v); scholars have long attributed the preface to Walton.
60. For an historical analysis of the shifting definitions of pastoral, see Garrard, *Ecocriticism*, 33–58.
61. Browne, preface to *Compleat Angler* (1750), viii.; McIlhaney, "Compleat Angler"; Westwood, *Chronicle of the "Compleat Angler*," xiii; *Collected Works of William Hazlitt*, 1:56.
62. Wordsworth, "Written upon a Blank Leaf in *The Compleat Angler*," in *William Wordsworth: Poems*, p. 398, lines 13 and 11; Cooper, *Art of "The Compleat Angler*," 94. Such analyses of Walton's fishing treatise support Terry Gifford's argument that from the Renaissance onward, "the term pastoral came to refer to any literature that described the countryside in contrast to the court or the city" ("Pastoral," 19).
63. Bevan, *Izaak Walton's "The Compleat Angler*," 51.
64. Passage from Sidney quoted in ibid., 51, to which I am applying Susan Snyder's insightful analysis of Du Bartas's phraseology (introduction to *Divine Weeks and Works*, 92).
65. Bush, *English Literature*, 239.
66. *The Compleat Angler* is first mentioned in an advertisement published in *The Perfect Diurnall* of May 9–16, 1653 (Bevan, introduction to *Compleat Angler*, 33). Sir Nicholas Harris Nicolas, in his celebrated 1836 edition of Walton's book, was the first editor to organize Walton's text into days, an innovation that has often been copied ever since (Horne, "Compleat Angler," 60).
67. In his text, Walton misidentifies Dennys as "Jo. Da[vors]" (77, 207, 386).
68. Cotton, *Compleat Angler, Part II*, 203. Throughout the seventeenth century the English used the Julian calendar, which was thirteen days behind our current Gregorian calendar; nonetheless, perhaps in part because global heating now causes mayflies (*Ephemera danica*) to emerge earlier, "May can stand as quoted" in this passage, "while June would be regarded as the peak month [for trout] in many managed fisheries" (Anthony Wilson, president emeritus, Izaak Walton Cottage Chapter [Staffordshire], Izaak Walton League of America, personal correspondence, January 29, 2020).
69. Blackburn and Holford-Strevens, *Oxford Companion to the Year*, 184.
70. Sparke, *Scintillula Altaris*, 275; Cressy, *Bonfires and Bells*, 3, 21. Sparke was

a Church of England clergyman who was ejected from his living in 1645; Walton contributed a prefatory poem to Sparke's book, which, as a celebration of "the FEASTS and FASTS" of the prewar church (*Scintillula Altaris*, title page), was politically transgressive when it was first published.

71. Stow, *Survay of London*, 72.
72. On the gathering of plant material as part of "maying," see Thomas, *Man and the Natural World*, 75; and Marcus, *Politics of Mirth*, 160. Thomas notes that puritans were "strongly hostile to the notion that vegetation might have any protective power and were unsympathetic to the symbolic use of plants" (78).
73. Stubbes, *Anatomie of Abuses*, M4r.
74. Hutton, *Rise and Fall of Merry England*, 145.
75. Whitaker, *Sunday in Tudor and Stuart Times*, 151, 149.
76. Quoted in Sharpe, *Personal Rule of Charles I*, 352. On the genesis of James I's Book of Sports, see also Semenza, *Sport, Politics, and Literature*, 93–96.
77. Hutton, *Rise and Fall of Merry England*, 196.
78. Firth and Rait, *Acts and Ordinances*, 1:421. Kevin Sharpe argues that "perhaps more than any of his injunctions," Charles's policy about the Book of Sports "raised opponents who were not natural enemies to the church" (*Personal Rule of Charles I*, 359). On earlier attempts by the Long Parliament to prohibit Sunday pastimes and condemn the Book of Sports, see Hutton, *Rise and Fall of Merry England*, 200–201.
79. Similarly, although he had certainly written it earlier in the year, Sir Thomas Browne dated his dedicatory preface to *The Garden of Cyrus* May 1, 1658, knowing full well that "the word 'May' [had become] almost a code-word for royalist sympathisers" (Preston, "Cyder and Sallets," 876).
80. Underdown, *Revel, Riot, and Rebellion*, 269.
81. Capp, *England's Culture Wars*, 214. On other transgressive May Day celebrations staged during the interregnum, see Capp, *England's Culture Wars*, 205; Hutton, *Rise and Fall of Merry England*, 219–21; and Underdown, *Revel, Riot, and Rebellion*, 264, 269.

82. I am indebted to A. R. Collins's online Historical Calendar—http://www.arc.id.au/Calendar.html—and Ian MacInnes's online English Calendar—https://aulis.org/Calendar/Welcome.html—for allowing me to make this discovery.
83. Durston, "'Preaching and Sitting Still,'" 206.
84. Durston and Maltby, introduction to *Religion in Revolutionary England*, 12.
85. Firth and Rait, *Acts and Ordinances*, 1:420.
86. Ibid., 1:599, 1:791, 2:384–85.
87. Capp, *England's Culture Wars*, 100, 109, 246.
88. Whitaker, *Sunday in Tudor and Stuart Times*, 158–59.
89. Enforcement of interregnum sabbatarian regulations depended on the zeal of local officials, and whereas travel on Sunday was regularly punished in Warwickshire and Northamptonshire, arrests in Hertfordshire focused instead on commercial activities that were illicitly conducted on the sabbath (ibid., 178–79; Capp, *England's Culture Wars*, 105; Hardy, preface to *Hertford County Records*, 1:xii). So the ability of Piscator and Viator to avoid prosecution for traveling on a Sunday in 1653 perhaps reflects Walton's personal knowledge of the legal landscape traversed by his characters.
90. In royalist Robert Herrick's poem "Corinna's *Going a Maying*," the sexualized May games that had scandalized Philip Stubbes decades earlier result in "Many a green-gown," that is, women's grass-stained skirts (*Complete Poetry of Robert Herrick*, vol. 1, p. 65, line 51).
91. Quoted in Davies, *Restoration of Charles II*, 342.
92. Cressy, *Bonfires and Bells*, 171.
93. For a more detailed account of the historical context of this narrative, see Alpers, *Singer of the "Eclogues*," 68.
94. Patterson, *Pastoral and Ideology*, 151, 171.
95. Similarly, in his pastoral dedicatory verses for a volume of poetry written by Alexander Brome, Walton's shepherds look forward to meeting the restored Charles II at "*yonder broad* beech tree"

("*To My Ingenious Friend Mr. Brome*," in Brome, *Songs and Other Poems*, A7v).

96. Thomas Flatman, "To My Worthy Friend Mr. Isaac Walton; On the Publication of This Poem," in *Works of John Chalkhill*, p. 84, line 7; I refer to the text of Virgil's first *Eclogue* found in Alpers, *Singer of the "Eclogues,"* p. 12, lines 46 and 51, and subsequent references to this edition of Virgil's poems appear parenthetically. Chalkhill, who died in 1642, was distantly related to Walton by marriage, and Walton included two poems by Chalkhill in all editions of his *Angler*. Tityrus has often been interpreted as a figure of Virgil himself since after the Battle of Philippi, the victorious Octavian prevented Virgil's farm from being expropriated (Alpers, *Singer of the "Eclogues,"* 68).

97. His revision of the first *Eclogue* is so radical that Jonquil Bevan questions whether Walton had actually read Virgil's poem, but Walton's reiterated description of a "broad *Beech tree*" replicates the wording of William Lathum's English translation (Bevan, *Izaak Walton's "The Compleat Angler,"* 70; *Virgils Eclogues*, 2). In the "Argument" prefacing his translation of eclogue 1, Lathum describes Meliboeus as "*an unfortunate miserable man, exiled and forced out of his owne Country*" (*Virgils Eclogues*, 1).

98. Mabey, *Flora Britannica*, 266. In Genesis, after Adam and Eve eat the forbidden fruit, "the eyes of them both were opened, and they knew that they *were* naked; and they sewed fig leaves together, and made themselves aprons" (3:7). And in another theologically loaded narrative that associates the sycamore with transformed perception, the tax collector Zacchaeus climbs a sycamore tree in order to get a good view of Jesus in Jericho (Luke 19:1–10).

99. Herbert, "The World," in *Complete English Poems*, p. 77, lines 11–12.

100. Gifford, "Pastoral," 53. My analysis of Walton's complex use of georgic develops Alastair Fowler's insight that the *Angler* "not only enlarges eclogue, but also . . . works toward a georgic modulation" (*Kinds of Literature*, 173).

101. Goodman, "Georgic," 557.

102. Low, *Georgic Revolution*, 221.

103. Thirsk, "Plough and Pen," 309; Thirsk discusses Blith on pp. 307–13. On Austen, see Preston, "Cyder and Sallets," 868; on Hartlib, see Warde, "Idea of Improvement," 137–39; on the religious rationales for seventeenth-century agricultural "improvement," see Harrison, *Bible*, 226–43.

104. Leslie and Raylor, introduction to *Culture and Cultivation*, 5; McRae, *God Speed the Plough*, 290.

105. Fussell, *Old English Farming Books*, 21–55; Sharrock, *History of the Propagation*; *Reformed Virginian Silk-Worm*.

106. Estienne and Liébault, *Maison Rustique*; on Walton's use of this source, see Bevan, introduction to *Compleat Angler*, 21–22 and 418.

107. On the identity of the willow-munching caterpillar that Piscator describes, see *Compleat Angler*, by Walton and Cotton, ed. Swann, 253.

108. *OED*, s.v. "dock, *n.1*."

109. In our own era, the treatment of livestock with parasiticides renders their feces insecticidal and thus inhospitable to invertebrates such as dung beetles (Sands and Wall, "Sustained Parasiticide Use").

110. Various kinds of tree bark containing tannic acid were used in the process of turning animal skins into leather. The female hairy-footed flower bee (*Anthophora plumipes*)—which is "jet black apart from her orange pollen brushes" on her hind legs—often nests "in the mortar of old walls" (Chinery, *Complete British Insects*, 350).

111. O'Connor, *Animals as Neighbors*, 1, 8.

112. Ibid., 4.

113. Dennys, *Secrets of Angling*, C2r; Bastard, *Chrestoleros*, p. 139, book 6, epigram 14: *De Piscatione*; Drayton, *Poly-Olbion*, in *Works of Michael Drayton*, vol. 4, p. 33, line 140.

114. The Eurasian otter (*Lutra lutra*), the only species of otter indigenous to England, is now protected throughout Great Britain. On the history of British otter hunting, see Lovegrove, *Silent Fields*, 244–50; for an account of how the species was saved from extinction in twentieth-century Britain, see Allen, *Otter*, 139–47.

115. Kruuk, *Otters*, 23, 42, 124.
116. *OED*, s.v. "gin, *n*.1."
117. *OED*, s.v. "fence, *n*."
118. From 1661 onward, Walton tweaked this passage so the owners of the nation's "Otter dogs"—large, shaggy hounds with webbed feet—would receive their reward from the newly restored "King" instead of Cromwell's regime (175).
119. On the statutes that Walton cites, see Walton and Cotton, *Complete Angler*, ed. Nicolas, 62–63. Sarah Robinson notes that "national legislation aimed at the protection of fish is on record from at least as early as 1285" in England ("Catching Fish, Making Law," 180).
120. Warde, *Invention of Sustainability*, 5.
121. Ibid., 58–101; Caradonna, *Sustainability*, 32–33.
122. *Treatyse of Fysshynge wyth an Angle*, 226; Samuel, *Arte of Angling*, D5v.
123. Mascall, *Booke of Fishing*, 45–46 (misprinted as 47).
124. Ibid., 45.
125. Quarles, *Shepheards Oracles*, 1.
126. Zwicker, *Lines of Authority*, 73.
127. David Cressy lists church celebrations and their dates in *Bonfires and Bells*, 6–7. Walton's evocation of the prohibited calendar represents one way in which interregnum decrees banning church festivals "were widely disregarded" (Morrill, *Nature of the English Revolution*, 153–54).
128. Walton, "To the Author."
129. *OED*, s.v. "watery, *adj.*"
130. *OED*, s.v. "discourse, *n*."
131. On the meaning of the term "smoking shower," see Swann, "Literary and Environmental References," 375–76.
132. On "May-butter," see ibid., 376.
133. Clarendon quoted in Trevor-Roper, *Catholics, Anglicans, and Puritans*, 216.
134. Cavendish quoted in Whitaker, *Mad Madge*, 137.
135. On Charles II's fantastical escape after his defeat at the Battle of Worcester, including his stint hiding in the Boscobel Oak in Shropshire, see Sherwood, *Civil War in the Midlands*, 174.
136. Lamb, *Climate, History, and the Modern World*, 211; Markley, "Summer's Lease," 135; Fagan, *Little Ice Age*, xiii. I have previously outlined the argument of this paragraph in Swann, "Literary and Environmental References," 376.
137. Thirsk, "Plough and Pen," 308–9.
138. Markham, *Pleasures of Princes*, 118.
139. Worster, *Nature's Economy*, 405.
140. Mentz, "Strange Weather in *King Lear*," 142.
141. Jones, *Shakespeare's Storms*, 2–4. John Adrian observes of the pragmatic resourcefulness of Walton's fishermen, "Perhaps more than anything else, the successful angler is marked by an ability to consider shifting variables and to adapt to them on the fly" (*Local Negotiations of English Nationhood*, 131).
142. Snider, "Hard Frost," 10, 19–20; Glover and Noble, *History and Gazetteer*, 615.
143. Cavert, "Winter and Discontent," 119–20.
144. Srigley, "Great Frost Fair," 848–49; Evelyn, *Diary*, 4:357.
145. Evelyn, *Diary*, 4:359; Duffy, *Frost Fair*, n.p.
146. Evelyn, *Diary*, 4:362; Rimbault, *Old Ballads*, 17.
147. Evelyn, *Diary*, 4:362.
148. Tryon, *Modest Observations*, 1.
149. Evelyn, *Diary*, 4:362–63, 364; Evelyn, "Abstract of a Letter," 562.
150. Evelyn, *Diary*, 4:363, 362; Plot and Bobart, "Discourse," 767–68.
151. Rimbault, *Old Ballads*, 8; Parochial Register of Ubley, Somerset, quoted in Srigley, "Great Frost Fair," 853.
152. "Izaak Walton's Will," 606.
153. Cavert, *Smoke of London*, 105–21.

CHAPTER 2

1. Bacon, *Advancement and Proficience of Learning*, 74–75.
2. On the "upsurge" of new types of social organizations after the British Civil Wars, see Clark, *British Clubs and Societies*, 26.
3. Wright, *Poetics of Angling*, 136.
4. The oldest surviving manuscript version of the *Treatyse*, dating from about 1450, is Yale Beinecke MS 171, a facsimile and transcription of which can be found in

McDonald, *Origins of Angling*, 133–73. The *Treatyse* was added to the second edition of the *Boke of Saint Albans*—a collection of treatises about hawking, hunting, and heraldry—by its printer, Wynkyn de Worde, in 1496.

5. As Richard Hoffmann explains in detail, the long-standing attribution of the *Treatyse* and its host text, the *Boke of Saint Albans*, to a nun named "Dame Juliana Berners" is spurious (*Fishers' Craft and Lettered Art*, 6–7), so I will treat both works as anonymous.

6. *Treatyse of Fysshynge wyth an Angle*, 188–89. Subsequent references appear parenthetically.

7. The interpolated gloss in this passage is from the modernized version of the *Treatyse* text found in McDonald, *Origins of Angling*, 66.

8. On Walton's use of previous angling texts, including the *Treatyse*, see Bevan, introduction to *Compleat Angler*, 15–24.

9. Samuel, *Arte of Angling*, B6r (facsimile of text included in this ed.). Subsequent references appear parenthetically. As H. J. Oliver observes, how-to books were structured by dialogue long before Samuel wrote his treatise ("Composition and Revisions," 298–300).

10. On William Samuel, a Marian exile who later served as the vicar of Godmanchester in Huntingdonshire, and his authorship of *The Arte of Angling*, see Harrison, "Author of *The Arte of Angling*."

11. Thomas, *Ends of Life*, 190; Bray, *Friend*, 61.

12. When Piscator's impatience with Viator's questions boils over again after dinner, Piscator's wife tells Viator that her husband has a long history of interpersonal conflict under similar circumstances: "I can tell you, my husband hath caste off many, and that some of his chiefest acquaintance, for their jesting, when he talketh of his cunning in angling" (E5v).

13. Coleby, preface to *Arte of Angling*, xiii–xiv.

14. Bacon, *Advancement and Proficience of Learning*, 75. On the title-page epigraph, see below, chapter 3.

15. Evelyn, *Diary*, 3:88.

16. Phineas Fletcher, *Piscatorie Eclogs*, eclog 4, in Fletcher and Fletcher, *Poetical Works*, 2:197.

17. Gardiner, *Booke of Angling*, 46–47. Subsequent references appear parenthetically. Andrew Hadfield discusses Gardiner's allegorical depictions of angling in "Drayton's Fish," 121–23.

18. From the second edition of 1655 onward, Piscator overtakes two men, a hunter (named "Venator" rather than "Viator") and the falconer Auceps at this point in the narrative.

19. Walton's nineteenth-century editor Sir Nicholas Harris Nicolas first noted this connection (Walton and Cotton, *Complete Angler*, ed. Nicolas, 19).

20. Morton, *Treatise of the Nature of God*, 1.

21. Ibid., 4.

22. *OED*, s.v. "overtake, *v*."

23. Walton, *Lives*, 303–4. Subsequent references appear parenthetically.

24. Morrill, *Nature of the English Revolution*, 151; Greenslade, "Compleat Angler," 365.

25. Walton added this description of Sheldon to his book in 1655. Both Payne and Sheldon had been ejected from positions at Oxford; Payne, who died in 1651, did not live to see Sheldon become archbishop of Canterbury after the Restoration.

26. Quoted in Greenslade, "Compleat Angler," 362–64.

27. Quoted in Bevan, *Izaak Walton's "The Compleat Angler,"* 28.

28. In an influential conduct book that was translated multiple times into English, Giovanni Della Casa advised that "if wee meete with a man, we never sawe before: with whome, upon some occasion, it behoves us to talke: without examining wel his worthines, most commonly, that wee may not offend in to[o] little, we give him to[o] much, and call him *Gentleman*, and otherwise *Sir*" (*Galateo*, 43).

29. Decades earlier, Gervase Markham had written of "young Scholars, and such as are but learners in the Art of Angling" (*Pleasures of Princes*, 129).

30. Green, *Christian's ABC*, 15.

31. Nowell, *Catechisme*, 1. Nowell's first

position after taking holy orders was as master of Westminster School.

32. Green, *Christian's ABC*, 66.

33. For accounts of how Nowell—a Marian exile who was later appointed dean of St. Paul's—came to write his catechism, see Lehmberg, "Nowell, Alexander"; and Green, *Christian's ABC*, 189.

34. From 1572 through 1647, editions of Nowell's catechism tailored for the student market bore the title *A Catechisme, or Institution of Christian Religion, to Bee Learned of all Youth Next After the Little Catechisme Appointed in the Booke of Common Prayer*.

35. Elspeth Graham notes that Walton also declares his political allegiance in this passage, as during the 1650s St. Paul was regarded as a model of "religious radicals, and prophesying sectaries, such as Fifth Monarchists and Quakers" ("Ways of Being," 357–58).

36. Bacon, *Advancement and Proficience of Learning*, 74–75.

37. My account of livery companies draws on Bucholz and Ward, *London*, 77–82; and Kathman, "Grocers, Goldsmiths, and Drapers," 3–4.

38. Walton's silence about his occupation contradicts seventeenth-century norms of behavior since men in early modern England "usually looked to their work as the source of their sense of identity"; yet by aligning Piscator's role in the Brotherhood of the Angle with Walton's own position as a "free brother" in a livery company, Walton demonstrates how "occupation shaped the individual's self-consciousness" (Thomas, *Ends of Life*, 106–7).

39. Quoted in Coon, "Life of Izaak Walton," 54. Walton had to pay fines because his apprenticeship was somehow irregular (55–58).

40. For the evidence of Walton's occupation, see ibid., 97–98.

41. *Camp-bell*, B4r; Dekker, *Londons Tempe*, A2r, B3v.

42. Quoted in Kathman, "Grocers, Goldsmiths, and Drapers," 4.

43. *OED*, s.v. "enter, v."

44. *OED*, s.v. "set, v.1."

45. The Ironmongers' records list Walton as "Master" of the apprentices Stephen Noell and Edward Blurton, who were admitted into the freedom of the Company in 1635 and 1649 respectively (Ironmongers, "Register of Freedom Admissions").

46. Bacon, *Advancement and Proficience of Learning*, 75.

47. For an analysis of Bacon's proposals, see Swann, *Curiosities and Texts*, 55–74.

48. Shapin, *Scientific Revolution*, 95. Detailed discussions of this scientific milieu include Eamon, *Science and the Secrets of Nature*, 323–32; and Webster, *Great Instauration*, 32–99.

49. Crombie, "Science and the Arts," 15; Dickson, *Tessera of Antilia*, 6.

50. Walton thus reflects the broader cultural ambivalence toward virtuosos analyzed by Craig Hanson (*English Virtuoso*, esp. 3–13).

51. Beginning in the 1655 edition, Piscator adds another fish-attractant formula, this one involving "the marrow of the Thigh-bone of an *Hern* [heron]," which he has likewise procured from his "friend of note" and has likewise not tried (289).

52. Records of 1633–34 note the existence of an "Oliver Henly of St. Mary Woolchurch, London, haberdasher aged 61" (Coldham, *English Adventurers and Emigrants*, 41).

53. Piscator here extrapolates far beyond Bacon's fish-free assertion that "*Water* may be the *Medium* of *Sounds*" (*Sylva Sylvarum*, p. 167, experiment 792).

54. "The other is this: *Vulnera hederae grandissimae inflicta sudant Balsamum oleo gelato, albicantique persimile, odoris vero longe suavissimi*" (Wounds made in a large branch of ivy exude a balsam congealed from the plant's oil that is very similar to whitewash and truly smells very sweet for a long time) (279; translation mine).

55. Smith, *Homosexual Desire in Shakespeare's England*, 83.

56. Quoted in Hunter, *John Aubrey*, 93. This discussion draws on my earlier analysis of Walton's engagement with the ideas and practices of seventeenth-century virtuosos (Swann, "Compleat Angler").

57. Shapin, *Social History of Truth*, 65–95.

58. See Walton, *Compleat Angler*, ed. Bevan, 389; and Walton and Cotton, *Compleat Angler*, ed. Swann, 248.

59. Bevan, "Izaak Walton and His Publisher," 345.
60. On the evidence that Walton edited *Reliquiae Wottonianae*, see Novarr, *Making of Walton's "Lives,"* 129–30. In his biography of Wotton, Walton mentions Wotton's "innate pleasure of *Angling*" once but discusses Wotton's social ties with "the *Virtuosi*" of Europe multiple times, stating that Wotton "was a most dear Lover, and a most excellent Judge" of "all manner of Arts"—including *"Chymistry"*—who loved "a tryal of natural Experiments" (*Lives*, 130, 120, 107, 113).
61. Wotton, *Life and Letters*, 2:405.
62. In the letter cited above, by contrast, Wotton addresses Walton as "My Worthy Friend" and signs off as "Your very hearty poor friend to serve you" (ibid., 2:404–5); and in his *Life* of Donne, Walton extols the long "friendship" between Wotton and Donne (*Lives*, 20). Walton refers to Sir Henry as his *"friend"* only once in his biography of Wotton (*Lives*, 97).
63. My analysis of Walton's portrayal of women develops my earlier discussion of gender in Walton's treatise (Swann, introduction to *Compleat Angler*, xiv–xv). Myra Wright likewise observes that Walton's fraternity of anglers "explicitly excludes women" (*Poetics of Angling*, 144).
64. On early modern portrayals of female anglers, see McIlhaney, "'Whole Shoals of Men'"; and Wright, *Poetics of Angling*, 101–5, 117–27, 143.
65. Gowing, "Twinkling of a Bedstaff," 288; Clark, *British Clubs and Societies*, 4; Whitaker, *Mad Madge*, 298.
66. On women's participation in early modern craft guilds, see Smith, *All Men and Both Sexes*, 73–107.
67. For an analysis of the early modern concept of female inferiority, see Fletcher, *Gender, Sex, and Subordination*, 60–82.
68. Bevan, *Izaak Walton's "The Compleat Angler,"* 39.
69. See *"To My Dear Brother Mr. Izaak Walton, upon His* Compleat Angler" by John Floud (427) and *"To My Dear Brother, Mr. Iz. Walton on His* Compleat Angler" by Robert Floud (431).
70. Walton, *Compleat Angler*, 3rd ed. (1661), 118–19.

71. Walton, *Lives*, 27–28. Subsequent references appear parenthetically.
72. Saintsbury, introduction to *Lives*, xiii.
73. Helen Wilcox suggests that "although this story is unlikely to be true, there was certainly something unusual about the timing of their marriage, with the drawing up of the bond . . . and the ceremony itself both occurring in Lent, and the period before the wedding being too short for banns to be called" ("Herbert, George"). Walton may also be trying to counter his readers' knee-jerk suspicions about the character of Jane Danvers, as seventeenth-century clergymen's wives were stereotypically regarded as unchaste (Hindle, "Shaming of Margaret Knowsley," 397).
74. Saintsbury, introduction to *Lives*, xiii.
75. A. S. McGrade fact-checks Walton's account of Hooker's marriage ("Hooker, Richard"), and David Novarr provides a detailed analysis of Walton's "mass of misinformation" about Hooker (*Making of Walton's "Lives,"* 267–75).
76. The two former students Walton names as visiting Hooker were Edwin Sandys and George Cranmer. Walton's aunt was Cranmer's sister, and it seems likely that the Cranmers were hostile toward the women in Richard Hooker's life because of legal action Hooker's daughters took against Sandys, whom Hooker had named as his literary executor (Novarr, *Making of Walton's Lives*, 269).
77. William Samuel's text was thus more typical of early modern depictions of female work, which usually "obscured much of women's economic activity. Women's work was taken for granted, something which they 'naturally' did" (Mendelson and Crawford, *Women in Early Modern England*, 258).
78. Ibid., 335; Flather, *Gender and Space*, 119. On women's roles in alehouse management, see also Clark, *English Alehouse*, 79–84.
79. *OED*, s.v. "honest, *adj.* and *adv.*"
80. *OED*, s.v. "cleanly, *adj.*" In the 1653 edition of Walton's *Angler*, the word "cleanly" first appears when Piscator

describes Bleak Hall to Viator as "an honest cleanly Ale house" (83); from 1655 onward, however, Walton revises this passage and instead commends "an honest cleanly Hostess" (215).

81. Herrick, "The Argument of His Book," in Complete Poetry of Robert Herrick, vol. 1, p. 7, line 6; OED, s.v. "handsome, adj., adv., and n."; OED, s.v. "conveniently, adv." Proverbial wisdom suggested that a physically attractive wife enhanced an alehouse-keeper's profits: "A handsome Hostesse makes the Reckoning deare" (quoted in McRae, Literature and Domestic Travel, 189).

82. According to early modern English gender norms, a virtuous woman was chaste, silent, and obedient, the lack of one of these characteristics indicating the absence of all three (Fletcher, Gender, Sex, and Subordination, 12–29).

83. In the fifth and final edition of 1676, "Eccho" seems to inhabit "a hollow tree" rather than a cave (231).

84. Ovid's Metamorphosis Englished, 55. Walton owned a copy of this edition of Ovid's work (Bevan, "Some Books," 262).

85. Keith, Rural Tradition, 33.

86. Fussell, English Dairy Farmer, 162.

87. Piscator and Viator meet Maudlin and her mother on the third day of their vacation, which commenced on Sunday, May 1, 1653 (see above, chapter 1). Earlier in the 1653 text, Piscator asks the Hostess of Bleak Hall to prepare his chub in the same way as she had dressed his fish when he stayed at the alehouse "about eight or ten days ago" (84), likewise placing Piscator in Hertfordshire at the beginning of a new grazing season.

88. Phythian-Adams, "Milk and Soot," 87.

89. Blith, English Improver Improved, C3v. On dairying as a normatively female occupation, see Fussell, English Dairy Farmer, 204; and Herbert, Female Alliances, 99–101. As Wendy Wall notes, the figure of the milkmaid undermines the dynamics of early modern English pastoral because "dairying emphasized an arduous manual labor at odds with courtly taste" (Staging Domesticity, 134).

90. OED, s.v. "white meat, n."

91. Brears, Cooking and Dining, 83.

92. Valenze, "Art of Women," 145.

93. Mendelson and Crawford, Women in Early Modern England, 270.

94. Beginning with the 1655 edition of his text, Walton reinforces this depiction of Piscator as an agent of charity when immediately before the anglers' second encounter with the milkwoman, Piscator lauds "Doctor Sh[eldon], whose [angling] skill is above others; and of that the Poor that dwell about him have a comfortable experience" (325).

95. Gervase Markham asserts that a "red Cow giveth the best milke" (Cheape and Good Husbandry, 43).

96. On the circulation and publication history of both poems, see Hester, "'Like a Spyed Spie,'" 25–26. As Jonquil Bevan notes, the attribution of the second text to Raleigh has been accepted largely on the basis of Walton's testimony in this passage (Walton, Compleat Angler, ed. Bevan, 390–91).

97. Walton included twenty-six quotations of poetry in the first edition of 1653; as he revised The Compleat Angler, he added more poems, and the fifth and final edition of his book published in 1676 contains thirty-six passages of verse.

98. Thomas, Ends of Life, 97.

99. Brathwaite, Whimzies, 12.

100. Milton, "L'Allegro," in John Milton: Complete Shorter Poems, p. 135, line 65; OED, s.v. "blithe, adj., n., and adv." Dorothy Osborne asserted that milkmaids "want nothing to make them the happiest People in the world, but the knoledge that they are soe" (Letters of Dorothy Osborne, 51–52).

101. Osborne, Letters of Dorothy Osborne, 51; Breton, "An Answere," in Poste, B1v. On early modern women singing while they worked, see McNeill, "Free and Bound Maids," 108–9.

102. Brears, Cooking and Dining, 81.

103. Watkins, Representing Elizabeth, 41.

104. Holinshed, Chronicles of England, 1158. Heywood repeats the story of Elizabeth at Woodstock in both If You Know Not Me, You Know Nobody, part 1 (1605) and Englands Elizabeth (1631).

105. Elizabeth I: Collected Works, 170, 188.

106. Watkins, Representing Elizabeth, 87, 97.

107. Louis Adrian Montrose argues that in Elizabeth's evocations of herself as a milkmaid, "the actual powerlessness and compulsory physical labor of the peasant are transformed into a paradoxical experience of power, freedom, and ease" ("'Eliza, Queene of Shepheardes,'" 164).

108. Ganey, "Milkmaids, Ploughmen, and Sex," 42.

109. Ray, *Collection of English Proverbs*, 69.

110. Ravenscroft, *Deuteromelia*, F1v, "Rounds or Catches of 4 Voices," no. 26. A slightly less explicit version of this song is sung in the play *The Two Merry Milkmaids* (J. C., *Pleasant Comedie*, B4v).

111. On early modern portrayals of Elizabeth I as queer, see Traub, *Renaissance of Lesbianism*, 125–57; and Swann, "Sex and the Single Queen."

112. Overbury did not actually write the descriptions of different types of people, including the sketch of "A fayre and happy Milke-mayd," that were published posthumously under his name in *New and Choise Characters* (London, 1615).

113. Phythian-Adams, "Milk and Soot," 90. In a seventeenth-century ballad titled "The Milk-maids life," Martin Parker observes milkmaids "Upon the first of May, / with garlands fresh and gay" (http://ebba.english.ucsb.edu/ballad/30170/transcription); the editors of the online English Broadside Ballad Archive believe this ballad was published sometime between 1633 and 1669 (http://ebba.english.ucsb.edu/ballad/30170/citation).

114. *OED*, s.v. "maudlin, *n.*" and "Magdalene, *n.*" On the complex figure of Mary Magdalene in seventeenth-century England, see Badir, *Maudlin Impression*.

115. Richard Fanshawe makes this mythological backstory explicit—to appallingly grotesque effect—when he remarks of a singing nightingale, "How prettily she tells a tale / Of rape and blood" ("An Ode upon Occasion of His Majesty's Proclamation in the Year 1630," in *Country House Poem*, ed. Fowler, p. 125, lines 115–16). We now know that it is the male (not the female) nightingale that sings loudly for prolonged periods of time, a behavior designed to claim territory and attract a female nightingale to live with him and be his love (Tree, *Wilding*, 184–85, 188–89).

116. Ganey, "Milkmaids, Ploughmen, and Sex," 61.

117. Quoted in Cooper, *Pastoral*, 58; italics indicate the phrase Malory added to his source.

118. Stevens, *Music and Poetry*, 424. Subsequent references appear parenthetically.

119. Walker, "Everyman or a Monster?," 17.

120. Walker, "Rereading Rape and Sexual Violence," 7; King, "Rape in England 1600–1800," 145.

121. Mendelson and Crawford, *Women in Early Modern England*, 211.

122. *OED*, s.v. "spoil, *v.*1."

123. Walton and Cotton, *Complete Angler*, ed. Hawkins, 71n. Hawkins comments on the 1676 edition of Walton's book, so he names Venator rather than Viator as the culprit, but the sequence of events and Piscator's command to his scholar remain unchanged from the first edition of 1653. Hawkins's editorial notes, including this one, were frequently replicated in later editions of Walton's treatise.

124. In seventeenth-century England, a syllabub "was a confection of white wine, cider or fruit juice, well sweetened with sugar and flavoured with lemon or nutmeg, to which cream or milk was added with considerable force," sometimes by "milking the cow directly on to the liquor in the syllabub pot" (Wilson, *Food and Drink in Britain*, 170).

125. Cunnar, "Donne's Witty Theory of Atonement," 83.

126. Petrarca, *Petrarch's Lyric Poems*, p. 340, no. 195, line 2; Spenser, *Yale Edition of the Shorter Poems*, p. 628, sonnet 47, lines 1, 4, 11–12.

127. Wilcox, "'Return unto Me!,'" 100. My analysis of the religiosity of this episode also draws on Cooper, *Art of "The Compleat Angler*," 102–3.

128. Geoffrey Galt Harpham observes that conversion "appears as an exemplary plot-climax, a reversal of a certain way of being and a recognition, an awakening to essential being, to one's truest self" ("Conversion and the Language of Autobiography," 43).

129. Bunyan declares, "*It is profitable to Christians to be often calling to mind the very beginnings of Grace with their Souls*" (*Grace Abounding*, A3v). Helen Wilcox observes that "in the mercantile early modern era of trading and exploring, the exchange of conversion experiences and the telling of travellers' tales about the spiritual pilgrimage were indeed seen to be 'profitable'" ("'Return unto Me!,'" 95).

130. Harpham, "Conversion and the Language of Autobiography," 44.

CHAPTER 3

1. Steven Shapin coins the phrase "edible environment" in "'You Are What You Eat,'" 391.
2. Carlton, *Going to the Wars*, 311; Hindle, "Dearth," 91; Hill, introduction to *Winstanley*, 22.
3. Hill, introduction to *Winstanley*, 22.
4. Hindle, "Dearth," 70; Gentles, *English Revolution*, 443.
5. Purkiss, *English Civil War*, 344; Gentles, *English Revolution*, 443.
6. Carlton, *Going to the Wars*, 246.
7. T. S., *True and Exact Relation*, 4; Carlton, *Going to the Wars*, 323; *Siege of Colchester*, 210.
8. Hyde, *Life of Edward Earl of Clarendon*, 1:251. Clarendon recounts the words of Sir Charles Cavendish.
9. A study conducted after World War II suggests that survivors of "semistarvation" develop and retain a "preoccupation with food" (Purkiss, *English Civil War*, 346–47).
10. Markham, *Pleasures of Princes*, 123.
11. Ibid.
12. Thomas Weaver, "*To My Dear Friend, Mr. Iz. Walton, in Praise of Angling, Which We Both Love*," in *Compleat Angler*, by Walton, ed. Bevan, 429; James Duport, "Ad Virum Optimum, & Piscatorem Peritissimum, *Isaacum Waltonum*," in *Compleat Angler*, by Walton and Cotton, ed. Swann, 14–16, 234 (translation mine).
13. John Evelyn, *Cook*, 147; Franck, *Northern Memoirs*, 276–77.
14. Manning, *Hunters and Poachers*, 131–32; Brears, *Cooking and Dining*, 201–2.
15. Brears, *Cooking and Dining*, 203.
16. Sociologists Josée Johnston and Shyon Baumann suggest that "foodies" regard food "not just as biological sustenance, but also as a key part of their identity, and a kind of lifestyle.... What unites foodies is the fact that food serves a key role in their 'narrative of self identity'" (*Foodies*, 1–2).
17. "Dinner," cooked and served at midday, was the main meal in most regions of early modern England (Flather, *Gender and Space*, 63).
18. Weston, "Freshwater Fish Fight."
19. Walton added this passage to the second edition of the *Angler* in 1655.
20. Walton added this description to his text in 1655.
21. In the 1653 text, Piscator immediately follows the formal binding of Viator as his "Scholer" by telling him how to catch a chub (84), but from 1655 onward, the first set of instructions that Piscator gives his new disciple is instead a recipe for how to *cook* a chub (218).
22. Hartle, "'Take a Long Spoon,'" 42.
23. This repetitive question-and-answer session counteracts Peter's three denials of Jesus before the Crucifixion (John 18:15–27).
24. Calvin, *Harmonie upon the Three Evangelists*, 455–56.
25. Hammond, *Paraphrase and Annotations*, 361. In the dedicatory letter to his *Life* of Robert Sanderson (1678), Walton mentions that he had known Hammond, who died in 1660 (*Lives*, 343).
26. Downame, *Annotations*, commentary on John 21:12, n.p.
27. Fissell, *Vernacular Bodies*, 120–30, esp. 130n46.
28. Browne, "Of the Fishes Eaten by Our Saviour with His Disciples After His Resurrection from the Dead," in *Works*, 3:54.
29. The previous two post-Resurrection appearances of Christ are depicted in John 20:11–23 and John 20:26–31. May 1—the day that Walton's 1653 narrative begins—was celebrated in the traditional Church of England calendar as the Feast of St. Philip and St. James the Less (see above, chapter 1). Philip had a history of mealtime faithlessness: he doubted that Jesus could supply enough bread to feed the five

thousand (John 6:5–7), and during the Last Supper, Philip asked Jesus to "shew us the Father" (John 14:8).

30. Chilton, "Friends and Enemies," 81.

31. McIlhaney, "Renaissance Acts and Images of Angling," 175.

32. On the contrasting politics of the Geneva and King James translations of the Bible, see Hill, *English Bible*, 60–65. The political defiance encoded by Walton's evocation of John 21 is further underlined by the fact that the epigraph vanishes from the title pages of all three editions of *The Compleat Angler* that Walton published after the Restoration.

33. Piscator himself catches seven trout: he brags that he and Viator "have caught but ten *Trouts*, of which my Scholer caught three" (147).

34. Morrill, *Stuart Britain*, 79.

35. The *Oxford English Dictionary* records the first appearance of the term "fish-day" in the early fourteenth century.

36. Evelyn, *Acetaria*, 74. On the biblical basis of early modern ideas about vegetarianism, see Harrison, *Bible*, 223–24.

37. Thomas, *Man and the Natural World*, 290; Boas, *Primitivism and Related Ideas*, 32. Acts 15:20, 15:29, and 21:25 echo the proscription of "blood" stated in Gen. 9:4.

38. Wilson, *Food and Drink in Britain*, 30–31.

39. Mennell, *All Manners of Food*, 27–28. The quarter days—the four dates spaced throughout the year when regular payments such as rent or interest were due—fell on March 25 (Lady Day), June 24 (Midsummer Day), September 29 (Michaelmas), and December 25 (Christmas) (Blackburn and Holford-Strevens, *Oxford Companion to the Year*, 588). Until the thirteenth century, members of monasteries were expected always to abstain from eating flesh unless they were ill (Wilson, *Food and Drink in Britain*, 26).

40. See 2 & 3 Edward VI, c. 19 and 5 Elizabeth I, c.5 in *Statutes of the Realm*, 4:65 and 4:424. On Elizabethan fish-days policy, see Sgroi, "Piscatorial Politics." Wednesday was dropped as a fish day in 1585, but under pressure from Parliament, Charles I ordered monthly Wednesday fasts in 1642 (27 Elizabeth I, c. 11 in *Statutes of the Realm*, 4:718–19; "An Ordinance for the Better Observation of the Monthly Fast," in Firth and Rait, *Acts and Ordinances of the Interregnum*, 1:22–24).

41. England and Wales, *Collection of Such Statutes*, 7–8. See also Brears, *Cooking and Dining*, 398–401; and Wilson, *Food and Drink in Britain*, 46. The four periods of Ember days occurred on the Wednesday, Friday, and Saturday following the first Sunday in Lent; Whitsunday; Holy Cross Day (September 14); and St. Lucia's Day (December 13) (*OED*, s.v. "ember, *n*.2").

42. Cogan, *Haven of Health*, 159.

43. The 1563 statute specifies that the consumption of "Sea Fishe of sundry kindes, either freshe or salte," fulfills the fish-days regulations (5 Elizabeth I, c. 5 in *Statutes of the Realm*, 4:426), but Tudor fish-day menus indicate that freshwater fish might also be consumed (see, e.g., Dawson, *Good Huswifes Jewell*, A2r–A3r).

44. 2 & 3 Edward VI, c. 19 in *Statutes of the Realm*, 4:65.

45. Ryrie, "Fall and Rise of Fasting," 105–6.

46. 5 Elizabeth I, c. 5 in *Statutes of the Realm*, 4:427; Cogan, *Haven of Health*, 159.

47. Ryrie, "Fall and Rise of Fasting," 108.

48. Featley, *Ancilla Pietatis*, 261.

49. Durston, "'For the Better Humiliation,'" 134. On changing seventeenth-century concepts of fasting, see also Dorey, "Controlling Corruption," 25–26; and Thomas, *Religion and the Decline of Magic*, 134–35.

50. "An Ordinance for Taking Away the Book of Common Prayer, and for Establishing and Putting in Execution of the Directory for the Publique Worship of God," January 4, 1644 [1645], in *Acts and Ordinances of the Interregnum*, ed. Firth and Rait, 1:604.

51. Walton added this passage to the second edition of *The Compleat Angler* in 1655.

52. *OED*, s.v. "tansy, *n*."; Brears, *Cooking and Dining*, 360. In his recipe (which Walton added to the *Angler* in 1655), Piscator explains how to prepare minnows so that they can be "*fryed with yolks of eggs, the flowers of Cowslips, and of Primroses,*

and a little Tansie" to make "a dainty dish of meat" (349).

53. Dobson, *Contours of Death and Disease*, 283.

54. Holland, "The Description of the Late Great Memorable and Prodigious Plague," in *Hollandi Post-huma*, E3v; Dobson, *Contours of Death*, 398, 400, 471–72.

55. Although recent posthumanist scholarship claims that "dominant Western and humanist understandings of embodiment" have conceived of human bodies as "fundamentally autonomous," humoral physiology necessarily "rejects a human separation from Nature 'out there'" (Neimanis, *Bodies of Water*, 2, 4).

56. On humoralism and health, see Wear, *Knowledge and Practice*, 37–39.

57. Lemnius, *Touchstone of Complexions*, 15; Lonie, "Fever Pathology," 28–29.

58. Shapin, *Changing Tastes*, 19; Cogan, *Haven of Health*, 215. My description of the humoral digestive process also draws on Albala, *Eating Right in the Renaissance*, 54–62.

59. Schoenfeldt, *Bodies and Selves*, 25–26; Cogan, dedicatory epistle to *Haven of Health*, 4r.

60. Evelyn, *Acetaria*, 68.

61. Cogan, *Haven of Health*, 199; OED, s.v. "meat, *n.*"

62. Cogan, *Haven of Health*, 199.

63. Albala, *Eating Right in the Renaissance*, 5–6, 63–77.

64. Moffett, *Healths Improvement*, 146.

65. Cogan, *Haven of Health*, 160.

66. Venner, *Via Recta*, 98.

67. Walton, *Lives*, 275, 328–29. On Herbert's avoidance of fish for the sake of his health, see Thorley, "'In All a Weak Disabled Thing,'" 3–4.

68. Venner, *Via Recta*, 98.

69. Albala, "Fish in Renaissance Dietary Theory," 11–12.

70. Cogan, *Haven of Health*, 161; Moffett, *Healths Improvement*, 142.

71. Albala, "Fish in Renaissance Dietary Theory," 12; Hart, *Klinike*, 88.

72. Moffett, *Healths Improvement*, 145.

73. Albala, "Fish in Renaissance Dietary Theory," 16.

74. OED, s.v. "pass, *v.*"

75. On the early modern construction of Englishmen as beef-eaters, see Appelbaum, *Aguecheek's Beef*, 1–8; and Shapin, "'You Are What You Eat,'" 384–87.

76. Goody, *Food and Love*, 133; Brears, *Cooking and Dining*, 609–10.

77. Albala, *Food in Early Modern Europe*, 39; Evelyn, *Acetaria*, 16.

78. Rabisha, *Whole Body of Cookery Dissected*, A2r, A8r, A3r. Robert May likewise dedicates *The Accomplisht Cook* to royalist aristocrats and gentlemen "*so well known to the Nation for their admired Hospitalities*" (A3r).

79. Markham, *English Huswife*, 43.

80. Ibid., 63.

81. The word "hogo" apparently does not enter the English language until 1649, and the *Oxford English Dictionary* cites Walton's pike recipe as the earliest use of the term to designate a "strong or piquant flavour" (s.v. "hogo, *n.*"). Similar politics of culinary diction also appear in Richard Franck's critique of decadent royalist foodies like Walton who prefer "an olio"—a spicy stew from Spain or Portugal—to "a broil'd haddock" (OED, s.v. "olio, *n.*"; Franck, *Northern Memoirs*, 223). The celebrated modern chef James Beard included Walton's recipe for roast pike in one of his cookbooks (*James Beard's New Fish Cookery*, 329–30).

82. Guibbory, *Christian Identity*, 14.

83. Ibid., 133–40.

84. See above, chapter 1.

85. Cogan, *Haven of Health*, 172. Careful selection of ingredients and mode of preparation were similarly crucial to the healthfulness of the "Herbs" and "Sallets" that Piscator also recommends. Like fish, many vegetables were regarded as cold and moist: lettuce was supposedly so phlegmatic in complexion that if eaten in great quantity, it could render a man impotent. The "acetous juice" of a vinegar-based dressing could help to counteract such qualities, but a cook nonetheless needed "skill and judgment" so as to combine salad ingredients that would "best agree with the constitution" of diners (Evelyn, *Acetaria*, 16, 50).

86. Franck, *Northern Memoirs*, 133–34.

87. Venner, *Via Recta*, 113.

88. My account of the humoralism of fish cookery follows Albala, "Fish in Renaissance Dietary Theory," 14–16.

89. Downame, *Annotations*, commentary on Luke 24:43, n.p.

90. On the humoral properties of thyme, see Venner, *Via Recta*, 209.

91. Jonquil Bevan points out that Walton thus evokes "traditional discussions of the four elements which occur in encyclopaedic works on Natural History" (Walton, *Compleat Angler*, ed. Bevan, 377).

92. Northrop Frye suggests that we should classify Walton's *Angler* as a Menippean satire, in part because of the work's "deipnosophistical interest in food" (*Anatomy of Criticism*, 312).

93. Markham, *English Huswife*, 36.

94. Powell, *Tom of All Trades*, 34; Evelyn, *Acetaria*, xv, 95.

95. In *Northern Memoirs*, Franck's alter ego Arnoldus and his companion Theophilus spend most of their time in Scotland but cross into England during the concluding third of the text. Franck seems to have taken this journey sometime between 1652 and 1654; although he did not publish his book until 1694, he probably wrote it in 1658 (Allan, "Franck, Richard").

96. Franck, *Northern Memoirs*, 175, 325, 58.

97. For typical recipes, see Brears, *Cooking and Dining*, 276–77.

98. As Viator prepares to catch his own chub after Piscator has tutored him, he tells his teacher that "Ile goe and observe your directions" (85).

99. Wall, *Recipes for Thought*, 3, 13–14, 227.

100. On the gendered politics of 1650s recipe books, see Spiller, "Printed Recipe Books."

101. Barker, "The Epistle to the Reader," in *Art of Angling*, n.p. Subsequent references appear parenthetically. Barker published a second edition of his book in 1653 that replicates the 1651 text but omits Barker's name from the title page and drops the "Epistle." On the publication history of Barker's treatise, see Westwood and Satchell, *Bibliotheca Piscatoria*, 21–23. The place Barker names as his residence—"Henry *the sevenths gifts, the next door to the Gate-house in Westminster*"—consisted of almshouses (Lowerson, "Barker, Thomas").

102. Barker says that he provides his address so he can be located by "*any Noble or Gentle Angler*" who might "*have a mind to discourse*" on the "*experiments*" that Barker discusses in his treatise ("Epistle to the Reader").

103. Jonquil Bevan outlines Walton's use of Barker's treatise in her commentary on Walton's text (Walton, *Compleat Angler*, ed. Bevan, 394–96).

104. *OED*, s.v. "scullion, *n*." In the expanded version of his treatise that he published in 1656, Barker revises this passage and reports instead that his lord "commanded me to turn Cook" (*Barker's Delight*, 14).

105. Barker, *Barker's Delight*, 46. Subsequent references appear parenthetically. Although its title page bears the date 1657, on the basis of an annotation on Thomason's copy, it seems *Barker's Delight* was actually published in 1656. A "Palmer" is an artificial fly fashioned to resemble a fuzzy caterpillar; the *OED* cites Barker as the first published author to use the term thus (s.v. "palmer, *n*.1").

106. Davies, "Montagu [Mountagu], Edward."

107. None of the sources for these recipes has been identified.

108. See *John Evelyn, Cook*; and Digby, *Closet*. Piscator uses the disparaging term "money-getting-men" near the beginning of his dialogue (64).

109. *OED*, s.v. "frumenty/furmety, *n*."; Wilson, *Food and Drink in Britain*, 199–200. In 1590, Leonard Mascall provided a recipe for a "speciall baite" that required the fisherman-chef to "take faire wheate and seeth it like furmantie: then take it out of the water and drie it, then frie it with hony, and good store of saffron, and then put it on your hooke" to catch roach (*Booke of Fishing*, 10–11).

110. Knight, *Reading Green in Early Modern England*, 117n10.

111. Markham, *English Huswife*, 64.

112. *OED*, s.v. "paste, *n*. and *adj*."; Mascall, *Booke of Fishing*, 8; Markham, *Pleasures of Princes*, 126. In his discussions

of bait, Barker refers to "paste" five times in the 1651 edition of his *Art of Angling*; in the final edition of *The Compleat Angler*, Walton uses the term eighteen times.

113. Piscator will scatter his ground bait on the bottom of a body of water to attract bream to that area. As Bevan explains, this section of Walton's treatise seems to be derived from a text written by another author identified only as "B.A." (Walton, *Compleat Angler*, ed. Bevan, 408).

114. In Claude Lévi-Strauss's classic formulation, "not only does cooking mark the transition from nature to culture, but through it and by means of it, the human state can be defined with all its attributes" (*Raw and the Cooked*, 164).

115. Walton here repeats a statement made by Albertus that was included in Edward Topsell's *Historie of Serpents* (180).

116. Bacon, *Sylva Sylvarum*, 153.

117. Walton, *Compleat Angler*, ed. Bevan, 389. Sea trout are a type of brown trout, and the adults actually eat fish and crustaceans (Wheeler, *Fishes of the British Isles*, 153).

118. Bacon, *Sylva Sylvarum*, 194; Topsell, *Historie of Serpents*, 180.

119. George Sandys coins the resonant term "foodful earth" in his translation of Psalm 49 (*Poetical Works of George Sandys*, 1:159). Walton, as he notes, derives his story of Elijah and the ravens from 1 Kings 17:6.

120. Moffett, *Theater of Insects*, 990. Walton revised and expanded this passage over multiple editions.

121. Steel, "Creeping Things," 224; Mortimer-Sandilands and Erickson, introduction to *Queer Ecologies*, 30.

122. Augustine, *City of God*, 691. Other church fathers made different theological uses of spontaneous generation: Lactantius, for example, argued that the existence of such nonsexual reproduction gave credence to the doctrine of the Virgin Birth (Vartanian, "Spontaneous Generation," 4:308).

123. Hale, *Primitive Origination of Mankind*, 287.

124. Aristotle believed that the sun performed a generative function parallel to that of the hot air (*pneuma*) in semen (Fry, *Emergence of Life on Earth*, 16); Browne, *Religio Medici*, in *Works*, 1:24; Moffett, *Theater of Insects*, 1040, 1102, 1097.

125. *OED*, s.v. "ecology, n."

126. Walton here draws on Pliny (*Historie of the World*, 329). Topsell likewise cites Pliny on this point (*Historie of Serpents*, 107).

127. Walton refers to a type of pondweed (*Potamogeton*), not the North American water plant also called "pickerel weed" (*OED*, s.v. "pickerel weed, n.").

128. Franck, *Northern Memoirs*, 176–77.

129. In a sixteenth-century anti-Catholic polemic, the naturalist William Turner stages a debate about spontaneous generation in which one character observes, "It is trulike that Dukkes and wilde Gese, and suche like of that water ha[u]nting kinde, cary ether the Rownes [roes] or Egges of fisshes or els yonge frie, upon their winges, billes, or fete; unto suche newe pondes, and diches, as ye have spoken of, where of come these fisshes, whereof ye make mencion" (*Huntyng of the Romyshe Wolfe*, A6v–A7r).

130. I owe this observation to Sean Herrera-Thomas's provocative discussion of homosociality in Walton's treatise ("Haunted by Authors," 166).

131. Remien, "Oeconomy and Ecology," 1118. Myra Wright links Walton's portrayal of the social process of conversion more generally with his depictions of "biological metamorphosis" (*Poetics of Angling*, 146).

132. Remien, "Oeconomy and Ecology," 1118.

133. Ibid., 1130.

CHAPTER 4

1. Cotton, prefatory epistle, *Compleat Angler, Part II*, 169. Subsequent references appear parenthetically. In this letter, dated March 10, Cotton recounts that Walton gave him "*a little more than ten days time*" to complete his work (169).

2. The final edition of Walton's text was issued as the centerpiece of *The Universal Angler*, which also included Cotton's new work on fly-fishing and the fourth edition of another angling treatise, Robert Venables's *The Experienc'd Angler*. On the

publication history of the 1676 edition, see Bevan, introduction to *Compleat Angler*, 38–40.

3. Schullery, *American Fly Fishing*, 9.

4. My analysis develops Jonquil Bevan's astute observation that if Piscator and Venator had "turned aside with Auceps at the park wall of Theobalds, a very different book would have ensued" (*Izaak Walton's "The Compleat Angler*," 79).

5. Goldring et al., *John Nichols's "The Progresses*," 1:706, 5:165n1; Lysons, "Theobalds."

6. Summerson, "Building of Theobalds," 114; Sutton, *Materializing Space*, 7; Andrews, "Theobalds Palace," 132 (site plan 4).

7. Sutton, "Decorative Program at Elizabethan Theobalds," 38–39, 44, 56. As Sutton notes, Burghley was actually a "Tudor parvenu" who "went to great lengths to fabricate his own ancient lineage" (35–36).

8. Sutton, *Materializing Space*, 8; Lysons, "Theobalds," 31. The historical currency converter on the National Archives website suggests that two to three thousand pounds in the 1590s would have been worth between £340,000 and £515,000 in 2017 ("Currency Converter: 1270–2017," National Archives, accessed October 23, 2022, https://www.nationalarchives.gov.uk/currency-converter).

9. Stone, "Building of Hatfield House," 102. Robert Cecil—who had been instrumental in securing James's succession—served as the king's secretary of state and eventually also as James's lord treasurer until Cecil's death in 1612 (Croft, "Cecil, Robert, First Earl of Salisbury"). Walton was certainly aware of the importance of Theobalds to the Stuart monarchy, telling the story of how John Donne was summoned to that royal palace one night by James's favorite, Robert Carr, who was "then at *Theobalds* with the King" (*Lives*, 45).

10. Thomson, "Progress, Retreat, and Pursuit," 95–96; Lysons, "Theobalds," 38.

11. Manning, *Hunters and Poachers*, 205–7; Phillips, "Theobalds Park Wall," 250; Rowe and Williamson, *Hertfordshire*, 138; Beaver, *Hunting and the Politics of Violence*, 74.

12. Thomson, "Progress, Retreat, and Pursuit," 96, 103.

13. Ibid., 95; Phillips, "Theobalds Park Wall," 260.

14. Manning, *Hunters and Poachers*, 207.

15. Andrews, "Theobalds Palace," 145.

16. Page, *Victoria History*, 3:449; Wilcher, "*Eikon Basilike*," 293.

17. Walford, *Greater London*, 1:381.

18. Lysons, "Theobalds," 33.

19. Page, *Victoria History*, 3:449.

20. Walford, *Greater London*, 1:384.

21. My analysis draws on Bates, *Masculinity and the Hunt*, 1–10; Bergman, "Spectacle of Beasts," 61; Berry, *Shakespeare and the Hunt*, 21; Crane, *Animal Encounters*, 103–19; and Norton, "Going to the Birds," 55.

22. I borrow the term "political ecology" from Beaver, *Hunting and the Politics of Violence*, 11.

23. MacGregor, "Animals and the Early Stuarts," 314.

24. Griffin, *Blood Sport*, 90; Berry, *Shakespeare and the Hunt*, 13.

25. MacGregor, *Animal Encounters*, 111; Berry, *Shakespeare and the Hunt*, 3–4, 29–30; Griffin, *Blood Sport*, 102–3.

26. Oggins, *Kings and Their Hawks*, 22–23, 30.

27. On the different early modern modes of deer hunting, see Manning, *Hunters and Poachers*, 23–27.

28. MacGregor, *Animal Encounters*, 161–70.

29. Ralph Sadler's estate was located at Standon in Hertfordshire; Walton knew members of Sadler's family who lived in Staffordshire.

30. Lovegrove, *Silent Fields*, 245.

31. MacGregor, "Animals and the Early Stuarts," 313.

32. Venator says he's been told by a friend that otter hunting "is much pleasanter than any other chase whatsoever; howsoever I mean to try it" (175); Viator's words in the 1653 text are very similar (64), but Walton's addition of the final clause in his 1655 revision emphasizes that Venator is an otter-hunt novice.

33. *The Compleat Angler* thus also rejects the ecosocial vision of Henry Peacham's *Compleat Gentleman*: Peacham likewise

notes that canon law traditionally forbade clergymen from hawking and hunting, but he nonetheless argues that these blood sports "are recreations very commendable and befitting a Noble or Gentleman to exercise; Hunting especially" (*Compleat Gentleman*, 182–84).

34. On "wit" as a masculine mode of debauched behavior, see Withington, *Society in Early Modern England*, 189–93.

35. On royalists and alehouses, see Capp, *England's Culture Wars*, 162–67.

36. Griffin, *Blood Sport*, 85; Thomas, *Man and the Natural World*, 160–65.

37. See above, chapter 2.

38. Markham, *Pleasures of Princes*, 103.

39. Kain, Chapman, and Oliver, *Enclosure Maps of England and Wales*, 1.

40. MacGregor, *Animal Encounters*, 101.

41. Manning, *Village Revolts*, 302.

42. Ibid.; McRae, "Pleasures of the Land," 169. Because the Crown owned the beds of all tidal stretches of English rivers, landlords of adjoining banks could not control usage (McRae, "Pleasures of the Land," 165). Although it was usually presumed that the owner of the bank of a nontidal river also owned the adjacent half of the river and thus the right to fish in that half of the watercourse, the property owner's right to the riverbed and/or right of fishing could be transferred. Sarah Robinson explains that "the owner of a river bank may own the soil of the river but not the right of fishing therein; he may own the right of fishing but not the soil; he may own both; and he may own neither" ("Catching Fish, Making Law," 49). From this perspective, Walton's anglers behave as if they own both the banks and the right to fish wherever they choose to go angling in the River Lea.

43. Houston, "People, Space, and Law," 86.

44. Manning, *Hunters and Poachers*, 123.

45. Houston, "People, Space, and Law," 85.

46. Ibid., 82; Blomley, "Making Private Property," 13; Stubbes, *Anatomie of Abuses*, P5r.

47. Piscator and Viator/Venator spend their first night in Hertfordshire at an inn—the Thatched House—in Hoddesdon (63, 79).

48. Shakespeare, *Midsummer Night's Dream*, 2.1.251.

49. Interpreting different plants as "painted Lectures of Gods sacred will," Henry Peacham writes that honeysuckle—which he dubs "woodbine"—signifies "that we should our friendship hold" (*Minerva Britanna*, 187).

50. McRae, "Pleasures of the Land," 164. My analysis of Walton's depiction of landownership also draws on Bevan, *Izaak Walton's "The Compleat Angler*," 77–81.

51. C. H. Firth outlines the legal problems faced by royalists with sequestered estates in "Royalists Under the Protectorate," 637–40.

52. Whitaker, *Mad Madge*, 231, 237.

53. Viator/Venator's speech anticipates—or was recycled by—Joseph Addison, who would assert in 1712 that "a Man of a Polite Imagination . . . often feels a greater Satisfaction in the Prospect of Fields and Meadows, than another does in the Possession. It gives him, indeed, a kind of Property in every thing he sees" (*Spectator*, no. 411, 3:538).

54. Traherne, "Wonder," in *Thomas Traherne: Selected Poems*, p. 6, lines 49–56.

55. Gerrard Winstanley et al., *The True Levellers' Standard Advanced* (1649), in Borlik, *Literature and Nature*, 410–11.

56. The Game Act of 1671, which granted sporting rights only to substantial landowners, at one stroke allowed the English gentry both to replace the Crown as "stewards of the game" and to disqualify their "social inferiors" from hunting (Landry, *Invention of the Countryside*, 4–5).

57. McRae, "Pleasures of the Land," 163.

58. Houston, "People, Space, and Law," 49.

59. "Short Discourse by Way of Post-Script," S1r–S1v. Subsequent references appear parenthetically.

60. Werner, *Studying Early Printed Books*, 39; Voss, "Printing Conventions," 100; Lesser, "Typographic Nostalgia," 107.

61. Voss, "Printing Conventions," 111n10.

62. McRae, "Pleasures of the Land," 165.

63. On their second day together,

Piscator Junior mentions to Viator that it is "the Seventh of *March*" (185).
64. See above, chapter 2.
65. Cotton, *The Wonders of the Peake*, in *Poetry of Charles Cotton*, 2:357, line 1264. Subsequent references to quotations of Cotton's poems from this edition appear parenthetically.
66. Tebbutt, "'In the Midlands,'" 165; "Peak District Plan," Peak District National Park Authority, accessed August 17, 2022, http://www.peakdistrict.gov.uk/looking-after/biodiversity/biodiversity-action-plan/peak-district.
67. Bull, *Peak District*, 1; "NCA Profile 53: South West Peak," Natural England, June 27, 2013, p. 3, http://publications.naturalengland.org.uk/publication/12392045.
68. For most of its course, the River Dove serves as the boundary between Staffordshire and Derbyshire as well as the line of demarcation between the White Peak and the Moorlands, but at Beresford Dale, the site of Cotton's country house, both banks of the Dove become encompassed by the White Peak (Tim Jacklin, "River Dove at Beresford Dale," Wild Trout Trust, 2015, sec. 2.1, https://www.wildtrout.org/av/river-dove-beresford-dale). In his fishing treatise, Cotton says that Beresford Hall is located "in the *More-Lands*, but within a spit, and a stride of the peak" (182).
69. Cope, "Metering Mineral Resources," 114.
70. Drayton, *Poly-Olbion*, in *Works of Michael Drayton*, 4:530, lines 379–80. On Drayton's gendered representation of the Peak and its influence, see Di Palma, *Wasteland*, 128–37.
71. Browne, "Journal," 27; *Journeys of Celia Fiennes*, 96; Plot, *Natural History of Stafford-shire*, 110.
72. In Cotton's *Wonders of the Peake*, the narrator's "ambivalence of stance" replicates the contrasting perspectives on the Peak that Cotton had voiced five years earlier through the separate characters of Viator and Piscator Junior (Hartle, "Defoe and *The Wonders*," 421).
73. Gerald Heywood provides both detailed analysis and a map of the travelers' route in his invaluable and lovely book *Charles Cotton and His River*, 19–34, 165.

74. Cotton refers to "*Peakish* Miles" in his *Wonders of the Peak* (*Poetry of Charles Cotton*, 2:334, line 401). Although the statute mile of 1,760 yards had been established since 1593, the "old British mile" of 2,428 yards was still widely used—especially in northern districts—throughout the seventeenth century (Morris, introduction to *Journeys of Celia Fiennes*, xxxix).
75. Piscator Junior says that it is "six Miles further to my House" (174), but as Gerald Heywood notes, in statute miles the travelers' route from Ashbourne to Beresford Hall is actually closer to nine miles (*Charles Cotton and His River*, 38n7).
76. Assessing the history of tourism in the Peak District, Trevor Brighton comments that "the anxieties aroused in the stranger as he entered the Peak on horseback for the first time are best portrayed" in Cotton's narrative (*Discovery of the Peak District*, 15).
77. *Journeys of Celia Fiennes*, 101.
78. Decades earlier, Thomas Hobbes had dubbed the Peak "the English Alps" (translation of the original Latin) at the beginning of his topographical poem *De Mirabilibus Pecci* (A1r).
79. On Cotton's implicit evocation of nightfall as the travelers arrive at Beresford Hall, see Heywood, *Charles Cotton and His River*, 34.
80. As Andy Wood observes, a similar sense of escaping from the inhospitable surroundings of the Peak into a bubble of civilization informs Cotton's description of Chatsworth in his *Wonders of the Peake* (*Politics of Social Conflict*, 5).
81. Buxton, introduction to *Poems of Charles Cotton*, xxvi; Heywood, *Charles Cotton and His River*, 45–46.
82. On the symbolism of trees in descriptions of early modern English estates, see Turner, *Politics of Landscape*, 97–101.
83. Kinder, *Historie of Darby-shire*, 22:23. The Gospel of Matthew reports that after he had betrayed Jesus, Judas "went and hanged himself" (27:5).
84. Cokain, "To the Same [Charles Cotton the Younger]," in *Chain of Golden Poems*, 132.
85. Gerald Heywood discusses the

location of the bowling green (*Charles Cotton and His River*, 47–48). Piscator Junior says he is "no very good bowler" but installed the green for "other men's" entertainment (184). Cotton had earlier written that a bowling green "is a place where three things are thrown away besides the Bowls, viz. Time, Money and Curses, and the last ten for one" (*Compleat Gamester*, 49).

86. Celia Fiennes advised would-be travelers to the Peak that "by reason of the steepness and hazard of the Wayes—if you take a wrong Way there is no passing—you are forced to have Guides" (*Journeys of Celia Fiennes*, 101).

87. As they prepared to stay at Bleak Hall in 1653, Piscator told Viator that "My Hostis has two beds, and I know you and I may have the best" (88). Sharing a bed with a same-sex "bedfellow" was a common practice in early modern England, and travelers were often expected to bunk with complete strangers, as Viator would probably have done if he had stayed at an Ashbourne inn as he had originally planned. Celia Fiennes complained that lodging in the Peak was so inadequate that individual rooms contained as many as four beds, with conditions being "sometymes ... so crowded that three must lye in a bed" (*Journeys of Celia Fiennes*, 103).

88. Although Piscator Junior is idiosyncratic in not consuming food at breakfast, Cotton's contemporaries normally drank ale or beer with this meal.

89. Thomas, *Ends of Life*, 117; Kinder, *Historie of Darby-shire*, 23:167.

90. Bull, *Peak District*, xiii. Cotton himself often expresses genteel scorn for "the Peak-rabble," as he calls his plebeian neighbors (*Wonders of the Peake*, in *Poetry of Charles Cotton*, 2:358, line 1280).

91. Kinder, *Historie of Darby-shire*, 22:182.

92. Browne, "Journal," 27.

93. See above, chapter 1.

94. My description of Cotton's fishing house draws on Heywood, *Charles Cotton and His River*, 49; Pevsner, *Staffordshire*, 68; and the building's entry on Historic England's National Heritage List, November 12, 1931, https://historicengland.org.uk/listing/the-list/list-entry/1006110.

95. As Gerald Heywood explains, between the site of Beresford Hall, which was located on "high ground," and the River Dove "rises the hill whose precipitous face—in places a sheer wall of rock—forms the western flank of Beresford Dale" (*Charles Cotton and His River*, 45).

96. In an editorial annotation on Cotton's text, Walton counters this passage's emphasis on property ownership by noting Cotton's failure to portray the natural setting of the fishing house holistically, observing that in Cotton's narrative, "*some part of the* Fishing-house *has been describ'd; but, the pleasantness of the River, Mountains, and Meadows about it, cannot* [be described]; *unless Sir Philip Sidney, or Mr. Cotton's Father were again alive to do it*" (184).

97. *OED*, s.v. "title, *n*."

98. *OED*, s.v. "junior, *adj*. and *n*."

99. See also Rom. 8:23, Gal. 4:4–5, and Eph. 1:4–5.

100. "To My Old, and Most Worthy Friend, Mr. IZAAK WALTON, on His Life of Dr. DONNE, &c.," in *Poetry of Charles Cotton*, 2:387–91, lines 19, 118, 117. Subsequent line references appear parenthetically. On the dating of this poem, see *Poetry of Charles Cotton*, 2:767.

101. Piscator Junior never mentions his mother either, although it was through her that Charles Cotton the Elder (and thus his son as well) gained possession of the Beresford estate (Hartle, introduction to *Poetry of Charles Cotton*, 1:xxiv).

102. Cotton's friendship with Walton exemplifies how, as I have discussed elsewhere, lineage became "a residual aspect of social authority" in seventeenth-century England (Swann, *Curiosities and Texts*, 143).

103. Hartle, "Cotton, Charles."

104. Cotton, "Epistle to John Bradshaw Esq.," in *Poetry of Charles Cotton*, 1:232, line 100; Turner, *Politics of Landscape*, 153.

105. *OED*, s.v. "house, *n*.1 and *int*."

106. Stone, *Family, Sex and Marriage in England*, 426.

107. Cotton's poem "The Retirement," which Walton included in the final edition of *The Compleat Angler*, provides the only hint of female presence in Cotton's treatise

when Cotton lovingly describes the River Dove—not a woman—as *"my beloved Nymph"* (226).

108. Nicolas, "Life of Charles Cotton," clxxxiv–clxxxv; Beresford Cotton was born in 1660 (clxxi).

109. Hartle, "Cotton, Charles." On the correct date of Cotton's second marriage, see Hartle's editorial comment in *Poetry of Charles Cotton*, 1:534.

110. Cotton, "Poverty," in *Poetry of Charles Cotton*, 1:332, line 44; Cotton writes of his *"beloved Caves"* as his *"safe retreat"* from *"all anxieties"* in "The Retirement" (2:394, lines 62–63); Beresford, introduction to *Poems of Charles Cotton*, 19–20; Nicolas, "Life of Cotton," clxxxiv. The historical currency converter on the National Archives website suggests that £1,500 in 1671 would have been worth about £170,000 in 2017 ("Currency Converter: 1270–2017," National Archives, accessed October 23, 2022, https://www.nationalarchives.gov.uk/currency-converter).

111. Here again, the presence of his servant bespeaks Piscator Junior's elite status, for Cotton observes that "in landing of a Fish . . . every one that can afford to Angle for pleasure, has some body to do for him" (189).

112. Fagan, *Fish on Friday*, 41, 43, 45; Thirsk, *Food in Early Modern England*, 269. Walton added a discussion of fishponds—which, as he notes, he drew from other authors—to the second edition of *The Compleat Angler* in 1655 (357–59).

113. Braham, *Institucion of a Gentleman*, E7r.

114. Quoted in MacGregor, *Animal Encounters*, 305.

115. *Boke of Saint Albans*, G3r. I am using the terms "hawking" and "falconry" interchangeably, but since hawks seize their quarry on the ground and falcons attack their prey in the air, the two activities were regarded in the early modern period as different modes of hunting (Grassby, "Decline of Falconry," 37).

116. *Boke of Saint Albans*, G3r.

117. Ibid., I4v.

118. Dennys, *Secrets of Angling*, B6r, C3v; see above, chapter 2; Venables, *Experienc'd Angler*, A6r, A2v.

119. On the church in Alstonefield and its connections with Cotton and his family, see Heywood, *Cotton and His River*, 30–32.

120. The second-century encyclopedist Aelian reported that Macedonian fishermen made highly effective artificial flies by attaching crimson wool and cock feathers to hooks, but Aelian's text—which was written in Greek—seems to have had no impact on anglers (Radcliffe, *Fishing from the Earliest Times*, 187–89).

121. In his slightly revised version of the *Treatyse*'s account of artificial flies, Leonard Mascall adds the "darce" (dace) and the chub to the list of fish that can be caught with such lures (*Booke of Fishing*, 16).

122. McDonald, *Origins of Angling*, 110–11, 224–25, 64n54.

123. Ibid., 111; McCully, *Fly-Fishing*, 64. The author of the *Treatyse* uses the verb "dubbe" to refer to the fabrication of flies but also uses the terms "dubbe" and "dubbyd hoke" as generic names for artificial flies (222–23, 190–91, 212–13).

124. On the different species of birds named in the *Treatyse*'s catalog of artificial flies, see McDonald, *Origins of Angling*, 111–12. As McDonald notes, the hackle (neck) feathers of a capon are softer than those of a rooster (a noncastrated male chicken) (112).

125. Mascall, *Booke of Fishing*, 16; Markham, *Pleasures of Princes*, 124, 123. Walton, who consistently follows Mascall, describes the items in the catalog as "Artificial made Flies" (254).

126. John McDonald explains how interpretation of this ambiguous passage affects the fabrication of the fly (*Origins of Angling*, 123). McDonald's book has color plates illustrating all the artificial flies described in the *Treatyse* (115–17), and Andrew Herd provides stunning close-up photographs of his interpretations of some of the same dressings (*History of Fly Fishing*, 1:54–55, 1:57–58).

127. Barker, *Art of Angling*, 15–16. Andrew Herd provides useful commentary on Barker's fly-tying method (*History of Fly Fishing*, 1:96–97). On the properties of the "wool" of animals' fur, see Carlos and Lewis, "Economic History of the Fur Trade."

128. Venables, *Experienc'd Angler*, 24; McCully, *Fly-Fishing*, 64. On Venables's other fly-tying innovations, see Herd, *History of Fly Fishing*, 1:102.

129. Venables, *Experienc'd Angler*, 29–30. *OED*, s.v. "mockado, *n.*1 and *adj.*"; Burnham, *Warp and Weft*, 52; *OED*, s.v. "hickwall, *n.*"; "Green Woodpecker," RSPB Wildlife Charity, accessed August 18, 2022, https://www.rspb.org.uk/birds-and-wildlife/wildlife-guides/bird-a-z/green-woodpecker.

130. An avid modern fly fisherman testifies that Cotton "is one of the few people who can describe exactly how to tie a fly without the benefit of any illustrations at all" (Brown, "Epitaph to Charles Cotton," 10).

131. Herd, *History of Fly Fishing*, 1:102.

132. For photographs of flies tied according to Cotton's instructions, see Herd, *History of Fly Fishing*, 1:97, 1:101.

133. Cotton, "On My Pretty Marten," in *Poetry of Charles Cotton*, 1:205, lines 83–86.

134. Cotton provides detailed general fly-tying instructions on pp. 190–91. Gerald Heywood outlines the fabrication principles for Cotton's different categories of artificial flies (*Charles Cotton and His River*, 97–98), and John McDonald explains Venables's and Cotton's contrasting methods of dubbing fly bodies (McDonald, *Origins of Angling*, 111).

135. On the lowly social status of dog-fur muffs, see Kathleen Walker-Meikle, "More Than One Way to Skin a Cat," *Renaissance Skin: Consuming*, accessed August 18, 2022, https://renaissanceskin.ac.uk/themes/consuming.

136. Herd, *History of Fly Fishing*, 1:103.

137. On the spaniel in early modern English culture, see MacInnes, "Mastiffs and Spaniels," 32–38.

138. Caius, *Englishe Dogges*, 40. On the early modern greyhound as an elite status symbol, see Russell, *Greyhound Nation*, 21–54.

139. A "Dun" is a dark-colored artificial fly that imitates the almost-adult (subimago) form of a mayfly (McCully, *Fly-Fishing*, 65). On the complex life cycle of mayflies, see McCully, *Fly-Fishing*, 129–30.

140. Animal hair that was added to early modern plaster as an aggregate became both waterproof and uniquely colored (Claire Gapper, "Chapter 1, Materials and Their Uses," *British Renaissance Plasterwork*, accessed August 18, 2022, http://clairegapper.info/materials-and-uses.html; Watson, *Angling with the Fly*, 93). Animal hides were dressed with lime as part of the tanning process.

141. Woven from wool, mohair, or silk, camlet was a luxurious lightweight fabric that often had a watered finish (*OED*, s.v. "camlet, *n.*"; Kerridge, *Textile Manufactures in Early Modern England*, 42).

142. In his poetic tribute to his pet pine marten, Cotton lovingly blazons Matty's body, including his "Back and Belly soft as Down" ("On My Pretty Marten," in *Poetry of Charles Cotton*, 1:203, line 41). Lovegrove notes that "Marten fur was prized more highly than almost any other, apart from imported Sable" (*Silent Fields*, 203).

143. Cotton also calls another fly, composed entirely of peacock feathers, "the Peacock-flie" (209). On Cotton's categorization of artificial flies, "which was to be used for another two centuries," see Herd, *History of Fly Fishing*, 1:103.

144. As Susan Frye argues, "The ideology of needlework is crucial to the study of gender roles in this period" ("Sewing Connections," 180n1).

145. Cotton, a royalist, claims Henry Jackson as his fly-tying progenitor despite Jackson's role during the civil wars as a parliamentarian officer (Baggs et al., "Alstonefield").

146. Markham, *Pleasures of Princes*, 125.

147. Later in *The Compleat Angler*, as a segue to Piscator's narrative ad for his favorite London tackle-vendors, Walton presents "an old Rhime out of an old Fish-book" that catalogs a fisherman's gear, including an "*Angling purse*" (155).

148. *OED*, s.v. "magazine, *n.*"

149. *Poetry of Charles Cotton*, 1:386, lines 19–21.

150. Grigson, *Menagerie*, 29–31.

151. Evelyn, *Diary*, 3:399, 175; Evelyn, *Elysium Britannicum*, 256.

152. Jackson, *Peacock*, 7, 21, 111; Grigson, *Menagerie*, 31.

153. Grigson, *Menagerie*, 18; Jackson, *Peacock*, 113–14; Cumming, "'Great Vanity and Excesse in Apparell,'" 346; Howey, "Vain, Exotic, and Erotic Feather," 215–16.
154. Cockayne, "Cockayne of Ashbourne Hall," 3. For images of all the coats of arms of Cotton and his relatives, see Heywood, *Charles Cotton and His River*, 12.
155. Cumming, "'Great Vanity and Excesse,'" 342.
156. MacGregor, *Animal Encounters*, 384–85, 388; Kathleen Walker-Meikle, "Furs for Earls," Renaissance Skin: Consuming, accessed August 18, 2022, https://renaissanceskin.ac.uk/themes/consuming.
157. Grigson, *Menagerie*, 22; Walker-Meikle, "Furs for Earls"; Cumming, "'Great Vanity and Excesse,'" 342.
158. MacGregor, *Animal Encounters*, 146–54.
159. Ibid., 205–9.
160. Jewitt, "Derby Signs," 232; Beresford and Beresford, *History of the Manor of Beresford*, 97. On the material culture of bearbaiting, see MacGregor, *Animal Encounters*, 206–7.
161. Howey, "Vain, Exotic, and Erotic Feather," 215; Ribeiro, *Fashion and Fiction*, 27–29; Cumming, "'Great Vanity and Excesse,'" 343.
162. Pope, *Rape of the Lock*, in *Major Works*, p. 82, canto 1, lines 135–36.
163. Heywood, *Charles Cotton and His River*, 12, 45.
164. Cotton's fishing house is registered on the National Heritage List for England as a Grade II* Listed Building, meaning it is legally protected as one of a small group of "particularly important buildings of more than special interest" (https://historicengland.org.uk/advice/hpg/has/listed-buildings).
165. Westwood, "The Fishing House," in *In Memoriam Izaak Walton*, n.p.

EPILOGUE

1. Maclean, *River Runs Through It*, 5. Subsequent references appear parenthetically.
2. Paul misreads *The Compleat Angler*: Walton's milkwomen sing songs for his anglers, not vice versa. His youthful erasure of female agency from Walton's narrative foreshadows Paul's inability as an adult to establish healthy relationships with women, one facet of his tragically "unthinking adherence to an outmoded myth" of "independent masculinity" (Lojek, "Casting Flies and Recasting Myths," 154–55). Robert Hayashi explores how this corrosive mythos has also underpinned ideas about race and ethnicity in the American West (*Haunted by Waters*).
3. The 1992 film version of *A River Runs Through It* excises all references to Walton and the *Angler* narrative other than cinematic Neal's brief mention of an otter. Although most commentators on the novella likewise ignore Maclean's allusions to *The Compleat Angler*, Ron McFarland observes that "in some ways 'A River Runs [T]hrough It' does amount to an antitype of Walton's pastoral celebration of angling" (*Norman Maclean*, 12).
4. Blew, "Mo-nah-se-tah," 196. On Old Rawhide as a transgressively positive character, see Peterson, "Prodigal Sons and Matriarchs," esp. 652–55.
5. The sequence 3-7-77, as Maclean's narrator explains, specifies the dimensions of a highwayman's grave: three feet by seven feet by seventy-seven inches (30).
6. On the otter hunt in Walton's *Angler*, see above, chapter 1. Neal's otter is presumably a northern river otter (*Lontra canadensis*) native to Montana, a different species than the Eurasian otter (*Lutra lutra*) hunted by Piscator. The otter's cougar DNA evokes the mountaineering leopard—which perished while ranging far above its normal altitude—that appears in Ernest Hemingway's epigraph to "The Snows of Kilimanjaro" (*Complete Short Stories*, 39).
7. The natural history of Paul's tale is as unsound as Neal's. The contrast between Paul's jackrabbit and "a snowshoe rabbit" makes sense only if Paul follows a black-tailed jackrabbit (*Lepus californicus*), which does not change color, because the white-tailed jackrabbit (*Lepus townsendii*), like the snowshoe rabbit (*Lepus americanus*) to which Paul compares his traveling companion, turns white in the

winter. Yet unlike the white-tailed jackrabbit, the range of the black-tailed jackrabbit does not extend to the area around Nevada Creek, Montana, through which Paul drives in his story. For information about all these animals and their ranges, see the "Montana Field Guide" website (http://fieldguide.mt.gov/default.aspx).

8. Hidy et al., *Great Northern Railway*, 124–25. The Great Northern's iconic mountain goat was dubbed "Rocky."

9. On the development of Marias Pass, see Hidy et al., *Great Northern Railway*, 74–75.

10. Meeker, *Comedy of Survival*, 29. Subsequent references appear parenthetically.

11. Stegner, "Haunted by Waters," 160. James E. Ford suggests that Maclean's novella is "neither tragedy nor comedy" but instead "a third kind of story" that parallels the ode in its structural complexity ("When 'Life . . . Becomes Literature,'" 531, 533).

BIBLIOGRAPHY

All early modern texts published before 1701 have been accessed through the Early English Books Online database (EEBO) unless otherwise noted.

All texts published between 1701 and 1800 have been accessed through the Eighteenth Century Collections Online database (ECCO) unless otherwise noted.

Addison, Joseph, and Richard Steele. *The Spectator*. Edited by Donald F. Bond. 5 vols. Oxford: Clarendon Press of Oxford University Press, 1987.

Adrian, John. *Local Negotiations of English Nationhood, 1570–1680*. Basingstoke, UK: Palgrave Macmillan, 2011.

Albala, Ken. *Eating Right in the Renaissance*. Berkeley: University of California Press, 2002.

———. "Fish in Renaissance Dietary Theory." In *Fish: Food from the Waters*, edited by Harlan Walker, 9–19. Totnes, UK: Prospect Books, 1998.

———. *Food in Early Modern Europe*. Westport, CT: Greenwood Press, 2003.

Allan, David. "Franck, Richard (c. 1624–c. 1708)." In *Oxford Dictionary of National Biography*. Online ed. Oxford: Oxford University Press, 2004.

Allen, Daniel. *Otter*. London: Reaktion, 2010.

Alpers, Paul. *The Singer of the "Eclogues": A Study of Virgilian Pastoral*. Berkeley: University of California Press, 1979.

Ambrose, Isaac. *Media: The Middle Things in Reference to the First and Last Things*. 2nd ed. London, 1652.

Andrews, Martin. "Theobalds Palace: The Gardens and Park." *Garden History* 21, no. 2 (Winter 1993): 129–49.

Anselment, Raymond A. "Feminine Self-Reflection and the Seventeenth-Century Occasional Meditation." *Seventeenth Century* 26, no. 1 (Spring 2011): 69–93.

Appelbaum, Robert. *Aguecheek's Beef, Belch's Hiccup, and Other Gastronomic Interjections: Literature, Culture, and Food Among the Early Moderns*. Chicago: University of Chicago Press, 2006.

Augustine. *The City of God Against the Pagans*. Edited and translated by R. W. Dyson. Cambridge: Cambridge University Press, 1998.

Bacon, Francis. *Of the Advancement and Proficience of Learning or The Partitions of Sciences, IX Bookes*. Translated by Gilbert Wat[t]s. Oxford, 1640.

———. *Sylva Sylvarum, or, A Naturall History*. London, 1651.

Badir, Patricia. *The Maudlin Impression: English Literary Images of Mary Magdalene, 1550–1700*. Notre Dame, IN: University of Notre Dame Press, 2009.

Baggs, A. P., M. F. Cleverdon, D. A. Johnston, and N. J. Tringham. "Alstonefield: Alstonefield." In *A History of the County of Stafford*, vol. 7, *Leek and the Moorlands*, edited by C. R. J. Currie and M. W.

Greenslade, 8–27. London: Victoria County History, 1996.
Barker, Thomas. *The Art of Angling*. 1651. Reprint, London: J. H. Burn, 1820.
———. *Barker's Delight*. London, 1656.
Bastard, Thomas. *Chrestoleros*. London, 1598.
Bates, Catherine. *Masculinity and the Hunt: Wyatt to Shakespeare*. Oxford: Oxford University Press, 2013.
Bauthumley, Jacob. *The Light and Dark Sides of God*. London, 1650.
Beard, James. *James Beard's New Fish Cookery*. Boston: Little, Brown, 1976.
Beatty, Bob. Afterword to *The Compleat Angler*, by Izaak Walton and Charles Cotton, 179–92. Revised by Eugene Burns. Harrisburg, PA: Stackpole, 1953.
Beaver, Daniel C. *Hunting and the Politics of Violence Before the English Civil War*. Cambridge: Cambridge University Press, 2008.
Beresford, John. Introduction to *Poems of Charles Cotton, 1630–1687*, edited by John Beresford, 7–34. New York: Boni and Liveright, n.d. [1923].
Beresford, William, and Samuel B. Beresford. *A History of the Manor of Beresford, in the County of Stafford*. Leek, UK: Eaton, 1908.
Bergman, Charles. "A Spectacle of Beasts: Hunting Rituals and Animal Rights in Early Modern England." In *A Cultural History of Animals in the Renaissance*, edited by Bruce Boehrer, 53–73. Oxford: Berg, 2007.
Berry, Edward. *Shakespeare and the Hunt: A Cultural and Social Study*. Cambridge: Cambridge University Press, 2001.
Bevan, Jonquil. Introduction to *The Compleat Angler, 1653–1676*, by Izaak Walton, edited by Jonquil Bevan, 1–54. Oxford: Clarendon Press of Oxford University Press, 1983.
———. "Izaak Walton and His Publisher." *The Library* 32, no. 4 (December 1977): 344–59.
———. *Izaak Walton's "The Compleat Angler": The Art of Recreation*. New York: St. Martin's Press, 1988.
———. "Some Books from Izaak Walton's Library." *The Library* 2, no. 3 (September 1980): 259–63.
Blackburn, Bonnie, and Leofranc Holford-Strevens. *The Oxford Companion to the Year*. Oxford: Oxford University Press, 1999.
Blew, Mary Clearman. "Mo-nah-se-tah, the Whore, and the Three Scottish Women." In *Norman Maclean*, edited by Ron McFarland and Hugh Nichols, 190–200. Lewiston, ID: Confluence Press, 1988.
Blith, Walter. *The English Improver Improved*. London, 1652.
Blomley, Nicholas. "Making Private Property: Enclosure, Common Right and the Work of Hedges." *Rural History* 18, no. 1 (2007): 1–21.
Boas, George. *Primitivism and Related Ideas in the Middle Ages*. Baltimore: Johns Hopkins University Press, 1997.
Boehrer, Bruce Thomas. *Animal Characters: Nonhuman Beings in Early Modern Literature*. Philadelphia: University of Pennsylvania Press, 2010.
———. *Shakespeare Among the Animals: Nature and Society in the Drama of Early Modern England*. New York: Palgrave, 2002.
Boke of Saint Albans. 2nd ed. London, 1496.
Borlik, Todd Andrew. *Ecocriticism and Early Modern English Literature: Green Pastures*. New York: Routledge, 2011.
———. Introduction to *Literature and Nature in the English Renaissance: An Ecocritical Anthology*, edited by Todd Andrew Borlik, 1–23. Cambridge: Cambridge University Press, 2019.
———, ed. *Literature and Nature in the English Renaissance: An Ecocritical Anthology*. Cambridge: Cambridge University Press, 2019.
Braham, Humfrey. *The Institucion of a Gentleman*. London, 1568.
Brathwaite, Richard. *Whimzies: Or, A New Cast of Characters*. London, 1631.

Bray, Alan. *The Friend.* Chicago: University of Chicago Press, 2003.
Brears, Peter. *Cooking and Dining in Tudor and Early Stuart England.* Totnes, UK: Prospect, 2015.
Breton, Nicholas. *A Poste with a Packet of Madde Letters: The Second Part.* London, 1606.
Brighton, Trevor. *The Discovery of the Peak District: From Hades to Elysium.* Chichester, UK: Phillimore, 2004.
Brome, Alexander. *Songs and Other Poems.* London, 1661.
Brown, Andrew. "Epitaph to Charles Cotton." *Waterlog* 4 (1997): 8–10.
Browne, Edward. "Journal of Edward and Thomas Browne's Tour into Derbyshire in 1662." In *The Works of Sir Thomas Browne,* edited by Simon Wilkin, vol. 1, 22–42. London: Henry G. Bohn, 1846.
Browne, Moses. Preface to *The Compleat Angler,* by Izaak Walton and Charles Cotton, edited by Moses Browne, iii–ix. London, 1750.
———. Preface to *The Compleat Angler,* by Izaak Walton and Charles Cotton, 2nd Ed., edited by Moses Browne, v–xiv. London, 1759.
Browne, Sir Thomas. *The Works of Sir Thomas Browne.* 2nd ed. Edited by Geoffrey Keynes. 4 vols. London: Faber & Faber, 1964.
Bucholz, Robert O., and Joseph P. Ward. *London: A Social and Cultural History, 1550–1750.* Cambridge: Cambridge University Press, 2012.
Buckmann, Carol A. *The First 50: The Story of the Iowa Division, Izaak Walton League of America, 1923–1973.* Lake Mills: Iowa Division, Izaak Walton League of America, 1973.
Buell, Lawrence. *The Environmental Imagination: Thoreau, Nature Writing, and the Formation of American Culture.* Cambridge, MA: Belknap Press of Harvard University Press, 1995.
Bull, John. *The Peak District: A Cultural History.* Oxford: Signal Books, 2012.
Bunyan, John. *Grace Abounding to the Chief of Sinners: or, A Brief and Faithful Relation of the Exceeding Mercy of God in Christ, to His Poor Servant John Bunyan.* London, 1666.
Burnham, Dorothy K. *Warp and Weft: A Textile Terminology.* Toronto: Royal Ontario Museum, 1980.
Bush, Douglas. *English Literature in the Earlier Seventeenth Century, 1600–1660.* 2nd ed. Oxford: Clarendon Press of Oxford University Press, 1962.
Buxton, John. Introduction to *Poems of Charles Cotton,* edited by John Buxton, xv–xxxiii. Cambridge, MA: Harvard University Press, 1958.
Byron, George Gordon Noël. *Byron's "Don Juan": A Variorum Edition.* 2nd ed. Edited by Truman Guy Steffan and Willis W. Pratt. 4 vols. Austin: University of Texas Press, 1971.
Caius, John. *Of Englishe Dogges.* Translated by Abraham Fleming. London, 1576.
Calvin, Jean. *A Harmonie upon the Three Evangelists Matthewe, Marke, and Luke . . . Whereunto Is Also Added a Commentarie upon the Evangelist S. John.* London, 1610.
Campana, Joseph, and Scott Maisano. Introduction to *Renaissance Posthumanism,* edited by Joseph Campana and Scott Maisano, 1–36. New York: Fordham University Press, 2016.
Camp-bell: or The Ironmongers Faire Field. London, 1609.
Capp, Bernard. *England's Culture Wars: Puritan Reformation and Its Enemies in the Interregnum, 1649–1660.* Oxford: Oxford University Press, 2012.
Caradonna, Jeremy. *Sustainability: A History.* New York: Oxford University Press, 2014.
Carlos, Ann M., and Frank D. Lewis. "The Economic History of the Fur Trade: 1670–1870." In *EH.Net Encyclopedia,* edited by Robert Whaples. March 16, 2008. http://eh.net/encyclopedia/the-economic-history-of-the-fur-trade-1670-to-1870.
Carlton, Charles. *Going to the Wars: The Experience of the British Civil Wars, 1638–1651.* London: Routledge, 1992.
Carson, James P. "The Great Chain of Being as an Ecological Idea." In

Animals and Humans: Sensibility and Representation, 1650–1820, edited by Katherine M. Quinsey, 99–118. Oxford: Voltaire Foundation, 2017.

Cavert, William M. *The Smoke of London: Energy and Environment in the Early Modern City*. Cambridge: Cambridge University Press, 2016.

———. "Winter and Discontent in Early Modern England." In *Governing the Environment in the Early Modern World*, edited by Sara Miglietti and John Morgan, 114–33. London: Routledge, 2017.

Cefalu, Paul, Gary Kuchar, and Bryan Reynolds. Introduction to *The Return of Theory in Early Modern English Studies, Volume 2*, edited by Paul Cefalu, Gary Kuchar, and Bryan Reynolds, 1–11. New York: Palgrave Macmillan, 2014.

Chalkhill, John. *The Works of John Chalkhill*. Edited by Charles Ryskamp and Scott D. Westrem. Princeton, NJ: Princeton University Press, 1999.

Chilton, Bruce. "Friends and Enemies." In *The Cambridge Companion to Jesus*, edited by Markus Bockmuehl, 72–86. Cambridge: Cambridge University Press, 2001.

Chinery, Michael. *Complete British Insects*. London: HarperCollins, 2005.

Clark, Peter. *British Clubs and Societies, 1580–1800: The Origins of an Associational World*. Oxford: Clarendon Press of Oxford University Press, 2000.

———. *The English Alehouse: A Social History, 1200–1830*. London: Longman, 1983.

Coates, Peter. *Nature: Western Attitudes Since Ancient Times*. Berkeley: University of California Press, 1998.

Cockayne, Andreas Edward. "Cockayne of Ashbourne Hall, Co. Derby; and Pooley Hall, Co. Warwick." In *Cockayne Memoranda: Collections Towards a Historical Record of the Family of Cockayne*, 1–62. Congleton, UK: Printed for private circulation, 1869.

Cogan, Thomas. *The Haven of Health*. London, 1636.

Cokain, Aston. *A Chain of Golden Poems Embellished with Wit, Mirth, and Eloquence*. London, 1658.

Coldham, Peter Wilson. *English Adventurers and Emigrants, 1609–1660*. Baltimore: Genealogical Publishing Company, 1984.

Coleby, R. J. W. Preface to *The Arte of Angling, 1577*, by William Samuel, edited by Gerald Eades Bentley, introduction by Carl Otto v. Kienbusch, explanatory notes by Henry L. Savage, vii–xx. Ashburton, UK: Flyfisher's Classic Library, 2000. Reprint of 2nd modern ed. (1958) with new preface.

Coon, Arthur Munson. "The Life of Izaak Walton." PhD diss., Cornell University, 1938.

Cooper, Helen. *Pastoral: Mediaeval into Renaissance*. Ipswich, UK: Brewer, 1977.

Cooper, John R. *The Art of "The Compleat Angler."* Durham, NC: Duke University Press, 1968.

Cope, Kevin L. "Metering Mineral Resources." In *Voice and Context in Eighteenth-Century Verse: Order in Variety*, edited by Joanna Fowler and Allan Ingram, 101–16. London: Palgrave Macmillan, 2015.

Cotton, Charles. *The Compleat Angler, Part II: Being Instructions How to Angle for a Trout or Grayling in a Clear Stream*. In *The Compleat Angler*, by Izaak Walton and Charles Cotton, edited by Marjorie Swann. Oxford: Oxford University Press, 2014.

———. *The Compleat Gamester*. London, 1674.

———. *The Poetry of Charles Cotton*. Edited by Paul Hartle. 2 vols. Oxford: Oxford University Press, 2017.

Crane, Susan. *Animal Encounters: Contacts and Concepts in Medieval Britain*. Philadelphia: University of Pennsylvania Press, 2013.

Cressy, David. *Bonfires and Bells: National Memory and the Protestant Calendar in Elizabethan and Stuart*

England. Berkeley: University of California Press, 1989.
Croft, Pauline. "Cecil, Robert, First Earl of Salisbury (1563–1612)." In *Oxford Dictionary of National Biography*. Online ed. Oxford: Oxford University Press, 2008.
Crombie, Alistair C. "Science and the Arts in the Renaissance: The Search for Truth and Certainty, Old and New." In *Science and the Arts in the Renaissance*, edited by John W. Shirley and F. David Hoeniger, 15–26. Washington, DC: Folger Shakespeare Library, 1985.
Cumming, Valerie. "'Great Vanity and Excesse in Apparell': Some Clothing and Furs of Tudor and Stuart Royalty." In *The Late King's Goods: Collections, Possessions and Patronage of Charles I in the Light of the Commonwealth Sale Inventories*, edited by Arthur MacGregor, 322–50. London: Alistair McAlpine in association with Oxford University Press, 1989.
Cummings, Brian. "Pliny's Literate Elephant and the Idea of Animal Language in Renaissance Thought." In *Renaissance Beasts: Of Animals, Humans, and Other Wonderful Creatures*, edited by Erica Fudge, 164–85. Urbana: University of Illinois Press, 2004.
Cunnar, Eugene R. "Donne's Witty Theory of Atonement in 'The Baite.'" *Studies in English Literature, 1500–1900* 29, no. 1 (Winter 1989): 77–98.
Curtius, Ernst Robert. *European Literature and the Latin Middle Ages*. Translated by Willard R. Trask. Princeton, NJ: Princeton University Press, 1973.
Davies, Godfrey. *The Restoration of Charles II, 1659–1660*. San Marino, CA: Huntington Library, 1955.
Davies, J. D. "Montagu [Mountagu], Edward, First Earl of Sandwich (1625–1672)." In *Oxford Dictionary of National Biography*. Online ed. Oxford: Oxford University Press, 2008.

Dawson, Thomas. *The Good Huswifes Jewell*. London, 1587.
De Grey, Thomas. *The Compleat Horseman and Expert Ferrier*. London, 1639.
Dekker, Thomas. *Londons Tempe, or, The Field of Happines*. London, 1629.
Della Casa, Giovanni. *Galateo of Maister John Della Casa, Archebishop of Beneventa. Or Rather, a Treatise of the Manners and Behaviours, It Behoveth a Man to Use and Eschewe, in His Familiar Conversation*. Translated by Robert Peterson. London, 1576.
Dennys, John. *The Secrets of Angling*. London, 1613.
Dickson, Donald R. *The Tessera of Antilia: Utopian Brotherhoods and Secret Societies in the Early Seventeenth Century*. Leiden: Brill, 1998.
Digby, Sir Kenelm. *The Closet of the Eminently Learned Sir Kenelme Digbie Kt. Opened Whereby Is Discovered Several Ways for Making of Metheglin, Sider, Cherry-Wine, &c.: Together with Excellent Directions for Cookery, as Also for Preserving, Conserving, Candying, &c*. London, 1669.
Di Palma, Vittoria. *Wasteland: A History*. New Haven, CT: Yale University Press, 2014.
Dobson, Mary J. *Contours of Death and Disease in Early Modern England*. Cambridge: Cambridge University Press, 1997.
Dorey, Margaret. "Controlling Corruption: Regulating Meat Consumption as a Preventative to Plague in Seventeenth-Century London." *Urban History* 36, no. 1 (May 2009): 24–41.
Downame, John, ed. *Annotations upon All the Books of the Old and New Testament*. 2nd ed. London, 1651.
Drayton, Michael. *The Works of Michael Drayton*. Rev. ed. Edited by J. W. Hebel, Kathleen Tillotson, and Bernard Newdigate. 5 vols. Oxford: Basil Blackwell for the Shakespeare Head Press, 1961.
Du Bartas, Guillaume de Salluste. *The Divine Weeks and Works of*

Guillaume de Saluste, Sieur Du Bartas. Translated by Josuah Sylvester and edited by Susan Snyder. 2 vols. Oxford: Clarendon Press of Oxford University Press, 1979.

Duckert, Lowell. "Recreation." In *Inhuman Nature*, edited by Jeffrey Jerome Cohen, 79–100. Washington, DC: Oliphaunt Books, 2014.

Duffy, Carol Ann. *Frost Fair*. London: Picador, 2019.

Durston, Christopher. "'For the Better Humiliation of the People': Public Days of Fasting and Thanksgiving During the English Revolution." *Seventeenth Century* 7, no. 2 (Fall 1992): 129–49.

———. "'Preaching and Sitting Still on Sundays': The Lord's Day During the English Revolution." In *Religion in Revolutionary England*, edited by Christopher Durston and Judith Maltby, 205–25. Manchester: Manchester University Press, 2006.

Durston, Christopher, and Judith Maltby. Introduction to *Religion in Revolutionary England*, edited by Christopher Durston and Judith Maltby, 1–16. Manchester: Manchester University Press, 2006.

Eamon, William. *Science and the Secrets of Nature: Books of Secrets in Medieval and Early Modern Culture*. Princeton, NJ: Princeton University Press, 1994.

Edwards, Thomas. *The First and Second Part of Gangraena*. London, 1646.

Egan, Gabriel. "Gaia and the Great Chain of Being." In *Ecocritical Shakespeare*, edited by Lynne Bruckner and Dan Brayton, 57–69. Farnham, UK: Ashgate, 2011.

Elizabeth I, Queen of England. *Elizabeth I: Collected Works*. Edited by Leah S. Marcus, Janel Mueller, and Mary Beth Rose. Chicago: University of Chicago Press, 2000.

England and Wales. *A Collection of Such Statutes as Are Now in Force. . . . Which Enjoyn the Observation of Lent, and Other Fish Days Throughout the Year*. London, 1685.

Estienne, Charles, and Jean Liébault. *Maison Rustique, Or, The Countrey Farme*. Translated by Richard Surflet, revised by Gervase Markham. London, 1616.

Evelyn, John. "An Abstract of a Letter from the Worshipful John Evelyn Esq; . . . Concerning the Dammage Done to His Gardens by the Preceding Winter." *Philosophical Transactions of the Royal Society* 14, no. 158 (April 20, 1684): 559–63.

———. *Acetaria: A Discourse of Sallets*. Edited by Christopher Driver. Totnes, UK: Prospect Books, 2005.

———. *The Diary of John Evelyn*. Edited by E. S. de Beer. 6 vols. Oxford: Clarendon Press of Oxford University Press, 1955.

———. *Elysium Britannicum, or The Royal Gardens*. Edited by John E. Ingram. Philadelphia: University of Pennsylvania Press, 2001.

———. *Fumifugium, or, The Inconveniencie of the Aer and Smoak of London Dissipated*. London, 1661.

———. *John Evelyn, Cook: The Manuscript Receipt Book of John Evelyn*. Edited by Christopher Driver. Totnes, UK: Prospect Books, 1997.

Fagan, Brian. *Fish on Friday: Feasting, Fasting, and the Discovery of the New World*. New York: Basic Books, 2006.

———. *The Little Ice Age: How Climate Made History, 1300–1850*. New York: Basic Books, 2000.

Featley, Daniel. *Ancilla Pietatis: Or, the Hand-Maid to Private Devotion*. London, 1626.

Fiennes, Celia. *The Journeys of Celia Fiennes*. Edited by Christopher Morris. London: Cresset Press, 1949.

Firth, C. H. "The Royalists Under the Protectorate." *English Historical Review* 52, no. 208 (October 1937): 634–48.

Firth, C. H., and R. S. Rait, eds. *Acts and Ordinances of the Interregnum, 1642–1660*. 3 vols. London: His Majesty's Stationery Office, 1911.

Fissell, Mary E. *Vernacular Bodies: The Politics of Reproduction in Early*

Modern England. Oxford: Oxford University Press, 2004.
Flather, Amanda. *Gender and Space in Early Modern England.* Woodbridge, UK: Boydell Press, 2007.
Fletcher, Anthony. *Gender, Sex, and Subordination in England, 1500–1800.* New Haven, CT: Yale University Press, 1995.
Fletcher, Giles, and Phineas Fletcher. *The Poetical Works of Giles and Phineas Fletcher.* Edited by Frederick S. Boas. 2 vols. Cambridge: Cambridge University Press, 1908–9.
Ford, James E. "When 'Life . . . Becomes Literature': The Neo-Aristotelian Poetics of Norman Maclean's 'A River Runs Through It.'" *Studies in Short Fiction* 30, no. 4 (Fall 1993): 525–34.
Foucault, Michel. *The Order of Things: An Archaeology of the Human Sciences.* 1970. Translated by Alan Sheridan. Reprint, London: Tavistock, 1986.
Fowler, Alastair, ed. *The Country House Poem.* Edinburgh: Edinburgh University Press, 1994.
———. *Kinds of Literature: An Introduction to the Theory of Genres and Modes.* Oxford: Clarendon Press of Oxford University Press, 1982.
Fox, Stephen R. *John Muir and His Legacy: The American Conservation Movement.* Boston: Little, Brown, 1981.
Franck, Richard. *Northern Memoirs, Calculated for the Meridian of Scotland: To Which Is Added, "The Contemplative and Practical Angler."* Edited by Sir Walter Scott. Edinburgh: Archibald Constable, 1821.
Fry, Iris. *The Emergence of Life on Earth: A Historical and Scientific Overview.* New Brunswick, NJ: Rutgers University Press, 2000.
Frye, Northrop. *Anatomy of Criticism: Four Essays.* Princeton, NJ: Princeton University Press, 1971.
Frye, Susan. "Sewing Connections: Elizabeth Tudor, Mary Stuart, Elizabeth Talbot, and Seventeenth-Century Anonymous Needleworkers." In *Maids and Mistresses, Cousins and Queens: Women's Alliances in Early Modern England,* edited by Susan Frye and Karen Robertson, 165–82. Oxford: Oxford University Press, 1999.
Fudge, Erica. *Brutal Reasoning: Animals, Rationality, and Humanity in Early Modern England.* Ithaca, NY: Cornell University Press, 2006.
Fussell, G. E. *The English Dairy Farmer, 1500–1900.* London: Frank Cass, 1966.
———. *Old English Farming Books, 1523–1793.* Collieston, UK: Aberdeen Rare Books, 1978.
Ganey, Robin. "Milkmaids, Ploughmen, and Sex in Eighteenth-Century Britain." *Journal of the History of Sexuality* 16, no. 1 (January 2007): 40–67.
Gardiner, Samuel. *A Booke of Angling, or Fishing.* London, 1606.
Garrard, Greg. *Ecocriticism.* New York: Routledge, 2004.
Geneva Bible. *The Bible, That Is, the Holy Scriptures Contained in the Old and New Testament Translated According to the Ebrew and Greeke, and Conferred with the Best Translations in Divers Languages; with Most Profitable Annotations upon All the Hard Places, and Other Things of Great Importance.* London, 1608.
Gentles, Ian. *The English Revolution and the Wars in the Three Kingdoms, 1638–1652.* Harlow, UK: Pearson Longman, 2007.
Gifford, Terry. "Pastoral, Anti-Pastoral, and Post-Pastoral." In *The Cambridge Companion to Literature and the Environment,* edited by Louise Westling, 17–30. Cambridge: Cambridge University Press, 2014.
Glacken, Clarence. *Traces on the Rhodian Shore: Nature and Culture in Western Thought from Ancient Times to the End of the Eighteenth Century.* Berkeley: University of California Press, 1967.
Glover, Stephen, and Thomas Noble, eds. *The History and Gazetteer of the County of Derby: Drawn Up from Actual Observation, and from the Best Authorities.* Part 1. Vol. 2.

Derby, UK: Printed for Stephen Glover by H. Mozley and Sons, 1831–33.

Goldring, Elizabeth, Faith Eales, Elizabeth Clarke, Jayne Elisabeth Archer, Gabriel Heaton, and Sarah Knight, eds. *John Nichols's "The Progresses and Public Processions of Queen Elizabeth I": A New Edition of the Early Modern Sources.* 5 vols. Oxford: Oxford University Press, 2014.

Goodman, K. "Georgic." In *The Princeton Encyclopedia of Poetry and Poetics*, 4th ed., edited by Roland Greene, Stephen Cushman, Clare Cavanagh, Jahan Ramazani, and Paul Rouzer, 556–57. Princeton, NJ: Princeton University Press, 2012.

Goody, Jack. *Food and Love: A Cultural History of East and West.* London: Verso, 1998.

Gowing, Laura. "The Twinkling of a Bedstaff: Recovering the Social Life of English Beds, 1500–1700." *Home Cultures* 11, no. 3 (2014): 275–304.

Graham, Elspeth. "Ways of Being, Ways of Knowing: Fish, Fishing, and Forms of Identity in Seventeenth-Century English Culture." In *Animals and Early Modern Identity*, edited by Pia F. Cuneo, 351–73. Farnham, UK: Ashgate, 2014.

Grassby, Richard. "The Decline of Falconry in Early Modern England." *Past and Present* 157 (November 1997): 37–62.

Green, Ian. *The Christian's ABC: Catechisms and Catechizing in England c. 1530–1740.* Oxford: Clarendon Press of Oxford University Press, 1996.

———. *Print and Protestantism in Early Modern England.* Oxford: Oxford University Press, 2000.

Greenslade, B. D. "*The Compleat Angler* and the Sequestered Clergy." *Review of English Studies*, n.s., 5, no. 20 (October 1954): 361–66.

Griffin, Emma. *Blood Sport: Hunting in Britain Since 1066.* New Haven, CT: Yale University Press, 2007.

Grigson, Caroline. *Menagerie: The History of Exotic Animals in England, 1100–1837.* Oxford: Oxford University Press, 2016.

Guibbory, Achsah. *Christian Identity, Jews, and Israel in Seventeenth-Century England.* Oxford: Oxford University Press, 2010.

Guiver, Robert. *Izaak Walton's Literary Legacy.* 2nd ed. Shallowford, UK: Izaak Walton Cottage Chapter of the Izaak Walton League of America, 2012.

Guyer, Benjamin M. "Izaak Walton's 'Holy War': *The Compleat Angler* in Polemical Context." *Sixteenth Century Journal* 47, no. 2 (Summer 2016): 283–303.

Hadfield, Andrew. "Drayton's Fish." In *"Poly-Olbion": New Perspectives*, edited by Andrew McRae and Philip Schwyzer, 112–31. Woodbridge, UK: D. S. Brewer, 2020.

Hale, Matthew. *The Primitive Origination of Mankind, Considered and Examined According to the Light of Nature.* London, 1677.

Hall, Joseph. *Bishop Joseph Hall and Protestant Meditation in Seventeenth-Century England: A Study With the Texts of "The Art of Divine Meditation" (1606) and "Occasional Meditations" (1633).* Edited by Frank Livingstone Huntley. Binghamton, NY: Center for Medieval and Early Renaissance Studies, 1981.

———. *Christian Moderation in Two Books.* London, 1640.

———. *The Devout Soul, or, Rules of Heavenly Devotion.* London, 1650.

Hammond, Henry. *A Paraphrase and Annotations upon All the Books of the New Testament.* London, 1653.

Hanson, Craig. *The English Virtuoso: Art, Medicine, and Antiquarianism in the Age of Empiricism.* Chicago: University of Chicago Press, 2009.

Hardy, W. J. Preface to *Notes and Extracts from the Sessions Rolls, 1581 to 1698*, edited by W. J. Hardy, compiled under the direction of the Hertfordshire County Council, i–xxxviii. Vol. 1 of *Hertford County Records*. Hertford, UK: Longmore, 1905.

Harpham, Geoffrey Galt. "Conversion and the Language of Autobiography." In *Studies in Autobiography*, edited by James Olney, 42–50. New York: Oxford University Press, 1988.

Harrison, Peter. *The Bible, Protestantism, and the Rise of Natural Science.* Cambridge: Cambridge University Press, 1998.

Harrison, Thomas P. "The Author of *The Arte of Angling*, 1577." *Notes and Queries* 7, no. 10 (October 1, 1960): 373–76.

Hart, James. *Klinike, or The Diet of the Diseased.* London, 1633.

Hartle, Paul. "Cotton, Charles (1630–1687)." In *Oxford Dictionary of National Biography*. Online ed. Oxford: Oxford University Press, 2004.

———. "Defoe and *The Wonders of the Peake*: The Place of Cotton's Poem in *A Tour Thro' the Whole Island of Great Britain*." *English Studies* 67, no. 5 (1986): 420–31.

———. Introduction to *The Poetry of Charles Cotton*, 1:xxi–xlvii. Edited by Paul Hartle. Oxford: Oxford University Press, 2017.

———. "'Take a Long Spoon': Culinary Politics in the English Civil War." In *At the Table: Metaphorical and Material Cultures of Food in Medieval and Early Modern Europe*, edited by Timothy J. Tomasik and Juliann M. Vitullo, 29–47. Turnhout: Brepols, 2007.

Hayashi, Robert T. *Haunted by Waters: A Journey Through Race and Place in the American West.* Iowa City: University of Iowa Press, 2007.

Hazlitt, William. *The Collected Works of William Hazlitt.* Edited by A. R. Waller and Arnold Glover. 12 vols. London: J. M. Dent, 1902–4.

Hemingway, Ernest. *The Complete Short Stories: The Finca Vigia Edition.* New York: Scribner, 2003.

Herbert, Amanda E. *Female Alliances: Gender, Identity, and Friendship in Early Modern Britain.* New Haven, CT: Yale University Press, 2014.

Herbert, George. *The Complete English Poems.* Edited by John Tobin. London: Penguin, 1991.

Herd, Andrew. *The History of Fly Fishing.* 2 vols. Ellesmere, UK: Medlar Press, 2011.

Herrera-Thomas, Sean. "Haunted by Authors: Pretexts and Pleasures in Early-Modern English and Late-Modern American Angling." PhD diss., University of California, Santa Cruz, 2006.

Herrick, Robert. *The Complete Poetry of Robert Herrick.* Edited by Tom Cain and Ruth Connolly. 2 vols. Oxford: Oxford University Press, 2013.

Hester, M. Thomas. "'Like a Spyed Spie': Donne's Baiting of Marlowe." In *Literary Circles and Cultural Communities in Renaissance England*, edited by Claude J. Summers and Ted-Larry Pebworth, 24–43. Columbia: University of Missouri Press, 2000.

Heywood, Gerald G. P. *Charles Cotton and His River.* Manchester: Sherratt and Hughes, 1928.

Hidy, Ralph W., Muriel E. Hidy, Roy V. Scott, and Don L. Hofsommer. *The Great Northern Railway: A History.* Minneapolis: University of Minnesota Press, 2004.

Hill, Christopher. *The English Bible and the Seventeenth-Century Revolution.* London: Allen Lane, 1993.

———. Introduction to *Winstanley: "The Law of Freedom" and Other Writings*, by Gerrard Winstanley, edited by Christopher Hill, 9–68. Cambridge: Cambridge University Press, 1983.

Hindle, Steve. "Dearth and the English Revolution: The Harvest Crisis of 1647–50." *Economic History Review* 61, no. S1 (2008): 64–98.

———. "The Shaming of Margaret Knowsley: Gossip, Gender and the Experience of Authority in Early Modern England." *Continuity and Change* 9, no. 3 (December 1994): 391–419.

Hobbes, Thomas. *De Mirabilibus Pecci.* London, 1627.

Hoffmann, Richard C. *Fishers' Craft and Lettered Art: Tracts on Fishing from the End of the Middle Ages.* Toronto: University of Toronto Press, 1997.

Holinshed, Raphael. *The Chronicles of England, from William the Conqueror . . . Untill the Yeare 1577.* London, 1585.

Holland, Abraham. *Hollandi Post-huma.* Cambridge, 1626.

Horne, Bernard S. *"The Compleat Angler," 1653–1967: A New Bibliography.* Pittsburgh: Pittsburgh Bibliophiles, 1970.

Houston, R. A. "People, Space, and Law in Late Medieval and Early Modern Britain and Ireland." *Past and Present* 230 (February 2016): 47–89.

Howey, Catherine. "The Vain, Exotic, and Erotic Feather: Dress, Gender, and Power in Sixteenth- and Seventeenth-Century England." In *Religion, Gender, and Culture in the Pre-Modern World,* edited by Alexandra Cuffel and Brian M. Britt, 211–40. New York: Palgrave Macmillan, 2007.

Hughes, Ann. "The Cromwellian Church." In *Reformation and Identity, c. 1520–1662,* edited by Anthony Milton, 444–56. Vol. 1 of *The Oxford History of Anglicanism,* edited by Rowan Strong. Oxford: Oxford University Press, 2017.

Hunter, Michael. *John Aubrey and the Realm of Learning.* London: Duckworth, 1975.

Huntley, Frank Livingstone. Introduction to *Bishop Joseph Hall and Protestant Meditation in Seventeenth-Century England: A Study with the Texts of "The Art of Divine Meditation" (1606) and "Occasional Meditations" (1633),* edited by Frank Livingstone Huntley, 3–63. Binghamton, NY: Center for Medieval and Early Renaissance Studies, 1981.

Hutton, Ronald. *The Rise and Fall of Merry England: The Ritual Year 1400–1700.* Oxford: Oxford University Press, 1994.

Hyde, Edward. *The Life of Edward Earl of Clarendon, Lord High Chancellor of England, and Chancellor of the University of Oxford.* 3 vols. Oxford, 1759.

Ironmongers, Worshipful Company of. "Register of Freedom Admissions, 1555–1740." London Metropolitan Archives CLC/L/IB/C/002/MS16977/001, 36, 41. Transcribed at https://www.findmypast.co.uk.

Jackson, Christine E. *Peacock.* London: Reaktion, 2006.

J. C. *A Pleasant Comedie, Called "The Two Merry Milke-Maids."* London, 1620.

Jewitt, Llewellynn. "Derby Signs, Described and Illustrated." *The Reliquary* 7 (1866–67): 175–80, 225–32.

Johnston, Josée, and Shyon Baumann. *Foodies: Democracy and Distinction in the Gourmet Foodscape.* 2nd ed. New York: Routledge, 2015.

Jones, Gwilym. "Environmental Renaissance Studies." *Literature Compass* 14, no. 10 (2017): 1–15.

———. *Shakespeare's Storms.* Manchester: Manchester University Press, 2015.

Jonson, Ben. *Ben Jonson: The Complete Poems.* Edited by George Parfitt. London: Penguin, 1996.

Kain, Roger J. P., John Chapman, and Richard R. Oliver. *The Enclosure Maps of England and Wales, 1595–1918.* Cambridge: Cambridge University Press, 2004.

Kathman, David. "Grocers, Goldsmiths, and Drapers: Freemen and Apprentices in the Elizabethan Theater." *Shakespeare Quarterly* 55, no. 1 (Spring 2004): 1–49.

Keith, W. J. *The Rural Tradition: A Study of the Non-Fiction Prose Writers of the English Countryside.* Toronto: University of Toronto Press, 1974.

Kerridge, Eric. *Textile Manufactures in Early Modern England.* Manchester: Manchester University Press, 1985.

Kinder, Philip. *The Historie of Darby-shire.* Edited by W. G. Dimock Fletcher. In *The Reliquary* 22 (1881–82): 17–24, 97–101, 181–84, 197–200; *The Reliquary* 23 (1882–83): 9–10, 117–20, 163–68.

King, Rebecca Frances. "Rape in England, 1600–1800: Trials, Narratives and the Question of Consent." MA thesis, Durham University, 1998.

Knight, Leah. *Reading Green in Early Modern England*. Farnham, UK: Ashgate, 2014.

Kruuk, Hans. *Otters: Ecology, Behaviour and Conservation*. Oxford: Oxford University Press, 1995.

Lamb, Charles, and Mary Lamb. *The Letters of Charles Lamb, to Which Are Added Those of His Sister, Mary Lamb*. Edited by E. V. Lucas. 3 vols. New Haven, CT: Yale University Press, 1935.

Lamb, H. H. *Climate, History, and the Modern World*. 2nd ed. London: Routledge, 1995.

Landry, Donna. *The Invention of the Countryside: Hunting, Walking, and Ecology in English Literature, 1671–1831*. New York: Palgrave, 2001.

Lehmberg, Stanford. "Nowell, Alexander (c. 1516/17–1602)." In *Oxford Dictionary of National Biography*. Online ed. Oxford: Oxford University Press, 2008.

Lemnius, Levinus. *The Touchstone of Complexions*. Translated by Thomas Newton. London, 1633.

Leslie, Michael, and Timothy Raylor. Introduction to *Culture and Cultivation in Early Modern England: Writing and the Land*, edited by Michael Leslie and Timothy Raylor, 1–12. Leicester: Leicester University Press, 1992.

Lesser, Zachary. "Typographic Nostalgia: Play-Reading, Popularity, and the Meanings of Black Letter." In *The Book of the Play: Playwrights, Stationers, and Readers in Early Modern England*, edited by Marta Straznicky, 99–126. Amherst: University of Massachusetts Press, 2006.

Lévi-Strauss, Claude. *The Raw and the Cooked*. Translated by John Weightman and Doreen Weightman. New York: Harper & Row, 1969.

Lewalski, Barbara Kiefer. *Protestant Poetics and the Seventeenth-Century Religious Lyric*. Princeton, NJ: Princeton University Press, 1984.

Lojek, Helen. "Casting Flies and Recasting Myths with Norman Maclean." *Western American Literature* 25, no. 2 (Summer 1990): 145–56.

Lonie, Iain M. "Fever Pathology in the Sixteenth Century: Tradition and Innovation." *Medical History* 25, no. S1 (1981): 19–44.

Loscocco, Paula. "Royalist Reclamation of Psalmic Song in 1650s England." *Renaissance Quarterly* 64, no. 2 (Summer 2011): 500–543.

Lovegrove, Roger. *Silent Fields: The Long Decline of a Nation's Wildlife*. Oxford: Oxford University Press, 2007.

Lovejoy, Arthur O. *The Great Chain of Being: A Study of the History of an Idea*. Cambridge, MA: Harvard University Press, 1982.

Low, Anthony. *The Georgic Revolution*. Princeton, NJ: Princeton University Press, 1985.

Lowerson, J. R. "Barker, Thomas (fl. 1651)." In *Oxford Dictionary of National Biography*. Online ed. Oxford: Oxford University Press, 2004.

Lysons, Daniel. "Theobalds." In *The Environs of London*, vol. 4, *Counties of Herts, Essex and Kent*, by Daniel Lysons, 29–39. London, 1796.

Mabey, Richard. *Flora Britannica*. London: Sinclair-Stevenson, 1996.

MacGregor, Arthur. *Animal Encounters: Human and Animal Interaction in Britain from the Norman Conquest to World War One*. London: Reaktion, 2012.

———. "Animals and the Early Stuarts: Hunting and Hawking at the Court of James I and Charles I." *Archives of Natural History* 16, no. 3 (1989): 305–18.

MacInnes, Ian. "Mastiffs and Spaniels: Gender and Nation in the English Dog." *Textual Practice* 17, no. 1 (March 2003): 21–40.

Maclean, Norman. *"A River Runs Through It" and Other Stories*. Chicago: University of Chicago Press, 2001.

Major, Philip. Introduction to *Literatures of Exile in the English Revolution and Its Aftermath, 1640–1690*, edited by

Philip Major, 1–13. Farnham, UK: Ashgate, 2010.

Maltby, Judith. "From *Temple* to *Synagogue*: 'Old' Conformity in the 1640s–1650s and the Case of Christopher Harvey." In *Conformity and Orthodoxy in the English Church, c. 1560–1660*, edited by Peter Lake and Michael Questier, 88–120. Woodbridge, UK: Boydell Press, 2000.

———. "Suffering and Surviving: The Civil Wars, the Commonwealth and the Formation of 'Anglicanism,' 1642–60." In *Religion in Revolutionary England*, edited by Christopher Durston and Judith Maltby, 158–80. Manchester: Manchester University Press, 2006.

Manning, Roger B. *Hunters and Poachers: A Social and Cultural History of Unlawful Hunting in England, 1485–1640*. Oxford: Clarendon Press of Oxford University Press, 1993.

———. *Village Revolts: Social Protest and Popular Disturbances in England, 1509–1640*. Oxford: Clarendon Press of Oxford University Press, 1988.

Marcus, Leah. *The Politics of Mirth: Jonson, Herrick, Milton, Marvell, and the Defense of Old Holiday Pastimes*. Chicago: University of Chicago Press, 1986.

Markham, Gervase. *Cheape and Good Husbandry for the Well-Ordering of All Beasts, and Fowles, and for the Generall Cure of Their Diseases*. London, 1614.

———. *The English Huswife*. In *Countrey Contentments*, by Gervase Markham. London, 1615.

———. *The Pleasures of Princes, or Good Mens Recreations*. In *Three Books on Fishing*, edited by J. Milton French. Gainesville, FL: Scholars' Facsimiles and Reprints, 1962. Originally published in London (1614). Page references are to the 1962 edition.

Markley, Robert. "Summer's Lease: Shakespeare in the Little Ice Age." In *Early Modern Ecostudies: From the Florentine Codex to Shakespeare*, edited by Thomas Hallock, Ivo Kamps, and Karen L. Raber, 131–42. New York: Palgrave Macmillan, 2008.

Martz, Louis L. *The Poetry of Meditation: A Study of English Religious Literature of the Seventeenth Century*. Rev. ed. New Haven, CT: Yale University Press, 1969.

Marvell, Andrew. *The Poems of Andrew Marvell*. 2nd ed. Edited by Nigel Smith. New York: Longman, 2007.

Mascall, Leonard. *A Booke of Fishing with Hooke and Line*. London, 1590.

May, Robert. *The Accomplist Cook, or The Art and Mystery of Cookery*. London, 1660.

McCabe, Richard A. "Hall, Joseph (1574–1656)." In *Oxford Dictionary of National Biography*. Online ed. Oxford: Oxford University Press, 2008.

McCully, C. B. *Fly-Fishing: A Book of Words*. Manchester: Carcanet, 1992.

McCutcheon, John T. "A Battle the Izaak Walton League Is Winning." Cartoon. *Outdoor America* 4, no. 12 (July 1926): 4.

McDonald, John. *The Origins of Angling*. Garden City, NY: Doubleday, 1963.

McFarland, Ron. *Norman Maclean*. Boise, ID: Boise State University, 1993.

McGrade, A. S. "Hooker, Richard (1554–1600)." In *Oxford Dictionary of National Biography*. Online ed. Oxford: Oxford University Press, 2004.

McIlhaney, Anne E. "*The Compleat Angler*." In *Sport in American Culture: From Ali to X-Games*, edited by Joyce D. Duncan, 90. Santa Barbara, CA: ABC-CLIO, 2004.

———. "Renaissance Acts and Images of Angling: An Anatomy of the British Piscatory, 1496–1653." PhD diss., University of Virginia, 1998.

———. "'Whole Shoals of Men': Representations of Women Anglers in Seventeenth-Century British Poetry." In *Reading the Earth: New Directions in the Study of Literature and Environment*, edited by Michael P. Branch, Rochelle Johnson, Daniel Patterson, and Scott Slovic, 55–66.

Moscow: University of Idaho Press, 1998.
McNeill, Fiona. "Free and Bound Maids: Women's Work Songs and Industrial Change in the Age of Shakespeare." In *Oral Traditions and Gender in Early Modern Literary Texts*, edited by Mary Ellen Lamb and Karen Bamford, 101–15. Aldershot, UK: Ashgate, 2008.
McRae, Andrew. *God Speed the Plough: The Representation of Agrarian England, 1500–1660*. Cambridge: Cambridge University Press, 1992.
———. *Literature and Domestic Travel in Early Modern England*. Cambridge: Cambridge University Press, 2009.
———. "The Pleasures of the Land in Restoration England: The Social Politics of *The Compleat Angler*." In *Essays in Memory of Richard Helgerson: Laureations*, edited by Roze Hentshell and Kathy Lavezzo, 163–79. Newark: University of Delaware Press, 2012.
Meeker, Joseph W. *The Comedy of Survival: In Search of an Environmental Ethic*. Los Angeles: Guild of Tutors Press, 1980.
Mendelson, Sara, and Patricia Crawford. *Women in Early Modern England*. Oxford: Clarendon Press of Oxford University Press, 1998.
Mennell, Stephen. *All Manners of Food: Eating and Taste in England and France from the Middle Ages to the Present*. Oxford: Basil Blackwell, 1986.
Mentz, Steve. "Strange Weather in *King Lear*." *Shakespeare* 6, no. 2 (June 2010): 139–52.
Milton, John. *John Milton: Complete Shorter Poems*. Edited by John Carey. Harlow, UK: Longman, 1984.
Miner, Earl. *The Cavalier Mode from Jonson to Cotton*. Princeton, NJ: Princeton University Press, 1971.
Moffett, Thomas. *Healths Improvement*. Corrected and enlarged by Christopher Bennet. London, 1655.
———. *Theater of Insects*. In *History of Four-Footed Beasts and Serpents*, by Edward Topsell. London, 1658.

Montrose, Louis Adrian. "'Eliza, Queene of Shepheardes,' and the Pastoral of Power." In *The Mysteries of Elizabeth I: Selections from "English Literary Renaissance,"* edited by Kirby Farrell and Kathleen Swaim, 162–91. Amherst: University of Massachusetts Press, 2003.
Morrill, John. *The Nature of the English Revolution*. London: Longman, 1993.
———. *Stuart Britain: A Very Short Introduction*. Oxford: Oxford University Press, 2000.
Morris, Christopher. Introduction to *The Journeys of Celia Fiennes*, edited by Christopher Morris, xiii–xliii. London: Cresset Press, 1949.
Mortimer-Sandilands, Catriona, and Bruce Erickson. Introduction to *Queer Ecologies: Sex, Nature, Politics, Desire*, edited by Catriona Mortimer-Sandilands and Bruce Erickson, 1–47. Bloomington: Indiana University Press, 2010.
Morton, Thomas, [of Berwick]. *A Treatise of the Nature of God*. London, 1599.
Neimanis, Astrida. *Bodies of Water*. London: Bloomsbury, 2017.
Newman, Lance. "Marxism and Ecocriticism." *Interdisciplinary Studies in Literature and Environment* 9, no. 2 (Summer 2002): 1–25.
Nicolas, Sir Nicholas Harris. "Life of Charles Cotton." In *The Complete Angler*, by Izaak Walton and Charles Cotton, 3rd ed., edited by Sir Nicholas Harris Nicolas, clxiii–cci. London: Chatto and Windus, 1875.
Norton, Marcy. "Going to the Birds: Birds as Things and Beings in Early Modernity." In *Early Modern Things: Objects and Their Histories*, edited by Paula Findlen, 53–83. London: Routledge, 2013.
Novarr, David. *The Making of Walton's "Lives."* Ithaca, NY: Cornell University Press, 1958.
———. Review of *The Compleat Angler, 1653–1676*, by Izaak Walton, edited by Jonquil Bevan. *Modern Language Review* 80, no. 1 (January 1985): 120–22.

Nowell, Alexander. *A Catechisme, or First Instruction and Learning of Christian Religion*. Translated by Thomas Norton. London, 1570.

O'Connor, Terry. *Animals as Neighbors: The Past and Present of Commensal Species*. East Lansing: Michigan State University Press, 2013.

Oggins, Robin S. *The Kings and Their Hawks: Falconry in Medieval England*. New Haven, CT: Yale University Press, 2004.

Oliver, H. J. "The Composition and Revisions of *The Compleat Angler*." *Modern Language Review* 42, no. 3 (July 1947): 295–313.

Osborne, Dorothy. *The Letters of Dorothy Osborne to William Temple*. Edited by G. C. Moore Smith. Oxford: Clarendon Press of Oxford University Press, 1928.

Ovid. *Ovid's Metamorphosis Englished by G. S.* Translated by George Sandys. London, 1626.

Page, William, ed. *The Victoria History of the County of Hertford*. 4 vols. London: Constable, 1902–14.

Park, Katharine, and Lorraine Daston. Introduction to *Early Modern Science*, 1–17. Vol. 3 of *The Cambridge History of Science*, edited by Katharine Park and Lorraine Daston. Cambridge: Cambridge University Press, 2006.

Parker, Geoffrey. *Global Crisis: War, Climate Change, and Catastrophe in the Seventeenth Century*. New Haven, CT: Yale University Press, 2013.

Patterson, Annabel. *Pastoral and Ideology: Virgil to Valéry*. Oxford: Clarendon Press of Oxford University Press, 1988.

Peacham, Henry. *The Compleat Gentleman*. London, 1622.

———. *Minerva Britanna*. London, 1612.

Peterson, John. "Prodigal Sons and Matriarchs: Gendered Homecomings in *A River Runs Through It*." *ISLE: Interdisciplinary Studies in Literature and Environment* 26, no. 3 (Summer 2019): 641–65.

Petrarca, Francesco. *Petrarch's Lyric Poems*. Edited and translated by Robert M. Durling. Cambridge, MA: Harvard University Press, 1976.

Pevsner, Nikolaus. *Staffordshire*. New Haven, CT: Yale University Press, 2002.

Phillips, Maberly. "Theobalds Park Wall." *Transactions of the East Hertfordshire Archaeological Society* 5 (1914): 248–62.

Phythian-Adams, Charles. "Milk and Soot: The Changing Vocabulary of a Popular Ritual in Stuart and Hanoverian London." In *The Pursuit of Urban History*, edited by Derek Fraser and Anthony Sutcliffe, 83–104. London: Edward Arnold, 1983.

Pliny. *The Historie of the World: Commonly Called, The Naturall Historie of C. Plinius Secundus*. Translated by Philemon Holland. London, 1634.

Plot, Robert. *The Natural History of Stafford-shire*. Oxford, 1686.

Plot, Robert, and Jacob Bobart. "A Discourse Concerning the Effects of the Great Frost, on Trees and Other Plants Anno 1683." *Philosophical Transactions of the Royal Society* 14, no. 165 (January 20, 1684): 766–79.

Pope, Alexander. *The Major Works*. Edited by Pat Rogers. Oxford: Oxford University Press, 2009.

Powell, Thomas. *Tom of All Trades; or The Plaine Path-way to Preferment*. London, 1631.

Preston, Claire. "Of Cyder and Sallets: The Hortulan Saints and *The Garden of Cyrus*." *Literature Compass* 3, no. 4 (July 2006): 867–83.

Purkiss, Diane. *The English Civil War: A People's History*. New York: Harper Perennial, 2006.

Puttenham, George. *The Arte of English Poesie*. Introduction by Baxter Hathaway. Kent, OH: Kent State University Press, 1970.

Quarles, Francis. *The Shepheards Oracles: Delivered in Certain Eglogues*. London, 1646 [1645].

Rabisha, William. *The Whole Body of Cookery Dissected*. London, 1661.

Radcliffe, David Hill. *Forms of Reflection: Genre and Culture as Meditational*

Writing. Baltimore: Johns Hopkins University Press, 1993.

———. "'Study to Be Quiet': Genre and Politics in Izaak Walton's *Compleat Angler*." *English Literary Renaissance* 22, no. 1 (Winter 1992): 95–111.

Radcliffe, William. *Fishing from the Earliest Times*. London: John Murray, 1921.

Ravenscroft, Thomas. *Deuteromelia: Or, The Second Part of Musicks Melodie, or Melodius Musicke*. London, 1609.

Ray, John. *Collection of English Proverbs*. Cambridge, 1678.

———. *The Wisdom of God Manifested in the Works of the Creation*. London, 1691.

The Reformed Virginian Silk-Worm. London, 1655.

Remien, Peter. "Oeconomy and Ecology in Early Modern England." *PMLA / Publications of the Modern Language Association of America* 132, no. 5 (October 2017): 1117–33.

Ribeiro, Aileen. *Fashion and Fiction: Dress in Art and Literature in Stuart England*. New Haven, CT: Yale University Press, 2005.

Richards, John F. *The Unending Frontier: An Environmental History of the Early Modern World*. Berkeley: University of California Press, 2003.

Rimbault, Edward F., ed. *Old Ballads Illustrating the Great Frost of 1683–4 and the Fair on the River Thames*. London: Printed for the Percy Society by T. Richards, 1844.

Robinson, Sarah P. "Catching Fish, Making Law: A History of Fishing Laws in Early Modern England and Colonial Massachusetts." JD thesis, Harvard Law School, 2000.

Rondelet, Guillaume. *Libri de Piscibus Marinis*. Lyon, 1554. https://doi.org/10.5962/bhl.title.155836.

Rowe, Anne, and Tom Williamson. *Hertfordshire: A Landscape History*. Hatfield, UK: Hertfordshire Publications, 2013.

Russell, Edmund. *Greyhound Nation: A Coevolutionary History of England, 1200–1900*. Cambridge: Cambridge University Press, 2018.

Ryrie, Alec. "The Fall and Rise of Fasting in the British Reformations." In *Worship and the Parish Church in Early Modern Britain*, edited by Natalie Mears and Alec Ryrie, 89–108. Farnham, UK: Ashgate, 2013.

Saintsbury, George. Introduction to *The Lives of John Donne, Sir Henry Wotton, Richard Hooker, George Herbert, and Robert Sanderson* by Izaak Walton, edited by George Saintsbury, v–xvii. 1927. Reprint, London: Oxford University Press, 1973.

Samuel, William. *The Arte of Angling, 1577*. Edited by Gerald Eades Bentley, introduction by Carl Otto von Kienbusch, and explanatory notes by Henry L. Savage. Facsimile and transcription with modernized spelling of only extant copy of original text. Princeton, NJ: Princeton University Library, 1956.

Sands, Bryony, and Richard Wall. "Sustained Parasiticide Use in Cattle Farming Affects Dung Beetle Functional Assemblages." *Agriculture, Ecosystems and Environment* 265 (2018): 226–35.

Sandys, George. *The Poetical Works of George Sandys*. Edited by Richard Hooper. 2 vols. London: John Russell Smith, 1872.

Scarpino, Philip V. *Great River: An Environmental History of the Upper Mississippi, 1890–1950*. Columbia: University of Missouri Press, 1985.

Schoenfeldt, Michael C. *Bodies and Selves in Early Modern England: Physiology and Inwardness in Spenser, Shakespeare, Herbert, and Milton*. Cambridge: Cambridge University Press, 1999.

Schullery, Paul. *American Fly Fishing: A History*. New York: Lyons Press, 1999.

Semenza, Gregory M. Colón. *Sport, Politics, and Literature in the English Renaissance*. Newark: University of Delaware Press, 2003.

Sgroi, R. C. L. "Piscatorial Politics Revisited: The Language of Economic Debate and the Evolution of Fishing

Policy in Elizabethan England." *Albion* 35, no. 1 (Spring 2003): 1–24.

Shakespeare, William. *As You Like It.* Edited by Juliet Dusinberre. London: Arden Shakespeare, 2006.

———. *A Midsummer Night's Dream.* Edited by Harold F. Brooks. London: Arden Shakespeare, 2007.

Shapin, Steven. *Changing Tastes: How Things Tasted in the Early Modern Period and How They Taste Now.* Hans Rausing Lecture 2011. Salvia Småskrifter 14. Uppsala: University of Uppsala, 2011.

———. *The Scientific Revolution.* Chicago: University of Chicago Press, 1996.

———. *A Social History of Truth: Civility and Science in Seventeenth-Century England.* Chicago: University of Chicago Press, 1994.

———. "'You Are What You Eat': Historical Changes in Ideas About Food and Identity." *Historical Research* 87, no. 237 (August 2014): 377–92.

Shapiro, Barbara J. *Probability and Certainty in Seventeenth-Century England: A Study of the Relationships Between Natural Science, Religion, History, Law, and Literature.* Princeton, NJ: Princeton University Press, 1983.

Sharpe, Kevin. *The Personal Rule of Charles I.* New Haven, CT: Yale University Press, 1992.

Sharrock, Robert. *The History of the Propagation and Improvement of Vegetables.* Oxford, 1660.

Sherwood, Roy. *The Civil War in the Midlands, 1642–1651.* Stroud, UK: Alan Sutton, 1992.

"A Short Discourse by Way of Post-Script, Touching the Lawes of Angling." In *The Compleat Angler*, by Izaak Walton, 3rd ed., S1r–S4r. London, 1661.

The Siege of Colchester. 1648. In *Transactions of the Essex Archaeological Society*, n.s., 4 (1893): 205–18.

Smith, Bruce R. *Homosexual Desire in Shakespeare's England: A Cultural Poetics.* Chicago: University of Chicago Press, 1994.

Smith, Hilda L. *All Men and Both Sexes: Gender, Politics, and the False Universal in England, 1640–1832.* University Park: Penn State University Press, 2002.

Smith, Nigel. "Bothumley, Jacob (1613–1692)." In *Oxford Dictionary of National Biography*. Online ed. Oxford: Oxford University Press, 2004.

———. Introduction to *A Collection of Ranter Writings from the 17th Century*, edited by Nigel Smith, 7–38. London: Junction Books, 1983.

———. *Literature and Revolution in England, 1640–1660.* New Haven, CT: Yale University Press, 1994.

Snider, Alvin. "Hard Frost, 1684." *Journal for Early Modern Cultural Studies* 8, no. 2 (Fall–Winter 2008): 8–32.

Snyder, Susan. Introduction to *The Divine Weeks and Works of Guillaume de Saluste, Sieur du Bartas*, vol. 1, 1–110. Edited by Susan Snyder and translated by Josuah Sylvester. Oxford: Clarendon Press of Oxford University Press, 1979.

Sparke, Edward. *Scintillula Altaris.* London, 1652.

Spenser, Edmund. *The Yale Edition of the Shorter Poems of Edmund Spenser.* Edited by William A. Oram, Einar Bjorvand, Ronald Bond, Thomas H. Cain, Alexander Dunlop, and Richard Schell. New Haven, CT: Yale University Press, 1989.

Spiller, Elizabeth. "Printed Recipe Books in Medical, Political, and Scientific Contexts." In *The Oxford Handbook of Literature and the English Revolution*, edited by Laura Lunger Knoppers, 516–33. Oxford: Oxford University Press, 2012.

Srigley, Michael. "The Great Frost Fair of 1683–4." *History Today* 10, no. 12 (December 1960): 848–55.

The Statutes of the Realm. 11 vols. London: Dawsons, 1963.

Steel, Karl. "Creeping Things: Spontaneous Generation and Material Creativity." In *Elemental Ecocriticism: Thinking with Earth, Air, Water, and Fire*, edited by Jeffrey Jerome Cohen and

Lowell Duckert, 209–36. Minneapolis: University of Minnesota Press, 2015.
Stegner, Wallace. "Haunted by Waters." In *Norman Maclean*, edited by Ron McFarland and Hugh Nichols, 153–60. Lewiston, ID: Confluence Press, 1988.
Stevens, John. *Music and Poetry in the Early Tudor Court*. Lincoln: University of Nebraska Press, 1961.
Stone, Lawrence. "The Building of Hatfield House." *Archaeological Journal* 112 (1965): 100–128.
———. *The Family, Sex and Marriage in England, 1500–1800*. Abridged ed. Harmondsworth, UK: Penguin, 1979.
Stow, John. *A Survay of London*. London, 1598.
Stubbes, Phillip. *The Anatomie of Abuses*. London, 1583.
Summerson, John. "The Building of Theobalds, 1564–1585." *Archaeologia* 97 (1959): 107–26.
Summit, Jennifer. "Active and Contemplative Lives." In *Cultural Reformations: Medieval and Renaissance in Literary History*, edited by James Simpson and Brian Cummings, 527–53. Oxford: Oxford University Press, 2010.
Sutton, James M. "The Decorative Program at Elizabethan Theobalds: Educating an Heir and Promoting a Dynasty." *Studies in the Decorative Arts* 7, no. 1 (Fall–Winter 1999–2000): 33–64.
———. *Materializing Space at an Early Modern Prodigy House: The Cecils at Theobalds, 1564–1607*. Aldershot, UK: Ashgate, 2004.
Swann, Marjorie. "*The Compleat Angler* and the Early Modern Culture of Collecting." *English Literary Renaissance* 37, no. 1 (December 2007): 100–117.
———. *Curiosities and Texts: The Culture of Collecting in Early Modern England*. Philadelphia: University of Pennsylvania Press, 2001.
———. Introduction to *The Compleat Angler*, by Izaak Walton and Charles Cotton, edited by Marjorie Swann, vii–xxv. Oxford: Oxford University Press, 2014.
———. "Literary and Environmental References in *The Compleat Angler*." *Notes and Queries* 61, no. 3 (September 2014): 373–76.
———. "Sex and the Single Queen: The Erotic Lives of Elizabeth Tudor in Seventeenth-Century England." In *Queens and Power in Medieval and Early Modern England*, edited by Carole Levin and Robert Bucholz, 224–41. Lincoln: University of Nebraska Press, 2009.
———. "Vegetable Love: Botany and Sexuality in Early Modern England." In *The Indistinct Human in Renaissance Literature*, edited by Jean E. Feerick and Vin Nardizzi, 139–58. New York: Palgrave, 2012.
Tebbutt, Melanie. "'In the Midlands but Not of Them': Derbyshire's Dark Peak—An Imagined Northern Landscape." In *Northern Identities: Historical Interpretations of "The North" and "Northernness*," edited by Neville Kirk, 163–94. Aldershot, UK: Ashgate, 2000.
Theis, Jeffrey S. *Writing the Forest in Early Modern England: A Sylvan Pastoral Nation*. Pittsburgh: Duquesne University Press, 2009.
Thirsk, Joan. *Food in Early Modern England: Phases, Fads, Fashions, 1500–1760*. London: Hambledon Continuum, 2006.
———. "Plough and Pen: Agricultural Writers in the Seventeenth Century." In *Social Relations and Ideas: Essays in Honour of R. H. Hilton*, edited by T. H. Aston, P. R. Coss, Christopher Dyer, and Joan Thirsk, 295–318. Cambridge: Cambridge University Press, 1983.
Thomas, Keith. *The Ends of Life: Roads to Fulfilment in Early Modern England*. New York: Oxford University Press, 2009.
———. *Man and the Natural World: Changing Attitudes in England, 1500–1800*. New York: Pantheon Books, 1983.

———. *Religion and the Decline of Magic*. Harmondsworth, UK: Penguin, 1985.

Thomson, Alan. "Progress, Retreat, and Pursuit: James I in Hertfordshire." In *Hertfordshire in History: Papers Presented to Lionel Munby*, edited by Doris Jones-Baker, 93–107. Hatfield, UK: Hertfordshire Publications, 1991.

Thorley, David. "'In All a Weak Disabled Thing': Herbert's Ill-Health and Its Poetic Treatments." *George Herbert Journal* 34, nos. 1–2 (Fall 2010–Spring 2011): 1–33.

Tillyard, E. M. W. *The Elizabethan World Picture*. New York: Random House, n.d. [1960s].

Topsell, Edward. *The Historie of Serpents*. London, 1608.

Traherne, Thomas. *Thomas Traherne: Selected Poems and Prose*. Edited by Alan Bradford. London: Penguin Books, 1991.

Tranter, Kirsten. "By the Rivers of Babylon: Biblical Allusion and the Politics of Pastoral in Izaak Walton's *The Compleat Angler*." In *Word and Self Estranged in English Texts, 1550–1660*, edited by Philippa Kelly and L. E. Semler, 195–204. Farnham, UK: Ashgate, 2010.

Traub, Valerie. *The Renaissance of Lesbianism in Early Modern England*. New York: Cambridge University Press, 2002.

Treatyse of Fysshynge wyth an Angle. Facsimile and transcription in *The Origins of Angling*, by John McDonald, 183–229. Garden City, NY: Doubleday, 1963. First published in the *Boke of Saint Albans*, 2nd ed. (London, 1496).

Tree, Isabella. *Wilding: The Return of Nature to a British Farm*. London: Picador, 2018.

Trefethen, James B. *An American Crusade for Wildlife*. New York: Winchester Press and the Boone and Crockett Club, 1975.

Trench, Charles Chenevix. *The Poacher and the Squire: A History of Poaching and Game Preservation in England*. London: Longmans, 1967.

Trevor-Roper, Hugh. *Catholics, Anglicans, and Puritans: Seventeenth-Century Essays*. Chicago: University of Chicago Press, 1988.

Tryon, Thomas. *Modest Observations on the Present Extraordinary Frost*. London, 1684.

T. S. *A True and Exact Relation of the Taking of Colchester*. London, 1648.

Turner, James. *The Politics of Landscape: Rural Scenery and Society in English Poetry, 1630–1660*. Cambridge, MA: Harvard University Press, 1979.

Turner, William. *The Huntyng of the Romyshe Wolfe*. Emden, 1555.

Underdown, David. *Revel, Riot, and Rebellion: Popular Politics and Culture in England, 1603–1660*. New York: Oxford University Press, 1985.

Valenze, Deborah. "The Art of Women and the Business of Men: Women's Work and the Dairy Industry c. 1740–1840." *Past and Present* 130 (February 1991): 142–69.

Vartanian, Aram. "Spontaneous Generation." In *Dictionary of the History of Ideas*, edited by Philip P. Wiener, 4:307–12. New York: Charles Scribner's Sons, 1973.

Venables, Robert. *The Experienc'd Angler: Or Angling Improv'd*. London, 1662.

Venner, Tobias. *Via Recta ad Vitam Longam*. London, 1650.

Virgil. *Virgils Eclogues Translated into English: By W. L. Gent*. Translated by William Lathum. London, 1628.

Voigt, William. *Born with Fists Doubled: Defending Outdoor America*. Iowa City: Izaak Walton League of America Endowment, 1992.

Voss, Paul J. "Printing Conventions and the Early Modern Play." *Medieval and Renaissance Drama in England* 15 (2003): 98–115.

Walford, Edward. *Greater London: A Narrative of Its History, Its People, and Its Places*. 2 vols. London: Cassell, 1894–95.

Walker, Garthine. "Everyman or a Monster? The Rapist in Early Modern England, c. 1600–1750." *History*

Workshop Journal 76 (Autumn 2013): 5–31.

———. "Rereading Rape and Sexual Violence in Early Modern England." *Gender and History* 10, no. 1 (April 1998): 1–25.

Wall, Wendy. *Recipes for Thought: Knowledge and Taste in the Early Modern English Kitchen*. Philadelphia: University of Pennsylvania Press, 2016.

———. *Staging Domesticity: Household Work and English Identity in Early Modern Drama*. Cambridge: Cambridge University Press, 2002.

Walsham, Alexandra. *The Reformation of the Landscape: Religion, Identity, and Memory in Early Modern Britain and Ireland*. Oxford: Oxford University Press, 2011.

Walton, Izaak. *The Compleat Angler*. 3rd ed. London, 1661.

———. *The Compleat Angler, 1653–1676*. Edited by Jonquil Bevan. Oxford: Clarendon Press of Oxford University Press, 1983.

———. "Izaak Walton's Will." Transcribed by Geoffrey Keynes. In *The Compleat Walton*, edited by Geoffrey Keynes, 605–9. London: Nonesuch Press, 1929.

———. *The Lives of John Donne, Sir Henry Wotton, Richard Hooker, George Herbert, and Robert Sanderson*. 1927. Edited by George Saintsbury. Reprint, London: Oxford University Press, 1973.

———. *"To the Author upon the Sight of the First Sheet of His Book."* In *Scintillula Altaris*, by Edward Sparke, n.p. London, 1652.

Walton, Izaak, and Charles Cotton. *The Compleat Angler*. Edited by Marjorie Swann. Oxford: Oxford University Press, 2014.

———. *The Complete Angler*. Edited by Sir John Hawkins. 4th ed. London: Printed for John, Francis, and Charles Rivington, 1784.

———. *The Complete Angler*. Edited by Sir Nicholas Harris Nicolas. 3rd ed. London: Chatto and Windus, 1875.

Warde, Paul. "The Idea of Improvement, *c*. 1520–1700." In *Custom, Improvement and the Landscape in Early Modern Britain*, edited by Richard W. Hoyle, 127–48. Farnham, UK: Ashgate, 2011.

———. *The Invention of Sustainability: Nature and Destiny, c. 1500–1879*. Cambridge: Cambridge University Press, 2018.

Watkins, John. *Representing Elizabeth in Stuart England: Literature, History, Sovereignty*. Cambridge: Cambridge University Press, 2002.

Watson, J. N. *Angling with the Fly: Flies and Anglers of Derbyshire and Staffordshire*. Yeadon, UK: Ken Smith, 2008.

Watson, Robert. *Back to Nature: The Green and the Real in the Late Renaissance*. Philadelphia: University of Pennsylvania Press, 2006.

Wear, Andrew. *Knowledge and Practice in English Medicine, 1550–1680*. Cambridge: Cambridge University Press, 2000.

Webster, Charles. *The Great Instauration: Science, Medicine, and Reform, 1626–1660*. 2nd ed. New York: Peter Lang, 2002.

Werner, Sarah. *Studying Early Printed Books, 1450–1800: A Practical Guide*. Hoboken, NJ: Wiley Blackwell, 2019.

Weston, Nick. "The Freshwater Fish Fight." *Word of Mouth* (blog). *The Guardian*, January 17, 2011. https://www.theguardian.com/lifeandstyle/wordofmouth/2011/jan/17/freshwater-fish-fight.

Westwood, Thomas. *The Chronicle of the "Compleat Angler" of Izaak Walton and Charles Cotton*. Edited by Thomas Satchell. London: W. Satchell, 1883.

———. *In Memoriam Izaak Walton, Obiit 15th December 1683*. London: William Satchell, 1884.

Westwood, Thomas, and Thomas Satchell. *Bibliotheca Piscatoria*. London: W. Satchell, 1883.

Wheeler, Alwyne. *The Fishes of the British Isles and North West Europe*. London: Macmillan, 1969.

Whitaker, Katie. *Mad Madge: The Extraordinary Life of Margaret Cavendish,*

Duchess of Newcastle, the First Woman to Live by Her Pen. New York: Basic Books, 2002.

Whitaker, W. B. *Sunday in Tudor and Stuart Times*. London: Houghton, 1933.

Wilcher, Robert. "*Eikon Basilike*: The Printing, Composition, Strategy, and Impact of 'The King's Book.'" In *The Oxford Handbook of Literature and the English Revolution*, edited by Laura Lunger Knoppers, 289–308. Oxford: Oxford University Press, 2012.

Wilcox, Helen. "Herbert, George (1593–1633).'" In *Oxford Dictionary of National Biography*. Online ed. Oxford: Oxford University Press, 2004.

———. "'Return unto Me!': Literature and Conversion in Early Modern England." In *Paradigms, Poetics and Politics of Conversion*, edited by Jan N. Bremmer, Wout J. van Bekkum, and Arie L. Molendijk, 85–105. Leuven: Peeters, 2006.

Williams, Raymond. *Keywords: A Vocabulary of Culture and Society*. London: Fourth Estate, 2014.

———. *Marxism and Literature*. Oxford: Oxford University Press, 1992.

———. *Problems in Materialism and Culture: Selected Essays*. London: NLB, 1980.

Wilson, C. Anne. *Food and Drink in Britain: From the Stone Age to the 19th Century*. Chicago: Academy Chicago Publishers, 1991.

Withington, Phil. *Society in Early Modern England: The Vernacular Origins of Some Powerful Ideas*. Cambridge, UK: Polity Press, 2010.

Wood, Andy. *The Politics of Social Conflict: The Peak Country, 1520–1770*. Cambridge: Cambridge University Press, 1999.

Wordsworth, William. *William Wordsworth: Poems*. Vol. 2. Edited by John O. Hayden. London: Penguin, 1977.

Worster, Donald. *Nature's Economy: A History of Ecological Ideas*. 2nd ed. Cambridge: Cambridge University Press, 2007.

Wotton, Sir Henry. *The Life and Letters of Sir Henry Wotton*. Edited by Logan Pearsall Smith. 2 vols. Oxford: Clarendon Press of Oxford University Press, 1966.

Wright, Myra E. *The Poetics of Angling in Early Modern England*. New York: Routledge, 2019.

Zwicker, Steven N. *Lines of Authority: Politics and English Literary Culture, 1649–1689*. Ithaca, NY: Cornell University Press, 1993.

INDEX

Italicized page references indicate illustrations. Endnotes are referenced with "n" followed by the endnote number.

Adam, 40, 90, 188, 211n98
Addison, Joseph, 224n53
Aelian (Claudius Aelianus), 227n120
Aesop, 23
agriculture, 40, 42-43, 46, 50, 136, 164, 194
  crop failure, 6, 40, 56, 107, 121
  improvement of, 6-7, 40-41, 166-67, 211n103
  See also dairying; dung; georgic
Albertus Magnus, 139, 222n115
alcohol, 3, 37-38, 65, 70, 86-87, 93, 103, 152-54, 167-69, 197-200, 204, 226n88
Aldrovandi, Ulisse (Aldrovandus), 143
alehouses, 73, 86, 88, 91-93, 111-12, 117, 125, 152-53, 157, 168, 215n80, 216n87, 226n87
Allen, Edmund, 74
angleworm. See earthworm
angling
  as art, 41, 44, 53, 63, 70-73, 76, 79, 82, 104, 112, 128, 154, 180, 191, 213n29
  as convivial, 8-9, 59-60, 65-105, 204 (see also conversion: fishers of men; voluntary associations: of anglers)
  as erotic metaphor, 102-3
  morality of, 30, 37, 68, 70-71, 109-10
  and property rights, 155-61, 171, 180, 224n42, 224n53, 226n96 (see also enclosure; hedges; poachers)
  social status of, 53, 153, 179-80
  as solitary, 8, 59-65
  as sport, 108
  superiority to other field sports, 16-17, 60, 128, 153-54, 179

  tackle, 63, 77, 82-84, 109, 131, 189, 228n147
  See also bait-fishing; fly-fishing; women: as anglers
angling manuals, 9, 49-50, 129, 179, 206n31
  See also Barker, Thomas; Cotton, Charles, the Younger; Dennys, John; Markham, Gervase: Pleasures of Princes; Mascall, Leonard; Samuel, William; "Short Discourse by Way of Post-Script, Touching the Lawes of Angling"; Treatyse of Fysshynge with an Angle; Venables, Robert; Walton, Izaak
animals (mammals), 6-7, 12-13, 18, 23, 119, 123, 154, 181, 187, 191-93, 198-99, 201, 206n31
  fur of, 10, 181-82, 185-88, 192-93, 227n127, 228n140
  hides, human use of, 211n110, 228n140
  See also individual species
anorexia. See food: inappetence
ant, 13, 18, 23, 25, 32, 41-42, 51
anthropocentrism, 7-8, 17-18, 22, 25, 27, 47-48, 109, 202, 204, 206n29, 208n38
Ardglass, Dowager Countess of (Mary Cromwell), 176
Aristotle, 30, 141, 222n124
Audubon Association, 2, 205n6
Augustine, Saint, 104, 141
Austen, Ralph, 40

Bacon, Sir Francis
  Advancement of Learning, 59-60, 66, 75, 77
  Baconian science, 7, 9, 77-78, 80, 207n23
  New Atlantis, 77
  Sylva Sylvarum, 80, 138-39, 214n53

badger, 185, 187
bait-fishing, 10, 24, 28-30, 41-42, 56, 87, 108,
    131, 147, 198, 203
  bait cookery, 51, 134-37, 189, 221n109,
    221n112
  bait oils, 78-82, 214n51, 214n54
  capturing of invertebrates for, 42-43,
    46, 109, 136, 180, 197
  cultivation of invertebrates for, 41-43,
    52, 136-37
  social status of, 181, 195, 197
barbel, 45-46, 54, 123, 135-36, 185
Barker, Thomas, 131-34, 221n101
  Art of Angling, The, 131-33, 136, 221n101,
    221n102, 221n112; artificial flies in,
    182-83, 188, 227n127
  Barker's Delight, 132-33, 221n104,
    221n105
Basse, William, 24, 85
Bastard, Thomas, 47
bat (mammal), 139
Baumann, Shyon, 218n16
Bauthumley, Jacob, 7, 206n34
bear, 183, 185, 187, 192-93
Beard, James, 220n81
beaver, 193
bedbug, 141
bee, 17, 23, 41, 45-46, 109, 134, 211n110
beech, 32, 39, 45, 53, 210n95, 211n97
beetle, 45, 109, 211n109
Berners, Dame Juliana (anonym), 213n5
Bevan, Jonquil, 32, 86, 207n6, 211n97,
    221n91, 221n103, 222n113, 223n4
Bible, 161
  Acts, 219n37
  Deuteronomy, 125-26
  Ecclesiastes, 26
  Ephesians, 226n99
  Exodus, 37
  I Kings, 222n119
  Galatians, 226n99
  Genesis, 16-17, 21, 24, 40, 118-19, 141,
    208n31, 211n98, 219n37
  John, 66, 114-18, 218n29, 219n32
  Leviticus, 125-26
  Luke, 27, 69, 114-15, 127, 207n14
  Matthew, 27, 66, 116, 159, 207n14, 225n83
  Psalms, 19-21, 27, 125, 140, 207n24,
    208n26, 208n29, 208n30, 222n119
  Romans, 172, 226n99
  translation of, Geneva, 21, 66, 114, 159,
    208n29, 208n30, 208n31, 219n32
  translation of, King James, 21, 117, 159,
    205n15, 208n29, 219n32
Bingley, Jane, 100-101
bird of paradise, 140
birds, 1, 7, 13, 17-18, 23, 35, 45, 57, 61, 93,
    139-40, 144, 181, 183, 191-93, 205n6,
    227n124
  feathers of, 10, 17, 26, 88, 109, 181-83,
    185, 187-88, 190-93, 227n120,
    227n124, 228n143
  See also individual species
blackberry, 44
Blith, Walter, 40, 211n103
blue cultural studies, 5
Boke of Saint Albans, 179-80, 193, 212n4,
    213n5
Book of Common Prayer, 5, 37, 71, 74-75,
    120, 161, 178, 206n19, 206n37
Book of Nature, 20-23, 25-27, 208n27
Book of Sports, 35-36, 38, 210n76, 210n78
Borlik, Todd, 8
Boyle, Robert, 78
bream, 24, 54, 87, 109, 134-36, 179, 222n113
Brears, Peter, 110
Breton, Nicholas, 96
Brighton, Trevor, 225n76
British Civil Wars, 5, 19, 21, 33, 36, 55, 98,
    121, 125, 149
  environmental impact of, 6-8, 33, 107, 151
Brome, Alexander, 103, 109, 210n95
Browne, Edward, 163
Browne, Moses, 14, 32
Browne, Sir Thomas, 7, 20, 206n30
  Garden of Cyrus, The, 210n79
  Religio Medici, 20, 141, 208n27
Buell, Lawrence, 15, 206n36
bullhead, 16
bulrush, 143
Bunyan, John, 105, 218n129
Burghley, Sir William Cecil, Baron, 148,
    150, 166, 223n7
butterfly, 138
buzzard, common (*Buteo buteo*), 181
Byron, George Gordon Noël, 30

caddis fly, 27-28, 42, 51
  caddisworm (larva), 42-44
calendar
  of artificial flies, 181, 183-84
  Church of England, 34, 51-52, 212n127,
    218n29
  Gregorian, 209n68

Julian, 209n68
   of Walton's *Angler*, 33-34, 94, 209n66, 216n87
   See also dairying: seasonal calendar of; May (month of); sabbath; seasonal change
Calvin, Jean, 115
Camden, William, 28
camel, 185-87, 192
carp, 41, 44, 52, 54, 87, 127, 134-36
Carr, Robert. *See* Somerset, Earl of
cat, 42, 134, 137, 185, 187
Cavendish, Margaret. *See* Newcastle, Duchess of
Cavendish, Sir Charles, 218n8
Cavendish, William. *See* Newcastle, 1st Duke of
Cecil, Robert. *See* Salisbury, 1st Earl of
Cecil, William. *See* Burghley, Sir William Cecil, Baron
cedar, 7
Chalkhill, John, 39, 211n96
chameleon, 140
Charles I, King, 6, 36, 38, 55, 117, 149, 192-93, 210n78, 219n40
Charles II, King, 38, 55, 125, 191-92, 210n95, 212n118, 212n135
Chatsworth, 166, 225n80
chicken, 23, 181-83, 188, 191-92, 227n120, 227n124
Children of Israel, 19-20, 44, 125-26, 208n38
chub, 42, 44-46, 52-53, 65, 73, 76, 95, 109, 111-13, 116, 120, 125, 127, 130-32, 135, 165, 168, 216n87, 218n21, 221n98, 227n121
Churchman, Joan (wife of Richard Hooker), 90-91
Church of England, 5, 8, 36, 66, 71, 74, 120
   Anglicanism, 8, 206n37, 209n70
   Anglicans, 9, 55, 71, 88, 115, 117-18, 209n70
   See also calendar: Church of England; Walton, Izaak: religious beliefs of
civil war. *See* British Civil Wars
Clarendon, 1st Earl of (Edward Hyde), 55, 218n8
Cleopas, 69-70
Cleopatra, 83
climate change, 204
   global heating, 58, 209n68
   Great Frost, 57-58

Little Ice Age, 6, 8, 55-58, 87, 107, 118
coal, 6, 58
cock. *See* chicken
Cogan, Thomas, 119, 122-23, 126
Cokain, Sir Aston, 166
Coleridge, Samuel Taylor, 14
collectors
   of curiosities, 78, 133-34, 191-92
   of exotic birds and animals, 191-93
   of secrets, 78-82, 132, 134
   See also virtuosos
comedy, 63-65, 86-87, 104, 163, 169, 197-204, 230n11
commensalism, 46-47, 50
conservation, 1-3, 8, 47-50, 106, 152-54, 204, 212n119
   fence months, 48-51
   See also hunting: otter; voluntary associations: of conservationists; wildlife management
contemplation. *See* meditation
Continental Divide, 200-201, 203-4
conversion, 9, 56, 60, 103-5, 111, 113-14, 130, 144, 162, 217n128, 218n129, 222n131
   catechism, 74-75, 161, 196, 214n34
   fishers of men, 66-72, 74-75, 83, 105, 114, 118
   See also Jesus
Cooper, Helen, 99
coot, 61, 185, 187
cormorant, 152
Cotton, Charles, the Elder, 166, 172-73, 176, 193, 226n96, 226n101
Cotton, Charles, the Younger
   Beresford Dale estate of, 10, 146-47, 161, 163-64, 166-67, 169, 171, 173-74, 176-78, 180, 186, 193-94, 225n68, 225n85, 226n95, 226n101
   Beresford Hall, 147, 161-62, 164, 166-72, 174, 176-78, 184, 189-91, 193-94, 225n68, 225n75, 226n95
   biography of, 146-47, 162-63, 166, 176, 192-94, 226n101
   Compleat Angler, Part II, The, reception of, 147; relationship to Walton's *Angler*, 147, 161-63, 168-69, 178, 184-85, 188-90; writing of, 9, 222n1
   Compleat Gamester, The, 225n85
   fishing house of, 170-71, 173-77, 190, 194, 204, 226n96, 229n164
   fly-tying of, 145, 182-94, 228n130, 228n132, 228n134, 228n143

Cotton, Charles, the Younger (*continued*)
   genteel identity of, 145, 167-73, 177-78, 180, 189-94, 226n102, 227n111
   lyric poetry of, 172-74, 185, 190, 194, 226n107, 227n110, 228n142
   relationship with Izaak Walton, 161, 170-77, 184, 194
   Wonders of the Peake, The, 163, 225n72, 225n74, 225n80, 226n90
cougar, 198-99, 229n6
cow, 18, 45-46, 94-96, 98-99, 100-101, 134, 136, 164, 183, 187, 191, 216n95
cowslip, 32-33, 35, 60, 219n52
Cranmer, George, 215n76
Crawford, Patricia, 95, 100
Cressy, David, 38, 212n127
Cromwell, Mary (2nd wife of Charles Cotton the Younger). *See* Ardglass, Dowager Countess of
Cromwell, Oliver, 19, 36, 107, 133, 191, 212n118
crow, 42-43
crustaceans, 141, 222n117
culverkey (flowering plant), 35

dace, 42, 81, 87, 134-35, 227n121
dairying
   daily schedule of, 95, 100
   dairy products, 94-95, 101, 103, 135-37
   seasonal calendar of, 94
   See also women: as dairyworkers
Danvers, Charles, 89
Danvers, Jane (wife of George Herbert), 89, 215n73
David, 21, 27
deer, 6, 23, 57-58, 149, 151, 192, 198
deforestation, 1-3, 6-7, 149
De Grey, Thomas, 207n1
Della Casa, Giovanni, 213n28
Dennys, John, 34, 180, 206n31, 209n67
diet
   continental cuisine, 124-25, 220n81
   humoral theory of, 121-24, 126-28, 220n55, 220n85
   Jewish dietary laws, 125-26
   piscivorous diet, 120-21, 123-28
   vegetarianism, 118-19
   See also fish days; recipes
Digby, Sir Kenelm, 108, 145
Dilg, Will H., 1-3, 205n2
Directory of Public Worship, 120
disease
   fevers, 121-23, 126

plague, 107
   typhus, 121
dock (plant), 45
dog, 18, 23, 183, 185-86
   See also individual breeds
Donne, John, 21, 82, 88-89, 172, 215n62, 223n9
   "The Baite," 102-3, 144
dove (bird), 23
   See also turtledove
Drayton, Michael, 28, 47, 163
Du Bartas, Guillaume de Salluste, 18, 20, 24, 140, 209n64
Dubravius, Jan, 143
duck, 61, 222n129
   mallard, 181-83, 185, 187-88
   teal, 183
   wigeon, 183
dung, 45-46, 57, 134, 136, 156, 211n109
Duport, James, 108

earthworm, 23, 45-46, 108-9, 135-37, 197-98
   brandling, 45-46
Echo (mythological figure), 93, 216n83
ecology, 8, 27-28, 44-45, 47, 49, 51, 141-42, 144-45, 204
   literary ecology, 10, 202
   non-equilibrium ecology, 56
   protoecology, 144-45
   queer ecology, 140-41
ecosystem, 5-6, 8, 11, 29, 44, 46-47, 53-54, 56, 106, 113, 180, 207n1
ecotourism, 163
Edward VI, King, 119
Edwards, Thomas, 7
eel, 12-13, 46, 54, 102, 126-27, 133, 139, 142, 144, 185
Egan, Gabriel, 207n21
elephant, 13, 18, 185, 193
Elijah, 140, 222n119
Elizabeth I, Queen, 74, 97-98, 119, 148, 193, 216n104, 217n107, 217n111
enclosure, 6, 155-56, 158
environmental education, 54, 56
environmental text, 8, 15, 29, 206n36
Erasmus, 14, 207n7
ermine, 198-99
Eve, 40, 211n98
Evelyn, John, 57-58, 67, 110, 118, 122, 124, 129, 134, 191
   Sylva, 49

falcon, 151, 227n115
falconry. *See* hawking
Fanshawe, Richard, 217n115
Featley, Daniel, 120
fern, 80, 186
  bracken, 186
Fiennes, Celia, 163, 165, 226n86, 226n87
fig tree, 40, 211n98
Firth, C. H. (Charles Harding), 224n51
fish, 7, 14, 16–18, 20–22, 27, 45–46, 50–51, 56–57, 64, 80, 135, 139–41, 143–44, 155, 158, 185, 193, 206n31, 207n22, 222n117, 122n129 (*see also individual species*)
  Christian miracles involving, 114–16, 218n29
  cooking of, 73, 91–92, 110–14, 126–27, 130–32, 168, 189, 216n87
  as foodstuff, 1, 3, 9, 45, 48, 65, 86, 95, 101, 106–24, 128, 144–45, 218n21 (*see also* diet: piscivorous diet)
  recipes for, 124–34
  salted, 110, 119, 123, 126, 219n43
fish days, 9, 118–21, 219n35, 219n40, 219n43
fishing, recreational. *See* angling
fishponds, 14, 41, 44, 179, 227n112
Flatman, Thomas, 39
flea, 141
Fletcher, Phineas, 67, 84
Floud, John, 14, 207n7
Floud, Rachel (1st wife of Izaak Walton), 14, 88, 145
flowers, 20, 24, 26, 30, 32–36, 38, 61, 88, 98–99, 142
  See also individual species
fly (insect), 23, 26, 28, 43–44, 51, 56, 109, 142, 158, 209n52
  See also individual species
fly-fishing, 1, 9–10, 39, 43–44, 53, 108, 129, 131, 179–80, 195–203
  flies, artificial, 63, 108, 132, 181–82, 184, 221n105, 227n120, 227n125, 227n126, 228n139, 228n143
  fly-tying, 10, 43–44, 182–93
  social status of, 10, 180–81, 194–95
  See also under Barker, Thomas: *Art of Angling*; calendar; Cotton, Charles, the Younger; Markham, Gervase: *Pleasures of Princes*; Mascall, Leonard; *Treatyse of Fysshynge with an Angle*; Venables, Robert; Walton, Izaak

food, 9, 17, 106–45
  dearth, 6, 40, 56, 58, 107, 218n9
  fasting, 120, 123
  food insecurity, 48–50, 106
  God as miraculous provider of, 9, 27, 137–40, 142
  inappetence, 29–30, 138–39
  meals (social acts of eating), 1, 3, 9, 12, 65, 86–87, 111, 116–17, 125, 127, 129, 168–69, 178, 218n17, 226n88
  politics of, 9, 124–26, 133
  See also dairying: dairy products; diet; fish: as foodstuff; recipes
Ford, James, 230n11
forests, 1–3, 6, 58, 150–51
fossil fuel. *See* coal
Fowler, Alastair, 211n100
fox, 6, 23, 48, 183, 185–86, 192
  See also hunting: fox
Foxe, John, 97
Franck, Richard, 129, 143–44, 220n81, 221n95
frog, 29–30, 109, 138–39, 141, 143, 185
Frye, Northrop, 221n92
Frye, Susan, 228n144
fungi, 18

gardens, 41, 51, 148, 167, 191
Gardiner, Samuel, 67–70, 72, 213n17
gender, 9, 60, 83–84, 86, 91–94, 100, 103, 105, 188–89, 205n14, 216n82, 228n144, 229n2
  and cookery, 129–32, 134, 136–37, 144, 189
georgic, 8, 15, 40–58, 97, 136–38, 156, 189, 193
  See also agriculture; conservation; dung; how-to manuals; rain; seasonal change
Gesner, Conrad, 28, 80, 142–43
Gifford, Terry, 209n62
gillyflower, 18
Glacken, Clarence, 27
goat, 187
  See also mountain goat
goose, 122n129
Graham, Elspeth, 214n35
grasshopper, 109, 140, 188
grayling, 51, 147, 170, 178, 181, 183, 185
Great Chain of Being, 7, 17–19, 22, 25, 106, 207n20, 207n21
Great Northern Railway, 199–200, 230n8
Green, Ian, 74

greyhound, 186, 189, 192
Grinsell, Thomas, 76
gudgeon, 65
Guibbory, Achsah, 125

haddock, 220n81
Hadfield, Andrew, 213n17
Hale, George, 104
Hale, Sir Matthew, 141
Hall, Joseph (bishop of Norwich), 21–26, 55, 208n33, 208n34, 208n38
Hammond, Henry, 115, 218n25
hare, 18, 23, 185–87, 189, 192
  See also jackrabbit; snowshoe rabbit
Harpham, Geoffrey Galt, 105, 217n128
harry-long-legs (crane fly), 187–88
Hartle, Paul, 114
Hartlib, Samuel, 40, 78, 211n103
Hastings, Sir George, 80–82, 138
hawk, 189, 227n115
hawking, 37, 60–61, 85, 128, 147, 151, 179, 189, 212n4, 213n18, 223n33, 227n115
Hawkins, Sir John, 101, 217n123
hawthorn fly, 43
Hayashi, Robert, 229n2
hedgehog, 18, 23
hedges, 6, 46, 53, 124, 156–59, 161, 169
  honeysuckle-hedge, 32, 157–58
Hemingway, Ernest, 229n6
Henly, Oliver, 79–80, 214n52
Henry, Prince of Wales, 21, 193
Henry VIII, King, 99, 119
heraldry, 179, 192–93, 212n4
  See also *Boke of Saint Albans*
Herbert, George, 17, 20, 24, 69, 89–90, 123, 208n41, 215n73
  "Man," 17, 207n18
  "Providence," 28–29
  "The World," 40, 211n99
herbs, 125, 127, 141–42
Herd, Andrew, 186, 227n126, 227n127
heron, 61, 143, 214n51
Herrera-Thomas, Sean, 222n130
Herrick, Robert, 92, 210n90
Hesiod, 40
Heywood, Gerald, 225n73, 225n75, 225n85, 226n95, 228n134
Heywood, Thomas, 97, 216n104
hickwall (European green woodpecker, *Picus viridis*), 183
Hobbes, Thomas, 225n78
Hoffmann, Richard, 213n5

holidays, 35–36
  See also Book of Sports; May (month of): May Day
Holinshed, Raphael, 97
Holland, Abraham, 121
honeysuckle (*Lonicera periclymenum*), 32, 104, 157, 224n49
  See also hedges: honeysuckle-hedge
Hooker, Richard, 71, 90–91, 215n75, 215n76
Horace, 12, 90, 207n4
horse, 18, 23, 41, 63, 136, 151, 164–65, 194, 196, 225n76
Hoskins, Sir John, 80
hound, 61, 185
how-to manuals, 8, 11–12, 41, 104, 206n1, 207n7, 212n4, 213n9
  See also angling manuals; *Boke of Saint Albans*
humoralism. See diet: humoral theory of
hunting, 7, 37, 60–61, 71, 85, 128, 153–54, 156, 162, 179, 189, 192, 197, 212n4, 223n33
  deer, 151
  fox, 6
  Game Act of 1671, 160, 224n56
  otter, 47–49, 52, 72, 92, 106, 111, 151–53, 156, 198, 200, 203, 211n114, 223n32
  as royal sport, 150–54
  See also James I, King: as blood-sport enthusiast
Huntley, Frank Livingstone, 25
Hutchinson, Isabella (1st wife of Charles Cotton the Younger), 176
Hyde, Edward. *See* Clarendon, 1st Earl of

insect larvae, 134
  caterpillars, 28, 44–45, 138, 141–42, 211n107 (*see also* silkworm)
  grubs, 42–43, 45–46, 51, 109
  maggots, 42–43, 51–52
  worms, 26, 42, 45, 51
insects, 28, 45, 108, 135, 139, 181–82, 188
  See also *individual subgroups and species*
interregnum (England), 5, 8, 19, 33, 36–37, 51, 55, 71, 98, 107–8, 115, 118, 121, 125, 131, 149, 158, 191, 206n35, 210n81, 210n89, 212n127
  environmental impact of, 149–51
Isaac, 21, 30, 208n31
ivy, 7, 78–80, 214n54
Izaak Walton League of America, 1–5, 105, 204, 205n8

jackrabbit, 198-200, 203, 229n7
Jackson, Henry, 189-90, 228n145
James, Saint, 66, 75
James I, King, 35, 38, 148, 192-93, 210n76, 223n9
  as blood-sport enthusiast, 148-52, 155
  See also Theobalds: as Jacobean royal estate
jasmine, 104
jay, Eurasian, 181-82
Jesus, 9, 21, 27, 66-67, 69, 99, 114-18, 127, 159, 211n98, 218n23, 218n29
  disciples of (see individual names; conversion: fishers of men)
John, Saint, 66, 75
Johnston, Josée, 218n16
Jonson, Ben, 207n4
Judas, 166, 225n83
Juxon, William (archbishop of Canterbury), 55

Ken, Anne (2nd wife of Izaak Walton), 88, 145, 208n42
Kinder, Philip, 166, 169
kingfisher, 28, 32
kite (bird), 137, 183

Lactantius, 222n122
lady's smock (flowering plant), 35
lamb. See sheep
Lamb, Charles, 14
lamprey, 46
Lathum, William, 211n97
lavender, 78
Leicester, 1st Earl of (Robert Dudley), 193
leopard, 229n6
Lévi-Strauss, Claude, 222n114
lily, 27, 33, 35, 142
lion, 18, 23, 193
livery companies. See trade guilds
Loscocco, Paula, 207n24
Lovegrove, Roger, 228n142

Maclean, Norman, 195-96, 203
  A River Runs Through It, 10, 195-204
Major, Philip, 206n35
Malory, Sir Thomas, 99, 217n117
mammals. See animals
Manning, Roger, 110
Markham, Gervase, 124-25, 129
  Cheape and Good Husbandry, 216n95
  English Huswife, The, 136

Pleasures of Princes, The, 56, 108, 136, 154, 213n29; artificial flies in, 182-83, 190
Marlowe, Christopher, 96, 99, 102, 137-38
Marriot, John, 209n59
Marriot, Richard, 132
Marvell, Andrew, 7, 206n30
Mary, Queen of Scots, 97
Mary I, Queen of England, 97
Mary Magdalene, 99, 217n114
Mascall, Leonard, 188
  A Booke of Fishing with Hooke and Line, 50, 136, 221n109; artificial flies in, 181-83, 188, 227n121, 227n125
masculinity, 9-10, 153, 201, 203, 224n34, 229n2
May (month of), 34, 38-39, 43, 50-51, 97, 210n79
May butter, 54
May Day, 34-38, 68, 94, 99, 210n81, 217n113, 218n29
May games, 35-36, 38, 210n90
maying customs, 35-38, 210n72
maypole, 35, 38
May, Robert, 125, 220n78
mayfly, 43, 51, 187, 209n68, 228n139
McCutcheon, John, 4
McDonald, John, 227n124, 227n126, 228n134
McFarland, Ron, 229n3
McGrade, A. S. (Arthur Stephen), 215n75
McIlhaney, Anne, 116
McRae, Andrew, 158, 160
meditation, 8, 19-30, 32, 37-40, 42-43, 53, 55, 71, 153, 208n29, 208n31, 208n33, 208n38, 208n40
  Ignatian, 20-21, 208n28
  Protestant, 21, 25, 27, 208n28
Meeker, Joseph, 10, 202
melon, 18
Mendelson, Sara, 95, 100
Milton, John, 5, 96
minnow, 16, 84, 114, 120, 125, 127, 189, 219n52
misogyny, 9, 84-85, 87, 90, 163, 215n67
Moffett, Thomas, 140
Montagu, Edward, 133
Montaigne, Michel de, 202
Montrose, Louis Adrian, 217n107
Moorhouse, Isabel, 100-101
More, Anne (wife of John Donne), 88-89
Morrill, John, 118

Morton, Thomas, of Berwick, 68
Moses, 125
mountain goat, 199–200
mountain lion. *See* cougar
mouse, 165, 185
mulberry, 44, 51
mullet (fish), 24
mushroom, 18
mussel, 108
myrtle, 104

Narcissus (mythological figure), 93
National Conservation Association, 205n6
natural history, 43–45, 51, 77, 206n36, 221n91
natural theology, 26–30, 209n46
nature, 5–6, 15–18, 48, 56, 206n28, 206n36
    God's relationship to, 7, 16–17, 22, 26–30, 47, 51, 57, 141, 180, 208n26
    Natura, goddess of, 16, 207n16
    oeconomy of, 145
    See also Book of Nature; Great Chain of Being; natural theology
nettle, 18
Newcastle, 1st Duke of (William Cavendish), 55, 158
Newcastle, Duchess of (Margaret Cavendish), 84
New Historicism, 5, 33
Nicolas, Sir Nicholas Harris, 209n66, 213n19
nightingale, 99, 217n115
Noah, 118, 141
Novarr, David, 215n75
Nowell, Alexander (dean of St. Paul's), 74–75, 95, 214n33, 214n34

oak, 6, 24, 55, 58, 208n41
oak fly, 43
Oliver, H. J. (Harold James), 213n9
orchard, 6, 41, 166
Osborne, Dorothy, 216n100
osprey, 152
ostrich, 185, 187, 191, 193
otter, 48, 80, 106, 152, 154, 197–200, 203, 211n114, 229n3, 229n6
    See also hunting: otter
otter dog (otter hound), 49, 152, 212n118
Overbury, Sir Thomas, 98, 217n112
Ovid, 93
ox, 23, 187

Parker, Martin, 217n113
parks, 6, 57, 107, 151, 156, 161
    See also Theobalds: park of
parliamentarians, 51, 98, 107, 149, 183, 228n145
partridge, 181, 183, 189
pastoral, 8, 15, 30–41, 43, 50, 83, 94, 96, 102, 137–38, 163, 209n60, 209n62, 210n95, 216n89, 229n3
    anti-pastoral, 45, 102–3
    piscatory pastoral, 31, 209n58
Paul, Saint, 75, 172, 214n35
Payne, Robert, 71–72, 213n25
Peacham, Henry, 207n1, 223n33, 224n49
peacock, 181–82, 187–88, 191–92, 228n143
Peak District, 10, 147, 162–67, 169–71, 174, 177–78, 184, 193–94, 225n68, 225n72, 225n76, 225n78, 225n80, 226n86, 226n87
    measurement of distances in, 163–64, 225n74, 225n75
    See also Chatsworth; Cotton, Charles, the Younger: Beresford Dale estate of
Peake, Robert, 193
perch (fish), 25, 51, 54, 65, 102, 108
Peter, Saint, 66–67, 75, 114–15, 218n23
Petrarch (Francesco Petrarca), 102–3
pheasant, 183
Philip, Saint, 34, 218n29
Philomela, 99, 217n115
pickerel. *See* pike (fish)
pickerel weed (*Potamogeton natans*), 142–43, 145, 222n127
pig, 18, 45, 183, 185–86
pike (fish), 29, 54, 78, 116, 125, 132, 134, 142–45, 179, 185, 220n81
pine marten (*Martes martes*), 185, 187, 192, 228n142
pink (flowering plant), 18
plants, 6–7, 17–18, 24, 26, 28, 35, 44, 58, 141–42, 224n49, 206n30, 210n72
    See also individual subgroups and species
Pliny, 17, 20, 141–42, 222n126
Plot, Robert, 163
plover, 183
Pluto (mythological figure), 99
poachers, 3, 58, 149, 156, 158, 178, 194
polecat (*Mustela putorius*), 185, 188
pollution
    air, 6
    water, 1

Pope, Alexander, 193
posthumanism, 206n29, 220n55
Powell, Edward, 159
Powell, Thomas, 129
presentism, 5, 205n16
primrose, 24, 32, 45, 53, 219n52
property
    landownership, 39, 211n96
    sequestration, 107-8
    See also angling: and property rights; Cotton, Charles, the Younger: Beresford Dale estate of; poachers
Proserpina, 99
puritanism, 35-38, 51, 77, 119-20, 201n72
puritans, 40, 154
Puttenham, George, 31, 33

Quarles, Francis, 31

rabbit, 134, 185, 192
Rabisha, William, 125
rain, 43, 52-57, 90, 102, 107, 117, 157, 163, 169, 204
Raleigh, Sir Walter, 96, 99, 102, 137-38
rank (social), 9, 60, 78-83, 105, 131-33, 154-56, 159, 173-74, 176, 178-80, 186, 188-90, 194, 223n33, 224n56, 226n102
    See also Cotton, Charles, the Younger: genteel identity of; terms of address
raven, 140, 222n119
Ray, John, 26, 209n47
recipes, 9, 129
    for fish, 12, 14, 120, 127, 130, 132-33, 219n52, 220n81
    See also bait-fishing: bait cookery; bait-fishing: bait oils; collectors: of secrets
Remien, Peter, 144
Restoration, 36, 38, 55, 125, 149-50, 158-60, 180, 183, 191, 212n118, 213n25, 219n32
rivers, 2, 5, 20, 26-27, 43-47, 49, 61, 95, 144, 180, 200
    Blackfoot, 196-98, 200-202
    Dove, 10, 146, 162, 165-66, 171, 174, 178, 180-81, 183, 191, 193-94, 204, 225n68, 226n95, 226n96, 226n107
    Lea, 32, 87, 93, 118, 156-57, 224n42
    Sow, 208n42
    Thames, 46-47, 57
roach (fish), 42, 46-47, 51, 65, 81, 87, 134-35, 221n109

Robinson, Sarah, 212n119, 224n42
Rondelet, Guillaume, 207n22
rook (bird), 18
Roosevelt, Teddy, 3-4, 205n13
rose, 18, 24, 104
roundheads. *See* parliamentarians
royalism, 36, 38-40, 55, 98, 210n79
royalists, 7, 9, 33, 39, 55, 107, 117, 124-25, 153-54, 158, 206n35, 207n24, 210n90, 220n81, 224n51, 228n145
Royal Society, 78, 84
ruffe (fish), 65
Ryrie, Alec, 120

sabbath, 35-38, 210n89
    sabbatarianism, 35-38, 49, 210n78, 210n89
sable (*Mustela zibellina*), 185, 188, 192-93, 228n142
Sadler, Ralph, 152, 223n29
Saintsbury, George, 89
Salisbury, 1st Earl of (Robert Cecil), 148-49, 223n9
salmon, 11, 28, 45-46, 48, 54, 79-80, 85, 110, 114, 126
Samuel, William, 63, 213n10
    The Arte of Angling, 50, 61-66, 68, 72, 85-88, 91-93, 111-12, 124, 129-30, 142-43, 156, 215n77
Sanderson, Robert (bishop of Lincoln), 89-90, 218n25
Sandys, Edwin, 215n76, 222n119
Sannazaro, Jacopo, 31
satire, Menippean, 14, 221n92
seasonal change, 50-52, 109
    See also calendar; georgic
sectarianism, 7, 159, 214n35
sedge, 143
sexual assault, 99-102, 217n115
sexuality, 7, 35, 38, 98-100, 102, 140-41, 217n111, 206n30, 210n90
Shakespeare, William, 5
    As You Like It, 208n40
    King Lear, 56
Shapin, Steven, 218n1
Sharpe, Kevin, 210n78
sheep, 18, 23, 32-33, 45, 90, 115, 118, 134-35, 164
Sheldon, Gilbert (archbishop of Canterbury), 71-72, 213n25, 216n94
"Short Discourse by Way of Post-Script, Touching the Lawes of Angling, A," 160-61

Sidney, Sir Philip, 32, 226n96
Sierra Club, 2, 205n6
silkworm, 41
snail, 51
snake, 170
snowshoe rabbit, 199, 229n7
Snyder, Susan, 209n64
Solomon, 26, 179
Somerset, Earl of (Robert Carr), 223n9
spaniel, 186-87, 192
Sparke, Edward, 34, 52, 209n70
Spenser, Edmund, 102
spider, 23
spirituality, 8, 11-12, 30
    See also conversion; meditation; natural theology
spontaneous generation, 9, 140-45, 222n122, 222n129
squirrel, 185-86
starling, 18
Stegner, Wallace, 203
Stow, John, 34
Stubbes, Philip, 35, 210n90
sustainability, 8, 14, 49-51
Sutton, James, 223n7
swallow (bird), 18, 23, 139
swan, 61
Swann, Marjorie, 205n17, 226n102
sycamore, 39-40, 53-54, 162, 169, 211n98

tansy, 120, 219n52
tench, 17, 41, 116
terms of address
    brother, 71, 73-77 (see also trade guilds)
    father, 171-72
    friend, 63-65, 72, 78-80, 83, 89, 214n51, 215n62
    master, 54, 71-77, 91, 104, 171, 214n45
    scholar, 24, 68-69, 71-77, 79, 91, 101, 104, 213n29
    sir, 54, 68, 70, 72-73, 167, 213n28
Theobalds, 10, 147-48, 153, 156, 160, 166, 178, 180, 194, 223n4
    as Elizabethan prodigy house, 148, 150
    as Jacobean royal estate, 148-50, 152, 192, 223n9
    park of, 148-50, 154-55
    post-Jacobean decline of, 149-51
Theocritus, 31
Thirsk, Joan, 211n103
Thomas, Keith, 7, 210n72
Thoreau, Henry David, 15

tiger, 23
toad, 7
Topsell, Edward, 139, 141, 222n115, 222n126
tortoise, 57-58, 193
trade guilds, 75-77, 84, 129, 214n38
    Ironmongers' Company, 76-77, 214n45
tragedy, 197, 201-4, 230n11
Traherne, Thomas, 159
Tranter, Kirsten, 19
travel, 37-38, 161, 163-67, 177, 210n89, 218n129, 225n76, 226n86, 226n87
    See also alehouses; Peak District: measurement of distances in
Treatyse of Fysshynge with an Angle, 50, 60-62, 108, 123, 135, 156, 179-80, 212n4, 213n5
    artificial flies in, 181-85, 188, 190, 193, 227n121, 227n123, 227n124, 227n126
    See also Worde, Wynkyn de
trees, 7, 44, 58, 142, 157-58, 166, 169, 225n82
    See also individual species
trout, 11-12, 17, 24, 26, 28, 34, 39, 43-45, 47, 52-54, 61, 72, 84-85, 101, 108, 110-13, 116-18, 120, 125, 131-33, 138-39, 141, 146-47, 157, 170, 181, 183, 185, 189, 191, 209n68, 222n117
Tryon, Thomas, 57
Turner, William, 222n129
turtledove, 23, 25

Underdown, David, 36

vegetables, 41, 142, 220n85
Venables, Robert, 183
    The Experienc'd Angler, 180, 183, 222n2;
    artificial flies in, 183, 186, 228n134
Venner, Tobias, 123, 126
Virgil, 31, 39, 211n96
    first Eclogue, 39-40, 211n97
    Georgics, 40
virtuosos, 9, 78, 80-83, 134, 138, 154, 180, 191, 215n60
    See also collectors
voluntary associations, 2, 84, 212n2
    of anglers, 3, 5, 8-9, 59-105, 110-14, 117-18, 127, 144-45, 155, 172-73
    of conservationists, 2, 204 (see also Audubon Association; Izaak Walton League of America; National Conservation Association; Sierra Club)
    of scientists, 77-78

wagtail, 139
walking (in the countryside), 37, 69, 208n38
Wall, Wendy, 216n89
Walton, Ann (surviving daughter of Izaak Walton), 22, 145
Walton, Izaak
　children of, 22, 145
　Compleat Angler, The, fly-fishing in, 39, 43–44, 53, 108, 131, 181, 183–84, 188, 190; illustrations in, 12–13, 207n5; literary modes in, 12–15, 207n3; posthumous editions of, 14, 32–33, 205n15, 207n6, 209n66; publication history of, 3, 12–13, 146, 174, 205n14, 207n5, 209n66, 222n2; reception history of, 3, 5, 9–10, 14–15, 31–33, 50, 101, 147, 161–63, 168–69, 178, 184–85, 188–90, 195–204, 205n17, 217n123, 229n3; sources of, 61–63, 65, 68, 72, 84–88, 91, 108, 111–12, 129–31, 138, 140, 142–43, 181, 183, 188, 195–204, 213n8, 222n113; title and subtitle of, 11–12, 19, 38, 106; title page of, 66, 114, 116–17, 219n32
　editor of John Chalkhill, *Thealma and Clearchus*, 39
　editor of Sir Henry Wotton, *Reliquiae Wottonianae*, 82, 215n60
　education of, 14, 74, 82
　library of, 22, 216n84
　Lives, 9, 69, 71, 82, 88–91, 123, 208n34, 215n60, 215n62, 215n75, 215n76, 218n25
　marital history of, 14, 25, 88, 145, 208n42
　occupation of, 14, 41, 76–77, 80, 83, 189, 214n38, 214n39, 214n45
　political beliefs of, 5, 19, 33, 36, 38–39, 51, 55, 98, 128, 133, 150–51, 206n19, 214n35, 219n32
　preface to Francis Quarles, *The Shepheards Oracles*, 31, 209n59
　prefatory poem for Alexander Brome, *Songs and Other Poems*, 210n95
　prefatory poem for Edward Sparke, *Scintillula Altaris*, 52, 210n70
　religious beliefs of, 5, 8, 19, 51, 74–75, 150, 159
　Stafford (hometown), links with, 25, 58, 143
　will of, 22, 58
Walton, Izaak (canon of Salisbury Cathedral, 8th son of Izaak Walton), 145
wasp, 134
water dog (retriever), 187
Watson, Robert, 206n28
weasel, 185
Weaver, Thomas, 17, 85, 108–9, 207n19
Westwood, Thomas, 194
whale, 17
Wight, Sarah, 116
Wilcox, Helen, 103, 215n73, 218n129
wildlife management, 2, 48
Wilkins, John, 78
Williams, Raymond, 207n13, 207n16
willow, 19, 44, 158, 211n107
wolf, 18
women, 9, 60, 83–103, 176, 215n77, 216n82, 216n101, 226n107
　as alewives, 91–93, 112–13, 130, 168, 215n78, 215n80, 215n81, 216n87
　as anglers, 83–84, 102, 215n64
　as dairyworkers, 45, 93–102, 216n89, 216n94, 216n100, 217n107, 217n113
　as members of trade guilds, 84, 215n66
　as wives, 84–91, 111, 129–30, 134, 136
　See also gender; misogyny; sexual assault
wonder, 27–30, 42, 44, 70, 208n30, 209n51
Wood, Andy, 225n80
woodbine. *See* honeysuckle
Worde, Wynkyn de, 179, 193, 212n4
worms. *See* earthworm; insect larvae: worms
Wotton, Sir Henry, 16, 81–83, 98, 154, 172, 208n34, 215n60, 215n62
Wright, Myra, 205n17, 206n31, 215n63, 222n131

Zacchaeus, 211n98

www.ingramcontent.com/pod-product-compliance
Lightning Source LLC
Chambersburg PA
CBHW022045290426
44109CB00014B/988